Tools
for
Teaching

Barbara Gross Davis

Tools for Teaching

JOSSEY-BASS
A Wiley Imprint
www.josseybass.com

Published by Jossey-Bass
A Wiley Imprint
989 Market Street, San Francisco, CA 94103-1741   www.josseybass.com

Jossey-Bass books and products are available through most bookstores. To contact Jossey-Bass directly call our Customer Care Department within the U.S. at 800-956-7739, outside the U.S. at 317-572-3986, or fax 317-572-4002.

Jossey-Bass also publishes its books in a variety of electronic formats. Some content that appears in print may not be available in electronic books.

Library of Congress Cataloging-in-Publication Data

Davis, Barbara Gross.
　　　Tools for teaching / Barbara Gross Davis.
　　　　　p.　cm. — (The Jossey-Bass higher and adult education series)
　　　Includes bibliographical references (p.　) and index.
　　　ISBN 1-55542-568-2
　　　　1. College teaching—United States—Handbooks, manuals, etc. 2. Classroom management—
　　United States—Handbooks, manuals, etc. 3. Curriculum planning—
　　United States—Handbooks, manuals, etc. I. Title. II. Series.
　　LB2331.D37　1993
　　378.1'25—dc20　　　　　　　　　　　　　　　　　　　　　　　　　　　93-19500

Printed in the United States of America
FIRST EDITION
HB Printing　　　　　20 19 18 17 16

A Publication in
THE JOSSEY-BASS
HIGHER AND ADULT EDUCATION SERIES

Contents

Contents

XI. Teaching Outside the Classroom

XII. Finishing Up

Preface

In the continuing debate over how to improve the quality of undergraduate education, two questions are of central importance: What should be taught? and How can that curriculum best be taught? *Tools for Teaching* addresses the latter question by providing a compendium of teaching strategies that focus on the major aspects of college and university teaching—from planning a course through assigning final grades.

The aim of the book is to encourage faculty to become more aware of how they teach and how they might teach more effectively, and to provide them with the tools for doing so. New faculty members who are teaching for the first time will find reassuring suggestions on how to design and offer a new course, how to write and grade an exam, and how to attend to the range of responsibilities involved in teaching and managing a large lecture course. Experienced faculty members who are faced with thorny teaching problems or are concerned about burning out or getting stale will find descriptions of various ways to revitalize their courses. Graduate student instructors and teaching assistants can also benefit from the ideas described in *Tools*.

Certain assumptions about you, the reader, have guided the design and organization of this book:

- You care about teaching and your students, and you want to improve your abilities to help your students develop their intellectual and cognitive skills.
- You want to learn about specific instructional strategies that other faculty members have used successfully and that educational researchers have found to be effective.
- You can figure things out for yourself. Once you are presented with the gist of a strategy, you can adapt it to your particular circumstances and needs—or reject it as inappropriate for you.
- You are busy and have little time to read through the burgeoning literature on teaching and learning. You want to be able to quickly

locate information and ideas for improving your teaching and your students' learning. (For those of you who wish to do further reading, each tool includes a reference list.)

Many of the ideas described in *Tools for Teaching* can be readily implemented; others require some planning or modifications in course design. Not all the suggestions are of equal importance, and no one instructor could possibly use even half of them—nor would any instructor want to. Rather, each entry was chosen to stimulate your thinking about teaching. *Tools* is truly a toolbox from which to select and adapt those ideas that match your teaching style and the needs of your students. Indeed, one of the premises of the book is that there are no pat answers, quick fixes, or sure-fire recipes for excellent teaching, only endless ways to improve your teaching skills.

Origin of Tools for Teaching

Every day, faculty in classrooms across the country acquire useful knowledge about teaching. This book is an attempt to catalogue those classroom-tested ideas and strategies in an easy-to-read format that lends itself to quick reference and skimming. In preparing *Tools for Teaching*, I reviewed hundreds of techniques, strategies, and ideas, and I selected those that seemed most sensible and worthwhile for encouraging students' learning and intellectual development in a wide range of disciplines.

The ideas in *Tools* come primarily from five sources: (1) my conversations with and classroom observations of faculty at the University of California, Berkeley (some of their ideas are catalogued in *The ABCs of Teaching Excellence*, 1983; the publication is now out of print, but the material is available through the computer network—INFOCAL—on the Berkeley campus); (2) articles and publications by faculty at this and other colleges and universities; (3) the research literature in higher education on teaching, learning, and theories of instruction; (4) the work of experienced faculty development consultants who publish newsletters, handouts, guidebooks, and other fugitive documents about good teaching; and (5) newspaper and magazine articles that describe what faculty are doing to improve teaching and undergraduate education.

I have made every effort to attribute each entry to a published source or to cite a reference that provides greater detail, although the source cited is not necessarily the originator of the technique. In some cases, though, the ideas form part of the general lore and common practices of faculty or reached me without attribution or evolved from my own experiences in teaching and working with faculty.

Though *Tools* derives from a substantial body of research and theory, I have deliberately kept discussions of research findings to a minimum to avoid disrupting the user's smooth reading of the text. The best teaching respects the purpose for using a particular technique. Therefore, I encourage those with the time and inclination to use the bibliographies at the end of each tool to delve more deeply into the background of a given area. I also encourage all readers not to grab techniques and insert them thoughtlessly into a course but to think about their function and impact—and then, like all good teachers, to evaluate their effectiveness.

Description and Organization of Tools for Teaching

Tools is a practical source book designed to be used as a reference book; it is not meant to be read cover to cover in two or three sittings. Although all the principles and suggestions derive from classroom experience and educational research and theory, the various tools focus on what instructors can do rather than on the theoretical underpinnings for the suggestions.

Those seeking discussions of theory and philosophy, essays on good teaching, personal reminiscences about classroom experiences, or case studies of typical teaching situations will want to look elsewhere. And indeed, there are useful resources on each of these subjects. Essays on good teaching have been compiled, for example, by Gullette (1983). Personal descriptions of teaching experiences can be found in publications such as *The Teaching Professor* and *College Teaching* or in discipline-specific periodicals related to college teaching, such as *Teaching of Psychology* and *Journal of College Science Teaching*. (Cashin and Clegg, 1993, have compiled a list of periodicals related to college teaching.) Christensen and Hansen (1987) have prepared a textbook of cases on such topics as establishing a learning contract with students, gaining students' respect, and leading a discussion. Theories, models, and alternative outlooks on teaching have been proposed by Axelrod (1973) and Jackson (1986), among others.

Tools for Teaching is unlike these other publications. The book consists of forty-nine tools organized into twelve sections that represent, in roughly chronological sequence, the key teaching responsibilities and activities of college instructors. The topics range from specific tasks (writing a course syllabus) to broad social issues (dealing with diversity on campus).

Each tool includes a brief introduction, a set of general strategies, and concise descriptions of practical ideas that faculty members can adapt and try out. The format lends itself to easy and efficient identification of major points and to quick reading or browsing. Moreover, each tool can be read independently of the others, and the tools can be read in any order.

As you will see, the groupings of tools within the sections are somewhat arbitrary. "Explaining Clearly," for example, is located in Section Four, "Lecture Strategies," but has obvious relevance to all types of classes. The table of contents, index, and cross-references within the tools should help you quickly locate the material you need. The following overview of the twelve sections may also help you decide where to delve.

Section One, "Getting Under Way," addresses planning issues: how to design a new course or revise an existing one, how to create a syllabus, and how to handle the first day of class. Section Two, "Responding to a Diverse Student Body," explores issues that arise in teaching students with disabilities, students from ethnic or cultural backgrounds different from your own, and older students returning to school after an extended absence. The final tool in this section looks at classes in which students have widely varying academic skills and abilities.

The next three sections focus on instructional strategies for different class formats. Section Three, "Discussion Strategies," provides ideas on how to lead a productive discussion, frame challenging questions, and encourage student participation. Section Four, "Lecture Strategies," addresses all aspects of the lecture method, particularly the large lecture class: how to prepare, how to deliver effective lectures, and how to create a positive classroom environment in a large impersonal auditorium. This section also describes supplements and alternatives to lecturing, to more actively engage students and overcome the passivity of one-way communication. The theme of active involvement is continued in Section Five, "Collaborative and Experiential Strategies." Here you will read about the advantages of group work for classes of all sizes and ways you can help students learn by doing, through role playing, case studies, and fieldwork.

Section Six, "Enhancing Students' Learning and Motivation," relies on current theories of learning for instructional strategies that help students learn and become more confident and independent in mastering course material. The section also addresses the thorny problem of motivating all students to do their best.

Section Seven, "Writing Skills and Homework Assignments," describes how faculty in all departments can help students develop their writing skills — and how to do so without spending enormous amounts of time grading students' papers. This section also offers helpful hints on how to design and grade problem sets.

For many faculty members, testing and grading are the most difficult aspects of teaching. Section Eight, "Testing and Grading," offers pointers on developing good exams, alleviating students' test anxieties, and assessing the merits of various grading methods.

Section Nine, "Instructional Media and Technology," explores low-tech media such as chalkboards, in addition to computers and multimedia presentations.

Perhaps the most important section in the book is Section Ten, "Evaluation to Improve Teaching," for in order to become a more effective instructor, you need to know what works for your students and what does not. The section describes a variety of quick methods for getting immediate feedback from students, as well as the use of videotape, colleague observation, and self-assessment.

Because a substantial part of an instructor's work with students takes place before and after class, Section Eleven, "Teaching Outside the Classroom," offers ideas on holding office hours, advising undergraduates, and working with graduate students as teaching assistants.

Finally, Section Twelve, "Finishing Up," covers end-of-term activities: review sessions, student ratings, and letters of recommendation.

Despite the size and scope of *Tools*, I was unable to address certain types of classroom situations (laboratory teaching, foreign language courses, freshman seminars, individualized instruction, team teaching). Some topics are not the subject of an individual tool but are discussed in various tools. For example, "dealing with troublesome behavior in the classroom" is not a stand-alone tool, but relevant strategies appear in "Encouraging Student Participation in Discussion," "Preparing to Teach the Large Lecture Course," and "Diversity and Complexity in the Classroom: Considerations of Race, Ethnicity, and Gender."

Since each tool is designed to be read on its own merits, there is a certain amount of overlap from one tool to another, which I hope the careful reader will not find annoying or distracting. Furthermore, not all the suggestions are fully compatible; they represent a variety of innovative strategies, from which you can select those that best meet your needs.

If you are a new instructor, you may want to focus first on Sections One, Three, and Four ("Getting Under Way," "Discussion Strategies," and "Lecture Strategies") and then select for more in-depth exploration tools that reflect your own situation. Refer to *Tools for Teaching* over the course of the term as a resource for handling common teaching challenges (for example, encouraging students to talk during discussion periods). Do not feel obligated to do everything immediately, but pick and choose from among the topics and try just a few things to start.

If you feel generally comfortable about your teaching but are looking for ways to inject some excitement into your courses, browse through the book and select topics you would like to explore or experiment with. Or skip to Section Three, "Discussion Strategies," and Section Five, "Collaborative and Experiential Strategies," or to the tools "Supplements and Alternatives to Lecturing" and "Helping Students Write Better in All Courses"—they all contain ideas for actively engaging students in your courses.

If you already have a sense of the areas you want to improve, read the tools that directly relate to those areas.

If you are unsure about your teaching strengths and weaknesses, begin by carefully assessing your teaching. By reviewing student rating forms from past classes, watching yourself on videotape, and asking a colleague or consultant to observe and comment on your teaching, you can begin to assess what you do well and what you could change. Other possibilities for assessment are described in "Self-Evaluation and the Teaching Dossier" in Section Ten. Once you have made your initial assessment, scan the table of contents and the index for the relevant topics.

All instructors can benefit from the tool "Fast Feedback," which offers new and experienced teachers practical advice on how to gauge students' comprehension of course material and how to elicit their opinions of the strengths and weaknesses of your teaching.

Regardless of how you use *Tools for Teaching*, whenever you find suggestions that you want to try, sketch out a plan. As Weimer (1990, p. 19) advises, "Articles on teaching should never be read without the simultaneous preparation of a to-do list that outlines proposed actions to be taken as a result of the reading."

What Is Effective Teaching?

For hundreds of years, college teaching was typified by a professor reading a lecture to an audience of note-taking students. The professor's duties were to compose and present authoritative lectures, to test students on their knowledge, and to assign grades. Over the last thirty years, however, this model has given way to a new understanding of what constitutes effective college-level instruction. Research on students' academic success and intellectual development and on theories of learning and cognitive development has demonstrated the effectiveness of modes of instruction that emphasize active learning and collaborative activities and engage students in intellectual discovery. According to this view, the instructor's task is to interact with students in ways that enable them to acquire new information, practice new skills, and reconfigure and expand on what they already know. One implication is that there is no one best instructional method—what constitutes effective teaching depends on the students, the context, the topic, and the discipline. Nonetheless, from the studies and reports on good teaching (Angelo and Cross, 1993; Centra and Bonesteel, 1990; Chickering and Gamson, 1991; Educational Testing Service, 1992; Murray, 1991; Ramsden, 1992; Reynolds, 1992; Schön, 1987; Shulman, 1987) and research on student achievement and academic success (Mow and Nettles, 1990; Noel, Levitz, Saluri, and Associates, 1985; Pascarella and Terenzini, 1991; Tinto, 1987), it is possible to identify four clusters of instructional skills, strategies, and attitudes that promote students' academic achievement.

1. *Organizing and explaining material in ways appropriate to students' abilities.* The heart of effective teaching is the instructor's understanding of the material. But knowledge of the subject matter, though essential, is not enough. Good teachers also understand what makes certain topics or concepts difficult for students, and they can explain those topics in plain, comprehensible terms. In addition, they are able to gauge their students' background knowledge and experiences, identify reasonable expectations for students' progress, select appropriate teaching methods and materials, devise examples and analogies that clarify key points, relate one topic to another, and assess whether students are learning what is being taught.

2. *Creating an environment for learning.* Effective teachers establish and maintain rapport with students, are attentive and responsive to students' needs, communicate high expectations, give appropriate feedback on stu-

dents' work, and respect diverse talents and ways of learning. Their instructional methods emphasize cooperation, collaboration, and strategies that actively engage students in learning.

3. *Helping students become autonomous, self-regulated learners.* Effective faculty communicate their goals and expectations to students, including the belief that the students can learn; direct students in establishing and developing their own connections to the course content; view the learning process as a joint venture; and stimulate students' intellectual interests and enthusiasm.

4. *Reflecting on and evaluating their teaching.* Effective teachers take time to critically examine why they are doing what they do and the effects of what they do on their students. On the basis of their conversations with and observations of their students, they can imagine ways to improve their teaching and help their students resolve whatever problems they may be encountering.

All the tools in this book are designed to help you assess and improve your skills in these areas. Of course, simply adopting a few new techniques or strategies will not immediately transform anyone into a masterful instructor. But every instructor can learn to be more effective by developing and practicing these key skills.

If you think back on the instructors who were most influential in your academic life, you will probably remember professors who knew the subject but seemed to have little awareness of how students learn. At times, you may have felt you were learning *despite* rather than *because of* the professor; and less ambitious classmates may not have learned much at all. *Tools* is intended to provide you with the repertoire of instructional strategies known and used by faculty who are the "because of" professors.

A Request

Since a theme of this book is that evaluation is critical for improvement, I would be grateful for your comments on the ideas presented in *Tools*. What works? What doesn't? Let me know what you think and please pass along the good ideas you use in your own courses (electronic mail: oed@violet. berkeley.edu or bgd@uclink.berkeley.edu).

Acknowledgments

This book could not have been written without the contributions of a great many people, and I am deeply indebted to each of them for their assistance and encouragement.

For sharing freely their ideas about good teaching: the faculty of the University of California, Berkeley. Berkeley has a great many outstanding and distinguished teachers, too many to list individually. I thank them collectively for their contributions to this book.

For reviewing and commenting on draft material at various stages. Many faculty members and administrators at the University of California, Berkeley, have reviewed earlier versions of various tools. I am grateful for their helpful suggestions and constructive criticisms. Several reviewers merit special recognition: Frederick C. Crews, Sam Davis, Marian Diamond, W. Russell Ellis, Sally Fairfax, Debra Fong, Ole Hald, Gary Handman, Michael Hardie, Francisco Hernandez, Sheila Humphreys, Helen Johnson, Peter Kerner, Matt Kondolf, Kristin Luker, Flora McMartin, Margarita Melville, William K. Muir, Kevin Padian, David Patterson, Matthew Rabin, Vincent Resh, K.V.S. Sastry, Michael Scriven, Daniele Spellman, Richard Sutch, Ronald Takaki, Stephen K. Tollefson, and Joanne Wile. Staff members from the following offices also provided valuable suggestions: Disabled Students' Program, Office of Media Services, Student Learning Center, Pre-Professional and Pre-Graduate Advising, and College Writing Program.

For reviewing and commenting on the entire manuscript: Larry Braskamp, Jo Keroes, John Ory, Mary Ann Shea, Mary Deane Sorcinelli, Marilla Svinicki, and Jon Wergin.

For editorial assistance: Amy Einsohn.

For bibliographic, research, and production assistance: Natalie Bosworth, Cherry Chaicharn, Leif Krauss, Michele Mattingly, Rose Nash, David Palumbo-Liu, McCrae Parker, Christi Zmich, and especially Debra Fong and Jana Woodard, who both hung in there from the very beginning to the end.

For design assistance: Chuck Byrne.

For ongoing advice and reality checks: Sam Davis, Rita Berro, Karen Gross McRoberts, Amy Einsohn, Stephen K. Tollefson, Larry Braskamp, Ole Hald, Daniele Spellman, Molly McRoberts, and Sam McRoberts.

I also want to acknowledge my debt to the authors of books that have become useful references in the field: Kenneth E. Eble, *The Craft of Teaching* (2nd ed., 1988); Barbara Schneider Fuhrmann and Anthony F. Grasha, *A Practical Handbook for College Teachers* (1983); Joseph Lowman, *Mastering the Techniques of Teaching* (1984); and Wilbert J. McKeachie, *Teaching Tips* (8th ed., 1986).

Finally, a very special thanks to my husband, Sam, professor of architecture and chair of the department at the University of California, Berkeley, for his steadfast encouragement, substantive contributions, and considerable patience, which enabled me to complete this book.

References

Angelo, T. A., and Cross, K. P. *Classroom Assessment Techniques: A Handbook for College Teachers.* (2nd ed.) San Francisco: Jossey-Bass, 1993.

Axelrod, J. *The University Teacher as Artist: Toward an Aesthetics of Teaching with Emphasis on the Humanities.* San Francisco: Jossey-Bass, 1973.

Cashin, W. E., and Clegg, V. L. "Periodicals Related to College Teaching." *Idea Paper*, no. 28. Manhattan: Center for Faculty Evaluation and Development, Kansas State University, 1993.

Centra, J. A., and Bonesteel, P. "College Teaching: An Art or a Science?" In M. Theall and J. Franklin (eds.), *Student Ratings of Instruction: Issues for Improving Practice.* New Directions for Teaching and Learning, no. 43. San Francisco: Jossey-Bass, 1990.

Chickering, A. W., and Gamson, Z. F. (eds.). *Applying the Seven Principles for Good Practice in Undergraduate Education.* New Directions for Teaching and Learning, no. 47. San Francisco: Jossey-Bass, 1991.

Christensen, C. R., and Hansen, A. J. *Teaching and the Case Method.* Boston: Harvard Business School, 1987.

Educational Testing Service. PRAXIS (Project to assess teacher performance). Described in "Classroom Performance Assessments: Creating a Portrait of the Beginning Teacher." *Educational Testing Service Developments*, 1992, *38*(1), 2–4.

Gullette, M. M. (ed.). *The Art and Craft of Teaching.* Cambridge, Mass.: Harvard University Press, 1983.

Jackson, P. W. *The Practice of Teaching.* New York: Teachers College Press, 1986.

Mow, S. L., and Nettles, M. T. "Minority Student Access to, and Persistence and Performance in, College: A Review of the Trends and Research Literature." In J. C. Smart (ed.), *Higher Education: Handbook of Theory and Research.* Vol. 6. New York: Agathon Press, 1990.

Murray, H. G. "Effective Teaching Behaviors in the College Classroom." In J. C. Smart (ed.), *Higher Education: Handbook of Theory and Research.* Vol. 7. New York: Agathon Press, 1991.

Noel, L., Levitz, R., Saluri, D., and Associates. *Increasing Student Retention: Effective Programs and Practices for Reducing the Dropout Rate.* San Francisco: Jossey-Bass, 1985.

Pascarella, E. T., and Terenzini, P. T. *How College Affects Students: Findings and Insights from Twenty Years of Research.* San Francisco: Jossey-Bass, 1991.

Ramsden, P. *Learning to Teach in Higher Education.* New York: Routledge, 1992.

Reynolds, A. "What Is Competent Beginning Teaching? A Review of the Literature." *Review of Educational Research*, 1992, *62*(1), 1–35.

Schön, D. A. *Educating the Reflective Practitioner: Toward a New Design for Teaching and Learning in the Professions.* San Francisco: Jossey-Bass, 1987.

Shulman, L. S. "Knowledge and Teaching: Foundations of the New Reform." *Harvard Educational Review*, 1987, *57*(1), 1–22.

Tinto, V. *Leaving College: Rethinking the Causes and Cures of Student Attrition.* Chicago: University of Chicago Press, 1987.

Weimer, M. "'Study' Your Way to Better Teaching." In M. D. Svinicki (ed.), *The Changing Face of College Teaching.* New Directions for Teaching and Learning, no. 42. San Francisco: Jossey-Bass, 1990.

The Author

Barbara Gross Davis is assistant vice chancellor, educational development, at the University of California, Berkeley. She received a B.A. degree (1968) in psychology, an M.A. degree (1973) in educational psychology, and a Ph.D. degree (1976), also in educational psychology, all from Berkeley.

Davis's main areas of interest have been program and curriculum evaluation, instructional improvement, and faculty development—all in higher education. She has conducted workshops and seminars on topics related to teaching, learning, and evaluation, and she has written about faculty evaluation, assessment, and teaching improvement.

Her books include *Evaluation of Composition Instruction* (1987, with M. Scriven and S. Thomas) and *Evaluating Intervention Programs* (1985, with S. Humphreys).

Tools
for
Teaching

I.

Getting Under Way

1. **Preparing or Revising a Course**
2. **The Course Syllabus**
3. **The First Day of Class**

Preparing or Revising a Course

1

In designing or revising a course, faculty are faced with at least three crucial decisions: what to teach, how to teach it, and how to ensure that students are learning what is being taught. Often, the most difficult step in preparing or revising a course is deciding which topics must be *excluded* if the whole is to be manageable. Many teachers, hoping to impart to students everything they know about a subject, attempt to include too much material by half. The following suggestions below are designed to help you limit the content of your course, structure and sequence the activities and assignments, set policies, and handle administrative tasks.

General Strategies

If the course is new to you but has been offered before, talk with faculty who have taught it previously. Ask your colleagues for their syllabus, list of assignments and papers, and old exams. Find out about the typical problems students have with the material and the difficulties the instructor encountered. If appropriate, look at past student evaluations of the course to help you identify its strengths and weaknesses.

If the course is new to you and has never been offered before, review textbooks on the topic of the course. Reviewing textbooks will give you a sense of the main themes and issues that your course might address, which is especially useful if you are preparing a course outside your areas of specialization. (Source: Brown, 1978)

If you have previously taught the course, begin by assembling everything associated with the course. Gather a copy of the syllabus, textbooks and readings, handouts, exams, your notes for each class session, and the past evaluations by students. Read the evaluations to get a sense of the course's strengths and weaknesses. Then take a look at the various course materials in light of students' comments, changes in the field, and your own changing interests. (Source: "Course Materials Review," 1987)

Identify the constraints in teaching the course. As you begin to design the course, ask yourself, How many hours are available for instruction? How many students will be enrolled? Are the students primarily majors or non-majors? At what level? What material can I safely assume that students will know? What courses have they already completed? What courses might they be taking while enrolled in mine? Will readers or graduate student instructors be available? What sorts of technological resources will be in the classroom? (Sources: Brown, 1978; Ory, 1990)

Think about how your course relates to other courses in your department's curriculum. Does your course serve as the introduction for more advanced classes? Is it a general education course that may provide the only exposure nonmajors will have to the content area? Is it an advanced course for majors?

Deciding What You Want to Accomplish

Establish goals. What do you expect your students to do or to produce as a result of taking the course? Writing down goals is important for at least four reasons (Erickson, n.d.): (1) the process forces you to clarify what you want your students to accomplish; (2) your list of goals will help you select appropriate teaching methods, materials, and assignments; (3) you can use your list of goals to communicate your expectations to students, to let them know what they are expected to accomplish; (4) your list of goals will be useful to colleagues who teach courses that rely on yours as a prerequisite. McKeachie (1986), however, warns faculty against becoming obsessed with writing detailed behavioral objectives. The chief purpose of writing goals is to help you plan your course and specify what you want to do.

Identify both content and noncontent goals. Fuhrmann and Grasha (1983) recommend identifying both content goals (for example, "understand the key forces affecting the rise of Japan as an economic power") and noncontent goals (for example, "become a good team member and work collaboratively with other students" or "learn to tolerate opposing points of view"). They advise faculty to start with a general list and then refine the goals to make them more specific. What do you expect from students? How will students demonstrate that they have mastered the goal? What will constitute acceptable performance? For example, if the general content goal is for students to understand the rise of Japan as an economic factor, a specific content goal might be that students will analyze in depth how technology has affected Japan's economic dominance. A specific noncontent goal might be that students will work in groups of three on an out-of-class project and prepare a joint report.

To get started in writing course goals, think about "the big picture." For example, imagine yourself overhearing a group of graduating seniors who have taken your course and are discussing why it was among the most valuable courses they have ever taken. What would they be saying about the course? Or imagine that several of your students will become local or national power brokers, or that half of them will have to drop out of school and work full-time. Would you change the way you are teaching your course? Why? Is there anything different you would like these students to learn? (Source: Bergquist and Phillips, 1977)

Scale down your goals to a realistic list. Adjust your ideal goals by taking into consideration the different abilities, interests, and expectations of your students and the amount of time available for class instruction. How many goals can your students accomplish in the time available? (Source: Lowman, 1984)

Defining and Limiting Course Content

After you have "packed" all your topics into a preliminary list, toss out the excess baggage. Designing a course is somewhat like planning a transcontinental trip. First, list everything that you feel might be important for students to know, just as you might stuff several large suitcases with everything that you think you might need on a trip. Then severely pare down the topics you have listed, just as you might limit yourself to one or two pieces of luggage. Research shows that too much detail and too many topics work against students' learning the material (Beard and Hartley, 1984).

Distinguish between essential and optional material. Divide the concepts or topics you want to cover into three groups: *basic* material should be mastered by every student, *recommended* material should be mastered by every student seeking a good knowledge of the subject, and *optional* material should be mastered by those students with special interests and aptitudes. Lectures and exams should focus on the basic elements of the course. Recommended and optional topics, labeled as such for students, can be included in lectures, supplementary materials, and readings.

Emphasize the core concepts. For example, in engineering, as one professor points out, there are thousands of formulas, but all of these are variations on a very limited number of basic ideas or theories. In a single course, students might encounter a thousand equations. Rote memorization is futile because no one can remember that many equations. Instead, the instructor repeatedly emphasizes the fundamentals by showing students how the thousand equations are embedded in a dozen basic ones.

Stress the classic issues, or the most enduring values or truths. Often the most interesting issues and themes for undergraduates turn out to be those that originally attracted *you* to the discipline.

Cut to the chase. Go for the most critical skills or ideas and drop the rest. For example, in solving mathematical problems, the most important task is setting up the problem—the rest is the mechanics. Not every problem needs to be worked through to completion. (Source: Svinicki, 1990–1991)

Give students a conceptual framework on which to hang major ideas and factual information. To the uninitiated, your field may look like an unruly mass of facts devoid of logic or unifying principles. To understand the relationship among concepts rather than simply memorize dozens of discrete points, students need a framework—a basic theory, a theme, a typology, or a controversial issue. Make this framework apparent to the students through repeated references to it.

Prepare a detailed syllabus. Share the conceptual framework, logic, and organization of your course with students by distributing a syllabus. See "The Course Syllabus."

Structuring the Course

Devise a logical arrangement for the course content. Material can be arranged chronologically, by topic or category, from concrete to abstract or vice versa, from theory to application or vice versa, by increasing level of skill or complexity, or by other schemes. Some courses—in history or literature—almost demand a chronological sequence. Here are some other strategies for organizing material (Bergquist and Phillips, 1977, pp. 146–149):

Micro/macro: Begin by describing a large complex phenomenon (macro perspective) or offer a detailed analysis of one aspect of the phenomenon (micro perspective). Establish a broad general base of knowledge and information (macro) or focus on a specific event or concern (micro).

Distal/proximal: Begin by presenting an immediate and pressing problem related to the field of study (proximal perspective) or by describing the origins, heritage or context (distal perspective). Begin with the relevance of the subject matter (proximal) or with historical or theoretical perspectives (distal).

Phenomenon/structure: Emphasize description and analysis of unique and significant events, people, or ideas (phenomenon) or emphasize description and analysis of theories, themes, and universal applications (structure). Focus on specific works, events, or people in their unique setting or focus on general patterns and concepts that are commonly shared by or expressed through different works, events, and people.

Stark and others (1990) offer additional sequencing patterns, suggesting that topics may be ordered according to the following:

- How relationships occur in the real world
- How students will use the information in social, personal, or career settings
- How major concepts and relationships are organized in the discipline
- How students learn
- How knowledge has been created in the field

List all class meetings. On your preliminary schedule mark university holidays, major religious holidays, breaks, and, if appropriate, college events that may preempt classes. Fill in this schedule with tentative topics and dates for exams. Keep in mind the rhythm of the term, including "down" times. Leave open at least part of the class before each exam to allow for catch-up or review. Leave extra time for complex or difficult topics. Schedule time during the middle of the semester for getting feedback from students on how well the course is going (see "Fast Feedback"). Also give special consideration to the first day of class (see "The First Day of Class"), the meetings right before exams, and the last two or three classes, which can be used to integrate and pull together the themes of the course (see "The Last Days of Class").

Select appropriate instructional methods for each class meeting. Instead of asking, What am *I* going to do in each class session? focus on What are *students* going to do? (Bligh, 1971). Identify which topics lend themselves to which types of classroom activities, and select one or more activities for each class session: lectures; small group discussions; independent work; simulations, debates, case studies, and role playing; demonstrations; experiential learning activities; instructional technologies; collaborative learning work, and so on. (See other tools for descriptions of these methods.) For each topic, decide how you will prepare the class for instruction (through reviews or previews), present the new concepts (through lectures, demonstrations, discussion), have students apply what they have learned (through discussion, in-class writing activities, collaborative work), and assess whether students can put into practice what they have learned (through testing, discussion, problem solving, and so on).

Design in-class and homework assignments. See "Designing Effective Writing Assignments," "Homework: Problem Sets," "Collaborative Learning: Group Work and Study Teams," and "Supplements and Alternatives to Lecturing: Encouraging Student Participation."

Selecting Textbooks and Readings

Choose textbooks and reading assignments that reflect your goals. The textbook exerts a greater influence on what students learn than the teaching method (McKeachie, 1986). Explain to your students how the readings relate to the course goals and classroom activities. Some faculty assign texts that repeat material covered in class — or vice versa — in order to reinforce the content. Some readings may be assigned to elaborate on the lectures by providing applications and examples. Some readings may be intended to convey additional material or to give contrasting points of view. (Source: "Selecting a Textbook," 1987)

Consider a range of criteria in selecting readings. If several textbooks, reports, or articles are appropriate to your course goals, select among them by judging the following (adapted from Lowman, 1984; "Selecting a Text-book," 1987; Wright, 1987):

- Accuracy and currency of content
- Coherence and clarity of content
- Level of difficulty and interest for students (challenging but not inappropriately difficult)
- Cost
    Choose the less expensive work if it is of comparable quality
    Choose paperbacks rather than hardbacks
    Limit the total cost of books for your course by placing some works on reserve in the library
- Size (heavy large texts are hard to carry)
- Format and layout (ease of reading)

McKeachie (1986) recommends selecting textbooks that match your own point of view because students may be annoyed or confused if you express disagreement with the text. To complement the principal textbook, however, and expose students to a range of perspectives, you could select articles and shorter texts that espouse points of view different from your own.

Assign a mix of texts and articles, including some current pieces. Advanced courses typically include journal articles, essays, research reports, or photocopied course readers. But even in lower-division courses, students should have an opportunity to read at least a few recent publications or journal articles. One faculty member in economics assigns the Tuesday editorial page of the *Wall Street Journal* each week. She uses these editorials as a basis for discussions and for exam questions that ask students to compare the editorials with textbook presentations on related topics.

Foster a habit of reading throughout college. Encourage students to explore beyond the reading material you assign. Eble (1988) recommends setting up in your office a shelf of books and articles selected for brevity, relevance, and interest. Invite students to browse through the materials and borrow items.

Follow the copyright laws. If you are compiling a photocopied reader, be sure to observe the copyright laws, available from your library or from photocopying vendors. Services have sprung up to handle faculty requests for permission to reproduce copyrighted material. For example, the Anthology Permissions Service in Salem, Massachusetts, authorizes copying of copyrighted material through blanket agreements with publishers. PUBNET Permissions, a project of the trade association Association of American Publishers, processes permissions requests by electronic mail to help faculty members reproduce copyrighted materials quickly and easily. (Source: Blum, 1991)

Take advantage of the new technologies in publishing. At least one national publisher lets professors order customized versions of its publications. The publisher will produce bound copies of chapters in its textbooks and supplementary articles, in any order the instructor requests. In some cases, if a professor orders only selected chapters of a textbook, the price is less than the cost of the entire text. Some publishers have gone a step farther and developed data bases of individual chapters from different texts, journal articles, case studies, and other material from which a faculty member can create a custom textbook. The materials are compiled, indexed, paginated, and bound within forty-eight hours. Other publishers offer low-cost versions of textbooks stripped of such frills as study questions and multicolor art and graphics. It may also be possible to make the content of scholarly print journals available electronically so that students need only have access to a computer and the campus network to complete the assigned reading. (Sources: Miller, 1990; "Stalled Economy Leads to 'No-Frills' Textbooks," 1992; Watkins, 1991)

Be conscious of workload. At most colleges, students are expected to spend two to three hours on outside work for each hour in class. For simple texts, you might estimate that students can read about twenty pages an hour—though, obviously, the rate will depend on your students' abilities and the nature of the reading material.

Setting Course Policies

"Extra credit" assignments. If you are offering extra credit assignments, announce them in class so that all students will be aware of the option. Some faculty allow only students who are doing satisfactory (C or higher) work on the regular assignments to undertake extra credit tasks. Here are some examples of extra credit options ("Extra Credit—Taking Sides and Offering Advice," 1991, pp. 5–6):

- One or two weeks before an exam, give students worksheets on the topics being studied in that unit. To receive extra credit, a student must complete the worksheet *and* bring it to the instructor's office for discussion and scoring.
- Offer a fixed number of extra credit points for a specified activity: attendance at a professional conference, submission of a book review in the topic area, and so on.
- Offer extra credit for completing problems in the textbook that were not assigned as homework.
- Offer students extra credit for keeping a journal account of all the relevant newspaper or magazine articles, books, or monographs they read in addition to the assigned readings. Journal entries should include the title, author, date, and source as well as some personal commentary. Journals are checked weekly on the spot and turned in at the end of the term.

Attendance. Let students know in the syllabus and on the first day of class that you expect them to come to class regularly. Do your best to make class time worthwhile—a time when real work takes place. Students are also more likely to attend if they know that exams will include items that have been discussed in class only. In most cases, however, attendance should not be mandatory or a factor in your grading policy. Grades should be based on students' mastery of the course content and not on such nonacademic factors as attendance. See "Grading Practices." If you must require attendance, let students know how you will determine whether they come to class. Give bonus points for perfect or near perfect attendance rather than subtracting points for absences (Professional and Organizational Development Network in Higher Education, 1989). The numerical result is the same but students will feel better having their attendance rewarded rather than their absences penalized. In addition to students' attendance, you should pay attention to your own patterns. Some observers recommend that instructors come early to class (to let students know you are interested and available), start on time (to reward the prompt), end on time (to enable students to leave for their next class), and stay late (to answer questions from students) (Heine and others, 1981).

Makeup exams. For advice on offering makeup tests—and ways to avoid having to do so—see "Quizzes, Tests, and Exams."

Late work. Be clear on whether you will accept late work and the penalties for missing deadlines. Some faculty members deduct an increasing number of points for each day an assignment is late. Others give a sufficient number of assignments so that a student is allowed to drop one or two without penalty (due to low grades or missing work). Still other faculty members give students two days of grace that they can apply to missed deadlines: a single assignment can be two days late or two assignments can each be a day late (Marincovich and Rusk, 1987).

Grading. See "Grading Practices."

Handling Administrative Tasks

Order books early and anticipate foul-ups. Double-check on the progress of your order with the bookstore a month or so before the term begins. Once the books have arrived, check back with the bookstore to see how many copies there are. No matter what precautions you take, there is always a chance that the books won't arrive before classes begin. You can make it easier on yourself and your class by not relying on books being available during the first two weeks of class. Instead, assign readings that you distribute, that are readily available on reserve in the library, or that students purchase from a photocopy vendor.

Place materials on reserve before the term begins or package reserve materials for students to purchase. Consult with campus librarians about the procedures for putting materials on reserve. Let your students know in which library the readings are located, the length of time they are available for use, and the number of copies on reserve. Because as many as 85 percent of the students check out reserve material to make their own photocopies rather than read it in the library ("Two Groups Tackle Reserve Book Problems," 1992), consider offering students the chance to purchase the reserve readings. (Sources: Janes and Hauer, 1988; "Two Groups Tackle Reserve Book Problems, 1992)

Make logistical arrangements in advance. Before the term begins, order audiovisual equipment, videos, or films, contact guest speakers, and arrange for field trips.

References

Beard, R. M., and Hartley, J. *Teaching and Learning in Higher Education.* (4th ed.) New York: HarperCollins, 1984.

Bergquist, W. H., and Phillips, S. R. *Handbook for Faculty Development.* Vol. 2. Washington, D.C.: Council for the Advancement of Small Colleges, 1977.

Bligh, D. A. *What's the Use of Lecturing?* Devon, England: Teaching Services Centre, University of Exeter, 1971.

Blum, D. E. "Use of Photocopied Anthologies for Courses Snarled by Delays and Costs of Copyright Permission Process." *Chronicle of Higher Education,* Sept. 11, 1991, A-19–A-20.

Brown, G. *Lecturing and Explaining.* New York: Methuen, 1978.

"Course Materials Review." *Teaching Professor,* 1(6), 3–4, 1987.

Eble, K. E. *The Craft of Teaching.* (2nd ed.) San Francisco: Jossey-Bass, 1988.

Erickson, B. L. "Instructional Objectives." Unpublished manuscript, Instructional Development Program, University of Rhode Island, n.d.

"Extra Credit—Taking Sides and Offering Advice." *Teaching Professor,* 1991, 5(3), 5–6.

Fuhrmann, B. S., and Grasha, A. F. *A Practical Handbook for College Teachers.* Boston: Little, Brown, 1983.

Heine, H., and others. *The Torch or the Firehose? A Guide to Section Teaching*. Cambridge: Undergraduate Academic Support Office of the Dean for Student Affairs, Massachusetts Institute of Technology, 1981.

Janes, J., and Hauer, D. *Now What? Readings on Surviving (and Even Enjoying) Your First Experience at College Teaching*. Littleton, Mass.: Copley, 1988.

Lowman, J. *Mastering the Techniques of Teaching*. San Francisco: Jossey-Bass, 1984.

McKeachie, W. J. *Teaching Tips*. (8th ed.) Lexington, Mass.: Heath, 1986.

Marincovich, M., and Rusk, L. *Excellence in Teaching Electrical Engineering*. Stanford, Calif.: Center for Teaching and Learning, Stanford University, 1987.

Miller, M. W. "Professors Customize Textbooks, Blurring Roles of Publisher, Seller and Copy Shop." *Wall Street Journal*, Aug. 16, 1990, pp. B1, B3.

Ory, J. C. *Teaching and Its Evaluation: A Handbook of Resources*. Urbana: Office of Instructional Resources, University of Illinois, 1990.

Professional and Organizational Development Network in Higher Education. *Bright Idea Network*, 1989. (For information contact David Graf, Iowa State University, Ames.)

"Selecting a Textbook." *Teaching Professor*, 1987, *1*(7), 2.

"Stalled Economy Leads to 'No-Frills' Textbooks." *Academic Leader*, 1992, *8*(9), 6.

Stark, J. S., and others. *Planning Introductory College Courses: Influences of Faculty*. Ann Arbor: National Center for Research to Improve Postsecondary Teaching and Learning, University of Michigan, 1990.

Svinicki, M. D. "So Much Content, So Little Time." *Teaching Excellence*, 1990–1991, *2*(8). (Publication of the Professional and Organizational Development Network in Higher Education, Teaching and Learning Center, University of Nebraska, Lincoln)

"Two Groups Tackle Reserve Book Problems." *Academic Leader*, 1992, *8*(9), 3.

Watkins, B. T. "San Diego Campus and McGraw-Hill Create Custom Texts." *Chronicle of Higher Education*, Dec. 6, 1991, p. A25.

Wright, D. L. "Getting the Most Out of Your Textbook." *Teaching at the University of Nebraska, Lincoln*, 1987, *8*(3), 1–3. (Newsletter available from the Teaching and Learning Center, University of Nebraska, Lincoln)

2

The Course Syllabus

A detailed course syllabus, handed out on the first day of class, gives students an immediate sense of what the course will cover, what work is expected of them, and how their performance will be evaluated. A typical syllabus includes the sequence of assigned readings and activities by date and topic and provides information on course policies and procedures.

All courses can benefit from a syllabus. The act of preparing a syllabus helps you decide what topics will be covered and at what pace. Further, by distributing a written explanation of course procedures, you can minimize misunderstandings about the due dates of assignments, grading criteria, and policies on missed tests. Finally, a well-prepared course syllabus shows students that you take your teaching seriously.

General Strategies

Look over the syllabi of other faculty members. Syllabi vary in format and content. If your department does not have a standard format, use your colleagues' syllabi as rough models. Birdsall (1989) provides examples of course syllabi.

Anticipate the general questions that will be in the minds of students. What will your students want to know about your course? The three most common concerns of students on the first day of class are likely to be: Will I be able to do the work? Will I like the professor? Will I get along with my classmates? (Knefelkamp, in Rubin, 1985). In terms of course-specific information, students most often want to know about the topics to be covered; number and types of tests and assignments; grading system; textbook and readings; policies pertaining to attendance, late work, and makeup work; purpose of the course; nature of class sessions; and level of preparation or background necessary to succeed in the course (Wilkerson and McKnight, 1978). In addition, as Rubin (1985) points out, students may be asking themselves, Why should I take *this* course? How does this course fit into the larger curriculum or the general education program? Where does it lead intellectually and practically?

Keep the syllabus flexible. Some classes move more quickly than others. Some classes get sidetracked on certain topics. You might anticipate such variations by indicating the topics to be covered week by week rather than session by session. Or you might plan to issue a revised schedule midway through the term to account for students' heightened interest in certain topics.

Creating a Syllabus

Include more rather than less material. Your syllabus need not include all the components mentioned here, but experienced faculty agree that a detailed syllabus is a valuable learning tool for students and lessens their initial anxieties about the course. Use lists, informal language, and headings to highlight major topics and help students locate information. If your syllabus is long, include a table of contents. (Sources: Birdsall, 1989; Lowther, Stark, and Martens, 1989; Rodgers and Burnett, 1981)

Provide basic information. Include the current year and semester, the course title and number, the number of units, the meeting time and location. Indicate any course meetings that are not scheduled for the assigned room. List your name, office address (include a map if your office is hard to locate), office phone number (and indicate whether you have voice mail), electronic address, fax number, and office hours. For your office hours, indicate whether students need to make appointments in advance or may just stop in. If you list a home telephone number, indicate any restrictions on its use (for example, "Please do not call after 10 P.M."). Include the names, offices, and phone numbers of any teaching or laboratory assistants. (Sources: Altman and Cashin, 1992; Birdsall, 1989)

Describe the prerequisites to the course. Help students realistically assess their readiness for your course by listing the knowledge, skills, or experience you expect them to have already or the courses they should have completed. Give students suggestions on how they might refresh their skills if they feel uncertain about their readiness. (Source: Rubin, 1985)

Give an overview of the course's purpose. Provide an introduction to the subject matter and show how the course fits in the college or department curriculum. Explain what the course is about and why students would want to learn the material. One faculty member writes an essay about the purpose of the course and includes it in the syllabus. He makes an effort to refer to the essay periodically during the term (Shea, 1990).

State the general learning goals or objectives. List three to five major objectives that you expect all students to strive for: What will students know or be able to do better after completing this course? What skills or competencies do you want to develop in your students? (Source: Johnson, 1988)

Clarify the conceptual structure used to organize the course. Students need to understand why you have arranged topics in a given order and the logic of the themes or concepts you have selected.

Describe the format or activities of the course. Let students know whether the course involves fieldwork, research projects, lectures, discussions with active participation, and the like. Which are required and which recommended?

Specify the textbook and readings by authors and editions. Include information on why the particular readings were selected. When possible, show the relationship between the readings and the course objectives, especially if you assign chapters in a textbook out of sequence (Rubin, 1985). Let students know whether they are required to do the reading before each class meeting. If students will purchase books or course readers, include prices and the names of local bookstores that stock texts. If you will place readings on reserve in the library, you might include the call numbers (McKeachie, 1986). If you do not have access to the call numbers or if they would make the reading list look too cluttered, give students as their first assignment the task of identifying the call numbers for the readings. Let students know that this will make it easier for them to locate each week's readings, and more importantly, it will give them practice in using the library's electronic card catalogue.

Identify additional materials or equipment needed for the course. For example, do students need lab or safety equipment, art supplies, calculators, computers, drafting materials? (Source: Altman and Cashin, 1992)

List assignments, term papers, and exams. State the nature and format of the assignments, the expected length of essays, and their deadlines. Give the examination dates and briefly indicate the nature of the tests (multiple-choice, essay, short-answer, take-home tests). How do the assignments relate to the learning objectives for the course? What are your expectations for written work? In setting up the syllabus, try to keep the work load evenly balanced throughout the term. (Source: Lowther, Stark, and Martens, 1989)

State how students will be evaluated and how grades will be assigned. Describe the grading procedures, including the components of the final grade and the weights assigned to each component (for example, homework, term papers, midterms, and final exams). Students appreciate knowing the weighting because it helps them budget their time (Altman, 1989). Will you grade on a curve or use an absolute scale? Will you accept extra-credit work to improve grades? Will any quiz grades be dropped? See "Grading Practices."

List other course requirements. For example, are students required to attend an office hour or form study groups?

Discuss course policies. Clearly state your policies regarding class attendance; turning in late work; missing homework, tests or exams; makeups; extra credit; requesting extensions; reporting illnesses; cheating and plagiarism. Some instructors give this information in a question-and-answer format (Schlesinger, 1987): "Is it true that makeup exams are given only during finals week? Yes, see page 6." Include a description of students' responsibilities in the learning process and the professor's and graduate student instructors' responsibilities. You might also list acceptable and unacceptable classroom behavior ("Please refrain from eating during class because it is disturbing to me and other students").

Invite students with special needs to contact you during office hours. Let students know that if they need an accommodation for any type of physical or learning disability, they should set up a time to meet with you to discuss what modifications are necessary.

Provide a course calendar or schedule. The schedule should include the sequence of course topics, the preparations or readings, and the assignments due. For the readings, give page numbers in addition to chapter numbers — this will help students budget their time. Exam dates should be firmly fixed, while dates for topics and activities may be listed as tentative. Provide an updated calendar as needed.

Schedule time for fast feedback from your students. Set a time midway through the term when you can solicit from students their reactions to the course so far. See "Fast Feedback" for ways to get feedback from students.

List important drop dates. Include on the course calendar the last day students can withdraw from the course without penalty.

Estimate student work load. Give students a sense of how much preparation and work the course will involve. How much time should they anticipate spending on reading assignments, problem sets, lab reports, or research?

Include supplementary material to help students succeed in the course. For example consider providing one or more of the following:

- Helpful hints on how to study, take notes, or do well in class
- Glossary of technical terms used in the course
- References on specific topics for more in-depth exploration
- Bibliography of supplemental readings at a higher or lower level of difficulty in case students find the required text too simple or too challenging
- Copies of past exams so students can see at the beginning of the term what they will be expected to know at the end
- Information on the availability of videotapes of lectures
- A list of campus resources for tutoring and academic support, including computer labs
- Calendar of campus lectures, plays, events, exhibits, or other activities of relevance to your course

Provide space for names and telephone numbers of two or three classmates. Encourage students to identify people in class they can call if they miss a session or want to study together. (Source: "What Did You Put in Your Syllabus?" 1985)

Using the Syllabus

Annotate your copy of the syllabus. For example, on your copy make notes of details that need special mention during the first class meeting. As the course progresses, note on the syllabus changes you would make in the future. For example, indicate those topics that could not be addressed in the time allotted. Add new topics that come up during the course.

Distribute the syllabus on the first day of class. Review the essential points and be prepared to answer questions about course requirements and policies. If you make any important changes, prepare and distribute a written addendum.

Bring extra copies of the syllabus the first few weeks of class. Use these extras to replace lost syllabi or give them to students who join the class after the first day.

References

Altman, H. B. "Syllabus Shares 'What the Teacher Wants.'" *Teaching Professor*, 1989, *3*(5), 1–2.

Altman, H. B., and Cashin, W. E. "Writing a Syllabus." *Idea Paper*, no. 27. Manhattan: Center for Faculty Evaluation and Development, Kansas State University, 1992.

Birdsall, M. *Writing, Designing and Using a Course Syllabus.* Boston: Office of Instructional Development and Evaluation, Northeastern University, 1989.

Johnson, G. R. *Taking Teaching Seriously.* College Station: Center for Teaching Excellence, Texas A & M University, 1988.

Lowther, M. A., Stark, J. S., Martens, G. G. *Preparing Course Syllabi for Improved Communication.* Ann Arbor: National Center for Research to Improve Postsecondary Teaching and Learning, University of Michigan, 1989.

McKeachie, W. J. *Teaching Tips.* (8th ed.) Lexington, Mass.: Heath, 1986.

"Preparing a Course Syllabus." *Illini Instructor Series*, no. 3. Urbana: Instructional and Management Services, University of Illinois, n.d.

Rodgers, C. A., and Burnett, R. E. *Student Manuals: Their Rationale and Design.* Syracuse, N.Y.: Center for Instructional Development, Syracuse University, 1981.

Rubin, S. "Professors, Students and the Syllabus." *Chronicle of Higher Education*, Aug. 7, 1985, p. 56.

Schlesinger, A. B. "One Syllabus That Encourages Thinking, Not Just Learning." *Teaching Professor*, 1987, *1*(7), 5.

Shea, M. A. *Compendium of Good Ideas on Teaching and Learning.* Boulder: Faculty Teaching Excellence Program, University of Colorado, 1990.

"What Did You Put in Your Syllabus?" *Teaching at the University of Nebraska, Lincoln*, 1985, *7*(1), 2. (Newsletter available from the Teaching and Learning Center, University of Nebraska, Lincoln)

Wilkerson, L., and McKnight, R. T. *Writing a Course Syllabus.* Chicago: Educational Development Unit, Michael Reese Hospital and Medical Center, 1978.

3

The First Day of Class

The first day of class sets the tone for the rest of the term. It is natural for both students and instructors to feel anticipation, excitement, anxiety, and uncertainty. To pique students' interest and anticipation, convey your enthusiasm for the material and stimulate students' curiosity about topics that will be covered during the term. To reduce students' anxiety and uncertainty, try to create a relaxed, open classroom environment conducive to inquiry and participation, and let students know what you will expect from them and what they can expect from you and the course. The following suggestions, intended to help you get your class off to a good start, address the three important tasks of the first day: handling administrative matters, creating an open friendly classroom environment, and setting course expectations and standards.

General Strategies

Visit the classroom before the first meeting. Locate and figure out how to work the lights, the blinds, and the ventilation. Check any audiovisual equipment (microphone, slide or overhead projector) you will be using. Find out how to obtain help if a bulb burns out or a piece of equipment malfunctions. Get comfortable speaking in the room and see how well your voice carries. Make sure your handwriting on the chalkboard is legible from the back row. (Source: Johnson, 1988)

Build a sense of community in the classroom. In general, students learn more and work harder in classes that spark their intellectual curiosity and allow for active involvement and participation. For the first day, plan an activity that provides opportunities for students to speak to one another or solve problems. Students also tend to work harder and respond more positively if they believe the instructor views them as individuals rather than as anonymous faces in the crowd (Wolcowitz, 1984). From the start, then, make an effort to get to know your students and express your interest in working with them during the semester.

Address students' concerns. Students enter a new class with several questions: Is this the right course for me? Does the teacher seem competent and fair? How much work will be required? How will I be evaluated? Use the first day to help your students understand how the class will serve their needs, and demonstrate your commitment to help them learn.

Set the tone for the rest of the semester. Greet students when they enter the classroom. Start and finish class on time. Encourage questions, and give students the opportunity to talk. Stay after class to answer questions, or invite students to walk with you back to your office.

Make the time worthwhile. Once administrative tasks are completed, plunge into substantive material. This signals to students that you are serious about making their time worthwhile and that you expect progress to be made at each session.

Expect some awkwardness. All teachers, especially beginning instructors, feel a twinge of apprehension before the first class. Do your best to assume a confident attitude. Keep in mind that to your students your nervousness is likely to be perceived as energy and enthusiasm. Arriving early on the first day of class and talking informally to students may help you relax. (Source: Marincovich and Rusk, 1987)

Taking Care of Administrative Tasks

Write the course name and number on the board. This message will alert any students who are in the wrong classroom to leave before you begin. (Source: Hilsen, 1988)

Take attendance. Call the roll or ask students to sign in. Have a contingency plan if more students than you can accommodate want to enroll. Check with your department to see whether policies exist for preferential enrollment. Some faculty give preference to graduating seniors. Others make certain that students have the prerequisites and then select enrollment by lottery. If your course is an elective, plan on admitting a few more students than you can comfortably accommodate; a small number will end up dropping your course.

Mention department course policies. Explain procedures for wait lists, adding and dropping courses, and so on. Know where to refer students who have problems in these areas.

Explain the procedures for the course's sections. If your course has sections, make sure that all students know which section they are enrolled in, who their graduate student instructor is, and when and where the section meets. Describe the relationship between the course and its sections and how sections will be run. Have the graduate student instructors introduce themselves.

Review any prerequisites for the course. Let students know what skills or knowledge they are expected to have and whether alternate experience or course work will be accepted. Is help available for those who do not have all the prerequisite skills? If computer work is part of the course, will training be provided?

Define your expectations for student participation. Besides turning in all written assignments and taking exams, what do you expect of students during class? See "Leading a Discussion."

Tell students about campus policies on academic honesty. State your expectations, and let students know what you regard as cheating and impermissible collaboration. See "Preventing Academic Dishonesty."

Hand out and discuss the course syllabus. One faculty member has students read the syllabus and then form groups to identify questions about the course or the instructor (Serey, 1989). Hearing these questions on the first day lets a professor know immediately what concerns are uppermost in students' minds.

Invite students to attend your office hours. Be sure students know where your office is and encourage them to stop by with questions and course-related problems. Make a special point of asking students who feel they may need academic accommodations for a physical or learning disability to see you so that appropriate arrangements can be made.

Review safety precautions. If your course requires lab work or fieldwork, review safe practices for using equipment and supplies and discuss emergency procedures. Show students how to use equipment safely and appropriately. (Source: Johnson, 1988)

Review emergency procedures. Let students know what to do in case of fire, tornado, earthquake, evacuation, or other emergency.

Bring copies of the required texts to the first class meeting. Know which stores besides the campus bookstore stock the texts. Are used copies available? Is the textbook on reserve in the library?

Tape the session, if appropriate. For students who miss the first day of class, make available a videotape or audiotape that they can review on their own. This way you do not have to keep repeating the material as new students join your class. If taping is impractical, ask students who enroll after the first day to obtain notes from someone who attended that session.

Creating a Positive Classroom Environment

Introduce yourself to your class. In addition to telling students how you wish to be addressed, say something about your background: how you first became interested in the subject, how it has been important to you, and why you are teaching this course. Convey your enthusiasm for the field and the subject. For many students, the instructor's enthusiasm about the course material is a key motivator for learning. (Sources: "The First Day of Class," 1989; Wolcowitz, 1984)

Ask students to fill out an introduction card. Have students indicate their name, campus address, telephone number, electronic mail address, year in school, and major field. You might also ask them to list related courses they have taken, prerequisites they have completed, other courses they are taking this semester, their reasons for enrolling in your course, what they hope to learn in the course, tentative career plans, and something about their outside interests, hobbies, or current employment. Make sure that students who later enroll in the course complete an introduction card.

Begin to learn students' names. By learning your students' names, you can create a comfortable classroom environment that will encourage student interaction. Knowing your students' names also tells them that you are interested in them as individuals. As you call roll, ask for the correct pronunciation and how the student prefers to be addressed. If your course enrolls fewer than forty students, call the roll for several class meetings to help you learn names. During the term, call students by name when you return homework or quizzes, and use names frequently in class. Ask students who are not called upon by name to identify themselves. Here are a variety of other strategies for learning students' names:

- *Photographs:* Consider grouping students for Polaroid pictures during the second week of class. In a single shot you may be able to photograph four or five people. The act of posing for a picture breaks the ice and creates an informal, relaxed environment. Circulate the photographs and have students write their name underneath their picture. If you do not have access to a camera, ask students to submit a small photograph of themselves (such as those taken in penny arcade photo booths or from their driver's license or student photo ID). Photocopies of photographs are fine. Place these photos on students' information sheets or introduction cards. Photographs are helpful in recalling a student before an appointment, or later on, when you are asked to write a recommendation for a student, you can refer back to the picture to jog your memory.

- *Name cards:* For a seminar class, use the United Nations model of place cards in front of each student. In a studio or lab course, post students' names above their workstations.
- *Seating chart:* Ask students to sit in the same seats for the first few weeks, and prepare a seating chart. Or block out on a piece of paper general locations within the room and write the names of students inside the appropriate blocks, instead of labeling exact seats. Try to memorize four or five names at each class session.
- *Name game:* In small classes, ask the first person to give her name. The second person gives the name of the first person and his own name, and the third person gives the names of the first two people followed by her own name. The chain continues until it returns to the first person, with the instructor preferably near the end. (Source: Scholl-Buckwald, 1985)
- *Introductions:* For large lecture classes, at the beginning of each class period, ask six or eight students to introduce themselves.

Give students an opportunity to meet each other. Ask students to divide themselves into groups of three to five and introduce themselves. Or have students group themselves by residence halls or living groups so that they can identify nearby classmates to study with (Heine and others, 1981). Or go around the room and ask all students to respond to one question, such as "What's the one thing you really want to learn from this course?" or "What aspect of the course seems most appealing to you?" Such questions are more interesting than those about students' majors or year in college.

Ask students to interview each other outside of class. If your course has a writing component, you might ask students to write a brief description of their partner. The class could agree on the interview questions beforehand, or each student could devise his or her own items. (Source: Scholl-Buckwald, 1985)

If your class is small, conduct a "people search." Students receive a sheet of paper with five to ten statements and a space for a signature near each statement. The statements should be relevant to students in your class and can be a mix of personal and academic attributes: "Someone who works and goes to school," "Someone who has taken (a related course)," "Someone who has already purchased the textbooks," "Someone who is left-handed," "Someone who knows the order of the planets" (or other content-related question). Students are given ten minutes to obtain as many signatures as possible. You can spend a few minutes debriefing to generate a class profile. Or you can compile the information for distribution at the next class meeting so students have a written record about their classmates. (Sources: Erickson and Strommer, 1991; Weisz, 1990)

Break students into small groups. An English professor divides the class into groups of six and gives each member of the group one line of a six-line poem. Students are asked to reassemble the poem and discuss what the poem means. A sociology professor asks groups of students to come up with a list of the ten most important events (or people) in history. After ten or fifteen minutes, the groups' responses are placed on the board for discussion and interpretation. (Source: Erickson and Strommer, 1991)

Encourage students to exchange phone numbers. If all students agree, ask them to write their name, telephone number, and electronic mail address on a plain sheet of paper and make copies of this roster for them. Encourage students to call their classmates about missed classes, homework assignments, and study groups. Or have students complete $3'' \times 5''$ cards and exchange cards with two or three classmates. (Source: "The First Day of Class," 1989)

Setting Course Expectations and Standards

Discuss the objectives of the course. As specifically as possible, tell your students what you wish to accomplish and why, but also ask for what they want to learn from you and what sorts of problems they would like to tackle. Be sure to acknowledge *all* contributions — your attentiveness to students' ideas will encourage student participation throughout the semester. (Source: McKeachie, 1986)

Ask students to list the goals they hope to achieve by taking the course. Have students, in small groups or individually, list three to five goals in the form of statements about knowledge, skills, appreciations, interests, or attitudes. Students can also rank their goals in terms of how difficult they may be to achieve. Use these lists to identify your class's interests and anticipated problem areas. (Source: Angelo and Cross, 1993)

Describe how you propose to spend class time. How will sessions be structured? How will discussions be organized? Will a specific time be set aside for questions, or may students ask questions as they arise? Should questions requiring a lengthy response be saved for office hours?

Give your students ideas about how to study and prepare for class. Study strategies are especially important in an introductory class. Give examples of questions students might wish to think about or strategies for approaching the material. Tell students how much time they will need to study for the course, and let them know about campus academic support services.

If appropriate, give a brief diagnostic pretest. Explain that this "test" will not be graded but is designed to give you information on topics students have mastered and areas in which they need additional review. You could present a list of key concepts, facts and figures, or major ideas and ask students to indicate their familiarity with each. In a writing course you might assign a short essay that will allow you to identify students' strengths and weaknesses.

Ask students to do a group exercise. Select a key word from the course title and have students generate word associations or related ideas. Put their responses on the board and use the list to give a thematic overview of the course. (Source: Wright, 1989)

Work through a problem or piece of material that illustrates the course content. Begin to teach students how to participate in your class. Engaging students in actual work during the first class session gives them an idea of what your class will be like. You might make a brief presentation of a core idea, pose a typical problem, or ask students to form working subgroups. (Source: Scholl-Buckwald, 1985)

Give an assignment for the next class session. By moving immediately into the first topic, you are indicating to students that the course is worthwhile, well organized, and well paced. Make sure that the assignment is ungraded, however, because students may be adding or dropping your course during the first week or so. (Sources: Johnson, 1988; Povlacs, 1986)

Ask students to write their reactions to the first day. Take two minutes at the end of class to have students jot down unsigned comments about what went well and what questions they have about the course. (Source: McKeachie, 1986)

References

Angelo, T. A., and Cross, K. P. *Classroom Assessment Techniques: A Handbook for College Teachers.* (2nd ed.) San Francisco: Jossey-Bass, 1993.

Erickson, B. L., and Strommer, D. W. *Teaching College Freshmen.* San Francisco: Jossey-Bass, 1991.

"The First Day of Class: Advice and Ideas." *Teaching Professor*, 1989, *3*(7), 1–2.

Heine, H., and others. *The Torch or the Firehose? A Guide to Section Teaching.* Cambridge: Undergraduate Academic Support Office of the Dean for Student Affairs, Massachusetts Institute of Technology, 1981.

Hilsen, L. "A Helpful Handout: Establishing and Maintaining a Positive Classroom Climate." In E. C. Wadsworth, L. Hilsen, and M. A. Shea (eds.), *A Handbook for New Practitioners from the Professional and Organizational Development Network in Higher Education.* Stillwater, Okla.: New Forums Press, 1988.

Johnson, G. R. *Taking Teaching Seriously.* College Station: Center for Teaching Excellence, Texas A & M University, 1988.

McKeachie, W. J. *Teaching Tips.* (8th ed.) Lexington, Mass.: Heath, 1986.

Marincovich, M., and Rusk, L. *Excellence in Teaching Electrical Engineering.* Stanford, Calif.: Center for Teaching and Learning, Stanford University, 1987.

Povlacs, J. T. "101 Things You Can Do the First Three Weeks of Class." *Teaching at the University of Nebraska, Lincoln*, 1986, *8*(1), 1–4. (Newsletter available from the Teaching and Learning Center, University of Nebraska, Lincoln)

Scholl-Buckwald, S. "The First Meeting of Class." In J. Katz (ed.), *Teaching as Though Students Mattered.* New Directions for Teaching and Learning, no. 21. San Francisco: Jossey-Bass, 1985.

Serey, T. "Meet Your Professor." *Teaching Professor*, 1989, *3*(1), 2.

Weisz, E. "Energizing the Classroom." *College Teaching*, 1990, *38*(2), 74–76.

Wolcowitz, J. "The First Day of Class." In M. M. Gullette (ed.), *The Art and Craft of Teaching.* Cambridge, Mass.: Harvard University Press, 1984.

Wright, D. L. "The Most Important Day: Starting Well." *Teaching at the University of Nebraska, Lincoln*, 1989, *11*(1), 1–3. (Newsletter available from the Teaching and Learning Center, University of Nebraska, Lincoln)

II.

Responding to a Diverse Student Body

Academic Accommodations for Students with Disabilities

4

Students who have a disability, particularly a learning disability, are a rapidly growing population on college campuses. Though it is difficult to obtain accurate figures, between 3 and 10 percent of college students report having physical or learning disabilities that require compensatory classroom teaching accommodations (City University of New York Committee for the Disabled, 1988; Project EASI, 1991; Smith, 1989). Such accommodations are neither difficult to provide nor distracting to the rest of the class. In fact, many of these accommodations may make learning easier for all your students.

General Strategies

Ask your students to clarify any special needs. At the beginning of each semester, you might make a general announcement: "Any student who feels that he or she may need accommodations for any sort of physical or learning disability, please speak to me after class, make an appointment to see me, or see me during my office hours." When you meet with a student, explain the course requirements and ask what classroom modifications would aid the student. Students are usually their own best advocates, and they know the techniques and adaptations that best suit their needs.

Remember that disabled students are students first, disabled second. It is natural for able-bodied people to feel hesitant or uneasy when first meeting people who are disabled. But disabled people are neither more or less emotionally fragile than able-bodied people. Thus you needn't worry about hurting the feelings of a student who is blind by mentioning the word *see*. Students who are blind "see" ideas or concepts, just as students who are deaf "hear" what someone means and wheelchair users "walk" to class. Offer physical assistance only if a student requests help or if the need is immediately obvious.

Be flexible about attendance and promptness. Students who use wheelchairs may encounter physical barriers in getting to class on time (broken elevators, late van transportation). Other students may sometimes feel fatigued or have difficulty concentrating as a result of their disability or their medication. Try to distinguish students' physical problems from apathetic behavior. (Source: City University of New York Committee for the Disabled, 1988)

Be sensitive to "nonvisible" or "hidden" disabilities. Three principal types of disabilities may not be immediately visible:

- *Learning disabilities* hinder students of average or above-average intelligence from easily and dependably processing various types of information. Dyslexic students, for example, have a perceptual deficit that prevents them from unerringly interpreting sequences of letters or numbers. It is important to realize that learning disabilities are *not* a reflection of a student's intelligence, physical or emotional health, or cultural or socioeconomic background. In general, using a variety of instructional modes enhances learning for such students, as it does for all students, by allowing them to master material that may be inaccessible in one particular mode. Most college students will know which forms or modalities of learning work best for them. (Sources: City University of New York Committee for the Disabled, 1988; Smith, n.d.)
- *Mild to moderate sensory deficits* (low-level vision, slight hearing impairment) should be accommodated by appropriate seating and room lighting.
- *Chronic disabilities* (diabetes, seizure disorders, cardiac or respiratory conditions, lupus, cancer, AIDS) may interfere with stamina, attention span, and alertness. The attendance and performance of affected students may be erratic, and they may need flexibility in the scheduling of assignments.

Check with your campus disabled students program for advice and guidance. Staff members can answer questions and provide helpful information about disabilities and academic accommodations.

Physical Access

Ensure classroom access. Most buildings on your campus should have entrances that are accessible to students who use mobility aids (wheelchairs, canes, crutches, and walkers). Individual classrooms and laboratories may differ in their accessibility. Contact your room scheduling office for assistance in obtaining an accessible classroom.

Observe seating needs. Students who use canes, crutches, or walkers appreciate having a chair or desk that is close to the door. Access to these seats should be flat: no steps, no uneven surfaces. Wheelchair users need flat or ramped access, and classroom tables or desks must have enough clearance for them to get their legs underneath. Lab tables and computer consoles should be set up so that wheelchair users can comfortably reach the equipment.

Make seating available for students' in-class aides. Students who are disabled usually locate and hire their own aides (note takers, lab assistants, readers), often through referrals from the campus disabled students program. You can help, at times, by announcing to your class that a note taker is needed or by referring qualified tutors and lab assistants to students who are disabled. The student and aide will reach their own arrangements about the type of help needed.

Ensure access to out-of-class activities. Be sensitive to questions of access when planning field trips, assigning lab and computer work, and recommending visits to museums, attendance at off-campus lectures and dramatic presentations, and the like.

Lecture and Laboratory Courses

Follow good teaching practices. Many techniques that will help students who have sensory or learning disabilities will also benefit all the students in your class. For example:

- Open each session with a brief review of the previous session's material and an outline of that day's topic. Conclude each session with a summary of key points.
- Emphasize new or technical vocabulary by presenting it visually (on the chalkboard, an overhead slide, or a handout) as well as orally.
- Describe all visual examples (board work, demonstrations, props). As you work at the board, instead of saying, "Adding this here and dividing by that gives us this," narrate what you are doing: "Adding all scores and dividing by the number of scores, gives us the mean."
- Give students opportunities for questions, clarification, and review.

(Sources: McGuire and O'Donnell, 1989; Smith, n.d.; Wren and Segal, 1985)

Be aware of students' cassette recorders. Students who cannot take notes in class may routinely record lectures. For their benefit, speak clearly and position yourself close enough to the microphone. Explain what you are writing on the board or what you are demonstrating. Students with hearing disabilities may ask you to wear a lapel microphone, linked to a headset that amplifies your voice.

Face the class when you are speaking. Deaf or hearing-disabled students who read lips cannot follow the lecture or conversation when your back or head is turned. If you are writing on the board or narrating a desktop demonstration, try to avoid talking when facing the board or the desktop. Remember that, at best, people who are deaf can read only 30 to 40 percent of spoken English by watching the speaker's lips. Augment their understanding by using facial expressions, gestures, and body language. (Sources: Fisher, 1985; Smith, n. d.)

Hand out written lists of technical terms for students who are deaf or hearing-disabled. Unfamiliar words are difficult to speech read and interpret. If possible, supply a list of these words or terms in advance to the student and interpreter. (Source: Smith, n.d.)

Make reading lists available in advance. Students who rely on readers or need Braille, large-print, and tape-recorded books will appreciate as much notice as possible. By midsemester, many students with disabilities try to obtain the reading lists for the courses they anticipate taking the following term.

Class Participation

Arrange for classroom participation or an alternative activity. Students who cannot raise their hand to answer or ask questions may feel isolated or ignored in class. During your first private meeting with such a student, ask how he or she wishes to be recognized in the classroom. Some students will want to be called on; others may prefer to meet periodically with you before or after class to ask questions about course content.

In class discussion and conversation directly address the student, not the student's aide or interpreter. In talking to deaf or hearing-disabled students, acknowledge the interpreter's presence but look at and address the student. When talking to a student in a wheelchair for more than a minute or two, it is best to sit down so that you can talk at eye level. (Source: Smith, n.d.)

Repeat comments or questions from participants as necessary and, as needed, identify the person who is speaking. When a student is speaking out of the range of vision of a deaf or hearing-disabled student, repeat the question or comment and indicate who is speaking (by motioning) so the student can follow the discussion. To accommodate students with visual disabilities, identify by name the student who is speaking or identify the person to whom you are speaking. (Source: Smith, n.d.)

Listen attentively when a student with a speech disability is speaking. Do not finish a student's sentences or interrupt. Never pretend to understand if you are having difficulty doing so. Instead, repeat what you have understood and allow the student to respond. (Source: National Center for Access Unlimited, 1992)

Give options for oral presentations, if needed. Oral presentations may pose difficulties for students who have speech disabilities. Students who wish to give their presentation without assistance should be encouraged to do so. But some students will want to give the presentation with the help of an interpreter, and others may want to write out their presentation and ask an interpreter or another student to read it to the class.

Written Materials and Exams

Ensure that students get the academic help they need to succeed in your class. Although a student may have an in-class aide (a note taker, sign-language interpreter, amanuensis), these aides are not academic tutors. Students with learning disabilities can often benefit from ongoing tutorial assistance.

Make the computer disks available to students. If you prepare your syllabus, assignments, or handouts on a computer, give copies of the disk to students who might need them. Students who are blind or partially sighted can take the disk to an adaptive computer that will prepare copy in Braille. If your campus is networked, you may be able to send the material through electronic mail, eliminating the need for disks. Use a computer or photo-copying enlarger to prepare large-type hard copy versions of your reading lists and other handouts for students who are partially sighted.

As appropriate, encourage students to use computers. Students with learning disabilities and students with reduced manual dexterity can benefit from drafting and revising their papers on a computer. Students with dyslexia and similar information-processing disabilities should be encouraged to use computers that have spell-checking features or to work with a proofreader or editor during the preparation of their final copy. Students who are partially sighted can use large point sizes on their computer screen and then reformat the text when they print out their papers.

Provide appropriate test-taking conditions. Federal law mandates academic accommodations. Some students with physical or learning disabilities may need one or more of the following kinds of accommodations to complete their exams:

- An in-class aide to read the test orally or to take down the student's dictated answers to exam questions
- A separate room that provides better lighting or fewer distractions or that houses special equipment (computer console, video magnifier, text-to-speech converter)
- An extended exam period to accommodate a student's slower writing speed or need to dictate answers to an aide or to equalize a student's reduced information-processing speed
- Option of substituting an oral exam for a written exam, or a written exam for an oral exam, or a multiple-choice exam for an essay exam
- Option of having exam questions presented in written or oral form

You and the student should agree early on how the student's progress in the course will be evaluated.

Assistive Instructional Technology

Find out what technological aids your institution makes available for students with disabilities. For example, some campuses have talking calculators, speech-activated computers, Braille workstations, and reading machines for use by students who are blind or visually disabled. One university has experimented with "stenocaptioning," a stenography machine hooked up to a computer for helping students with hearing disabilities read from the computer as the lecturer speaks ("New Technology Boosts Hearing-Impaired Students," 1992).

Make certain that adaptive computer equipment is available for students with disabilities. Check with your disabled students program or your computer center for information and advice. Adaptive technologies for people with mobility disabilities include modifications of keyboards, mouthsticks and headwands for striking keys, and floppy disk guides that make it easier to handle disks. For students with visual disabilities, equipment includes speech synthesizers, Braille or large-print output devices, and screen-reading programs. Students with learning disabilities can benefit from special software. Berliss (1991) offers advice and information for making computer laboratories and equipment accessible. (Source: Project EASI, 1991)

If you assign films or videos, make sure they are close captioned. Check with your media center about the Captioned Films Program, which distributes captioned theatrical, short subject, documentary, and educational films. (Source: Smith, n.d.)

References

Berliss, J. R. "Checklists for Implementing Accessibility in Computer Laboratories at Colleges and Universities." Madison: Trace Research and Development Center, University of Wisconsin, 1991.

City University of New York Committee for the Disabled. *Reasonable Accommodations: A Faculty Guide to Teaching College Students with Disabilities.* New York: Professional Staff Congress/City University of New York, 1988. (Available from Professional Staff Congress/City University of New York, 25 West 43rd St., New York, N.Y.)

Fisher, M. (ed.). *Teaching at Stanford.* Stanford, Calif.: Center for Teaching and Learning, Stanford University, 1985.

McGuire, J. M., and O'Donnell, J. M. "Helping Learning Disabled Students to Achieve: Collaboration Between Faculty and Support Services." *College Teaching,* 1989, *37*(1), 29–32.

National Center for Access Unlimited. "Ten Commandments for Communicating with People with Disabilities." In B. P. Noble, "When Businesses Need Not Fret." *New York Times,* June 7, 1992, p. F25.

"New Technology Boosts Hearing-Impaired Students." *National On-Campus Report,* 1992, *20*(10), 3.

Project EASI (Equal Access to Software for Instruction). *Computers and Students with Disabilities: New Challenges for Higher Education.* (2nd ed.) Washington, D.C. EDUCOM, 1991.

Smith, D. G. *The Challenge of Diversity: Involvement or Alienation in the Academy?* Report No. 5. Washington, D.C.: School of Education and Human Development, George Washington University, 1989.

Smith, L. M. *The College Student with a Disability: A Faculty Handbook.* Sacramento: Health and Welfare Agency, California Employment Development Department, n.d.

Wren, C., and Segal, L. *College Students with Learning Disabilities: A Student Perspective.* Chicago: Project Learning Strategies, DePaul University, 1985.

Diversity and Complexity in the Classroom: Considerations of Race, Ethnicity, and Gender

5

Since the 1960s and the rise of the civil rights movement, American colleges and universities have been engaged in an ongoing debate about how best to enroll, educate, and graduate students from groups historically underrepresented in higher education: women, African Americans, Chicanos and Latinos, Native Americans, American-born students of Asian ancestry, and immigrants. As enrollment statistics show, changes in both the demographics of the applicant pool and college admissions policies are bringing about a measure of greater diversity in entering classes (Levine and Associates, 1990).

Once they are on campus, though, many of these students feel that they are treated as unwelcome outsiders, and they describe having encountered subtle forms of bias (Cones, Noonan, and Janha, 1983; Fleming, 1988; Green, 1989; Hall and Sandler, 1982; Pemberton, 1988; Sadker and Sadker, 1992; Simpson, 1987; Woolbright, 1989). Some students of color have labeled this bias "the problem of ignorance" or the "look through me" syndrome (Institute for the Study of Social Change, 1991). As reported by the Institute for the Study of Social Change, students talk about subtle discrimination in certain facial expressions, in not being acknowledged, in how white students "take over a class" and speak past students of color, or in small everyday slights in which they perceive that their value and perspective are not appreciated or respected. Though often unwitting or inadvertent, such behaviors reinforce the students' sense of alienation and hinder their personal, academic, and professional development.

There are no universal solutions or specific rules for responding to ethnic, gender, and cultural diversity in the classroom, and research on best practices is limited (Solomon, 1991). Indeed, the topic is complicated, confusing, and dynamic, and for some faculty it is fraught with uneasiness, difficulty, and discomfort. Perhaps the overriding principle is to be thoughtful and sensitive and do what you think is best. The material in this section is intended to help you increase your awareness of matters that some faculty and students have indicated are particularly sensitive for women and students of color. Some of these problems affect all students, but they may be exacerbated by ethnic and gender differences between faculty members and their students.

The following ideas, based on the teaching practices of faculty across the country and on current sociological and educational research, are intended to help you work effectively with the broad range of students enrolled in your classes.

General Strategies

Recognize any biases or stereotypes you may have absorbed. Do you interact with students in ways that manifest double standards? For example, do you discourage women students from undertaking projects that require quantitative work? Do you undervalue comments made by speakers whose English is accented differently than your own? Do you assume that most African-American, Chicano/Latino, or Native American students on your campus are enrolled under special admissions programs? Do you assume that most students of color are majoring in Ethnic Studies?

Treat each student as an individual, and respect each student for who he or she is. Each of us has some characteristics in common with others of our gender, race, place of origin, and sociocultural group, but these are outweighed by the many differences among members of any group. We tend to recognize this point about groups we belong to ("Don't put me in the same category as all those other New Yorkers/Californians/Texans you know") but sometimes fail to recognize it about others. However, any group label subsumes a wide variety of individuals—people of different social and economic backgrounds, historical and generational experience, and levels of consciousness. Try not to project your experiences with, feelings about, or expectations of an entire group onto any one student. Keep in mind, though, that group identity can be very important for some students. College may be their first opportunity to experience affirmation of their national, ethnic, racial, or cultural identity, and they feel both empowered and enhanced by joining monoethnic organizations or groups. (Source: Institute for the Study of Social Change, 1991)

Rectify any language patterns or case examples that exclude or demean any groups. Do you

- Use terms of equal weight when referring to parallel groups: men and women rather than men and ladies?
- Use both *he* and *she* during lectures, discussions, and in writing, and encourage your students to do the same?
- Recognize that your students may come from diverse socioeconomic backgrounds?
- Refrain from remarks that make assumptions about your students' experiences, such as, "Now, when your parents were in college . . ."?
- Refrain from remarks that make assumptions about the nature of your students' families, such as, "Are you going to visit your parents over spring break?"
- Avoid comments about students' social activities that tacitly assume that all students are heterosexual?
- Try to draw case studies, examples, and anecdotes from a variety of cultural and social contexts?

Do your best to be sensitive to terminology. Terminology changes over time, as ethnic and cultural groups continue to define their identity, their history, and their relationship to the dominant culture. In the 1960s, for example, *negroes* gave way to *blacks* and *Afro-Americans*. In the 1990s, the term *African American* gained general acceptance. Most Americans of Mexican ancestry prefer *Chicano* or *Latino* or *Mexican American* to *Hispanic*, hearing in the last the echo of Spanish colonialism. Most Asian Americans are offended by the term *Oriental*, which connotes British imperialism; and many individuals want to be identified not by a continent but by the nationality of their ancestors—for example, *Thai American* or *Japanese American*. In California, *Pacific Islander* and *South Asian* are currently preferred by students whose forebears are from those regions. To find out what terms are used and accepted on your campus, you could raise the question with your students, consult the listing of campuswide student groups, or speak with your faculty affirmative action officer.

Get a sense of how students feel about the cultural climate in your classroom. Let students know that you want to hear from them if any aspect of the course is making them uncomfortable. During the term, invite them to write you a note (signed or unsigned) or ask on midsemester course evaluation forms one or more of the following questions (adapted from Cones, Janha, and Noonan, 1983):

- Does the course instructor treat students equally and evenhandedly?
- How comfortable do you feel participating in this class? What makes it easy or difficult for you?
- In what ways, if any, does your ethnicity, race, or gender affect your interactions with the teacher in this class? With fellow students?

Introduce discussions of diversity at department meetings. Concerned faculty can ask that the agenda of department meetings include topics such as classroom climate, course content and course requirements, graduation and placement rates, extracurricular activities, orientation for new students, and liaison with the English as a second language (ESL) program.

Tactics for Overcoming Stereotypes and Biases

Become more informed about the history and culture of groups other than your own. Avoid offending out of ignorance. Strive for some measure of "cultural competence" (Institute for the Study of Social Change, 1991): know what is appropriate and inappropriate behavior and speech in cultures different from your own. Broder and Chism (1992) provide a reading list, organized by ethnic groups, on multicultural teaching in colleges and universities. Beyond professional books and articles, read fiction or nonfiction works by authors from different ethnic groups. Attend lectures, take courses, or team teach with specialists in Ethnic Studies or Women's Studies. Sponsor mono- or multicultural student organizations. Attend campuswide activities celebrating diversity or events important to various ethnic and cultural groups. If you are unfamiliar with your own culture, you may want to learn more about its history as well.

Convey the same level of respect and confidence in the abilities of all your students. Research studies show that many instructors unconsciously base their expectations of student performance on such factors as gender, language proficiency, socioeconomic status, race, ethnicity, prior achievement, and appearance (Green, 1989). Research has also shown that an instructor's expectations can become self-fulfilling prophecies: students who sense that more is expected of them tend to outperform students who believe that less is expected of them—regardless of the students' actual abilities (Green, 1989; Pemberton, 1988). Tell all your students that you expect them to work hard in class, that you want them to be challenged by the material, and that you hold high standards for their academic achievement. And then *practice* what you have said: *expect* your students to work hard, be challenged, and achieve high standards. (Sources: Green, 1989; Pemberton, 1988)

Don't try to "protect" any group of students. Don't refrain from criticizing the performance of individual students in your class on account of their ethnicity or gender. If you attempt to favor or protect a given group of students by demanding less of them, you are likely to produce the opposite effect: such treatment undermines students' self-esteem and their view of their abilities and competence (Hall and Sandler, 1982). For example, one faculty member mistakenly believed she was being considerate to the students of color in her class by giving them extra time to complete assignments. She failed to realize that this action would cause hurt feelings on all sides: the students she was hoping to help felt patronized, and the rest of the class resented the preferential treatment.

Be evenhanded in how you acknowledge students' good work. Let students know that their work is meritorious and praise their accomplishments. But be sure to recognize the achievements of all students. For example, one Chicana student complained about her professor repeatedly singling out her papers as exemplary, although other students in the class were also doing well. The professor's lavish public praise, though well intended, made this student feel both uncomfortable and anxious about maintaining her high level of achievement.

Recognize the complexity of diversity. At one time the key issue at many colleges was how to recruit and retain African-American students and faculty. Today, demographics require a broader multicultural perspective and efforts to include many underrepresented groups. Although what we know about different ethnic groups is uneven, avoid generalizing from studies on African-American students (Smith, 1989).

Course Content and Material

Whenever possible, select texts and readings whose language is gender-neutral and free of stereotypes. If the readings you assign use only masculine pronouns or incorporate stereotypes, cite the date the material was written, point out these shortcomings in class, and give your students an opportunity to discuss them.

Aim for an inclusive curriculum. Ideally, a college curriculum should reflect the perspectives and experiences of a pluralistic society. At a minimum, creating an inclusive curriculum involves using texts and readings that reflect new scholarship and research about previously underrepresented groups, discussing the contributions made to your field by women or by various ethnic groups, examining the obstacles these pioneering contributors had to overcome, and describing how recent scholarship about gender, race, and class is modifying your field of study. This minimum, however, tends to place women, people of color, and non-European or non-American cultures as "asides" or special topics. Instead, try to recast your course content, if possible, so that one group's experience is not held up as the norm or the standard against which everyone else is defined. (Sources: Coleman, n.d.; Flick, n.d.; Jenkins, Gappa, and Pearce, 1983)

Do not assume that all students will recognize cultural, literary, or historical references familiar to you. As the diversity of the student and faculty populations increases, you may find that you and your students have fewer shared cultural experiences, literary allusions, historical references, and metaphors and analogies. If a certain type of cultural literacy is prerequisite to completing your course successfully, consider administering a diagnostic pretest on the first day of class to determine what students know. Of course, you may choose to refer deliberately to individuals or events your students may not know to encourage them to do outside reading.

Consider students' needs when assigning evening or weekend work. Be prepared to make accommodations for students who feel uncomfortable working in labs or at computer stations during the evening because of safety concerns. Students who are parents, particularly those who are single parents, may also appreciate alternatives to evening lab work or weekend field trips, as will students who work part-time.

Bring in guest lecturers. As appropriate, you can broaden and enrich your course by asking faculty or off-campus professionals of different ethnic groups to make presentations to your class.

Class Discussion

Emphasize the importance of considering different approaches and viewpoints. One of the primary goals of education is to show students different points of view and encourage them to evaluate their own beliefs. Help students begin to appreciate the number of situations that can be understood only by comparing several interpretations, and help them appreciate how one's premises, observations, and interpretations are influenced by social identity and background. For example, research conducted by the

Institute for the Study of Social Change (1991) shows that white students and African-American students tend to view the term *racism* differently. Many white students, for example, believe that being friendly is evidence of goodwill and lack of racism. Many African-American students, however, distinguish between prejudice (personal attitudes) and racism (organizational or institutional bias); for them, friendliness evidences a lack of prejudice but not necessarily a wholehearted opposition to racism.

Make it clear that you value all comments. Students need to feel free to voice an opinion *and* empowered to defend it. Try not to allow your own difference of opinion prevent communication and debate. Step in if some students seem to be ignoring the viewpoints of others. For example, if male students tend to ignore comments made by female students, reintroduce the overlooked comments into the discussion (Hall and Sandler, 1982).

Encourage all students to participate in class discussion. During the first weeks of the term, you can prevent any one group of students from monopolizing the discussion by your active solicitation of alternate viewpoints. Encourage students to listen to and value comments made from perspectives other than their own. You may want to have students work in small groups early in the term so that all students can participate in nonthreatening circumstances. This may make it easier for students to speak up in a larger setting. See "Collaborative Learning: Group Work and Study Teams," "Leading a Discussion," and "Encouraging Student Participation in Discussion."

Monitor your own behavior in responding to students. Research studies show that teachers tend to interact differently with men and women students (Hall and Sandler, 1982; Sadker and Sadker, 1990) and with students who are—or whom the instructor perceives to be—high or low achievers (Green, 1989). More often than not, these patterns of behavior are unconscious, but they can and do demoralize students, making them feel intellectually inadequate or alienated and unwelcome at the institution.

As you teach, then, try to be evenhanded in the following matters:

- Recognizing students who raise their hands or volunteer to participate in class (avoid calling on or hearing from only males or only members of one ethnic group)
- Listening attentively and responding directly to students' comments and questions
- Addressing students by name (and with the correct pronunciation)

- Prompting students to provide a fuller answer or an explanation
- Giving students time to answer a question before moving on
- Interrupting students or allowing them to be interrupted by their peers
- Crediting student comments during your summary ("As Akim said . . .")
- Giving feedback and balancing criticism and praise
- Making eye contact

Also, refrain from making seemingly helpful offers that are based on stereotypes and are therefore patronizing. An example to avoid: an economics faculty member announced, "I know that women have trouble with numbers, so I'll be glad to give you extra help, Jane."

You might want to observe your teaching on videotape to see whether you are unintentionally sending different messages to different groups. Sadker and Sadker (1992) list questions to ask about your teaching to explore gender and ethnic differences in treatment of students. (Sources: Hall and Sandler, 1982; Sadker and Sadker, 1990; Sadker and Sadker, 1992)

Reevaluate your pedagogical methods for teaching in a diverse setting. Observers note that in discussion classes professors tend to evaluate positively students who question assumptions, challenge points of view, speak out, and participate actively (Collett, 1990; Institute for the Study of Social Change, 1991). Recognize, however, that some of your students were brought up to believe that challenging people who are in positions of authority is disrespectful or rude. Some students may be reluctant to ask questions or participate out of fear of reinforcing stereotypes about their ignorance. The challenge for teaching a diverse student body is to be able to engage both verbally assertive students and those with other styles and expressions of learning. See "Leading a Discussion," "Encouraging Student Participation in Discussion," and "Learning Styles and Preferences" for suggestions on how to actively involve all students. (Source: Institute for the Study of Social Change, 1991)

Speak up promptly if a student makes a distasteful remark, even jokingly. Don't let disparaging comments pass unnoticed. Explain why a comment is offensive or insensitive. Let your students know that racist, sexist, and other types of discriminatory remarks are unacceptable in class. For example, "What you said made me feel uncomfortable. Although you didn't mean it, it could be interpreted as saying. . . ."

Avoid singling out students as spokespersons. It is unfair to ask a student to speak for his or her entire race, culture, or nationality. To do so not only ignores the wide differences in viewpoints among members of *any* group but also reinforces the mistaken notion that every member of a minority group is an ad hoc authority on his or her group (Pemberton, 1988). An example to avoid: after lecturing on population genetics and theories of racial intelligence, a faculty member singled out an African-American student in the class to ask his reactions to the theories. Relatedly, do not assume all students are familiar with their ancestors' language, traditions, culture, or history. An example to avoid: asking an American-born student of Chinese descent, "What idiom do you use in Chinese?" (Sources: Flick, n.d.; Pemberton, 1988)

Assignments and Exams

Be sensitive to students whose first language is not English. Most colleges require students who are nonnative speakers of English to achieve oral and written competency by taking ESL courses. Ask ESL specialists on your campus for advice about how to grade papers and for information about typical patterns of errors related to your students' native languages. For example, some languages do not have two-word verbs, and speakers of those languages may need extra help — and patience — as they try to master English idioms. Such students should not be penalized for misusing, say, *take after*, *take in*, *take off*, *take on*, *take out*, and *take over*.

Suggest that students form study teams that meet outside of class. By arranging for times and rooms where groups can meet, you can encourage students to study together. Peer support is an important factor in student persistence in school (Pascarella, 1986), but students of color are sometimes left out of informal networks and study groups that help other students succeed (Simpson, 1987). By studying together, your students can both improve their academic performance and overcome some of the out-of-class segregation common on many campuses. See "Collaborative Learning" for suggestions on how to form study teams.

Assign group work and collaborative learning activities. Students report having had their best encounters and achieved their greatest understandings of diversity as "side effects" of naturally occurring meaningful educational or community service experiences (Institute for the Study of Social Change, 1991). Consider increasing students' opportunities for group projects in which three to five students complete a specific task, for small group work during class, or for collaborative research efforts among two or three students to develop instructional materials or carry out a piece of a research study. Collaborative learning can be as simple as randomly grouping (by counting off) two or three students in class to solve a particular problem or to answer a specific question. See "Collaborative Learning," "Leading a Discussion," and "Supplements and Alternatives to Lecturing" for ideas about incorporating group work into instruction.

Give assignments and exams that recognize students' diverse backgrounds and special interests. As appropriate to your field, you can develop paper topics or term projects that encourage students to explore the roles, status, contributions, and experiences of groups traditionally underrepresented in scholarly research studies or in academia (Jenkins, Gappa, and Pearce, 1983). For example, a faculty member teaching a course on medical and health training offered students a variety of topics for their term papers, including one on alternative healing belief systems. A faculty member in the social sciences gave students an assignment asking them to compare female-only, male-only, and male-female work groups.

Advising and Extracurricular Activities

Meet with students informally. Frequent and rewarding informal contact with faculty members is the single strongest predictor of whether or not a student will voluntarily withdraw from a college (Tinto, 1989). Ongoing contact outside the classroom also provides strong motivation for students to perform well in your class and to participate in the broad social and intellectual life of the institution. In addition to inviting groups of your students for coffee or lunch, consider becoming involved in your campus orientation and academic advising programs or volunteering to speak informally to students living in residence halls or to other student groups. See "Academic Advising and Mentoring Undergraduates."

Encourage students to come to office hours. Of course, all students can benefit from the one-to-one conversation and attention that only office hours provide. In addition, students who feel alienated on campus or uncomfortable in class are more likely to discuss their concerns in private. (Source: Chism, Cano, and Pruitt, 1989)

Don't shortchange any students of advice you might give to a member of your own gender or ethnic group. Simpson (1987) reports the following unfortunate incident. A white male faculty member was asked by a female African-American student about whether she should drop an engineering class in which she was having difficulties. Worried that if he advised a drop, he might be perceived as lacking confidence in the intellectual abilities of African-American women, he suggested that she persevere. Had the student been a white male, the professor acknowledged, he would have placed the student's needs ahead of his own self-doubts and unhesitatingly advised a drop.

Advise students to explore perspectives outside their own experiences. For example, encourage students to take courses that will introduce them to the literature, history, and culture of other ethnic groups. (Source: Coleman, n.d.)

Involve students in your research and scholarly activities. Whenever you allow students to see or contribute to your own work, you are not only teaching them about your field's methodology and procedures but also helping them understand the dimensions of faculty life and helping them feel more a part of the college community (Blackwell, 1987). Consider sponsoring students in independent study courses, arranging internships, and providing opportunities for undergraduates to participate in research.

Help students establish departmental organizations. If your department does not have an undergraduate association, encourage students to create one. Your sponsorship can make it easier for student groups to obtain meeting rooms and become officially recognized. Student organizations can provide peer tutoring and advising as well as offer social and academic programs. In fields in which women and certain ethnic groups have traditionally been underrepresented, some students may prefer to form caucuses based on their gender or cultural affinities (for example, women in architecture). Research by the Institute for the Study of Social Change (1991) has documented the importance of associations for students of color as a basis for collective identification and individual support.

Provide opportunities for all students to get to know each other. Research shows that both African-American and white students, for example, would like greater interracial contact. African-American students tend to prefer institutional programs and commitments, while most white students prefer opportunities for individual, personal contacts. (Source: Institute for the Study of Social Change, 1991)

References

Blackwell, J. E. "Faculty Issues Affecting Minorities in Education." In R. C. Richardson and A. G. de los Santos (eds.), *From Access to Achievement: Strategies for Urban Institutions*. Tempe: National Center for Postsecondary Governance and Finance, Arizona State University, 1987.

Broder, L.L.B., and Chism, N.V.N. "The Future Is Now: A Call for Action and List of Resources." In L.L.B. Broder and N.V.N. Chism (eds.), *Teaching for Diversity*. New Directions for Teaching and Learning, no. 49. San Francisco: Jossey-Bass, 1992.

Chism, N.V.N., Cano, J., and Pruitt, A. S. "Teaching in a Diverse Environment: Knowledge and Skills Needed by TAs." In J. D. Nyquist, R. D. Abbott, and D. H. Wulff (eds.), *Teaching Assistant Training in the 1990s*. New Directions for Teaching and Learning, no. 39. San Francisco: Jossey-Bass, 1989.

Coleman, L. *The Influence of Attitudes, Feeling and Behavior Toward Diversity on Teaching and Learning*. Boulder: Faculty Teaching Excellence Program, University of Colorado, n.d.

Collett, J. "Reaching African-American Students in the Classroom." In L. Hilsen (ed.), *To Improve the Academy*. Vol. 9. Stillwater, Okla.: New Forums Press, 1990.

Cones, J. H., Janha, D., and Noonan, J. F. "Exploring Racial Assumptions with Faculty." In J. H. Cones, J. F. Noonan, and D. Janha (eds.), *Teaching Minority Students*. New Directions for Teaching and Learning, no. 16. San Francisco: Jossey-Bass, 1983.

Fleming, J. *Blacks in College*. San Francisco: Jossey-Bass, 1988.

Flick, D. *Developing and Teaching an Inclusive Curriculum*. Boulder: Faculty Teaching Excellence Program, University of Colorado, n.d.

Green, M. F. (ed.). *Minorities on Campus: A Handbook for Enriching Diversity*. Washington, D. C.: American Council on Education, 1989.

Hall, R. M., and Sandler, B. R. *The Classroom Climate: A Chilly One for Women?* Washington, D. C.: Association of American Colleges, 1982.

Institute for the Study of Social Change. *The Diversity Project: Final Report*. Berkeley: University of California, 1991.

Jenkins, M. L., Gappa, J. M., and Pearce, J. *Removing Bias: Guidelines for Student-Faculty Communication*. Annandale, Va.: Speech Communication Association, 1983.

Levine, A., and Associates. *Shaping Higher Education's Future*. San Francisco: Jossey-Bass, 1990.

Pascarella, E. T. "A Program for Research and Policy Development on Student Persistence at the Institutional Level." *Journal of College Student Personnel*, 1986, 27(2), 100–107.

Pemberton, G. *On Teaching Minority Students: Problems and Strategies.* Brunswick, Maine: Bowdoin College, 1988.

Sadker, M., and Sadker, D. "Confronting Sexism in the College Classroom." In S. L. Gabriel and I. Smithson (eds.), *Gender in the Classroom: Power and Pedagogy.* Urbana: University of Illinois Press, 1990.

Sadker, M., and Sadker, D. "Ensuring Equitable Participation in College Classes." In L.L.B. Border and N.V.N. Chism (eds.), *Teaching for Diversity.* New Directions for Teaching and Learning, no. 49. San Francisco: Jossey-Bass, 1992.

Simpson, J. C. "Black College Students Are Viewed as Victims of a Subtle Racism." *Wall Street Journal*, Apr. 3, 1987, p. 1.

Smith, D. G. *The Challenge of Diversity: Involvement or Alienation in the Academy?* Report No. 5. Washington, D.C.: School of Education and Human Development, George Washington University, 1989.

Solomon, B. B. "Impediments to Teaching a Culturally Diverse Undergraduate Population." In J. D. Nyquist, R. D. Abbott, D. H. Wulff, and J. Sprague (eds.), *Preparing the Professoriate of Tomorrow to Teach: Selected Readings for TA Training.* Dubuque, Iowa: Kendall/Hunt, 1991.

Tinto, V. "Principles of Effective Retention." Paper presented at the University of California Student Research Conference, Asilomar, Calif., Apr. 23–24, 1989.

Woolbright, C. (ed.). *Valuing Diversity on Campus: A Multicultural Approach.* Bloomington, Ind.: Association of College Unions-International, 1989.

6

Reentry Students

Adults over the age of twenty-five who have been away from formal education for at least two years make up an increasingly large proportion of the undergraduate student body, and their numbers are rapidly rising at many campuses (Schlossberg, Lynch, and Chickering, 1989). These students represent a wide range of ages, attitudes, and interests and no longer conform, if they ever did, to the stereotype of the reentry student—a white, middle-class, middle-aged woman. Bean and Metzner (1985) and Bishop-Clark and Lynch (1992) report several key differences between reentry students and younger students. Although there are wide variations, in general, reentry students tend to be less involved in the social and extracurricular life of the campus, are more likely to treat their professors as peers, are more intrinsically motivated to learn, bring a more practical, problem-solving orientation to learning, and are clearer about their educational goals. Faculty have reported that reentry students often provide some of their most satisfying teaching experiences: these students are motivated, interested, and excited about learning (Giczkowski, 1992). The suggestions below are designed to help you meet the challenges and opportunities of working with reentry students.

General Strategies

Help reentry students develop a sense of belonging to the campus. All students thrive when they feel comfortable and connected to the intellectual life of the campus. Reentry students, in particular, are likely to wonder, Will I fit in? See "Academic Advising and Mentoring Undergraduates" for advice on how to introduce students to the campus and make them feel a part of campus life.

Recognize that some reentry students may feel inadequately prepared for college work. Those reentry students who have never attended college or who did poorly in college the first time around may lack self-confidence or feel nervous about their ability to perform in the classroom. Help these students feel comfortable in your classroom by offering reassurance and expressing confidence in their abilities, as you would for all your other students. (Sources: Bishop-Clark and Lynch, 1992; Cross, 1981)

Be evenhanded in how you relate to students of different ages. See "Diversity and Complexity in the Classroom" for guidance on avoiding bias and unfairness.

Seek advice from your campus's reentry program. If your campus has a program for reentry students, seek advice and assistance from the staff. If no program exists on your campus, contact your local community center.

Class Participation

Encourage your students to get to know one other. Helping your students become acquainted will decrease any barriers among the age-groups and increase the chances that students can learn from one another. See "The First Day of Class" for suggestions.

Be sensitive to the time pressures reentry students face. More so than younger students, reentry students may have competing and multiple demands on their time: family responsibilities, job commitments, social and community obligations, and commuting. Keep in mind that field trips and weekend or evening activities may be especially problematic for these students.

Be aware of the dynamics between younger and older students. Older and younger students may not always work well together. Younger students may resent older students, perceiving them to be more motivated, knowledgeable, and collegial with the professor. Older students may unwittingly distance themselves from younger students by acting like a parent or authority figure. Watch for such tendencies and do your best to minimize the opportunities for tensions to surface. (Source: Bishop-Clark and Lynch, 1992; Watkins, 1990)

Teaching Tactics

Adopt participatory pedagogical styles. All students benefit from active learning strategies where they can learn by discussing, writing, or doing, but reentry students, in particular, are less likely to tolerate passive lecturing. They learn more effectively by talking about issues than by being talked at. They want to interact. See "Supplements and Alternatives to Lecturing,"

"Encouraging Student Participation in Discussion," and "Helping Students Write Better in All Courses" for suggestions on how to make instruction an active enterprise.

Incorporate group work into instruction. The life experiences of reentry students can enrich classroom discussion. Older students can often provide real-life examples that illustrate theories and general principles students are reading about. Capitalize on the resources of experience within your class by assigning collaborative learning activities that permit students to work together in small groups. See "Encouraging Student Participation in Discussion" and "Collaborative Learning" for ideas on group work.

Take advantage of reentry students' capacity for self-direction. Reentry students are used to functioning autonomously as independent, self-directed adults. Independent study opportunities or choices in assignments will acknowledge and reinforce these students' autonomous learning abilities and styles.

Vary the way you present course content. One business professor explains that with traditional-age students he introduces a new concept or idea by first discussing the theory and then presenting some applications. With older students, in contrast, he begins with the applications and then moves to the theory. This approach is both more engaging to older students and more motivating. (Source: Watkins, 1990)

References

Bean, J. P., and Metzner, B. S. "A Conceptual Model of Nontraditional Undergraduate Student Attrition." *Review of Educational Research*, 1985, 55(4), 485–540.

Bishop-Clark, C., and Lynch, J. M. "The Mixed-Age College Classroom." *College Teaching*, 1992, 40(3), 114–117.

Cross, K. P. *Adults as Learners: Increasing Participation and Facilitating Learning.* San Francisco: Jossey-Bass, 1981.

Giczkowski, W. "The Influx of Older Students Can Revitalize College Teaching." *Chronicle of Higher Education*, March 25, 1992, p. B3.

Schlossberg, N. K., Lynch, A. Q., and Chickering, A. W. *Improving Higher Education Environments for Adults.* San Francisco: Jossey-Bass, 1989.

Watkins, B. T. "Growing Number of Older Students Stirs Professors to Alter Teaching Styles." *Chronicle of Higher Education*, Aug. 1, 1990, pp. A1, A12.

Teaching Academically Diverse Students

7

All classes, but particularly large undergraduate introductory or survey courses, will include students with a range of academic abilities, interests, skills, and goals. The crucial question for instructors is how best to promote learning in a class of academically diverse students. Very bright students may become bored if they fail to find your class intellectually challenging. But less capable students may be overwhelmed by the material and lose interest. The suggestions below are intended to help you meet the needs of both groups.

General Strategies

Determine entry-level knowledge required for students to succeed in your course. Make those expectations explicit in your course description and syllabus, and underscore them during the first class meeting.

Give students an indication of whether they have the requisite skills and knowledge to succeed in the class. For instance, give a pretest on the first day of class that covers the material you expect the students to know already. If you want students to stretch a bit, add a few items you assume they don't know. Ask for a sample of their writing if your class has a writing component. Direct students who lack essential skills or knowledge to courses that will provide them with those skills, or assign supplementary work early in the semester. (Source: Angelo, 1991; Angelo and Cross, 1993)

Prepare a reading list that reflects the academic diversity of the class. You might want to divide your reading list into three categories: background reading for students who need to review or acquire skills or knowledge to succeed in class, basic reading essential to the course, and in-depth reading, grouped by topic, for students who wish to delve deeper into particular subjects.

Identify early on students who may have difficulty in the class. It is helpful to give a test or exam in the first two or three weeks so that you and your students know how well they are doing. Watch class attendance as well. When students feel lost or overwhelmed by a course, they may stay away.

Plan a variety of assignments appropriate to various kinds of learning styles. Students differ in their preferred styles of learning. Four types of styles are *abstract*—preference for learning theories and generating hypotheses that focus on general principles and concepts; *concrete*—preference for learning tangible, specific, practical tasks with a focus on skills; *individual*—preference for learning or working alone with an emphasis on self-reliance and solitary tasks such as reading; and *interpersonal*—preference for learning in a well-organized, teacher-directed class with expectations, assignments, and goals clearly identified. See "Learning Styles and Preferences." (Source: Fuhrmann and Grasha, 1983)

Teach to the level you expect students to reach. For most classes, you will probably gear the material for the B student, the bright middle range. When in doubt, it is better to overestimate rather than underestimate the level of the class. Students tend to learn more when a course is conducted just above the level at which they are functioning. (Source: Lucas, 1990)

Observing How Well Students Are Learning the Material

Ask questions during class. Try to get a sense of whether students are keeping up or falling behind. Instead of simply asking students whether they understand the material, ask pointed questions that require them to demonstrate their understanding. Focus on key concepts and complex ideas by having students give definitions, associations, and applications of the ideas. Ask a student to explain something you have presented, and gauge the response in terms of detail and accuracy. Go over material a second time, as needed.

Give frequent short in-class assignments. For example, pose a question or problem, ask students to respond in writing, and then have students correct their own answer or their neighbor's.

Ask students to write a "minute paper." Toward the end of a class session, pose two questions for your students: "What is the most significant thing you learned today?" and "What question is uppermost in your mind at the end of today's class?" If you have students turn in their answers anonymously, you will be able to evaluate how well they are grasping the material. (Source: Davis, Wood, and Wilson, 1983)

Ask students to list key concepts or ideas. After you have finished discussing or lecturing on a particular topic, ask students to jot down three or four key concepts or main ideas about the topic. You can have students turn in their lists, which you can review, or tell students to keep their lists to review for exams. You can also use the lists to start a class discussion. (Source: Angelo and Cross, 1993)

Ask students to give definitions and applications for difficult concepts. At the end of the class period, hand out a brief questionnaire of the following type:

- As I understand it, the main idea (concept or point) of today's session was . . .
- A good example of an application of this idea is . . .
- In my mind, the main point of today's lecture is most closely related to the following concepts, ideas, people, places, processes, events, or things. . . (Have students list several items.)

(Source: Lancaster, 1974)

Ask students to summarize the main ideas. Take five minutes at the beginning of a class period to have students summarize in writing that day's reading assignment. Or take five minutes at the end and ask them to summarize the lecture or discussion.

Collect students' lecture notes at random. Tell students that you would like to occasionally collect their lecture notes to get a sense of which ideas you are getting across and how well the class is following your presentations. This activity may also encourage your students to take good notes.

Be aware of who is talking most in class. Do the bright students tend to dominate the discussion? If so, be sure to direct your comments and questions to the entire class, and ask follow-up questions of all students. See "Leading a Discussion."

Watch for nonverbal cues from students. If you see students having trouble taking notes or you detect blank or quizzical looks on their faces, stop and say, "I seem to be losing some of you; let me explain this point another way."

Arrive early for class. Use the time before class to chat with students about how well they are understanding the material and to answer questions they may have from the last session or from the readings.

Helping Students Who Are Having Difficulty

Prepare supplementary materials. If students find the assigned readings too challenging or unclear, recommend other texts that explain the concepts in a different way. Consider preparing a glossary of terms that isolate key concepts and give short definitions or examples.

Hold review sessions during office hours. Instead of slowing the pace of the class, invite students having trouble with a particular topic to meet for a group review during your office hours or schedule a classroom if your office is too small.

Show students how to do the tasks you set for the class. Students who are struggling are unlikely to benefit from broad admonitions to "work harder." Often they need help with specific skills (how to read critically a journal article, how to move from topic to thesis in writing a paper). Peters (1990) gives suggestions for offering a series of supplemental two-hour workshops during the first weeks of class on four topics: reading text material, taking notes, studying, and taking exams. During the workshops, students practice the skills on the actual course material.

Distribute copies of good (B or B+) papers, lab reports, or book reviews. Handing out copies of good (but not extraordinary) work helps students understand your standards and expectations. Students can also compare their own work against the models.

Refer students to campus or department resources. Students in trouble do not always seek help on their own. Ask a student who is having problems to come to your office, and urge the student to seek assistance: "You could benefit a lot from individual or group tutoring. Why don't you go over to the student learning center now and see what they can do? Tell me what arrangements you've made by early next week."

Encourage students to learn from each other. Use class time to help students organize study groups of five or six members. Give students an overview of how study groups operate and what your expectations are for the members. See "Collaborative Learning." Or assign class partners who can work together on projects. Brighter students will have the opportunity to develop their skills in explaining and analyzing material, and struggling students will have a source of peer tutoring. If you assign papers or essays, you might also want to encourage students to exchange drafts with classmates for peer editing. See "Helping Students Write Better in All Courses."

Write "see me" on the papers or tests of students who are doing poorly. Don't just make an announcement in class that you want to see students whose scores fall below a C. Instead put an encouraging word on their work, "I have some advice that will help you do better work. See me during my office hours."

Encouraging Your Best Students

Prepare supplementary materials. Give your top students special assignments such as recommended reading, additional papers or problem sets, or fieldwork. While some students may not follow through on the extra work, they will relish the extra attention.

Use office hours for advanced exploration of a topic. During an office hour, provide a group of students with an in-depth analysis of a topic that was covered only briefly in class. Suggest follow-up independent study. For students who wish to pursue aspects of the course in more detail, recommend enrollment in an independent research course the following term.

References

Angelo, T. A. (ed.). *Classroom Research: Early Lessons from Success*. New Directions for Teaching and Learning, no. 46. San Francisco: Jossey-Bass, 1991.

Angelo, T. A., and Cross, K. P. *Classroom Assessment Techniques: A Handbook for College Teachers*. (2nd ed.) San Francisco: Jossey-Bass, 1993.

Davis, B. G., Wood, L., and Wilson, R. *ABCs of Teaching Excellence*. Berkeley: Office of Educational Development, University of California, 1983.

Fuhrmann, B. S., and Grasha, A. F. *A Practical Handbook for College Teachers*. Boston: Little, Brown, 1983.

Lancaster, O. E. *Effective Teaching and Learning*. New York: Gordon and Breach, 1974.

Lucas, A. F. "Using Psychological Models to Understand Student Motivation." In M. D. Svinicki (ed.), *The Changing Face of College Teaching*. New Directions for Teaching and Learning, no. 42. San Francisco: Jossey-Bass, 1990.

Peters, C. B. "Rescue the Perishing: A New Approach to Supplemental Instruction." In M. D. Svinicki (ed.), *The Changing Face of College Teaching*. New Directions for Teaching and Learning, no. 42. San Francisco: Jossey-Bass, 1990.

III.

Discussion Strategies

Leading a Discussion

8

Class discussion provides students with opportunities to acquire knowledge and insight through the face-to-face exchange of information, ideas, and opinions. A good give-and-take discussion can produce unmatched learning experiences as students articulate their ideas, respond to their classmates' points, and develop skills in evaluating the evidence for their own and others' positions. Initiating and sustaining a lively, productive discussion are among the most challenging of activities for an instructor.

General Strategies

Keep in mind the purpose of discussion. Discussions are useful for actively involving students in learning. Through discussion, students gain practice in thinking through problems and organizing concepts, formulating arguments and counterarguments, testing their ideas in a public setting, evaluating the evidence for their own and others' positions, and responding thoughtfully and critically to diverse points of view.

Plan how you will conduct each discussion session. A stimulating discussion is spontaneous and unpredictable, yet a good discussion requires careful planning. You will want to devise assignments to prepare students for discussion, compose a list of questions to guide and focus the discussion, and prepare specific in-class activities such as pair work and brainstorming. Have in mind three or four ways to begin the discussion (see below); if your first approach fails, try the next. To renew students' attention and heighten their motivation, plan to shift activities after twenty minutes or so if student interest and participation are waning (Frederick, 1989). Your plan should also allow time for a wrap-up so that students can synthesize what they have discussed.

Discuss your expectations at the beginning of the term. On the first day of class or in the syllabus, define the role discussion will play in the course. Describe students' responsibilities: let them know you expect everyone to participate, that class time is a "safe place" to test ideas and react to new perspectives, and that the discussion will be more worthwhile if students come prepared. Some faculty establish teaching/learning contracts that include the values, assumptions, and ideals of how the class will operate. (Sources: Hansen, 1991; Tiberius, 1990)

Setting the Context for Discussion

Explain the ground rules for participation. For example, do students have to raise their hand to speak? If you will call on students to speak, do they have a right to "pass" without penalty? One faculty member offers students a choice of responses when they don't want to answer when called on: "I prefer not to talk just now" or "Please call on me later" (Hansen, 1992). Another faculty member asks those students who do not wish to be called on to write their name on a piece of paper. She places a star next to their name as a reminder to skip over them. She finds that few students exercise this option and some change their mind over the course of the term.

Give pointers about how to participate in a discussion. Students need to understand the value of listening carefully, tolerating opposing viewpoints, suspending judgment until all sides have spoken, realizing that often there is no one right answer or conclusion, and recognizing when they have not understood a concept or idea. Deemer (1986, p. 41) distributes a list of principles to students:

- I am critical of ideas, not people. I challenge and refute the ideas. . . but I do not indicate that I personally reject them.
- . . . I focus on coming to the best decision possible, not on winning.
- I encourage everyone to participate. . . .
- I listen to everyone's ideas even if I don't agree.
- I restate what someone has said if it is not clear to me.
- I first bring out all ideas and facts supporting all sides, and then I try to put them together in a way that makes sense.
- I try to understand all sides of the issue.
- I change my mind when the evidence clearly indicates that I should do so.

Tiberius (1990) also recommends distributing a handout on group skills (adapted from pp. 67–68):

- Seek the best answer rather than try to convince other people.
- Try not to let your previous ideas or prejudices interfere with your freedom of thinking.
- Speak whenever you wish (if you are not interrupting someone else, of course), even though your idea may seem incomplete.
- Practice listening by trying to formulate in your own words the point that the previous speaker made before adding your own contribution.
- Avoid disrupting the flow of thought by introducing new issues; instead wait until the present topic reaches its natural end; if you wish to introduce a new topic, warn the group that what you are about to say will address a new topic and that you are willing to wait to introduce it until people are finished commenting on the current topic.
- Stick to the subject and talk briefly.
- Avoid long stories, anecdotes, or examples.
- Give encouragement and approval to others.
- Seek out differences of opinion; they enrich the discussion.
- Be sympathetic and understanding of other people's views.

One faculty member in sociology asks students to agree that no one will express an opinion on a subject until that person has (1) indicated an understanding of the previous speaker's views by briefly restating them to the latter's satisfaction and (2) inquired whether the speaker had something further to add. This instructor reminds the students of the agreement until the procedures become habitual (Thompson, 1974).

Help students prepare for discussion. Discussions are more lively and satisfying if students are prepared. Some faculty distribute four to six study questions for each reading assignment. Or you can ask students to conduct a "fact finding" mission to search the texts for factual evidence that clarifies a particular concept or problem (Clarke, 1988). Or ask students to come to class with a one- or two-paragraph position piece or several questions they would like to hear discussed. Hill (1969, pp. 55–56) recommends asking students to write out one or more of the following for each article they read:

- List all unfamiliar words or terms, and look up and write down the definitions.
- Write your version of the author's message or thesis.
- Identify the subtopics in the article, and design a question that you would ask for each.

- Indicate what other ideas the reading substantiates, contradicts, or amplifies.
- Summarize your reactions and evaluation of the article.

A professor of business administration assigns a weekly "reaction" paper, one to two pages on a specific topic. The papers are graded and also used as the basis for class discussion.

Show a videotape of a good discussion session. Consider showing the class segments from Public Broadcasting System's "Ethics in America" or other PBS shows in which people with a variety of perspectives and political viewpoints discuss important issues. The impact of the videotapes will be greater if the content area relates to the subject matter of your course.

Starting a Discussion

Refer to any study questions you may have distributed. Begin the discussion by launching into one of the study questions or by asking the class which of the study questions they found most provocative or most difficult to answer.

Ask for students' questions. Tell students to come to the discussion session with one or two questions about the reading: "Bring a provocative, intriguing question to class and a sentence or two about why you would like to hear the question discussed." From these questions, pick one at random to start the discussion. Or have students divide into small groups to discuss their questions. For a change of pace, have students generate questions during class time, in pairs or in small groups. (Source: Frederick, 1981)

Pair students to discuss assigned reading materials in a question-and-answer format. Ask students to come to the discussion session with four complex questions that are phrased like good essay exam questions (you may need to give them models of good test questions). During class, have the students pair off and alternate asking and answering the questions. Move from pair to pair, listening or occasionally joining in. (Source: McKeachie, 1986)

Phrase questions so students feel comfortable responding. Lowman (1984) and McKeachie (1986) recommend formulating questions that probe students' understanding but do not have a single correct answer. For example, instead of asking for a definition ("What is entropy?"), ask the students to relate something new that they learned ("What about entropy stands out in your mind?") or to give an example of the concept.

Pose an opening question and give students a few minutes to write down an answer. Once students start to gather their thoughts and write, additional questions and issues will arise. After students have finished writing, ask for volunteers or call on several students. (Sources: Clarke, 1988; Frederick, 1989)

Ask students to describe a "critical incident." Begin the discussion by asking volunteers to recall an event in their own lives that pertains to the topic under discussion. When several students have related incidents, explore their commonalities and differences and connect the discussion to the readings. (Source: Brookfield, 1990)

Ask students to recall specific images from the reading assignment. Ask students to volunteer one memorable image / scene / event / moment from the reading: "What images remain with you after reading the account of Wounded Knee?" List these on the board and explore the themes that emerge. (Source: Frederick, 1981)

Ask students to pose the dumbest question they can think of. One faculty member uses this device to unleash students' creativity and to minimize their fears in speaking up. After he has asked this question a few times during the beginning of the term, it becomes a game that everyone is willing to play. The class sifts through the questions, weeding out the irrelevant and focusing on the good ones. A variation of this technique is to pose a question and ask students for their "first approximations" — not a detailed answer, just a glint of useful information.

Pose questions based on a shared experience. A shared experience — a field trip, slide show, demonstration, film, exhibit — can stimulate an exchange that reveals students' different perceptions and reactions to the same event. The discussion can then focus on how and why their perceptions differ.

Make a list of key points. "Let's list the important points (or arguments that support a particular position) from the reading." Then list the points on the board and use these as a starting point for the discussion by asking students which points are or are not important.

Use brainstorming. Brainstorming encourages students to consider a range of possible causes, consequences, solutions, reasons, or contributing factors to some phenomenon. Make the rules known to students: anyone can contribute an idea (no matter how bizarre or farfetched), and each idea is written on the board. Free association, creativity, and ingenuity are the goal; no idea is questioned, praised, or criticized at this point. After a set period of time (five minutes, for example) or when students have run out of ideas, the group begins critically evaluating all the ideas.

Pose a controversial question. Have students group themselves by the pro or con position they take. Ask each group to identify two or three arguments or strong examples to support their position. Write each group's statements on the board and then open the discussion for comments from all. (Source: Frederick, 1981)

Generate "truth statements." Divide students into groups and have each group compose three true statements about some particular topic. "It is true that Marxism . . ." or "It is true that high-density housing . . ." or "It is true that Executive Order 9066. . . ." List their responses on the board and open the discussion to the full class. (Source: Frederick, 1981)

Have students divide into small groups to discuss a question you pose. Give pairs, trios, or small groups of students an explicit task: "Identify the two most obvious differences between today's and last week's readings" or "Identify three themes common to the reading assignments" or "Make a list of as many comparisons (or contrasts) as you can in ten minutes." Give the groups a time limit and ask them to select a spokesperson who will report back to the entire class. (Source: Frederick, 1981)

Ask students to respond to a brief questionnaire. Distribute a brief set of questions to students, and use their signed responses as the basis for discussion. "Ellen, I see you answered the first question in the negative. Daniele, I note that you disagree with Ellen" or "Amber, your answer to question four is intriguing. Can you tell us more?" (Source: Davis, 1976)

Use student panels. Assign each student a different role on the panel (for example, experts in particular topics or representatives of particular points of view). Give panel members a week or more to prepare, completing whatever readings, research, or other activities you may suggest for them. Some faculty require all students to serve on a panel during the term; others offer panels as an option to a written paper or exam, or for extra credit.

Use storyboarding. Divide a particular problem into three to five subtopics or questions, post each subtopic or question in large type on a flipchart, and place the flipcharts around the classroom. Divide the class into as many subgroups as there are charts. Students are to read the question on their flipchart, write solutions on slips of paper or Post-its—one idea per note—and attach the slips to the chart. After ten minutes, the groups move on to the next flipchart and post notes there. Continue until all groups have visited all flipcharts. This technique encourages the free flow of ideas and keeps students actively involved. Here are examples of questions from a business administration course: "How can the sales reps increase sales?" "What methods can be used to recruit new distributors in underdeveloped markets?" (Source: "Storyboarding," 1988)

Stage a role play. See "Role Playing and Case Studies."

Guiding the Discussion

Take rough notes. Jot down key points that emerge from the discussion and use these for summarizing the session. You might also note problem areas that need clarification or students' contributions that can be used as a segue to subsequent points.

Keep the discussion focused. List the day's questions or issues on the board so that the class can see where the discussion is heading. Brief interim summaries of the discussion are helpful, as long as the summaries do not cut off the discussion prematurely.

Use nonverbal cues to maintain the flow. For example, hold up your hand to signal stop, to prevent one student from interrupting another. Step back from a student who is speaking so that he or she will see the other faces in the room. Prompt students to speak by an expectant look in your eye, a nod of your head, or slight motion of your hand. Interpose your body between two students in a heated exchange. To shift the mood and pace of the class, you can move around, sit down, stand up, make notes, or write on the board. (Source: Rosmarin, 1987)

Bring the discussion back to the key issues. If the discussion gets off track, stop and describe what is happening: "We seem to have lost sight of the original point. Let's pick up the notion again that. . . ." "Peter, you have a good point, but does it directly apply to the issue of censorship?" "This is all very provocative, but we also need to talk about the NEA's response before we end today."

Listen carefully to what students say. Be aware of the following:

- Content, logic, and substance (Is the student sensitive to the strengths and weaknesses of his or her presentation?)
- Nuance and tone, including the speaker's degree of authority or doubt and degree of emotion or commitment (Is the student involved with or removed from the subject matter?)
- How the comment relates to the overall discussion (Does it build on previous points and strengthen the flow of the discussion?)
- Opportunities for moving the discussion forward (Do students agree or disagree with what has been said?)
- The mood of the class as a whole
- What is left unsaid

(Sources: Christensen, 1991; Jacobson, 1981)

Clarify students' confusions. Don't let the discussion become bogged down in confusing information. "Let's clear up this misunderstanding before we continue." "We've covered some important points so far. Are you persuaded or troubled by this line of thinking?" (Source: Lowman, 1984)

Prevent the discussion from deteriorating into a heated argument. Remind students to focus on ideas, not on personal attacks, and to show tolerance for divergent points of view. Don't allow students to cut each other off or to make extraneous comments. If the discussion becomes too free-wheeling and heated, ask students to raise their hand if they wish to speak. Defuse arguments with a calm remark:

- Let's slow down a moment.
- Hold on. It's not helpful when five people jump all over what their classmate says. Let's give Russ a break.
- It seems like we need to identify those areas we can agree upon and those areas where we disagree. Let's start with those things we all agree with.
- This isn't getting us anywhere. Those who want to continue on this point can do so outside of class. Let's move on to a new topic.

You can also use conflicts as the basis for a homework assignment, to be written out away from the heat of the moment. (Source: McKeachie, 1986)

But do not shut off disagreement as soon as it occurs. A certain amount of disagreement can stimulate discussion and thought. Lively exchanges can be generated by asking, "Who doesn't agree with what's being said?" or "Will someone present an opposite point of view or counterposition?" or "What would a devil's advocate say?"

Change the task if the discussion begins to stagnate. Expect one or two lulls in the discussion. Students need time to think about what they have said and to take a breath. However, move on to a different task when students' attention is wandering. To refresh their thinking, pair students off for a short task or move from theory to application or from method to findings.

Be alert for signs that a discussion is breaking down. Indications that a discussion is not going well include the following:

- Excessive hair splitting or nit-picking
- Repetition of points
- Private conversations
- Members taking sides and refusing to compromise
- Ideas being attacked before they are completely expressed
- Apathetic participation

Introducing a new question or activity can jump start the discussion. It may also be useful to confront the problem directly by asking students to talk about why the discussion is faltering. (Sources: Hyman, 1980; Tiberius, 1990)

Vary the emotional tone of the discussion. To spark a discussion, ask specific rather than general questions; call on individual students known for their strong opinions. To calm a discussion, pose abstract or theoretical questions, slow the tempo of your voice, and avoid calling on specific individuals. For example, to heat a discussion, ask, "Should gays and lesbians be able to join the military?" To cool a discussion, ask, "What political and social factors affect the debate on gays and lesbians in the military?" (Sources: Christensen, 1991; Rosmarin, 1987)

Bring closure to the discussion. Announce that the discussion is ending: "Are there any final comments before we pull these ideas together?" The closing summary should then show students how the discussion progressed, emphasize two or three key points, and provide a framework for the next session. End by acknowledging the insightful comments students have made. (Source: Clarke, 1988)

Assign students responsibility for summarizing the major points. At the beginning of the discussion, select one or two students to be the "summarizers" of the major issues, concerns, and conclusions generated during discussion. A variation of this technique is to tell the class that someone will be called on at the end of class to summarize. This strategy encourages students to listen more carefully for the main ideas because they may be called upon to give the summary.

Ask students to write down a question that is uppermost in their minds. During the closing minutes of class, ask students to list one or two questions they have as a result of the day's discussion. Have students turn in these questions anonymously, and use the questions to start the next class meeting.

Evaluating the Discussion

Ask students to write briefly on how their thinking changed as a result of the discussion. You can also ask students to put the discussion in the context of issues previously discussed. Have students turn in their paragraphs, and review a sample to see what they have learned.

Make your own informal evaluation of the discussion. Did everyone contribute to the discussion? How much did the teacher dominate the session? What was the quality of students' comments? What questions worked especially well? How satisfied did the group seem about the progress that was made? Did students learn something new about the topic?

Occasionally save time at the end of the period to assess the day's discussion. You can hold an informal conversation or ask students to respond in writing to one or more of the following questions:

- What are some examples of productive or helpful contributions?
- When did the group stray from the subject?
- Whom do people look at when they talk?
- Does everyone who wants to speak have the opportunity to do so?

(Source: Davis, 1976)

Videotape the discussion. If you are interested in making a detailed analysis of how you conduct discussions, videotape a session. There are a number of ways to analyze a tape, one of which is to examine who undertakes which of the following activities (adapted from Davis, 1976, pp. 85–86):

- *Initiating:* proposing tasks or procedures, defining problems, identifying action steps
- *Eliciting:* requesting information, inviting reactions, soliciting ideas
- *Informing:* offering information, expressing reactions, stating facts
- *Blocking:* introducing irrelevancies, changing the subject, questioning others' competence
- *Entrenching:* expressing cynicism, posing distractions, digging in
- *Clarifying:* clearing up confusions, restating others' contributions, suggesting alternative ways of seeing problems or issues
- *Clouding:* creating confusion, claiming that words can't "really" be defined, remaining willfully puzzled, quibbling over semantic distinctions, obscuring issues
- *Summarizing:* pulling together related ideas, offering conclusions, stating implications of others' contributions
- *Interpreting:* calling attention to individual actions and what they mean
- *Consensus proposing:* asking whether the group is nearing a decision, suggesting a conclusion for group agreement
- *Consensus resisting:* persisting in a topic or argument after others have decided or lost interest, going back over old ground, finding endless details that need attention
- *Harmonizing:* trying to reconcile disagreements, joking at the right time to reduce tensions, encouraging inactive members
- *Disrupting:* interfering with the work of the group, trying to increase tensions, making jokes as veiled insults or threats
- *Evaluating:* asking whether the group is satisfied with the proceedings or topic, pointing out implicit or explicit standards the group is using, suggesting alternative tasks and practices

As you observe your students' behavior and your own, think about ways to increase productive activities and decrease counterproductive ones. Ask a trusted colleague or a faculty development expert on your campus to analyze and review your tape with you.

References

Brookfield, S. D. *The Skillful Teacher.* San Francisco: Jossey-Bass, 1990.

Christensen, C. R. "The Discussion Teacher in Action: Questioning, Listening, and Response." In C. R. Christensen, D. A. Garvin, and A. Sweet (eds.), *Education for Judgment: The Artistry of Discussion Leadership.* Boston: Harvard Business School, 1991.

Clarke, J. H. "Designing Discussions as Group Inquiry." *College Teaching*, 1988, *36*(4), 140–143.

Davis, J. R. *Teaching Strategies for the College Classroom*. Boulder, Colo.: Westview Press, 1976.

Deemer, D. "Structuring Controversy in the Classroom." In S. F. Schomberg (ed.), *Strategies for Active Teaching and Learning in University Classrooms*. Minneapolis: Office of Educational Development Programs, University of Minnesota, 1986.

Frederick, P. "The Dreaded Discussion: Ten Ways to Start." *Improving College and University Teaching*, 1981, *29*(3), 109–114.

Frederick, P. "Involving Students More Actively in the Classroom." In A. F. Lucas (ed.), *The Department Chair's Role in Enhancing College Teaching*. New Directions for Teaching and Learning, no. 37. San Francisco: Jossey-Bass, 1989.

Hansen, A. J. "Establishing a Teaching/Learning Contract." In C. R. Christensen, D. A. Garvin, and A. Sweet (eds.), *Education for Judgment: The Artistry of Discussion Leadership*. Boston: Harvard Business School, 1991.

Hansen, F. "Laying the Groundwork for Class Discussions." *National Teaching and Learning Forum*, 1992, *1*(3), 6–7.

Hill, W. F. *Learning Through Discussion*. Newbury Park, Calif.: Sage, 1969.

Hyman, R. T. *Improving Discussion Leadership*. New York: Teachers College Press, 1980.

Jacobson, R. L. "Asking Questions Is the Key Skill Needed for Discussion Teaching." *Chronicle of Higher Education*, July 25, 1981, p. 20.

Lowman, J. *Mastering the Techniques of Teaching*. San Francisco: Jossey-Bass, 1984.

McKeachie, W. J. *Teaching Tips*. (8th ed.) Lexington, Mass.: Heath, 1986.

Rosmarin, A. "The Art of Leading a Discussion." In C. R. Christensen and A. J. Hansen (eds.), *Teaching and the Case Method*. Boston: Harvard Business School, 1987.

"Storyboarding: A New Way to Brainstorm." *Personal Report*, July 1988, pp. 2–3.

Thompson, G. W. *Discussion Groups in University Courses: Ideas and Activities*. Washington, D.C.: American Sociological Association, 1974.

Tiberius, R. G. *Small Group Teaching: A Trouble-Shooting Guide*. Toronto: Ontario Institute for Studies in Education Press, 1990.

Encouraging Student Participation in Discussion

9

Students' enthusiasm, involvement, and willingness to participate affect the quality of class discussion as an opportunity for learning. Your challenge is to engage all students, keep them talking to each other about the same topic, and help them develop insights into the material. Roby (1988) warns against falling into quasi discussions—encounters in which students talk but do not develop or criticize their own positions and fail to reflect on the process and outcomes of the session. Two common forms of quasi discussion are quiz shows (where the teacher has the right answers) and bull sessions (characterized by clichés, stereotypes, empty generalizations, lack of standards for judging opinions, and aimless talking). The following suggestions are intended to help you create a classroom in which students feel comfortable, secure, willing to take risks, and ready to test and share ideas.

General Strategies

Encourage students to learn each other's names and interests. Students are more likely to participate in class if they feel they are among friends rather than strangers; so at the beginning of the term, ask students to introduce themselves and describe their primary interests or background in the subject (Tiberius, 1990). These introductions may also give you some clues about framing discussion questions that address students' interests. See "The First Day of Class" for ideas on helping students get to know one another.

Get to know as many of your students as class size permits. In classes of thirty or less, learn all your students' names. ("The First Day of Class" lists several ways to do this.) If you require students to come to your office once during the first few weeks of class, you can also learn about their interests. Class participation often improves after students have had an opportunity to talk informally with their instructor.

Arrange seating to promote discussion. If your room has movable chairs, ask students to sit in a semicircle so that they can see one another. At a long seminar table, seat yourself along the side rather than at the head. If appropriate, ask students to print their names on name cards and display them on their desk or the table. Research reported by Beard and Hartley (1984) shows that people tend to talk to the person sitting opposite them, that people sitting next to each other tend not to talk to one another, that the most centrally placed member of a group tends to emerge as leader, and that leaders tend to sit in the least crowded parts of a room.

Allow the class time to warm up before you launch into the discussion. Consider arriving two to three minutes early to talk informally with students. Or open class with a few minutes of conversation about relevant current events, campus activities, or administrative matters. (Sources: Billson, 1986; Welty, 1989)

Limit your own comments. Some teachers talk too much and turn a discussion into a lecture or a series of instructor-student dialogues. Brown and Atkins (1988) report a series of studies by various researchers that found that most discussion classes are dominated by instructors. In one study (p. 53) faculty talked 86 percent of the time. Avoid the temptation to respond to every student's contribution. Instead, allow students to develop their ideas and respond to one another.

Tactics to Increase Student Participation

Make certain each student has an opportunity to talk in class during the first two or three weeks. The longer a student goes without speaking in class, the more difficult it will be for him or her to contribute. Devise small group or pair work early in the term so that all students can participate and hear their own voices in nonthreatening circumstances.

Plan an icebreaker activity early in the semester. For example, a professor teaching plant domestication in cultural geography asks students to bring to class a fruit or vegetable from another culture or region. The discussion focuses on the countries of origin and the relationship between food and culture. At the end of class students eat what they brought. See "The First Day of Class" for other suggestions.

Ask students to identify characteristics of an effective discussion. Ask students individually or in small groups to recall discussions and seminars in which they have participated and to list the characteristics of those that were worthwhile. Then ask students to list the characteristics of poor discussions. Write the items on the board, tallying those items mentioned by more than one student or group. With the entire class, explore ways in which class members can maximize those aspects that make for a good discussion and minimize those aspects that make for a poor discussion.

Periodically divide students into small groups. Students find it easier to speak to groups of three or four than to an entire class. Divide students into small groups, have them discuss a question or issue for five or ten minutes, and then return to a plenary format. Choose topics that are focused and straightforward: "What are the two most important characteristics of goal-free evaluation?" or "Why did the experiment fail?" Have each group report orally and record the results on the board. Once students have spoken in small groups, they may be less reluctant to speak to the class as a whole.

Assign roles to students. Ask two or three students to lead a discussion session sometime during the term. Meet with the student discussion leaders beforehand to go over their questions and proposed format. Have the leaders distribute three to six discussion questions to the class a week before the discussion. During class the leaders assume responsibility for generating and facilitating the discussion. For discussions you lead, assign one or two students per session to be observers responsible for commenting on the discussion. Other student roles include periodic summarizer (to summarize the main substantive points two or three times during the session), recorder (to serve as the group's memory), timekeeper (to keep the class on schedule), and designated first speaker. (Source: Hyman, 1980)

Use poker chips or "comment cards" to encourage discussion. One faculty member distributes three poker chips to each student in her class. Each time a student speaks, a chip is turned over to the instructor. Students must spend all their chips by the end of the period. The professor reports that this strategy limits students who dominate the discussion and encourages quiet students to speak up. Another professor hands out a "comment card" each time a student provides a strong response or insightful comment. Students turn back the cards at the end of the period, and the professor notes on the course roster the number of cards each student received. (Source: Sadker and Sadker, 1992)

Use electronic mail to start a discussion. One faculty member in the biological sciences poses a question through electronic mail and asks the students to write in their responses and comments. He then hands out copies of all the responses to initiate the class discussion.

Tactics to Keep Students Talking

Build rapport with students. Simply saying that you are interested in what your students think and that you value their opinions may not be enough. In addition, comment positively about a student's contribution and reinforce good points by paraphrasing or summarizing them. If a student makes a good observation that is ignored by the class, point this out: "Thank you, Steve. Karen also raised that issue earlier, but we didn't pick up on it. Perhaps now is the time to address it. Thank you for your patience, Karen" (Tiberius, 1990). Clarke (1988) suggests tagging important assertions or questions with the student's name: the Amy argument or the Haruko hypothesis. Tiberius (1990) warns against overdoing this, however, because a class may get tired of being reminded that they are discussing so-and-so's point.

Bring students' outside comments into class. Talk to students during office hours, in hallways, and around campus. If they make a good comment, check with them first to see whether they are willing to raise the idea in class, then say: "Jana, you were saying something about that in the hall yesterday. Would you repeat it for the rest of the class."

Use nonverbal cues to encourage participation. For example, smile expectantly and nod as students talk. Maintain eye contact with students. Look relaxed and interested.

Draw all students into the discussion. You can involve more students by asking whether they agree with what has just been said or whether someone can provide another example to support or contradict a point: "How do the rest of you feel about that?" or "Does anyone who hasn't spoken care to comment on the plans for People's Park?" Moreover, if you move away from—rather than toward—a student who makes a comment, the student will speak up and outward, drawing everyone into the conversation. The comment will be "on the floor," open for students to respond to.

Give quiet students special encouragement. Quiet students are not necessarily uninvolved, so avoid excessive efforts to draw them out. Some quiet students, though, are just waiting for a nonthreatening opportunity to speak. To help these students, consider the following strategies:

- Arrange small group (two to four students) discussions.
- Pose casual questions that don't call for a detailed correct response: "What are some reasons why people may not vote?" or "What do you

remember most from the reading?" or "Which of the articles did you find most difficult?" (McKeachie, 1986).

- Assign a small specific task to a quiet student: "Carrie, would you find out for next class session what Chile's GNP was last year?"
- Reward infrequent contributors with a smile.
- Bolster students' self-confidence by writing their comments on the board (Welty, 1989).
- Stand or sit next to someone who has not contributed; your proximity may draw a hesitant student into the discussion.

Discourage students who monopolize the discussion. As reported in "The One or Two Who Talk Too Much" (1988), researchers Karp and Yoels found that in classes with fewer than forty students, four or five students accounted for 75 percent of the total interactions per session. In classes with more than forty students, two or three students accounted for 51 percent of the exchanges. Here are some ways to handle dominating students:

- Break the class into small groups or assign tasks to pairs of students.
- Ask everyone to jot down a response to your question and then choose someone to speak.
- If only the dominant students raise their hand, restate your desire for greater student participation: "I'd like to hear from others in the class."
- Avoid making eye contact with the talkative.
- If one student has been dominating the discussion, ask other students whether they agree or disagree with that student.
- Explain that the discussion has become too one-sided and ask the monopolizer to help by remaining silent: "Larry, since we must move on, would you briefly summarize your remarks, and then we'll hear the reactions of other group members."
- Assign a specific role to the dominant student that limits participation (for example, periodic summarizer).
- Acknowledge the time constraints: "Jon, I notice that our time is running out. Let's set a thirty-second limit on everybody's comments from now on."
- If the monopolizer is a serious problem, speak to him or her after class or during office hours. Tell the student that you value his or her participation and wish more students contributed. If this student's comments are good, say so; but point out that learning results from give-and-take and that everyone benefits from hearing a range of opinions and views.

Tactfully correct wrong answers. Any type of put-down or disapproval will inhibit students from speaking up and from learning. Say something positive about those aspects of the response that are insightful or creative and point out those aspects that are off base. Provide hints, suggestions, or follow-up questions that will enable students to understand and correct their own errors. Billson (1986) suggests prompts such as "Good—now let's take it a step further"; "Keep going"; "Not quite, but keep thinking about it."

Reward but do not grade student participation. Some faculty members assign grades based on participation or reward student participation with bonus points when assigning final grades. Melvin (1988) describes a grading scheme based on peer and professor evaluation: Students are asked to rate the class participation of each of their classmates as high, medium, or low. If the median peer rating is higher than the instructor's rating of that student, the two ratings are averaged. If the peer rating is lower, the student receives the instructor's rating. Other faculty members believe that grading based on participation is inappropriate, that is, subjective and not defensible if challenged. They also note that such a policy may discourage free and open discussion, making students hesitant to talk for fear of revealing their ignorance or being perceived as trying to gain grade points. In addition, faculty argue, thoughtful silence is not unproductive, and shy students should not be placed at a disadvantage simply because they are shy.

There are means other than grades to encourage and reward participation: verbal praise of good points, acknowledgment of valued contributions, or even written notes to students who have added significantly to the discussion. One faculty member uses lottery tickets to recognize excellent student responses or questions when they occur. He doesn't announce this in advance but distributes the first ticket as a surprise. Tickets can be given to individuals or to small groups. Over the term, he may hand out fifteen to twenty lottery tickets. In a small class, you may be able to keep notes on students' participation and devote some office hours to helping students develop their skills in presenting their points of view and listening to their classmates (Hertenstein, 1991).

References

Beard, R. M., and Hartley, J. *Teaching and Learning in Higher Education.* (4th ed.) New York: Harper & Row, 1984.

Billson, J. M. "The College Classroom as a Small Group: Some Implications for Teaching and Learning." *Teaching Sociology*, 1986, *14*(3), 143–151.

Brown, G., and Atkins, M. *Effective Teaching in Higher Education*. London: Methuen, 1988.

Clarke, J. H. "Designing Discussions as Group Inquiry." *College Teaching*, 1988, *36*(4), 140–143.

Hertenstein, J. H. "Patterns of Participation." In C. R. Christensen, D. A. Garvin, and A. Sweet (eds.), *Education for Judgment: The Artistry of Discussion Leadership*. Boston: Harvard Business School, 1991.

Hyman, R. T. *Improving Discussion Leadership*. New York: Teachers College Press, 1980.

McKeachie, W. J. *Teaching Tips*. (8th ed.) Lexington, Mass.: Heath, 1986.

Melvin, K. B. "Rating Class Participation: The Prof/Peer Method." *Teaching of Psychology*, 1988, *15*(3), 137–139.

"The One or Two Who Talk Too Much." *Teaching Professor*, 1988, *2*(7), 5.

Roby, T. W. "Models of Discussion." In J. T. Dillon (ed.), *Questioning and Discussion: A Multidisciplinary Study*. Norwood, N.J.: Ablex, 1988.

Sadker, M., and Sadker, D. "Ensuring Equitable Participation in College Classes." In L.L.B. Border and N.V.N. Chism (eds.), *Teaching for Diversity. New Directions for Teaching and Learning*, no. 49. San Francisco: Jossey-Bass, 1992.

Tiberius, R. G. *Small Group Teaching: A Trouble-Shooting Guide*. Toronto: Ontario Institute for Studies in Education Press, 1990.

Welty, W. M. "Discussion Method Teaching." *Change*, 1989, *21*(4), 40–49.

10

Asking Questions

Asking and answering questions are central to the learning process and to effective teaching. Yet studies show that faculty devote less than 4 percent of class time to asking questions and that the questions they do ask are rarely of the type that require students to think (Barnes, 1983). The types of questions posed and the sequencing of questions should capture students' attention, arouse their curiosity, reinforce important points, and promote active learning. When students respond to questions, you also gain insight into how well they are learning the material. Like other aspects of teaching, the ability to develop good questioning skills can be learned.

General Strategies

Identify your key questions in advance. As you prepare for class, formulate questions and anticipate the range of possible student responses. Put the list in some logical order (specific to general, simple to complex, or convergent — questions with a single correct answer — to divergent — questions with many valid answers). Hyman (1982, p. 3) argues for a carefully planned sequence of major questions. For example, in a class discussion on the Falkland Islands, he suggests not jumping in with "Why did Argentina invade the Falkland Islands?" Instead, build up to that important question with a series of questions: "According to Argentina, what is its historical claim to the Falklands? What previous attempts did Argentina and Britain make to settle their dispute? Who did Argentina believe would support its action? What did Argentina believe would be Britain's reaction to the invasion? What function, then, did the invasion serve for Argentina?" When composing questions, include a few that you are not quite sure how to answer. You may be impressed by your students' ideas. Don't stick solely to your list — add questions that occur to you during class or modify your list as you go along.

Prepare strategies for asking questions. Think about different ways to use your questions: Will you pose questions to the class as a whole, to pairs of students, to small groups? Will the question be a prompt for brainstorming, consensus building, or debate? (Source: Kasulis, 1984)

Decide whether you want to call on students individually. Some faculty members believe that students need to be drawn into the discussion. Others strongly believe that calling on students who may not wish to speak intimidates students and may deter others from making contributions. Still other faculty compromise by distributing a few study questions for which all students will be responsible; this gives shy students a chance to think through their responses before class. If you decide to call on students, pause after asking a question, and then call on someone at random. If you go around the room calling on students in order, some students' attention may wander until it is their turn.

Be aware of the manner in which you ask questions and treat responses. Your tone of voice and nonverbal cues (facial expressions, gestures) strongly affect whatever you say. Act as though you are seeking knowledge, not interrogating the troops.

Keep a journal on the class. Take a few minutes after each class session to jot down names of students who spoke up, who responded to whose points, and the kinds of questions that generated the most lively exchange. Use this information in preparing future sessions. (Source: Kasulis, 1984)

Levels and Types of Questions

Balance the kinds of questions you ask. Move from simple questions to those that require more thought. Experienced discussion leaders have found it helpful to develop a typology or inventory of questions such as these:

- *Exploratory questions* probe facts and basic knowledge: "What research evidence supports the theory of a cancer-prone personality?"
- *Challenge questions* examine assumptions, conclusions, and interpretations: "How else might we account for the findings of this experiment?"
- *Relational questions* ask for comparisons of themes, ideas, or issues: "What premises of *Plessy* v. *Ferguson* did the Supreme Court throw out in deciding *Brown* v. *Board of Education*?
- *Diagnostic questions* probe motives or causes: "Why did Jo assume a new identity?"
- *Action questions* call for a conclusion or action: "In response to a sit-in at California Hall, what should the chancellor do?"

- *Cause-and-effect questions* ask for causal relationships between ideas, actions, or events: "If the government stopped farm subsidies for wheat, what would happen to the price of bread?"
- *Extension questions* expand the discussion: "How does this comment relate to what we have previously said?"
- *Hypothetical questions* pose a change in the facts or issues: "Suppose Gregg had been rich instead of poor; would the outcome have been the same?"
- *Priority questions* seek to identify the most important issue: "From all that we have talked about, what is the most important cause of the decline of American competitiveness?"
- *Summary questions* elicit syntheses: "What themes or lessons have emerged from today's class?"

(Sources: Christensen, 1991; Jacobson, 1981; Rosmarin, 1987)

Vary the cognitive skills your questions call for. Different questions require different levels of thinking. Lower-level questions are appropriate for assessing students' preparation and comprehension or for reviewing and summarizing content. Higher-level questions encourage students to think critically and to solve problems. Various researchers have developed cognitive schemes for classifying questions. Bloom's (1956) system of ordering thinking skills from lower to higher has become a classic:

- Knowledge skills (remembering previously learned material such as definitions, principles, formulas): "Define *shared governance*." "What are Piaget's stages of development?"
- Comprehension skills (understanding the meaning of remembered material, usually demonstrated by restating or citing examples): "Explain the process of mitosis." "Give some examples of alliteration."
- Application skills (using information in a new context to solve a problem, answer a question, perform a task): "How does the concept of price elasticity explain the cost of oat bran?" "Given the smallness of the sample, how would you analyze these data?"
- Analysis skills (breaking a concept into its parts and explaining their interrelationships; distinguishing relevant from extraneous material): "What factors affect the price of gasoline?" "Point out the major arguments Shelby Steele uses to develop his thesis about affirmative action."
- Synthesis skills (putting parts together to form a new whole; solving a problem requiring creativity or originality): "How would you design an

experiment to show the effect of receiving the Distinguished Teaching Award on a faculty member's subsequent career progress?" "How would you reorganize Bloom's taxonomy in light of new research in cognitive science?"

- Evaluation skills (using a set of criteria to arrive at a reasoned judgment of the value of something): "To what extent does the proposed package of tax increases resolve the budget deficit?" "If cocaine were legalized, what would be the implications for public health services?"

Also include questions that ask for hunches, intuitive leaps, and educated guesses. Stimulate students' thinking by varying the intellectual approach of your questions.

Tactics for Effective Questioning

Ask one question at a time. Sometimes, in an effort to generate a response, instructors attempt to clarify a question by rephrasing it. But often the rephrasing constitutes an entirely new question. Keep your questions brief and clear. Long complex questions may lose the class. For example, "How is the theory of Jacques Lacan similar to Freud's?" rather than "How are Lacan and Freud alike? Are they alike in their view of the unconscious? How about their approach to psychoanalysis?" (Sources: Hyman, 1982; "Successful Participation Strategies," 1987)

Avoid yes/no questions. Ask "why" or "how" questions that lead students to try to figure out things for themselves. Not "Is radon considered a pollutant?" but "Why is radon considered a pollutant?" You cannot get a discussion going if you ask questions that only require a one-syllable or short-phrase response.

Pose questions that lack a single right answer. A history professor includes questions for which a number of hypotheses are equally plausible — for example, "Why did the birthrate rise in mid-eighteenth-century England?" or "Why did Napoleon III agree to Cavour's plans?" She emphasizes to students that the answers to these questions are matters of controversy or puzzlement to scholars and asks the class to generate their own hypotheses. She embellishes what students suggest by adding historians' theories and by showing how different answers to the questions lead in very different directions. She concludes by stressing that the answer to the question remains unresolved.

Ask focused questions. An overly broad question such as "What about the fall of the Berlin Wall?" can lead your class far off the topic. Instead ask, "How did the reunification of Germany affect European economic conditions?"

Avoid leading questions. A question such as "Don't you all think that global warming is the most serious environmental hazard we face?" will not lead to a free-ranging discussion of threats to the environment. Similarly, avoid answering your own question: "Why can't we use the chi-square test here? Is it because the cells are too small?"

After you ask a question, wait silently for an answer. Do not be afraid of silence. Be patient. Waiting is a signal that you want thoughtful participation. Count to yourself while your students are thinking; the silence rarely lasts more than ten seconds. If you communicate an air of expectation, usually someone will break the silence, even if only to say, "I don't understand the question." If a prolonged silence continues, ask your students what the silence means: "Gee, everyone has been quiet for a while — why?" Or encourage students by saying, "It's not easy to be the first one to talk, is it?" Someone will jump in with a comment or response. Don't feel you have to call on the first person who volunteers. You might want to wait until several hands are raised to let students know that replies do not have to be formulated quickly to be considered. Consider choosing the student who has spoken least. After the first student is finished, call on the other students who had raised their hands, even if their hands are down. (Sources: Kasulis, 1984; Lowman, 1984; Swift, Gooding, and Swift, 1988)

Search for consensus on correct responses. If one student immediately gives a correct response, follow up by asking others what they think. "Do you agree, Hadley?" is a good way to get students involved in the discussion.

Ask questions that require students to demonstrate their understanding. Instead of "Do you understand?" or "Do you have any questions about evaluation utilization?" ask, "What are the considerations to keep in mind when you want your evaluation results to be used?" Instead of "Do you understand this computer software?" ask, "How would we change the instructions if we wanted to sort numbers in ascending rather than descending order?" Instead of "Does everybody see how I got this answer?" ask, "Why did I substitute the value of delta in this equation?" If you want to ask, "Do you have any questions?" rephrase it to "What questions do you have?" The latter implies that you expect questions and are encouraging students to ask them.

Structure your questions to encourage student-to-student interaction.
"Sam, could you relate that to what Molly said earlier?" Be prepared to help
Sam recall what Molly said. Students become more attentive when you ask
questions that require them to respond to each other. (Source: Kasulis, 1984)

Draw out reserved or reluctant students. Sometimes a question disguised
as an instructor's musings will encourage students who are hesitant to speak.
For example, instead of "What is the essence or thesis of John Dewey's work?"
saying, "I wonder if it's accurate to describe John Dewey's work as learning by
doing?" gives a student a chance to comment without feeling put on the spot.

Use questions to change the tempo and direction of the discussion.
Kasulis (1984) identifies several ways to use questions.

- To lay out perspectives: "If you had to pick just one factor . . ." or "In a
  few words, name the most important reason . . ." This form of questioning can also be used to cap talkative students.
- To move from abstract to concrete, or general to specific: "If you were
  to generalize . . ." or "Can you give some specific examples?"
- To acknowledge good points made previously: "Sandra, would you
  tend to agree with Francisco on this point?"
- To elicit a summary or give closure: "Beth, if you had to pick two
  themes that recurred most often today, what would they be?"

Use probing strategies. Probes are follow-up questions that focus students'
attention on ideas or assumptions implicit in their first answer. Probes can
ask for specifics, clarifications, consequences, elaborations, parallel examples, relationship to other issues, or explanations. Probes are important
because they help students explore and express what they know, even when
they aren't sure they know it (Hyman, 1980). Here are some examples of
probing from Goodwin, Sharp, Cloutier, and Diamond (1985, pp. 15–17):

Instructor:	What are some ways we might solve the energy crisis?
Student:	Peak-load pricing by utility companies.
Instructor:	What assumptions are you making about consumer behavior when you suggest that solution?
Instructor:	What does it mean to devalue the dollar?
Student:	I'm not really sure, but doesn't it mean, that, um, like say last year the dollar could buy a certain amount of goods and this year it could buy less—does that mean devalued?

Instructor: Well, let's talk a little bit about another concept, and this is inflation. Does inflation affect the dollar in that way?

Instructor: What is neurosis?

Students: [no response]

Instructor: What are the characteristics of a neurotic person?

Instructor: How far has the ball fallen after three seconds, Christi?

Student: I have no idea.

Instructor: Well, Christi, how would we measure distance?

Move around the room to include students in the discussion. When a student asks a question, it is natural for an instructor to move toward that student without realizing that this tends to exclude other students. To draw others into the conversation, look at the student who is speaking but move away from that student.

Tactics for Handling Students' Responses to Your Questions

Listen to the student. Do not interrupt a student's answer, even if you think the student is heading toward an incorrect conclusion. Interrupting signals your impatience and hinders participation. Instead, wait a second or two after a student responds to be sure that the student is finished speaking.

Use nonverbal gestures to indicate your attention. Maintain eye contact with the student who is speaking. Nod your head, use facial expressions or hand gestures to prompt the student to continue, or adopt a physical stance that signals you are ready to move on.

Vary your reactions to students' answers. When a student has spoken, you can respond in the following ways:

- Restate what the speaker has said to reinforce the point.
- Ask for clarification: "Could you be more specific about. . ."
- Invite the student to elaborate: "We'd like to hear more about. . ."
- Expand the student's contribution: "That's absolutely correct, and following up on what you said. . ."

- Acknowledge the student's contribution but ask for another view: "You're right about children's linguistic capabilities, but what about their social development?"
- Acknowledge the originality of a student's ideas: "Self-selection factors could be responsible for the outcome; I didn't think of that."
- Nod or look interested but remain silent.

You needn't give a verbal response to every student. By nodding or pointing, you can keep the focus on your students' responses rather than shift attention to yourself. Collect a number of student comments. Condense and combine them, and relate them to each other. You don't want students to feel that they need your comment after each response. (Sources: Hyman, 1982; "Successful Participation Strategies," 1987; Yelon and Cooper, 1984)

Praise correct answers. Students look to their instructors for guidance and support. Teachers who are indifferent to students' responses or who chastise students soon find that participation drops off. Be enthusiastic, replying with "Excellent answer" or "Absolutely correct" rather than a bland "OK," "yes," "all right." But be aware that most students will stop thinking about a question once the instructor has indicated that someone's response is correct. If you want to elicit more responses, say, "Combustion? That's good. What other outcomes are possible?" Moreover, Tiberius (1990) warns against praising every answer because that turns the instructor into the official dispenser of rewards and makes it awkward when a student gives a vague or irrelevant answer. (Source: Hyman, 1982)

Tactfully correct wrong answers. Correct the answer, not the student: "I don't believe that answer is correct" instead of "Michele, you are wrong." Look beyond the answer to the thought process: "This is a hard concept to grasp; let's take this a step at a time"; "You're right about one part, but let's figure out the rest together." Encourage the student to rephrase or revise the answer. If one student needs assistance in answering a question, look to another student to provide help rather than providing it yourself.

References

Barnes, C. P. "Questioning in College Classrooms." In C. L. Ellner and C. P. Barnes (eds.), *Studies of College Teaching*. Lexington, Mass.: Lexington Books, 1983.

Bloom, B. S. (ed.). *Taxonomy of Educational Objectives*. Vol. 1: *Cognitive Domain*. New York: McKay, 1956.

Christensen, C. R. "The Discussion Teacher in Action: Questioning, Listening, and Response." In C. R. Christensen, D. A. Garvin, and A. Sweet (eds.), *Education for Judgment: The Artistry of Discussion Leadership.* Boston: Harvard Business School, 1991.

Goodwin, S. S. , Sharp, G. W., Cloutier, E. F., and Diamond, N. A. *Effective Classroom Questioning.* Urbana: Office of Instructional Resources, University of Illinois, 1985.

Hyman, R. T. *Improving Discussion Leadership.* New York: Teachers College Press, 1980.

Hyman, R. T. "Questioning in the College Classroom." *Idea Paper*, no. 8. Manhattan: Center for Faculty Evaluation and Development in Higher Education, Kansas State University, 1982.

Jacobson, R. L. "Asking Questions Is the Key Skill Needed for Discussion Teaching." *Chronicle of Higher Education*, July 25, 1981, p. 20.

Kasulis, T. P. "Questioning." In M. M. Gullette (ed.), *The Art and Craft of Teaching.* Cambridge, Mass.: Harvard University Press, 1984.

Lowman, J. *Mastering the Techniques of Teaching.* San Francisco: Jossey-Bass, 1984.

Rosmarin, A. "The Art of Leading a Discussion." In C. R. Christensen and A. J. Hansen (eds.), *Teaching and the Case Method.* Boston: Harvard Business School, 1987.

"Successful Participation Strategies." *Teaching Professor*, 1987, *1*(7), 5–6.

Swift, J. N., Gooding, C. T., and Swift, P. R. "Questions and Wait Time." In J. T. Dillon (ed.), *Questioning and Discussion: A Multidisciplinary Study.* Norwood, N.J.: Ablex, 1988.

Tiberius, R. G. *Small Group Teaching: A Trouble-Shooting Guide.* Toronto: Ontario Institute for Studies in Education Press, 1990.

Yelon, S. L., and Cooper, C. R. "Discussion: A Naturalistic Study of a Teaching Method." *Instructional Science*, 1984, *13*(3), 213–224.

Fielding Students' Questions

11

As Rosmarin (1987) points out, it is hard to pose a good question — and even harder to answer one. Instructors have to think on their feet, answering questions in ways that nurture students' curiosity and encourage them to develop their intellectual abilities.

General Strategies

Explicitly request questions from students. Show your genuine interest in having students ask questions by giving students prompts. "What questions do you have about the Tydings-McDuffie Act of 1934?" Give students time to formulate their questions, and look around the room to make certain you don't miss somebody's hand.

Be aware of how your behavior and offhand remarks set the tone for students' questions. Sometimes students refrain from asking questions because they sense that their teacher doesn't want to hear them. A teacher's negative response to students' questions — "We discussed that last time" or "That question is not really on point" — discourages future questions. Other discouraging behaviors include looking at your watch while students ask questions, avoiding eye contact, answering questions hurriedly or incompletely, and treating questions as interruptions rather than contributions to the learning process. (Source: Hyman, 1982)

Tactics for Answering Questions

Thank or praise the student for having asked a question. "Good question" and "Thanks for asking that" are comments that engage students and reinforce the behavior of asking questions. Some faculty members award extra credit to students who ask perceptive questions about the material covered in the class. For example, a faculty member teaching a large lecture class in chemistry asks students to write out their questions. He discusses the best ones in class at the next session. At the end of the term, he awards extra credit to those who submitted questions. (Watkins, 1990).

Call on questioners in the order in which they sought recognition. Say, "Debbie first, then Leif, then McCrae" so students know they will have their turn. If several students want to comment, keep a written list of the order and stick to it. Remember that students mentally stop participating once their hands go up and they think of what they want to say. For students whose hands have been up for a while, ask, "Have we gone past your comment?" (Source: Rosmarin, 1987)

Make sure that everyone can hear students' questions. Repeat the question if necessary, and briefly paraphrase a long or complex question. In some cases your paraphrase may help the student think out loud and answer his or her own question. Try, however, to avoid repeating or paraphrasing every question. Such repetition invites students to listen to you and not their fellow students. In addition, you run the risk of boring the class. (Source: Goodwin, Sharp, Cloutier, and Diamond, 1985)

Clarify students' questions. If you don't understand a student's question, ask for clarification: "Give me an example" or "Do you mean . . . ?" Or instead of "Your question isn't clear," say, "I'm sorry, I don't understand your question."

Answer students' questions directly. Students ask questions because they want a response from their teacher. By responding directly you indicate that the question is worthwhile. Place your one-sentence direct answer either first or last in your response: "Yes, I do think that historians have portrayed the 'trail of tears' inaccurately." If you redirect a question to the class at large, let the questioner know that you are not avoiding or dismissing the question: "After we hear what everyone else wants to say, I'll see if there's anything left to add." (Source: Hyman, 1982)

But encourage students to try to answer their own questions. Sometimes you can rephrase a student's question in a way that points toward an answer, or you can provide a clue by asking, "Leslie, have you thought about . . . ?" A faculty member in architecture turns students' questions about design issues back to them. When a student asks, "Should I put the kitchen on the north or south end?" the instructor asks the student, "Why might you want the kitchen on the north end?" Or you can turn some students' questions back to the class: "What do others of you think are the reasons the treaty of Guadalupe Hidalgo was ignored?" In this way, you not only encourage more student participation but also announce that peers are a resource. If no one can answer, you can probe the difficulty.

When responding, talk to the whole class. Don't focus solely on the questioner but look around the room to include all the students in your comments.

When students raise complex or tangential questions, ask them to stop by after class. Sometimes students ask questions that go beyond the topic of discussion: questions that anticipate an upcoming topic, seek more detail, or raise a new issue. The question may be important to the student but irrelevant to the current discussion. You could immediately offer a response, but questions requiring a lengthy response or detour from the topic are usually best answered after class or during office hours.

Delay answers to questions that will be covered later. If the question will be addressed later during the class, mention this and return to the question at the appropriate time. When you reach the subject, let the student know you have remembered the question: "Here is the answer to the question you asked before, Lynn."

Check back with the student to make sure the question has been answered. After giving an answer, confirm with the student that the question has been answered satisfactorily: "Was that what you were asking?" or "Has your question been answered?"

Tactics for Handling Difficult Questions and Questioners

Be diplomatic. Resist the temptation to use humor at students' expense or embarrass a questioner. As Sprague and Stuart (1988) point out, the class's empathy is with the questioner. Your efforts to put a nervous or confused questioner at ease will win you the class's goodwill. Consider the following two sets of responses from Sprague and Stuart (p. 331):

> *Not*: "Well, as I already said..."
> *But*: "Let me go over those graphs more slowly."

> *Not*: "You've totally confused fission and fusion."
> *But*: "Many of those problems relate to nuclear fission. The fusion reaction is quite different. It works like this..."

Admit when you don't know the answer. If you don't know the answer to a student's question, say so: "I don't know about that. It's a good question." Then you could follow up in one of these ways:

- Ask whether someone in the class can answer the question (and check the answer before the next class).
- Suggest resources that would enable the student to answer the question (but note that assigning students the task of looking up answers to their questions may lead students to ask fewer questions).
- Show students how to think out loud about the answer.
- Volunteer to find the answer yourself and report back to the class at the next session.

Similarly, if you are not sure of an answer, it is better to say, "I'm not sure, let me think about it" than to give a wrong answer and have to correct yourself later. (Source: Goodwin, Sharp, Cloutier, and Diamond, 1985)

Be patient with students who ask questions you have already answered. Although you may have already discussed a topic or even answered an identical question, students may not have understood the point at the time. Only later, when the material makes sense to them, does the particular point become meaningful. When answering repetitive questions, try to use different language and examples so that you don't bore students who grasped the idea earlier. Or consider asking another student in class to answer the question.

Preempt long-winded questioners. Occasionally, a student may filibuster when asking a question, using the occasion to vent his or her views on a variety of topics. One way to respond is to jump in and answer what appears to be the student's main point, and then recognize another student. For example: "You want to know why the university refuses to divest. The regents' position is that the Sullivan principles are sufficient. Let's hear from Flora; she's had her hand up for a long time." (Sources: Sprague and Stuart, 1988; Watkins, 1983)

Cut off students who want an extended dialogue. Some students are reluctant to relinquish the floor; they'll pose follow-up questions or make additional comments. The best strategy is to end the exchange forcefully but with a compliment or invitation. "You've raised quite a number of excellent points. Maybe you can come to my office later and talk with me further." Or "You've made a number of good comments; why don't we hear from someone else as well?" (Source: Sprague and Stuart, 1988)

References

Cashin, W. E., Brock, S. C., and Owens, R. E. "Answering and Asking Questions." Manhattan: Center for Faculty Evaluation and Development in Higher Education, Kansas State University, 1976.

Goodwin, S. S., Sharp, G. W., Cloutier, E. F., and Diamond, N. A. *Effective Classroom Questioning*. Urbana: Office of Instructional Resources, University of Illinois, 1985.

Hyman, R. T. "Questioning in the College Classroom." *Idea Paper*, no. 8. Manhattan: Center for Faculty Evaluation and Development in Higher Education, Kansas State University, 1982.

Rosmarin, A. "The Art of Leading a Discussion." In C. R. Christensen and A. J. Hansen (eds.), *Teaching and the Case Method*. Boston: Harvard Business School, 1987.

Sprague, J., and Stuart, D. *The Speaker's Handbook*. (2nd ed.) Orlando, Fla.: Harcourt Brace Jovanovich, 1988.

Watkins, B. T. "Credit for Ingenious Questions About Chemistry." *Chronicle of Higher Education*, July 5, 1990, p. A16.

Watkins, K. "Handling Difficult Questions and Situations." *Innovation Abstracts*, 1983, 5(24), 1–2.

IV.

Lecture Strategies

Preparing to Teach the Large Lecture Course

12

A sizable portion of the work involved in teaching a large lecture course takes place well before the first day of classes. For example, in a seminar you can make a spur-of-the-moment assignment, but in large classes you may need to distribute written guidelines. Similarly, in small classes students can easily turn in their homework during class. In large lectures you must decide how to distribute and collect papers without consuming precious class time. All these tasks take planning and organization. Many of the following suggestions for teaching large classes will also work for small classes: good teaching practices apply to classes of any type.

General Strategies

Become comfortable with the material. In an introductory survey course you may be covering topics outside your specialty area. Read up on those topics and try to anticipate questions that beginning students might ask. Review the course materials, assignments, and reading lists of colleagues who have taught the course before. Consider sitting in on courses taught by colleagues who are especially effective teachers of large classes to see what ideas and techniques work well, or ask them about their experiences teaching the course.

Don't plan to lecture for a full period. The average student's attention span is between ten and twenty minutes (Penner, 1984). After that, students have difficulty concentrating on the speaker. For each lecture, plan to change the pace every fifteen minutes or so to relieve the monotony and recapture students' interest. For example: ask students to solve a problem at their seats or in groups of two or three, give a demonstration, use an audiovisual aid, or tell a story or anecdote.

Be clear about what can reasonably be accomplished by lecturing. Research shows that lecturing is as effective as other instructional methods, such as discussion, in transmitting information but less effective in promoting independent thought or developing students' thinking skills (Bligh, 1971). In addition to presenting facts, try to share complex intellectual analyses, synthesize several ideas, clarify controversial issues, or compare and contrast different points of view.

Budget your own time carefully. Teaching a large lecture class takes a great deal of time and energy. Set up weekly work schedules for yourself so that you are prepared for the onslaught of midterms and finals. Find ways to scale back other obligations, if you can, so that you have time to deal with the complexities of teaching such courses.

Organizing the Course

Decide what content to cover. After reviewing your department's guidelines or sample curricula, set your broad goals for the course. The goals of an introductory survey course might include stimulating students' interest in the field and providing them with sufficient foundation to pursue that interest. Next, make a list of topics you feel are important to include. Estimate the amount of time required to address these topics, and then increase your estimate by 50 percent to allow time for entertaining questions from students and for the inevitable slippage in large groups (Christensen, 1988). For suggestions on how to reduce the number of topics to fit the length of the course, see "Preparing or Revising a Course."

Organize the topics in a meaningful sequence. Lurching from one topic to another makes it difficult for students to assimilate and retain the material (Dubrow and Wilkinson, 1984). Arrange the course topics thematically, chronologically, spatially, in ascending or descending order, by cause and effect or problem and solution, or according to some other conceptual rationale. Here are some examples of course organizational patterns:

- *Topical:* A psychology course examines how four groups of theorists approach human behavior: social learning theorists, developmental theorists, psychoanalytic theorists, and cognitive theorists.
- *Causal:* An economics course explores various factors that affect the distribution of wealth: the labor market, tax policy, investment policy, and social mobility.
- *Sequential:* A course on education in the United States covers the school system from preschool to elementary school, secondary school, college, and graduate school.

- *Symbolic or graphic:* An integrative biologist begins each lecture by projecting the same transparency of a diagram of the human brain. Using a plastic overlay, she then draws in those structural details relevant to that day's lecture.
- *Structural:* A physiologist discusses anatomical systems in the same consistent format: the organs, the functions of the organs, how the organs are regulated, the relationship of the system to other systems, and so on.
- *Problem-solution:* An engineering course looks at a series of structural failures in various types of buildings.

Make the course structure explicitly known to students throughout the term. Describe the organizational structure in the syllabus, at the beginning of the course, and throughout the term. Periodically devote a part of the lecture to the broader view.

Vary the types of lectures you deliver. Choose formats that suit the content (adapted from Frederick, 1986, pp. 45–47):

- The *expository lecture* is the traditional lecture that treats a single question or problem, typically with a hierarchical organization of major and minor points. This approach allows you to present broad concepts and factual information efficiently but runs the risk of reducing students to passive spectators.
- The *interactive lecture* evolves around orderly brainstorming in which students generate ideas in response to a question or prompt ("Call out what you know about DNA"). The instructor and the class then sort the responses into categories. The flow of examples and counterexamples, generalizations and specifics, or rules and exceptions encourages students to grapple actively with the topic.
- *Problem solving, demonstrations, proofs, and stories* begin with the instructor posing a question, paradox, or enigma—some provocative problem that whets students' interest: "What would happen if. . .?" The suspenseful answer unfolds during the class period, with students actively or passively anticipating or pointing toward solutions.
- The *case study method* follows a realistic situation step by step to illustrate a general principle or problem-solving strategy. Depending on the level of the students, either the instructor takes the lead or the students themselves generate the questions and principles.
- *Short lectures framing discussion periods* allow an instructor to shift the energy to students. The instructor begins with a twenty-minute lecture

setting the stage for some issue, then opens up a fifteen-minute discussion of implications and effects, and closes with another short lecture that pulls together the major themes or issues. In large classes, the discussion segment may be turned over to students working in trios or small groups.

(Sources: Bligh, 1971; Brown, 1978; Brown and Atkins, 1988; Frederick, 1986; Lowman, 1984; Penner, 1984)

Consider the abilities and interests of your students. In preparing your course, ask yourself How much will the class know about the subject matter? How interested will they be in the material? What experiences or attitudes might students have that I can use to draw them into the subject?

Prepare a detailed syllabus for students. The more information you give in writing, the fewer problems you will have later on. During the term, try to stick to the course schedule. If you must deviate, make it clear when and why you are departing from the schedule.

Meet with your graduate student instructors before the term begins. Discuss course procedures, their responsibilities, grading, and the most effective ways for them to conduct sections. See "Guiding, Training, and Supervising Graduate Student Instructors."

Visit the classroom before the first meeting. Notice the instructor's area, placement of light switches, chalkboards, and other details. Make arrangements for whatever instructional equipment you will need: overhead projector, microphone, slide projector. When you visit the classroom, stand where you will lecture, practice using the equipment, and write on the board. Check whether your board work can be seen from the back of the room. (Source: Johnson, 1988)

Preparing Lecture Notes

Carefully prepare your lectures. Thorough preparation can prevent last-minute headaches. You need time to arrange your points, develop your examples, write out definitions, solve equations, and so on. Some faculty prepare their lectures well in advance and revise them during the term to take into account students' reactions to previous lectures. Other faculty believe that the best time to prepare a lecture is immediately after class, when the experience of what worked and what didn't is still fresh (Eble, 1988). New faculty typically complete the bulk of preparatory reading before the course starts and then keep about one or two weeks ahead of their students (Dubrow and Wilkinson, 1984).

Avoid lecturing verbatim from a script. If you simply read from a prepared text, you will find yourself disengaged from the material (you won't be thinking about what you are saying) and your students will feel disengaged as well (Day, 1980). Moreover, reading prevents you from maintaining eye contact with students, and it casts your voice down toward your notes instead of up and out toward the lecture hall. Writing out lectures is also extremely time-consuming. If you do feel the need to write out your lectures, reduce the completed text to a brief outline of key words and phrases. Lecture from this outline—you will naturally produce sentences more for the ear than for the eye, thereby making it easier for students to grasp the material. See "Delivering a Lecture."

Experiment with different formats for your lecture notes. Some formats are more suited to certain subjects and disciplines than others (adapted from Day, 1980, pp. 101–104).

- An *outline* is especially useful in organizing a talk and providing an overview of the general structure of subordinate points and transitions.
- A list of *major points* is closer to extemporaneous speech than a detailed outline; this format is appropriate for a speaker who knows the material well.
- A *tree diagram* (such as a flowchart or network) provides a system of pathways through important points with optional stopovers, tangents, useful illustrations, or examples.

Honjo (1989) describes one faculty member in engineering who blocks out a single sheet of paper for each session. He reserves the uppermost left-hand block for the outline of the day's lecture (this outline is also placed on the board). The remaining blocks each correspond to a panel of the board, enabling him to visualize how the board will look as he works through all the examples.

Prepare your notes to aid your delivery. If you are writing an outline of key words or phrases, 5″ × 8″ index cards are easier to use than smaller cards or sheets of paper. Color code your notes to highlight difficult points, distinctions between major examples, and important information. Include notations that indicate times to pause, ask questions, raise your voice, and so on. Write in the margin, "Put this on the board" or "Have students jot down a response at their seats" or "If less than ten minutes left at this point, skip to card 7." Examples boxed in red could mean "Include this if students seem uncertain about my point."

Write down facts and formulas for easy reference. Within the body of your lecture notes or on a separate sheet of paper, copy out all the key facts, quotations, computations, or complex analyses.

Write down vivid examples. Clear, straightforward, memorable examples reinforce the points you are trying to make. Experienced faculty recommend that you give special attention to preparing examples, illustrations, and demonstrations—more than you might need, to be able to respond to students' confusions or questions (Erickson and Strommer, 1991). Research shows that an important characteristic of an effective teacher is the ability to take difficult concepts and transform them in ways that students can understand, through the use of metaphors, analogies, and examples (Shulman, 1987). See "Explaining Clearly."

Prepare your lecture for the ear, not the eye. Oral presentations are very different from written presentations. When students are listening to you speak, they cannot go back and "reread" a troublesome sentence or look up a difficult word in the dictionary. Use these techniques to facilitate oral comprehension:

- Use short, simple words and informal diction, including personal pronouns and contractions.
- Speak succinctly, in short, straightforward sentences.
- Offer signposts for transitions and structure—"the third objection," "let's look at this argument from another angle," "in contrast," "as we have seen," "now we can turn to . . ."
- Restate and periodically summarize key points.

To prevent students from sinking into passive listening, also engage students' active listening skills by interspersing questions throughout your lecture.

Rehearse your lecture. A run-through will give you a sense of how comfortable you are with the material and the length of your presentation. To save time, practice only the most difficult sections, the opening and the ending.

Structuring a Lecture

Structure the lecture to suit your audience and the subject matter. Consider the difficulty of the material and students' level of ability as you make decisions about the amount of information to cover, the amount of detail, and the number of examples you present.

Begin by writing out the main theme and why students should learn about it. Identify what you most want your students to remember about the topic. It is better to teach two or three major points well than to inundate students with information they are unlikely to remember. Brown and Atkins (1988, pp. 36–39) recommend the following process for writing a lecture:

- Specify the main topic or topics.
- Free associate words, facts, ideas, and questions as they come to you.
- State a working title or a general question based on the groupings from your free association.
- Prepare a one-page sketch of the lecture.
- Read selectively, as needed, and jot down notes on important ideas and organizational structure.
- Structure the lecture in outline form and flesh it out with examples and illustrations; identify your key points.
- Check the opening and ending.

Provide a logical progression for the material. Some lectures lend themselves to a chronological or sequential approach. At other times, you can move from the general principle to specific instances, build up from the parts to the whole, trace one idea across time or space, describe a problem and then illustrate its solution, or announce your thesis and then step back to provide evidence for your argument.

Structure your lectures to help students retain the most important material. Research shows that students' retention is greatest at the beginning of a fifty-minute class, decreases to low levels as the period wears on, and then increases slightly in anticipation of the end (Ericksen, 1978). Plan your classes so that the main points come at a time when students are most attentive. Structure them to include these elements:

- Attention-getting introduction
- Brief overview of main points to be covered
- Quick statement of background or context

- Detailed explanation of no more than three major points, the most important first, with a change of pace every ten or fifteen minutes
- Concluding summary of main points to reinforce key themes

Design your lectures in ten- or fifteen-minute blocks. Each block should cover a single point with examples and end with a brief summary and transition to the next section. If you find yourself running out of time, cut an entire block or shorten the middle section of a block rather than rush the summary.

Budget time for questions. Whether or not you formally open the floor for questions, leave time for students to ask you to repeat material or to supply additional explanations. Some faculty ask for students' questions at the beginning of class and list these on the board to be answered during the hour.

Begin and end with a summary statement. Continuity and closure are important: students need to see how each new topic relates to what they have already learned as well as to what they will be learning in the coming weeks. To bring your points home, use different words and examples in your opening and closing summaries.

Managing a Large Lecture Course

Establish reasonable rules for student behavior. Instructors in large classes usually find it helpful to announce policies about latecomers, eating and talking during class, and other disruptive behavior. Explain your rules early on and stress the value of cooperation and consideration. For example, some faculty set limits on when students can pack up and leave: "You're mine until 2 P.M." or "When the cartoon appears on the overhead you can go" or "After the class has posed three good questions about the material, students can leave" (Hilsen, 1988). Let students know that you expect them to arrive promptly but use the first couple of minutes to discuss a related issue, to take account of stragglers. For example, a geography faculty member discusses the nation's weather. Shea (1990) describes a faculty member in political science who begins class with discussion of a relevant news item.

Plan how to grade and return homework. If homework is an essential part of your course and you do not have a graduate student instructor, grade samples of homework assignments to save time. For the assignments you do not grade, distribute an answer sheet so students can assess their own performance. If you have graduate student instructors, have students turn in and receive their homework in section. Otherwise, collect homework in a locked box in the department office. Distribute homework in alphabetical folders in boxes on the side of the lecture hall. Call out one or two letters at a time and let the people whose last names begin with those letters go get their papers. Or label a set of manila envelopes with row numbers, and ask students to choose a row for the term and to sit in that row when taking exams, turning in homework, and picking up homework (Chism, 1989).

Stagger due dates for essay or research papers. One faculty member requires all three hundred of his students to write one paper during the semester, but students write on different topics and the papers are due on different dates. At the beginning of the term, he randomly divides the class into, say, ten groups of thirty students each. He announces the dates when the various groups are to turn in their papers. All students receive their paper topics two weeks before their due date. Using this approach, the instructor is able to read and respond to all three hundred papers but never reads more than thirty or so in any given week (Source: Erickson and Strommer, 1991).

Use multiple-choice tests, if possible. Machine-scored multiple-choice exams can save time and minimize grading errors, but students also need practice in writing and grappling with complex questions. If you can, then, include two or three questions that call for a few paragraphs of explanation or analysis.

Avoid giving makeup exams. Scheduling makeup exams is logistically difficult and time-consuming. Instead, try to give enough exams or quizzes so that students can drop their lowest score. Some faculty give shorter final exams and use the last hour for makeup tests. See "Allaying Students' Anxieties About Tests."

Consider forming a student exam review committee. The committee, made up of four or five elected members of the class, is charged with identifying specific test questions that may have been problematic for the class and with suggesting possible remedies. During the exam, students who so wish anonymously complete a brief comment sheet that they turn in with their exam. Members of the student exam review committee meet after the test has been administered to review the exam and look at students' comment sheets. They then meet with the professor to negotiate possible adjustments. For example, if over half the class felt question 3 was unfair, the committee may suggest tossing it out. The instructor makes the final decision after hearing from the committee. All students in the class are made aware of subsequent adjustments. (Source: Holmgren, 1992)

Consider using computerized record-keeping and communications systems. Software such as BIJOU (Wiseman, 1986) can facilitate the storage and retrieval of information related to enrolling students into sections, coordinating the preparation and delivery of materials with staff and office support, and maintaining rosters and grade records.

Sample Lecture Outline

Below is a sample outline (adapted from Scott, 1990, p. 35) for a lecture on DNA.

Opening: While you may be familiar with DNA, did you know that the story surrounding its structure, the double helix, is one of the greatest detective stories of all time?

Thesis: Crick and Watson's discovery of the genetic code radically changed our views about all forms of life.

Connection: If you plan to take other science courses, this topic will be invaluable in helping you understand genetics and molecular biology. But even if this is the last science course you will ever take, the DNA in your body will influence your life and life span. The genetic code also holds the key to cures for life-threatening diseases and has ethical ramifications, especially regarding efforts to alter the genes of a human fetus.

Organizers: There are three things I want to discuss.
    a.   Double helix
    b.   Human genomes
    c.   The book of life project

Body: (Elaboration of three topics with opportunities for small group work during the session)

Summary: (Brief recap about each of the three topics and why the discoveries are so important)

Closing: Let me close by posing a question: If you could genetically alter a vegetable or piece of fruit, what would you change and why?

References

Bligh, D. A. *What's the Use of Lecturing?* Devon, England: Teaching Services Centre, University of Exeter, 1971.

Brown, G. *Lecturing and Explaining*. New York: Methuen, 1978.

Brown G., and Atkins, M. *Effective Teaching in Higher Education*. London: Methuen, 1988.

Chism, N.V.N. "Large-Enrollment Classes: Necessary Evil or Not Necessary Evil." *Notes on Teaching*. Columbus: Center for Teaching Excellence, Ohio State University, June 1989, pp. 1–7.

Christensen, N. "Nuts and Bolts of Running a Lecture Course." In A. L. Deneff, C. D. Goodwin, and E. S. McCrate (eds.), *The Academic Handbook*. Durham, N.C.: Duke University Press, 1988.

Day, R. S. "Teaching from Notes: Some Cognitive Consequences." In W. J. McKeachie (ed.), *Learning, Cognition, and College Teaching*. New Directions for Teaching and Learning, no. 2. San Francisco: Jossey-Bass, 1980.

Dubrow, H., and Wilkinson, J. "The Theory and Practice of Lectures." In M. M. Gullette (ed.), *The Art and Craft of Teaching* Cambridge, Mass.: Harvard University Press, 1984.

Eble, K. E. *The Craft of Teaching*. (2nd ed.) San Francisco: Jossey-Bass, 1988.

Ericksen, S. C. "The Lecture." *Memo to the Faculty*, no. 60. Ann Arbor: Center for Research on Teaching and Learning, University of Michigan, 1978.

Erickson, B. L., and Strommer, D. W. *Teaching College Freshmen*. San Francisco: Jossey-Bass, 1991.

Frederick, P. J. "The Lively Lecture—8 Variations." *College Teaching*, 1986, *34*(2), 43–50.

Hilsen, L. "A Helpful Handout: Establishing and Maintaining a Positive Classroom Climate." In E. C. Wadsworth, L. Hilsen, and M. A. Shea (eds.), *A Handbook for New Practitioners from the Professional and Organizational Development Network in Higher Education*. Stillwater, Okla.: New Forums Press, 1988.

Holmgren, P. "Avoiding the Exam-Return Question 'Wall'—Working with Your SERC Committee." *Journal of College Science Teaching*, 1992, *20*(4), 214–216.

Honjo, R. T. *Speak of the GSI: A Handbook on Teaching*. Berkeley: Department of Mechanical Engineering, University of California, 1989.

Johnson, G. R. *Taking Teaching Seriously*. College Station: Center for Teaching Excellence, Texas A&M University, 1988.

Lowman, J. *Mastering the Techniques of Teaching*. San Francisco: Jossey-Bass, 1984.

Marincovich, M., and Rusk, L. *Excellence in Teaching Electrical Engineering*. Stanford, Calif.: Center for Teaching and Learning, Stanford University, 1987.

Penner, J. G. *Why Many College Teachers Cannot Lecture.* Springfield, Ill.: Thomas, 1984.

Scott, M. D. *Agents of Change: A Primer for Graduate Teaching Assistants.* Chico: College of Communication, California State University, 1990.

Shea, M. A. *Compendium of Good Ideas on Teaching and Learning.* Boulder: Faculty Teaching Excellence Program, University of Colorado, 1990.

Shulman, L. S. "Knowledge and Teaching: Foundations of the New Reform." *Harvard Educational Review*, 1987, *57*(1), 1–22.

Wiseman, M. "The BIJOU Teaching Support System." *Perspectives in Computing*, 1986, *6*(1), 5–13.

Delivering a Lecture

13

Lecturing is not simply a matter of standing in front of a class and reciting what you know. The classroom lecture is a special form of communication in which voice, gesture, movement, facial expression, and eye contact can either complement or detract from the content. No matter what your topic, your delivery and manner of speaking immeasurably influence your students' attentiveness and learning. Use the following suggestions, based on teaching practices of faculty and on research studies in speech communication, to help you capture and hold students' interest and increase their retention.

General Strategies

Watch yourself on videotape. Often we must actually see our good behaviors in order to exploit them and see our undesirable behaviors in order to correct them. If you want to improve your public speaking skills, viewing a videotape of yourself can be an invaluable way to do so. See "Watching Yourself on Videotape."

Learn how not to read your lectures. At its best, lecturing resembles a natural, spontaneous conversation between instructor and student, with each student feeling as though the instructor is speaking to an audience of one. If you read your lectures, however, there will be no dialogue and the lecture will seem formal, stilted, and distant. Even if you are a dynamic reader, when you stick to a script you forfeit the expressiveness, animation, and give-and-take spontaneity of plain talking. Reading from notes also reduces your opportunities to engage your class in conversation and prevents you from maintaining eye contact. On this point all skilled speakers agree: don't read your presentation. See "Preparing to Teach the Large Lecture Course" for advice on preparing lecture notes.

Prepare yourself emotionally for class. Some faculty play rousing music before lecturing. Others set aside fifteen or thirty minutes of solitude to review their notes. Still others walk through an empty classroom gathering their thoughts. Try to identify for yourself an activity that gives you the energy and focus you need to speak enthusiastically and confidently. (Source: Lowman, 1984)

Opening a Lecture

Avoid a "cold start." Go to class a little early and talk informally with students. Or walk in the door with students and engage them in conversation. Using your voice informally before you begin to lecture helps keep your tone conversational.

Minimize nervousness. A certain amount of nervousness is normal, especially right before you begin to speak. To relax yourself, take deep breaths before you begin or tighten and then release the muscles of your body from your toes to your jaw. Once you are under way your nervousness will lessen.

Grab students' attention with your opening. Open with a provocative question, startling statement, unusual analogy, striking example, personal anecdote, dramatic contrast, powerful quote, short questionnaire, demonstration, or mention of a recent news event. Here are some sample openings:

- "How many people would you guess are sent to prison each week in the state of California? Raise your hand if you think 50 people or fewer. How about 51 to 100? 101 to 150? Over 150? (Pause) In fact, over 250 people are placed in custody every week." (sociology lecture)
- "Freddie has been with the company for nearly four years and is considered a good worker. Recently, though, he's been having problems. He's late for work, acts brusque, and seems sullen. One morning he walks into the office, knocks over a pile of paper, and leaves it lying on the floor. His supervisor says, 'Freddie, could you please pick up the material so that no one trips over it?' Freddie says loudly, 'Pick it up yourself.' If you were the supervisor, what would you do next?" (business lecture)
- "The number-one fear of Americans—more terrifying than the fear of death—is public speaking." (rhetoric lecture)
- An economist shows a slide of farmers dumping milk from trucks or burning cornfields and asks, "Why would people do this?" (economics lecture)
- "Watch what happens to this balloon when the air is released." (physics lecture)

- "Take two minutes to complete the ten true-false items on the question-naire that I'm distributing. We'll use your answers as part of today's lecture." (psychology lecture)
- "How many of you believe that high-rise housing means high-density housing?" (architecture lecture)
- "Nearly three-quarters of all assaults, two-thirds of all suicide at-tempts, half of all suicides, and half of all rapes are committed by people under the influence of what drug? How many think crack? Heroin? Marijuana? None of the above? The correct answer is alcohol." (social welfare lecture)

Vary your opening. Any dramatic technique loses impact upon repetition.

Announce the objectives for the class. Tell your students what you expect to accomplish during the class, or list your objectives on the board. Place the day's lecture in context by linking it to material from earlier sessions.

Establish rapport with your students. Warmth and rapport have a positive effect on any audience. Students will feel more engaged in the class if the opening minutes are personal, direct, and conversational. (Source: Knapper, 1981)

Capturing Students' Interest

During class, think about and watch your audience—your students. Focus on your students as if you were talking to a small group. One-on-one eye contact will increase students' attentiveness and help you observe their facial expressions and physical movements for signs that you are speaking too slowly or too quickly, or need to provide another example. A common mistake lecturers make is to become so absorbed in the material that they fail to notice whether students are paying attention.

Vary your delivery to keep students' attention. Keeping students' attention is among the most important facets of helping them learn (Penner, 1984). Studies show that most people's attention lapses after ten minutes of passive listening (Wolvin, 1983). To extend students' attention spans, do the following:

- Ask questions at strategic points or ask for comments or opinions about the subject.

- Play devil's advocate or invite students to challenge your point of view.
- Have students solve a problem individually, or have them break into pairs or small four-person groups to answer a question or discuss a topic.
- Introduce visual aids: slides, charts, graphs, videotapes, and films.

Make the organization of your lecture explicit. Put an outline on the board before you begin, outline the development of ideas as they occur, or give students a handout of your major points or topics. Outlines help students focus on the progression of the material and also help them take better notes. If their attention does wander, students can more readily catch up with the lecture if they have an outline in front of them.

Convey your own enthusiasm for the material. Think back to what inspired you as an undergraduate or to the reasons you entered the field you are in. Even if you have little interest in a particular topic, try to come up with a new way of looking at it and do what you can to stimulate students' enthusiasm. If you appear bored with the topic, students will quickly lose interest.

Be conversational. Use conversational inflections and tones, varying your pitch just as you do in ordinary conversation. If you focus on the meaning of what you are saying, you'll instinctively become more expressive. Choose informal language, and try to be natural and direct.

Use concrete, simple, colorful language. Use first-person and second-person pronouns (I, we, you). Choose dramatic adjectives, for example, "*vital* point" rather than "main point" or "*provocative* issue" rather than "next issue." Eliminate jargon, empty words, and unnecessary qualifiers ("little bit," "sort of," "kind of"). (Source: Bernhardt, 1989)

Incorporate anecdotes and stories into your lecture. When you are in a storytelling mode, your voice becomes conversational and your face more expressive, and students tend to listen more closely. Use anecdotes to illustrate your key points.

Don't talk into your notes. If you are not using a lectern and you need to refer to your note cards, raise the cards (rather than lower your head) and take a quick glance downward, keeping your head steady. This movement will be easier if your notes are brief and in large letters. (Source: Bernhardt, 1989)

Maintain eye contact with the class. Look directly at your students one at a time to give them a sense that you are speaking to each individual. Look at a student for three to five seconds — a longer glance will make most students uncomfortable. Beware of aimless scanning or swinging your head back and forth. Mentally divide the lecture hall into three to five sections, and address comments, questions, and eye contact to each section during the course of your lecture, beginning in the center rear of the room. Pick out friendly faces, but also try to include nonlisteners. However, don't waste your time trying to win over the uninterested; concentrate on the attentive. If real eye contact upsets your concentration, look between two students or look at foreheads. (Source: Bernhardt, 1989)

Use movements to hold students' attention. A moving object is more compelling than a static one. Occasionally, move about the room. Use deliberate, purposeful, sustained gestures: hold up an object, roll up your sleeves. To invite students' questions, adopt an open, casual stance. Beware of nervous foot shifting, however, and aimless, distracting gestures.

Use movements to emphasize an important point or to lead into a new topic. Some faculty move to one side of the table or the lectern when presenting one side of an argument and to the other side when presenting the opposing view. This movement not only captures students' attention but reinforces the opposition between the two points of view (Harris, 1977). Other faculty indicate tangential points by standing off to the side of the room (Weimer, 1988).

Use facial expressions to convey emotions. If you appear enthusiastic and eager to tell students what you know, they are more likely to be enthusiastic about hearing it. Use your facial features: eyes, eyebrows, forehead, mouth, and jaw to convey enthusiasm, conviction, curiosity, and thoughtfulness. (Source: Lowman, 1984)

Laugh at yourself when you make a mistake. If you mispronounce a word or drop your notes, your ability to see the humor of the situation will put everyone at ease. Don't let your confidence be shaken by minor mistakes.

Keep track of time. How long is it taking you to cover each point? Where should you be in the material halfway through the class period? If you seem to be running out of time, what will you leave out? If time runs short, do not speed up to cover everything in your notes. Have some advance plan of what to omit: If I don't have fifteen minutes left when I reach this heading, I'll give only one example and distribute a handout with the other examples.

Mastering Delivery Techniques

Vary the pace at which you speak. Students need time to assimilate new information and to take notes, but if you speak too slowly, they may become bored. Try to vary the pace to suit your own style, your message, and your audience. For example, deliver important points more deliberately than anecdotal examples. If you tend to speak quickly, try to repeat your major points so that students can absorb them.

Project your voice or use a microphone. Ask students whether they can hear you, or have a graduate student instructor sit in the back corner to monitor the clarity and volume of your speaking voice. Try not to let the volume of your voice drop at the ends of sentences. When using a microphone, speak in a normal voice and do not lean into the microphone.

Vary your voice. Consider the pitch, volume, duration of words, intonation, and the intensity of your voice. Experiment with vocal techniques by reading aloud. Lowman (1984, chap. 4) describes a series of voice exercises to improve projection, articulation, and tonal quality.

Pause. The pause is one of the most critical tools of public speaking. It is an important device for gaining attention. Pauses can be used as punctuation— to mark a thought, sentence, or paragraph—and also for emphasis, before or after a key concept or idea. If you suddenly stop in midsentence, students will look up from their notes to see what happened. Planned pauses also give you and your audience a short rest. Some faculty take a sip of coffee or water after they say something they want students to stop and think about. Other faculty deliberately pause, announce, "This is the really important consideration," and pause again before proceeding.

Watch out for vocalized pauses. Try to avoid saying "um," "well," "you know," "OK," or "so." Silent pauses are more effective.

Adopt a natural speaking stance. Balance yourself on both feet with your toes and heels on the ground. Beware of shifting movements or unconscious rocking to and fro. Keep your knees slightly relaxed. Shoulders should be down and loose, with elbows cocked, and your hands at waist level. If you use a lectern, don't grip the sides, elbows rigid; instead, keep your elbows bent and lightly rest your hands on the lectern, ready for purposeful gestures. (Source: Bernhardt, 1989)

Breathe normally. Normal breathing prevents vocal strain that affects the pitch and quality of your speech. Keep your shoulders relaxed, your neck loose, your eyes fully open, and your jaw relaxed.

Closing a Lecture

Draw some conclusion for the class. Help students see that a purpose has been served, that something has been gained during the last hour. A well-planned conclusion rounds out the presentation, ties up loose ends, suggests ways for students to follow up on the lecture, and gives students a sense of closure.

Finish forcefully. Don't allow your lecture to trail off or end in midsentence because the period is over, and avoid the last-minute "Oh, I almost forgot. . . ." An impressive ending will echo in students' minds and prompt them to prepare for the next meeting. End with a thought-provoking question or problem; a quotation that sets an essential theme; a summation of the major issue as students now understand it, having had the benefit of the lecture just delivered; or a preview of coming attractions. For example, a physics professor ended a lecture by asking a volunteer to come up to the front, stand with his back to the wall, and try to touch his toes. She challenged the class to think about why the volunteer was not successful in this task. The topic of the next lecture, center of gravity, was thus introduced in a vivid, memorable way. Don't worry if you finish a few minutes early; explain that you have reached a natural stopping point. But don't make it a habit.

End your lecture with the volume up. Make your voice strong, lift your chin up, keep your eyes facing the audience. Be sure to stay after class for a few minutes to answer students' questions.

Improving Your Lecturing Style

Make notes to yourself immediately after each lecture. Consider the timing, the effectiveness of your examples, the clarity of your explanations, and the like. Jot down questions students asked or any comments they made. These notes will help you be more effective the next time you give that lecture.

Use a cassette recorder. Record a practice session or an actual lecture. Listen to your pacing, inflection, tone emphasis, and use of pauses. Is your tone conversational? Are the transitions clear? Are the vocalized pauses ("um," "well," "you know") at a minimum? Lowman (1984) describes the following procedure for comparing your conversational style and your lecturing style. Ask a friend to meet you in a moderate-sized room. Sit down, start the recorder, and begin a conversation by stating your name, age, and birthplace. Then talk for four or five minutes about a favorite book, movie, restaurant, exhibit, or hobby. Have your friend ask you some questions. Now move to a classroom, stand up, and give a short lecture (five to eight minutes) to your friend. Several days later listen to the recordings.

- Listen first straight through, without stopping the tape or taking notes. What is your overall impression of the voice you are hearing?
- Replay the recording of the conversation, and jot down words that best describe your voice.
- Replay the conversation again, this time focusing on the use of extraneous words, the level of relaxation and fluency in the voice, patterns of breathing, pitch and pace, emphasis and articulation.
- The next day replay the recording of the lecture and make a set of notes on it.
- Review your notes to identify the differences between the two recorded segments. Consider style, use of language, pacing, volume, fluency, expressiveness, and so on. Any differences you note will help you decide how to improve.

Use a video recorder. When reviewing a videotape of yourself lecturing, you can watch the entire tape, watch the tape with the sound turned off, or listen to the tape without watching it. Adopt the procedures outlined above for reviewing and analyzing your videotape. Most of the time you will be pleasantly surprised: you may have felt nervous during the lecture, but the videotape will show you that your nervousness was not apparent to your class. Seeing yourself on tape can be a good confidence builder. See "Watching Yourself on Videotape."

Work with a speech consultant. Speech consultants can help you develop effective delivery skills. Ask your campus faculty development office for names of consultants or a schedule of workshops on lecturing.

References

Bernhardt, D. Workshop on Public Speaking, University of California at Berkeley, Aug. 1989.

Harris, R. J. "The Teacher as Actor." *Teaching of Psychology*, 1977, *4*, 185–187.

Knapper, C. K. "Presenting and Public Speaking." In M. Argyle (ed.), *Social Skills and Work*. New York: Methuen, 1981.

Lowman, J. *Mastering the Techniques of Teaching*. San Francisco: Jossey-Bass, 1984.

Penner, J. G. *Why Many College Teachers Cannot Lecture*. Springfield, Ill.: Thomas, 1984.

Weimer, M. G. "Ways and Means of Communicating Structure." *Teaching Professor*, 1988, 2(7), 3.

Wolvin, A. D. "Improving Listening Skills." In R. B. Rubin (ed.), *Improving Speaking and Listening Skills*. New Directions for College Learning Assistance, no. 12. San Francisco: Jossey-Bass, 1983.

14

Explaining Clearly

Before launching into an explanation, give your students the context, structure, and terminology they will need to understand the new concept and to relate it to what they already know. Use repetition and examples to help them focus on the essential points. Try to refrain from introducing too many new concepts at the same time.

General Strategies

Place the concept in the larger context of the course. To give students a sense of continuity and meaning, tell them how today's topic relates to earlier material. A brief enthusiastic summary will help the class see the relevance of the new concept and its relationship to the course's main themes.

Give students a road map. You don't want students spending the hour wondering, Why is the professor talking about that? or Where does this fit in? So, at the beginning of class, put a brief outline on the board or provide a handout that will help students follow along. Refer to the outline to alert students to transitions and to the relationships between points. Some faculty give students a list of questions to be addressed during the class. Handouts can also include new terms, complex equations, formulas, and copies of detailed overhead transparencies or slides shown in class.

Avoid telling students everything you know. Students become confused, lost, anxious, or bored when inundated with information. Be selective: deliver the most essential information in manageable chunks.

Set an appropriate pace. Talk more slowly when students are taking notes and when you are explaining new material, complex topics, or abstract issues. You can pick up the pace when relating stories, summarizing a previous lecture, or presenting an example.

Aiding Students' Comprehension

Don't make assumptions about what students know. Define not only technical terms but also unusual words or expressions, and review key terms from previous lectures. Introduce new terms one at a time, and write each on the board.

Acknowledge the difficulty of concepts students are likely to find hard to understand. Cue students to the most difficult ideas by saying, "Almost everyone has difficulty with this one, so listen closely." Because the level of students' attention varies throughout the hour, it is important to get everyone listening carefully before explaining a difficult point.

Create a sense of order for the listener. In written texts, organization is indicated by paragraphs and headings. In lectures, your voice must convey the structure of your lectures. Use verbal cues to do the following:

- Forecast what you will be discussing: "Today I want to discuss three reasons why states are mandating assessments of student learning in higher education."
- Indicate where you are in the development of your ideas: "The first reason, then, is the decline of funds available for social and educational programs. Let's look at the second reason: old-fashioned politics."
- Restate main ideas: "We've looked at the three pressures on colleges and universities to institute assessment procedures: the legislature's desire to get maximum effectiveness for limited dollars, the appeal of campaign slogans such as 'better education,' and public disenchantment with education in general. We've also explored two possible responses by colleges and universities: compliance and confrontation."

Begin with general statements followed by specific examples. Research shows that students generally remember facts or principles if they are presented first with a concise statement of the general rule and then with specific examples, illustrations, or applications (Bligh, 1971; Knapper, 1981). To present a difficult or abstract idea, experienced faculty recommend that you first give students an easy example that illustrates the principle, then provide the general statement and explanation of the principle, then offer a more complex example or illustration. Finally, address any qualifications or elaborations. (Source: Brown, 1978)

Move from the simple to complex, the familiar to unfamiliar. Lay out the most basic ideas first and then introduce complexities. Start with what students know and then move to new territory.

Presenting Key Points and Examples

Limit the number of points you make in a single lecture. Research shows that students can absorb only three to five points in a fifty-minute period and four to five points in a seventy-five-minute class (Lowman, 1984). Even the most attentive students retain only small quantities of new information (Knapper, 1981). Be ruthless in paring down the number of major points you make, and be more generous with examples and illustrations to prove and clarify your arguments. Cut entire topics rather than condense each one. As necessary, supplement your lecture with a handout that students can study for a more detailed treatment.

In introductory courses, avoid the intricacies of the discipline. To avoid confusing a class of beginning undergraduate students, focus on the fundamentals, use generalizations, and do not give too many exceptions to the rule.

Demonstrate a complex concept rather than simply describe it. For example, instead of telling students how to present a logical argument, present a logical argument and help them analyze it. Instead of describing how to solve a problem, solve it on the board and label the steps as you go along.

Use memorable examples. Vivid examples will help students understand and recall the material. Spend time developing a repertoire of examples that link ideas and images. Use examples that do the following (adapted from Bernstein, n.d., pp. 27–28):

- Draw upon your students' experiences or are relevant to their lives (to explain depreciation, a professor uses the drop in prices of new versus used textbooks)
- Represent the same phenomena (to explain aerodynamic oscillation, an instructor cites a scarf held out a window of a moving car, a thin piece of paper placed near an air conditioner, and a suspension bridge battered by gale winds)
- Dramatize concepts (in defining a particular body organ, a professor compares its size or texture to familiar objects, such as a walnut or grapefruit; an economics professor defines a trillion by saying, "It takes 31,700 years to count a trillion seconds.")
- Engage students' empathy ("Imagine yourself as Hamlet. How does the poison feel? How does it affect your speech?")

Liberally use metaphors, analogies, anecdotes, and vivid images. Students tend to remember images longer than they remember words (Lowman, 1984). You can help students recall important concepts by pairing abstract content with a vivid image or a concrete association. For example, in describing velocity a physics professor uses the example of a speeding bullet.

Call attention to the most important points. Your students may not grasp the importance of a point unless you announce it: "This is really important, so listen up" or "The most important thing to remember is . . ." or "This is so important that every one of you should have it engraved on a plaque hung over your bed" or "You don't have to remember everything in this course, but you should remember . . ." or "This is something you will use so many times that it's worth your special attention." It is also useful to follow through by explaining why a particular point is important—saying so may not be enough.

Using Repetition to Your Advantage

Stress important material through repetition. Students' attention wanders during class. Indeed, research suggests that students are focally aware of the lecture content only about 50 to 60 percent of the time. To underscore the importance of a point, you will need to say it more than once. (Source: Pollio, 1984)

Use different words to make the same point. No single explanation will be clear to all students. By repeating major points several times in different words, you maximize the chances that every student will eventually understand. In some disciplines you may be able to develop the same point in two or three different modes: mathematically, verbally, graphically. In others, you may want to say things twice: formally and colloquially.

Use redundancy to let students catch up with the material. Students will have trouble understanding a second topic if they are still grappling with the first. Give students a chance to catch up by building in redundancy, repetition, and pauses.

References

Bernstein, H. R. *Manual for Teaching*. Ithaca, N.Y.: Center for the Improvement of Undergraduate Education, Cornell University, n.d.

Bligh, D. A. *What's the Use of Lecturing?* Devon, England: Teaching Services Centre, University of Exeter, 1971.

Brown, G. *Lecturing and Explaining.* New York: Methuen, 1978.

Knapper, C. K. "Presenting and Public Speaking." In M. Argyle (ed.), *Social Skills and Work.* New York: Methuen, 1981.

Lowman, J. *Mastering the Techniques of Teaching.* San Francisco: Jossey-Bass, 1984.

Pollio, H. R. "What Students Think About and Do in College Lecture Classes." *Teaching–Learning Issues* 1984, *3*, 3–18. (Publication available from the Learning Research Center, University of Tennessee, Knoxville)

Personalizing the Large Lecture Class

15

Lecture classes of more than a hundred students pose special challenges for instructors. It is easy for students to feel anonymous or isolated in large courses and difficult for them to get to know one another for support and group study. By nature, large courses include students of varying abilities but offer little opportunity for individual attention. The following suggestions are designed to help you help your students feel that their presence is noted and does matter.

General Strategies

Be as flexible as your class plan will allow. Provide a "warm" classroom environment—allow time to entertain students' comments and give immediate responses to their questions.

Let your personality and interests come through. The best lecturers give the impression that they are talking to a few friends, sharing their humor and their enthusiasm for their field. Let your students see that you are a person whose interests, emotions, and values extend beyond the classroom. Before class begins, one science faculty member who loves music plays the music of the composer or musician whose birthday is closest to that day. (Source: Marincovich and Rusk, 1987)

Be attentive to the physical environment of the classroom. Make sure that the lights are adequate for note taking, that glare does not interfere with the students' view of the chalkboard, that the room temperature is comfortable. Encourage students to adjust the room to their needs: to close the blinds or open the windows, for example.

Make the space small. A large lecture room will seem smaller if you stand in front of the lectern, not behind it. Move about the space as you lecture, using the aisles if appropriate. If you have graduate student instructors, join with them in distributing class materials. (Source: Gleason, 1986)

Creating a Sense of Community

Encourage students to get to know one another. In an impersonal classroom, students feel less responsibility toward other class members and the instructor (Gleason, 1986). Students who feel anonymous in class are less motivated to learn and less likely to do the required work (Brock, 1976). Conversely, students who feel a sense of community pay more attention and participate more. On the first day of class, consider having students introduce themselves to one or two others sitting nearby. If your class does not have sections, explain how study groups can work, and set aside class time to organize such groups (see "Collaborative Learning"). Help students get to know one another by giving short group assignments. Or have the class form teams of two or three students to submit test questions, work on in-class projects, and so on. Ask students to exchange telephone numbers with at least two other people in the class. See "The First Day of Class."

Make an attempt to meet informally with students. While it will not be possible to meet all students in a large lecture class, nor should you feel compelled to try, it is worthwhile to get to know a few students. Some faculty extend an open invitation for students to drop by a café for coffee and conversation. Others randomly select two or three students a week from the class roster and invite them to lunch. Still others hold afternoon teas in their offices throughout the semester. One faculty member purchases twenty-five cheap bleacher seats for a ball game and gives them to the first twenty-five students who want to attend. After those tickets are gone, other students can join the group by purchasing their own (Padian, 1992).

Try to learn the names of some students and refer to students by name. While it is impossible to learn the names of all the students in a large class, students seem to appreciate instructors' attempts to learn the names of a few. If a student brings up a point, ask for the student's name, and refer to that point or question as his or hers. The effect of this personal address carries over to all the students. (Source: Benjamin, 1991)

Ask students to complete autobiographical information sheets. During the first week of class ask students to fill out a one-page sheet with their name, address, year in college, hometown, reasons for taking the course, expectations, hobbies, work experience, and so on. Use this information to select course activities or match examples to students' interests. (Source: Benjamin, 1991)

Help the students forge a common identity as "the class." Each class has a distinctive personality that emerges during the term. Encourage the group to develop its own culture. For example, one term a faculty member began each class session by asking students, "Are you awake? Are you ready to learn?" and waiting until all students responded with a resounding yes.

Distribute a course newsletter. A one-page newsletter distributed electronically or by hard copy every three or so weeks can be a forum for announcements, more detailed explanations of topics covered in class, errata, inspirational messages, study tips, and so on. Encourage students to place comments or questions in your mailbox, in an envelope taped to your office door, or through electronic mail. Answer students' questions in the newsletter.

Establish a "help" room or course center. Make available to students old tests and homework assignments (with the answers), supplementary textbooks, readings, and other materials they can use to review the course content and prepare for examinations. If possible, assign a graduate student instructor or advanced undergraduate to assist students with problems or answer their questions. (Source: Brock, 1976)

Hold an in-class orientation just for freshmen and transfer students. One science faculty member teaching a large lower-division lecture course uses a portion of class time during the second week to meet with new students. He dismisses class twenty minutes early but invites new students to stay. During that time, he reintroduces himself and the graduate student instructors, reviews office hours and course requirements, learns a little bit about the backgrounds of the new students, and gives them practical advice on how to study, the importance of attending class, the need for forming study groups, where to seek help, and how to get to know professors at a large university. (Source: Padian, 1992)

Minimizing the Distance Between Teacher and Student

Let students know that they are not faces in an anonymous audience. In large courses students often think that their classroom behavior (eating, talking, sleeping, reading the newspaper, arriving late, leaving early) goes unnoticed. Tell students that you are aware of what is happening in class and act accordingly.

Ask students to refrain from sitting in certain rows of the classroom. For example, one math professor asks students to sit only in rows 1, 2, 4, 5,

7, 8, and so on. With rows 3, 6, and 9 empty, he can walk through the audience between the rows, which is especially important while students are working at their seats. Of course this suggestion is only possible if your course is not maximally enrolled or oversubscribed and if your classroom is large enough.

Recognize students' outside accomplishments. Read your campus newspaper, scan the dean's list, pay attention to undergraduate awards and honors, and let students know you are aware of their achievements.

Occasionally attend lab or discussion sections. Sections give you an opportunity to meet students and answer questions in a smaller setting.

Capitalize on outside events or situations, as appropriate. Relate major world events or events on campus both to topics in your class and to the fabric of your students' lives outside the classroom. Consider distributing a calendar or setting aside class time to mention community events and resources that will enhance their understanding of the subject matter: plays, lectures, performances, demonstrations, and the like.

Arrive early and chat with students. Ask how the course is going, whether they are enjoying the readings, whether there is anything they want you to include in lectures. Or ask students to walk back with you to your office after class.

Read a sampling of assignments and exams. If you have graduate student instructors who do most of the grading, let students know you will be reading and grading some of their assignments and exams.

Seek out students who are doing poorly in the course. Write "I know you can do better; see me during my office hours" on all exams graded C – or below. Offer early assistance to students having difficulty.

Acknowledge students who are doing well in the course. Write "Good job! See me after class" on all exams graded A – or above. Take a moment after class to compliment students who are excelling. Some teachers send "A" students a letter of congratulations at the end of the semester.

Schedule topics for office hours. If students are reluctant to come, periodically schedule a "help session" on a particular topic rather than a free-form office hour. See "Holding Office Hours."

Talk about questions students have asked in previous terms. Mention specific questions former students have asked and explain why they were excellent questions. This lets students know that you take their questions seriously and that their questions will contribute to future offerings of the course. (Source: Gleason, 1986)

Listen attentively to all questions and answer them directly. If the answer to a question is contained in material you will cover during the remainder of the lecture, acknowledge the aptness of the question, ask the student to hold onto the question for a bit, and answer the question directly when you arrive at that subject. See "Fielding Students' Questions."

Try to empathize with beginners. Remember that not all of your students are as highly motivated and interested in the discipline as you were when you were a student. Slow down when explaining complex ideas, and acknowledge the difficulty and importance of certain concepts or operations. Try to recall your first encounter with a concept—what examples, strategies, or techniques helped clarify it for you? By describing that encounter and its resolution to your students, you not only explain the concept but also convey the struggle and rewards of learning. (Source: Gleason, 1986)

Monitoring Students' Progress

Ask questions. By asking questions, you turn students into active participants in the class and you can also get a sense of their interest and comprehension. For example, you might leave the last ten or fifteen minutes for students' questions and if several questions concern one topic, incorporate a brief lecture on that topic into your next lecture. If your class is too large for an open discussion, identify participation areas of the room (the northeast quadrant one period, the southwest the next) and engage that day's group in discussion. You can involve the entire class by asking a true-false or multiple-choice question and having students respond by calling out or using their fingers (thumbs up or thumbs down, one for A, two for B, and so on). Scan the responses to see whether students understood your point. (Source: Gleason, 1986)

Look at the class, especially at key points of the lecture. Be alert to nonverbal reactions that indicate that you have lost your audience. For example, are students talking to their neighbors to catch a point they missed? If so, ask for questions or opinions, or ask students to supply elaborations or illustrations.

If you have graduate student instructors, ask for periodic reports on problems students are having. For example, at the end of each week ask your graduate student instructors to list two or three points that caused students the most difficulty in discussion sections. You might also ask for their observations about students' responses to your lectures.

Give frequent quizzes and two or more midterms. Frequent quizzes (graded or ungraded) give students a greater opportunity to do well in your course and give you an ongoing sense of their progress.

Gather feedback during the semester. See "Fast Feedback" for a variety of informal ways to check students' progress and gauge how and what they are learning.

References

Benjamin, L. T. "Personalization and Active Learning in the Large Introductory Psychology Class." *Teaching of Psychology*, 1991, *18*(2), 68–74.

Brock, S. C. *Practitioners' Views on Teaching the Large Introductory College Course.* Manhattan: Center for Faculty Evaluation and Development in Higher Education, Kansas State University, 1976.

Gleason, M. "Better Communication in Large Courses." *College Teaching*, 1986, *34*(1), 20–24.

Marincovich, M., and Rusk, L. *Excellence in Teaching Electrical Engineering.* Stanford, Calif.: Center for Teaching and Learning, Stanford University, 1987.

Padian, K. "Three Suggestions for Improving Contact with Students." *Journal of College Science Teaching*, 1992, *21*(4), 205–206.

Supplements and Alternatives to Lecturing: Encouraging Student Participation

16

Traditional lecturing suffers from a major defect: it is one-way communication in which the student is a passive participant—merely a listener. Students learn best when they take an active role: when they discuss what they are reading, practice what they are learning, and apply concepts and ideas. The following techniques have been used successfully by faculty in various fields to engage large undergraduate classes in student-student and student-faculty interaction, both to enhance learning and to break up the potential tedium of straight lecturing. Though oriented toward large lecture courses, these ideas can be implemented in classes of any size.

Breaking the Class into Small Groups

Group students into pairs or trios. At the beginning of a class session, ask students to pair off with someone sitting nearby or behind them. Let students know that during class they will discuss material or solve a problem with their partner. You can then ask pairs to define a term ("Describe the Doppler effect to your partner"), to pose a "why" or "how" question from the reading, to solve a problem, to answer a question you raise, or to identify the major points in the lecture. To ensure that partners' misinformation does not go uncorrected, offer a brief recapitulation or answer to the whole class. Faculty who use this technique report that students use the time wisely, learn effectively from one another, and can concentrate above the din of everyone talking at once. This change-of-pace activity also recaptures students' attention. (Source: Pestel, 1990)

Use learning dyads. Give the entire class an assignment to be carried out before the next class meeting. The assignment may entail reading, completing a problem set, doing a field trip or laboratory experiment, or any other activity. Ask the students to prepare two copies of four or five questions about the assignment: for example, "Why did Congress pass the Repatriation Act of 1935?" At the next class, students turn in to you one set of their questions, which you use to evaluate the students' performance. Then have the students pair off and ask their partners a question from the list they have prepared; students should alternate in the roles of questioner and responder. At successive meetings, have students form new partnerships. (Source: McKeachie, 1986)

Form small subgroups. Ask your class to form subgroups of three or four students, and pose a specific question or task that the groups can resolve in two or three minutes. For instance, ask the groups to generate examples that illustrate a particular point, to rank order several items, to identify reasons for an event or occurrence, or to suggest ways to remedy or change something. In a cognitive psychology class, a faculty member asks subgroups to "identify which aspect of artificial intelligence has the greatest impact on our lives: robotics, expert systems, pattern recognition, or natural language." In a math class, a faculty member hands out a short problem for the subgroups to solve at their seats. He distributes only one copy per group, which forces the students to discuss and collaborate rather than starting to work on the solution on their own. If class size permits, let students know that you will be soliciting responses from each group. If the class is too large, ask one or two groups to state their conclusions, and ask how many of the groups agree. Subgroups give students a chance to move from passive listening to active learning, give the instructor a breather from lecturing, and provide students with a chance to get to know one another.

Use the snowball discussion technique. Ask the class to pair off. Pose a general question that will generate several ideas from even the least sophisticated student: "Who are the key professionals, besides the architect, involved in designing, financing, and constructing a building?" Ask each pair to generate as many responses as possible during a designated period (three or four minutes), with one member recording the responses on a piece of paper. When time is up, ask each pair to join with a nearby pair to form a four-person group. The quartet can combine their ideas into one list and add new ideas to it. If desired, the quartets can combine again to form octets. During the last round, ask the students to select one member of the group to be the recorder-spokesperson who reports back to the class. This technique is especially good early in the semester because it gets students thinking about the subject matter, lets you see how much they already know about the field, helps students overcome the isolation and impersonality of a large class, and sets a pattern of student participation for the term. The process can be repeated—with a more sophisticated topic—at a later date.

Convene simultaneous discussion groups. Have students divide into discussion sections (twenty to twenty-five people) that meet in corners of the lecture hall or move into empty neighboring classrooms. Start the whole class off with a common task, and then sit in with each group briefly to answer questions, comment on the topic, and get the groups started or back on track. It is helpful to distribute to students guidelines on how to participate in a discussion. (See "Leading a Discussion.") If desired, bring the entire class back together to summarize the groups' activities.

Use the twenty-five/five rule. When 25 percent of the groups have completed an in-class task, the remaining groups have about five more minutes to finish. (Source: Michaelsen, 1983)

Engaging the Entire Class

Ask students to brainstorm. Some faculty, even in classes of up to four hundred students, pose a general open-ended question to the class as a whole and ask students to brainstorm, that is, to offer as many suggestions as possible without judging their validity. For example, "What factors contributed to the formation of OPEC?" Give your students these guides for brainstorming:

- Criticism is ruled out; no one should criticize anyone else's suggestions.
- Freewheeling is welcome.
- Quantity is desired: the more ideas, the more likelihood of obtaining good ones.

Write your students' ideas on the board or on an overhead transparency. It is helpful if you arrange the comments, as they occur, in rough categories (for example, social, economic, political factors) and later ask the students to identify the categories or themes that have emerged from their suggestions. You can also sift through the list, combine related ideas, and provide the major conclusions yourself. A variation on brainstorming is to stop in the middle of your lecture and ask students to write down all their thoughts on the subject being discussed. (Source: Frederick, 1986)

Post problems. Begin the period by asking students to raise questions or problems. Write these on the board, but do not answer the questions—just help your students clarify their problems. Once the list is finished, you can sort the items into related categories. If the list is long and time is limited, ask the class to vote on which problems should be given priority. You can then either respond to the questions yourself or assign questions to subgroups. Some of the benefits of posting questions include increased participation, an attitude of problem solving in which problems are clarified and seen as challenges rather than as evidence of inadequacy, and increased self-confidence as students help others and are helped by them. (Source: McKeachie, 1986)

Devise a questionnaire for students to complete during class. Create a short questionnaire covering one or more controversial topics (theories, research findings, positions on issues) in your course. After each controversial statement, list five response categories: strongly agree, agree, neither agree nor disagree, disagree, strongly disagree. Pass these questionnaires out at the beginning of a class meeting and tally them after class. Throughout the semester, reveal selected results from the survey as they relate to new concepts or issues covered in lectures or readings. Offer the class a snapshot or profile of itself so that each student can see how his or her views match those of classmates. If time permits, ask one or more members of the class who took a "strongly agree" or "strongly disagree" position to state briefly their reasons and evidence. Such discussions bring controversies to life, and students tend to be quite interested in hearing the opinions and reasoning of fellow students.

Pause during your lecture to pose a "thought problem" or ask a question. Give students a few minutes to solve a problem at their seats; after you explain the answer, proceed with your lecture. Or ask a true-false or multiple-choice question and have students respond by calling out or raising their hand. Or if class size permits, give students colored index cards (yellow, white, blue) and periodically call for a vote on an issue by asking for a simultaneous show of cards. You can also ask questions that have a one- or two-word answer—"What's the next number in the Fibonacci Series 1,1,2,3,5,8,___?" "Who painted 'Expulsion from Paradise'?"—in a quick, energetic way. Move about the class when asking questions (it helps to have a portable microphone) and call on people with direct eye contact. (Sources: Gleason, 1986; "Participation in Large Classes," 1990; Povlacs, 1986)

Pause during your lecture for an ungraded writing activity. See "Helping Students Write Better in All Courses" for a variety of informal in-class writing activities.

Ask students to become experts on key words. At the beginning of the term distribute a list of key concepts, ideas, people, organizations, or events. Ask each student to select one word (in very large classes groups of students may choose the same word). For their first assignment, students submit a one-page "definition" of their word. Throughout the semester, students are encouraged to read in depth on their key word and to serve as in-house experts when the term comes up in lecture. (Source: Christensen, 1988)

Encourage students to ask questions. If the class is too large for you to take oral questions, have students write out their questions during the lecture and pass them to the aisles. If there are only a few questions, you can quickly sort them and give your answers on the spot. If you receive many questions, tell students you will address them during the next session. (Source: McKeachie, 1986)

Stage a daytime "talk show." One faculty member offers students the opportunity to earn extra credit by participating in a group role-playing activity. The group consists of five to six speakers who play the roles of participants discussing a controversial topic that might be found on the "Donahue Show." For example, one group topic was "All Tobacco and Alcohol Advertising Should Be Banned." Students played various roles, from an attorney for the American Civil Liberties Union to a spokesperson for the American Lung Association to a corporate representative from a tobacco company. After researching their positions, the students assume the roles of the talk show participants, with the instructor as host circulating through the "audience" fielding questions with a microphone. (Source: Geske, 1992)

Conduct a large group discussion. To hold a discussion with several hundred students, let disagreement play a major part. After a student expresses a point of view, ask the rest of the class to indicate whether or not they agree: "How many of you think that this is a sound position to take?" Once agreement is registered by a show of hands, ask for points of disagreement or alternative views and put these to a show of hands. Keep the discussion moving by searching for different ideas instead of inviting speeches that support a majority point of view. (Source: Maier, 1963)

Periodically cut short your lecture. For example, occasionally end half an hour early and use that time for informal discussion. One faculty member makes attendance optional for that half hour. Some students elect to leave, but for those who stay, he reports holding lively discussions about the lectures, reading assignments, and the discipline. (Source: Padian, 1992)

Avoid starting a serious discussion near the end of the period. As class draws to a close, students' questions or comments may be stifled by peer pressure for the dismissal of class.

Allow time for students to write a summary of what has been presented. At the end of the period, ask students to jot down the two or three key points of the day's lecture or the question that is uppermost in their minds. Collect their responses and review a sample as a check on what they have learned.

Making Use of Alternatives to Lecturing

Invite guest speakers to class. Arrange visits by outside guests or faculty colleagues who have relevant expertise or practical experience. An English professor sometimes invites professional actors to talk about their interpretations of a scene or role from a play the students are studying. Instead of having the guest speaker deliver a lecture, you or two or three students could interview the speaker in front of the class. If the speaker's work is familiar to your students, ask them to submit a set of questions for the speaker. When possible, encourage students to join you and the guest for coffee after class (McKeachie, 1986). Use a portion of the next class session to emphasize the speaker's contributions.

As a courtesy to each guest speaker, make arrangements well in advance, give the speaker relevant background information about your course and your students, discuss the format for the guest's presentation, confirm the time and place, provide a map of the campus, arrange for campus parking, and promptly send each speaker a thank-you note. (Source: "The Guest Lecturer," 1991)

Set up a conference call in class. Invite a content expert, author of the course readings, elected official, or writer or director of a film shown in class to speak with your students by telephone. Use an open mike and speaker phone and have students ask questions they have prepared, or you can pose the students' questions to the speaker. Some campuses are equipped with teleconferencing facilities that can be used for this purpose. (Source: "Phone Interviews," 1989).

Arrange a debate. Two people exchanging points of view can often hold a class's attention far more effectively than a single speaker. Invite a colleague to debate you on some issue relevant to your course. Or involve all your students in a debate by dividing the class in half. Students can either support the side of an issue assigned to the half of the hall where they happen to be sitting, or they can be told to come to class prepared to take a seat on a particular side of a debate. You can also have small groups debate an issue by giving instructions such as the following (Deemer, 1986, p. 41):

> Your group needs to identify the four best arguments for outlawing (or mandating) the use of IQ tests. Start by sharing your views and making a list of all the arguments you can identify. Don't be critical or evaluate the arguments that are proposed at this time. Put your energy into helping each other identify and communicate ideas, regardless of how absurd they may sound. When your list is relatively complete, then go back and select the four best arguments. You have about 30 minutes.

If class size permits, ask for volunteers to make a statement on the pro side and on the con. For some topics, create pro, con, and neutral groups. (Source: Frederick, 1986)

Stage a role play. See "Role Playing and Case Studies."

Play simulation games. Simulation or educational games duplicate certain features of a physical, social, historical, or political environment and allow students to engage in activities that approximate realistic situations. Simulation games have been developed in a range of disciplines: business, international relations, history, sociology, urban planning. For example, in a simulation game on the Russian Revolution, students volunteer to join one of four parties and are asked to caucus to decide on courses of action for the upcoming 1917 election (McKeachie, 1986). In the game Prisoner's Dilemma, students are arrested and charged with a serious crime. This simulation introduces students to plea bargaining, decision making based on self-interest versus social benefit, and the workings of the criminal justice system (Hyman, 1981). In other simulations, students are citizens of a society in which they have fixed economic and social roles, or students simulate politicians conducting international negotiations.

A typical simulation game involves competing groups of students and takes about one to two hours to complete. Be sure to budget enough time for a thorough discussion of what students learned from the game and what generalizations they drew from the particular sequence of play.

Research findings indicate that simulations have a favorable effect on students' motivation and involvement (McKeachie, 1986). However, simulations are not more effective than conventional methods for achieving cognitive objectives and thus are best used as adjuncts to other methods of teaching. Simulation or educational games and computer simulations are reported in the teaching journals of the disciplines (for example, *Teaching Sociology, Teaching Political Science, Journalism Educator*) as well as in specialized journals (*Simulation and Games*). Abt (1970) and Bratley, Fox, and Schrage (1987) provide overviews of simulations in various disciplinary areas. Ramsden (1992) describes a simulation using electronic mail. For those interested in developing simulation games, Fuhrmann and Grasha (1983, chap. 9) describe the procedures.

References

Abt, C. *Serious Games*. Washington, D. C.: University Press of America, 1970.

Bratley, P., Fox, B. L., and Schrage, L. E. *A Guide to Simulations*. (2nd ed.) New York: Springer-Verlag, 1987.

Christensen, T. "Key Words Unlock Students' Minds." *College Teaching*, 1988, *36*(2), 61.

Deemer, D. "Structuring Controversy in the Classroom." In S. F. Schomberg (ed.), *Strategies for Active Teaching and Learning in University Classrooms*. Minneapolis: Office of Educational Development Programs, University of Minnesota, 1986.

Frederick, P. J. "The Lively Lecture—8 Variations." *College Teaching*, 1986, *34*(2), 43–50.

Fuhrmann, B. S., and Grasha, A. F. *A Practical Handbook for College Teachers*. Boston: Little, Brown, 1983.

Geske, J. "Overcoming the Drawbacks of the Large Lecture Class." *College Teaching*, 1992, *40*(4), 151–154.

Gleason, M. "Better Communication in Large Courses." *College Teaching*, 1986, *34*(1), 20–24.

"The Guest Lecturer: Do's and Don'ts." *Teaching Professor*, 1991, *5*(6), 2.

Hyman, R. T. "Using Simulation Games in the College Classroom." *Idea Paper*, no. 5. Manhattan: Center for Faculty Evaluation and Development in Higher Education, Kansas State University, 1981.

McKeachie, W. J. *Teaching Tips*. (8th ed.) Lexington, Mass.: Heath, 1986.

Maier, N.R.F. *Problem-Solving Discussions and Conferences*. New York: McGraw-Hill, 1963.

Michaelsen, L. K. "Team Learning in Large Classes." In C. Bouten and R. Y. Garth (eds.), *Learning in Groups*. New Directions for Teaching and Learning, no. 14. San Francisco: Jossey-Bass, 1983.

Padian, K. "Three Suggestions for Improving Contact with Students." *Journal of College Science Teaching*, 1992, *21*(4), 205–206.

"Participation in Large Classes." *Teaching Professor*, 1990, *4*(2), 3.

Pestel, B. C. "Students 'Participate' with Each Other." *Teaching Professor*, 1990, *4*(5), 4.

"Phone Interviews." *Teaching Professor*, 1989, *3*(2), 7.

Povlacs, J. T. "101 Things You Can Do the First Three Weeks of Class." *Teaching at the University of Nebraska, Lincoln*, 1986, *8*(1), 1–4. (Newsletter available from the Teaching and Learning Center, University of Nebraska, Lincoln)

Ramsden, P. *Learning to Teach in Higher Education*. New York: Routledge, 1992.

17

Maintaining Instructional Quality with Limited Resources

Given the financial situation of many colleges and universities today, faculty are often faced with teaching their large lecture courses under increasingly difficult conditions. Money for guest lecturers, duplicating materials, media resources, laboratory sessions, and field trips is disappearing. Graduate student instructors (GSIs) and readers are no longer routinely available for classes. Are there alternatives to simply decreasing the amount of writing you assign and forgoing sections and small group discussions? How can you continue to provide quality education in the face of budget constraints?

One approach to smaller budgets is for departments to consider structural changes in the size and nature of courses that are offered. Another strategy is for you to adopt teaching techniques that do not depend on GSIs or readers. For example, "Personalizing the Large Lecture Class" and "Supplements and Alternatives to Lecturing" contain many suggestions for giving students opportunities for discussion when GSI-led sections are eliminated or reduced.

Testing and Grading Students Without Support from Readers and GSIs

Consider group testing. See "Quizzes, Tests, and Exams."

Ask students to generate test items. Faculty who use this technique have had some success in adapting students' items for midterm exams. See "Quizzes, Tests, and Exams." (Sources: Buchanan and Rogers, 1990; Fuhrmann and Grasha, 1983)

Use optical scanning to score tests. Multiple-choice tests can measure both simple knowledge and complex concepts. Scanning devices make scoring easy and reliable. See "Multiple-Choice and Matching Tests."

Assigning and Grading Writing Assignments Without Support from Readers and GSIs

Don't feel as though you have to read and grade every piece of your students' writing. Students are writing primarily to learn a subject. It is better to have students write than not to have them write, even if you cannot respond to each piece of writing. Ask students to analyze each other's work during class, or ask them to critique their work in small groups. Or simply have students write for their own purposes, without any feedback. Students will learn that they are writing in order to think more clearly, not to obtain a grade. Keep in mind, too, that you can collect students' papers and skim their work. (Source: Watkins, 1990)

Assign brief in-class writing assignments. Before discussing a topic, ask students to write a brief account of what they already know about the subject or what opinions they hold. You need not collect these; the purpose is to focus students' attention. Or you can ask students to respond in writing to short-answer questions you pose during class. The questions might call for a review of material previously covered or test students' recall of the assigned readings. (Source: Tollefson, 1988)

During class, pause for a three-minute write. Periodically ask students to write for three minutes on a specific question or topic. Tell them to write freely about whatever pops into their mind without worrying about grammar, spelling, phrasing, or organization. Writing experts believe that this kind of free writing helps students synthesize diverse ideas and identify points they don't understand. You need not collect these exercises. (Source: Tollefson, 1988)

Use peer response groups. Divide the class into groups of three or four students, no larger. Tell the students to bring to class enough copies of a rough draft of a paper for each member of their group. Give students guidelines for responding to the drafts. See "Helping Students Write Better in All Courses."

Assigning and Grading Problem Sets Without Support from Readers and GSIs

Give frequent homework but do not grade every assignment. Instead, grade one or two problems without telling the students in advance which ones those will be. Or collect two or three problems a week for grading. Some faculty ask their students to accumulate homework in a notebook, which is called in for checking from time to time, or they give short quizzes on the problem sets and grade those. For assignments you do not grade, distribute an answer sheet on the day the homework is due so that students can check their own work. (Source: Committee on the Teaching of Undergraduate Mathematics, 1979)

Encourage students to work collaboratively on their homework. Students can learn from each other by working together. To cut down on grading, ask a small group of students to submit a single homework assignment. (Sources: Marincovich and Rusk, 1987; Reznick, 1985)

Evaluate some class requirements on a pass/not pass basis. You need not assign a letter grade to every piece of homework. Consider check, check plus, or zero as well as pass/not pass.

Creating a Sense of Community in Large Classes Without Discussion Sections

Help students become acquainted with one another. On the first day of class, ask students to introduce themselves to one or two others sitting nearby. Help students get to know one another by giving short group assignments. Or have the class form study teams or groups of four or six students to submit test questions, work on in-class projects, and so on. Ask students to exchange telephone numbers with at least two other people in the class.

Try to meet with groups of students outside class. Extend an invitation to your students to meet you somewhere for informal conversation, or randomly select two or three students a week from the class roster and invite them to lunch, or turn some office hours into "open house" teas. While you will not be able to meet informally with all students, your efforts will be appreciated by the entire class.

Keep in touch with students electronically. For example, if your campus is networked, distribute an informal newsletter. Or set up an electronic mail forum for students in your course, so that they can communicate with one another. See "Computers and Multimedia."

Restructuring Departmental Courses and Course Offerings

Reduce class sizes, if possible. Enrolling fewer students is one way to compensate for a decline in support, particularly in large lecture classes where GSI and/or reader support is eliminated. For example, large lower-division courses enrolling three or four hundred students might be offered in multiple simultaneous versions, with different faculty teaching each version (enrolling a hundred or so students). At the upper-division level, some classes might be restricted to department majors only. Keep in mind, though, that reducing enrollments in some courses will lead to higher enrollments in others.

Find alternative ways for students to satisfy course requirements. If a particular course is a breadth or major requirement, consider the possibility of allowing students to satisfy the requirement in other ways. Identify courses in other departments and colleges that would be acceptable, or provide students with a list of courses offered in summer session or at other institutions that would meet the requirement.

Cut back on sparsely enrolled courses. Departments might consider temporarily redirecting instructors to oversubscribed offerings (for example, offer additional sections of a large lecture class) and postponing less popular courses.

Offer a substitute for discussion sections. If funds do not permit small weekly section meetings, each with its own GSI, offer a few larger open-ended sections that any student in the class can attend whenever he or she wishes.

References

Buchanan, R. W., and Rogers, M. "Innovative Assessment in Large Classes." *College Teaching*, 1990, *38*(2), 69–73.

Committee on the Teaching of Undergraduate Mathematics. *College Mathematics: Suggestions on How to Teach It.* Washington, D.C.: Mathematical Association of America, 1979.

Deemer, D. "Structuring Controversy in the Classroom." In S. F. Schomberg (ed.), *Strategies for Active Teaching and Learning in University Classrooms.* Minneapolis: Office of Educational Development Programs, University of Minnesota, 1986.

Fuhrmann, B. S., and Grasha, A. F. *A Practical Handbook for College Teachers.* Boston: Little, Brown, 1983.

Marincovich, M., and Rusk, L. *Excellence in Teaching Electrical Engineering.* Stanford, Calif.: Center for Teaching and Learning, Stanford University, 1987.

Padian, K. "Three Suggestions for Improving Contact with Students." *Journal of College Science Teaching*, 1992, *21*(4), 205–206.

Reznick, B. A. *Chalking It Up: Advice to a New TA.* New York: Random House, 1985.

Tollefson, S. K. *Encouraging Student Writing.* Berkeley: Office of Educational Development, University of California, 1988.

Walvoord, B. F. *Helping Students Write Well: A Guide for Teachers in All Disciplines.* (2nd ed.) New York: Modern Language Association, 1986.

Watkins, B. T. "More and More Professors in Many Academic Disciplines Routinely Require Students to Do Extensive Writing." *Chronicle of Higher Education*, 1990, 36(44), pp. A13–A14, A16.

V.

Collaborative and Experiential Strategies

Collaborative Learning: Group Work and Study Teams

18

Students learn best when they are actively involved in the process. Researchers report that, regardless of the subject matter, students working in small groups tend to learn more of what is taught and retain it longer than when the same content is presented in other instructional formats. Students who work in collaborative groups also appear more satisfied with their classes. (Sources: Beckman, 1990; Chickering and Gamson, 1991; Collier, 1980; Cooper and Associates, 1990; Goodsell, Maher, Tinto, and Associates, 1992; Johnson and Johnson, 1989; Johnson, Johnson, and Smith, 1991; Kohn, 1986; McKeachie, Pintrich, Lin, and Smith, 1986; Slavin, 1980, 1983; Whitman, 1988)

Various names have been given to this form of teaching, and there are some distinctions among these: cooperative learning, collaborative learning, collective learning, learning communities, peer teaching, peer learning, reciprocal learning, team learning, study circles, study groups, and work groups. But all in all, there are three general types of group work: informal learning groups, formal learning groups, and study teams (adapted from Johnson, Johnson, and Smith, 1991).

Informal learning groups are ad hoc temporary clusterings of students within a single class session. Informal learning groups can be initiated, for example, by asking students to turn to a neighbor and spend two minutes discussing a question you have posed. You can also form groups of three to five to solve a problem or pose a question. You can organize informal groups at any time in a class of any size to check on students' understanding of the material, to give students an opportunity to apply what they are learning, or to provide a change of pace.

Formal learning groups are teams established to complete a specific task, such as perform a lab experiment, write a report, carry out a project, or prepare a position paper. These groups may complete their work in a single class session or over several weeks. Typically, students work together until the task is finished, and their project is graded.

Study teams are long-term groups (usually existing over the course of a semester) with stable membership whose primary responsibility is to provide members with support, encouragement, and assistance in completing course requirements and assignments. Study teams also inform their members about lectures and assignments when someone has missed a session. The larger the class and the more complex the subject matter, the more valuable study teams can be.

The suggestions below are designed to help you set up formal learning groups and study teams. If you have never done group work in your classes, you might want to experiment first with informal learning groups. Two other tools, "Leading a Discussion" and "Supplements and Alternatives to Lecturing: Encouraging Student Participation," describe a variety of easy ways to incorporate informal learning groups into your courses. "Helping Students Write Better in All Courses" discusses informal collaborative writing activities.

General Strategies

Plan for each stage of group work. When you are writing your syllabus for the course, decide which topics, themes, or projects might lend themselves to formal group work. Think about how you will organize students into groups, help groups negotiate among themselves, provide feedback to the groups, and evaluate the products of group work.

Carefully explain to your class how the groups will operate and how students will be graded. As you would when making any assignment, explain the objectives of the group task and define any relevant concepts. In addition to a well-defined task, every group needs a way of getting started, a way of knowing when its task is done, and some guidance about the participation of members. Also explain how students will be graded. Keep in mind that group work is more successful when students are graded against a set standard than when they are graded against each other (on a curve). See "Grading Practices." (Source: Smith, 1986)

Give students the skills they need to succeed in groups. Many students have never worked in collaborative learning groups and may need practice in such skills as active and tolerant listening, helping one another in mastering content, giving and receiving constructive criticism, and managing disagreements. Discuss these skills with your students and model and reinforce them during class. Some faculty use various exercises that help students gain skills in working in groups (Fiechtner and Davis, 1992). See "Leading a Discussion" for examples of guidelines for participating in small groups. (Sources: Cooper, 1990; Johnson, Johnson, and Smith, 1991)

Consider written contracts. Some faculty give students written contracts that list members' obligations to their group and deadlines for tasks (Connery, 1988).

Designing Group Work

Create group tasks that require interdependence. The students in a group must perceive that they "sink or swim" together, that each member is responsible to and dependent on all the others, and that one cannot succeed unless all in the group succeed. Knowing that peers are relying on you is a powerful motivator for group work (Kohn, 1986). Strategies for promoting interdependence include specifying common rewards for the group, encouraging students to divide up the labor, and formulating tasks that compel students to reach a consensus. (Source: Johnson, Johnson, and Smith, 1991)

Make the group work relevant. Students must perceive the group tasks as integral to the course objectives, not just busywork. Some faculty believe that groups succeed best with tasks involving judgment. As reported by Johnson, Johnson, and Smith (1991), for example, in an engineering class, a faculty member gives groups a problem to solve: Determine whether the city should purchase twenty-five or fifty buses. Each group prepares a report, and a representative from each group is randomly selected to present the group's solution. The approaches used by the various groups are compared and discussed by the entire class. Goodsell, Maher, Tinto, and Associates (1992, pp. 75–79) have compiled a detailed bibliography of discipline-specific efforts in collaborative learning that can be useful for developing tasks and activities.

Create assignments that fit the students' skills and abilities. Early in the term, assign relatively easy tasks. As students become more knowledgeable, increase the difficulty level. For example, a faculty member teaching research methods begins by having students simply recognize various research designs and sampling procedures. Later, team members generate their own research designs. At the end of the term, each team prepares a proposal for a research project and submits it to another team for evaluation. (Source: Cooper and Associates, 1990)

Assign group tasks that allow for a fair division of labor. Try to structure the tasks so that each group member can make an equal contribution. For example, one faculty member asks groups to write a report on alternative energy sources. Each member of the group is responsible for research on one source, and then all the members work together to incorporate the individual contributions into the final report. Another faculty member asks groups to prepare a "medieval newspaper." Students research aspects of life in the Middle Ages, and each student contributes one major article for the newspaper, which includes news stories, feature stories, and editorials. Students conduct their research independently and use group meetings to share information, edit articles, proofread, and design the pages. (Sources: Smith, 1986; Tiberius, 1990)

Set up "competitions" among groups. A faculty member in engineering turns laboratory exercises into competitions. Students, working in groups, design and build a small-scale model of a structure such as a bridge or column. They predict how their model will behave when loaded, and then each model is loaded to failure. Prizes are awarded to the groups in various categories: best predictions of behavior, most efficient structure, best aesthetics. (Source: Sansalone, 1989)

Consider offering group test taking. On a group test, either an in-class or take-home exam, each student receives the score of the group. Faculty who have used group exams report that groups consistently achieve higher scores than individuals and that students enjoy collaborative test taking (Hendrickson, 1990; Toppins, 1989). Faculty who use this technique recommend the following steps for in-class exams:

- Assign group work at the beginning of the term so that students develop skills for working in groups.
- Use multiple-choice tests that include higher-level questions. To allow time for discussion, present about twenty-five items for a fifty-minute in-class exam.
- Divide students into groups of five.
- Have students take the test individually and turn in their responses before they meet with their group. Then ask the groups to arrange themselves in the room and arrive at a group consensus answer for each question. Score the individual and group responses and prepare a chart showing the average individual score of each group's members, the highest individual score in each group, and the group's consensus score.

Ninety-five percent of the time, the group consensus scores will be higher than the average individual scores (Toppins, 1989).

For more information on group exams, see "Quizzes, Tests, and Exams."

Organizing Learning Groups

Decide how the groups will be formed. Some faculty prefer randomly assigning students to groups to maximize their heterogeneity: a mix of males and females, verbal and quiet students, the cynical and the optimistic (Fiechtner and Davis, 1992; Smith, 1986). Some faculty let students choose with whom they want to work, although this runs the risk that groups will socialize too much and that students will self-segregate (Cooper, 1990). Self-selected groups seem to work best in small classes, for classes of majors who already know one another, or in small residential colleges (Walvoord, 1986). Still other instructors prefer to form the groups themselves, taking into account students' prior achievement, levels of preparation, work habits, ethnicity, and gender (Connery, 1988). They argue for making sure that members of each group are exclusively graded students or exclusively pass/not pass students and that well-prepared students be placed in groups with other well-prepared students. Other faculty, however, try to sprinkle the more able students evenly among the groups (Walvoord, 1986). A middle ground, proposed by Walvoord (1986), is to ask students to express a preference, if they wish, then make the assignments yourself. You could, for example, ask students to write down the names of three students with whom they would most like to work.

Be conscious of group size. In general, groups of four or five members work best. Larger groups decrease each member's opportunity to participate actively. The less skillful the group members, the smaller the groups should be. The shorter amount of time available, the smaller the groups should be. (Sources: Cooper, 1990; Johnson, Johnson, and Smith, 1991; Smith, 1986)

Keep groups together. When a group is not working well, avoid breaking it up, even if the group requests it. The addition of the floundering group's members to ongoing groups may throw off their group process, and the bailed-out troubled group does not learn to cope with its unproductive interactions. (Source: Walvoord, 1986)

Guiding Learning Groups

Help groups plan how to proceed. Ask each group to devise a plan of action: who will be doing what and when. Review the groups' written plans or meet with each group to discuss its plan.

Regularly check in with the groups. If the task spans several weeks, you will want to establish checkpoints with the groups. Ask groups to turn in outlines or drafts or to meet with you.

Provide mechanisms for groups to deal with uncooperative members. Walvoord (1986) recommends telling the class that after the group task is completed, each student will submit to the instructor an anonymous assessment of the participation of the other group members: who did extra work and who shirked work. If several people indicate that an individual did less than a fair share, that person could receive a lower grade than the rest of the group. This system works, says Walvoord, if groups have a chance in the middle of the project to discuss whether any members are not doing their share. Members who are perceived as shirkers then have an opportunity to make amends. Here are some other options for dealing with shirkers:

- Keep the groups at three students: it is hard to be a shirker in a small group.
- Make it clear that each group must find its own way to handle unproductive group behavior.
- Allow the groups, by majority vote, to dismiss a member who is not carrying a fair share. Students who are dropped from a group must persuade the group to reconsider, find acceptance in another group, or take a failing grade for the project.

Perhaps the best way to assure comparable effort among all group members is to design activities in which there is a clear division of labor and each student must contribute if the group is to reach its goal. (Sources: Connery, 1988; Walvoord, 1986)

Evaluating Group Work

Ensure that individual student performance is assessed and that the groups know how their members are doing. Groups need to know who needs more assistance in completing the assignment, and members need to know they cannot let others do all the work while they sit back. Ways to ensure that students are held accountable include giving spot quizzes to be completed individually and calling on individual students to present their group's progress. (Source: Johnson, Johnson, and Smith, 1991)

Give students an opportunity to evaluate the effectiveness of their group. Once or twice during the group work task, ask group members to discuss two questions: What action has each member taken that was helpful for the group? What action could each member take to make the group even better? At the end of the project, ask students to complete a brief evaluation form on the effectiveness of the group and its members. The form could include items about the group's overall accomplishments, the student's own role, and suggestions for changes in future group work. Rau and Heyl (1990) have developed a form that can be used for an interim or final evaluation. (Sources: Johnson, Johnson, and Smith, 1991; Walvoord, 1986)

Decide how to grade members of the group. Some faculty assign all students in the group the same grade on the group task. Grading students individually, they argue, inevitably leads to competition within the group and thus subverts the benefits of group work. Other faculty grade the contribution of each student on the basis of individual test scores or the group's evaluation of each member's work. If you assign the same grade to the entire group, the grade should not account for more than a small part of a student's grade in the class (perhaps a few bonus points that would raise a test score from a B − to a B). (Sources: Cooper, 1990; Johnson, Johnson, and Smith, 1991)

Dealing with Student and Faculty Concerns About Group Work

"I paid my tuition to learn from a professor, not to have to work with my classmates, who don't know as much." Let students know at the beginning of the term that you will be using some group techniques. Students who are strongly antagonistic can drop your class and select another. Inform students about the research studies on the effectiveness of collaborative learning and describe the role it will play in your course. Invite students to try it before deciding whether to drop the class. (Source: Cooper and Associates, 1990)

"Our group just isn't working out." Encourage students to stick with it. Changing group membership should really be a last resort. Help your students learn how to be effective group members by summarizing for them some of the information in "Leading a Discussion" and "Encouraging Student Participation in Discussion."

"Students won't want to work in groups." Some students may object, in part because most of their education has been based on individual effort, and they may feel uncomfortable helping others or seeking help. The best advice is to explain your rationale, design well-structured meaningful tasks, give students clear directions, set expectations for how team members are to contribute and interact, and invite students to try it. (Source: Cooper and Associates, 1990)

"Students won't work well in groups." Most students can work well in groups if you set strong expectations at the beginning of the term, informally check in with groups to see how things are going, offer assistance as needed, and provide time for groups to assess their own effectiveness. Some groups may indeed have problems, but usually these can be resolved. See "Encouraging Student Participation in Discussion" for suggestions on how to minimize monopolizers, draw out quiet students, and generally engage all students in active participation.

"If I do group work, I won't be able to cover as much material during the semester as I do when I lecture." Yes, adding group work may mean covering fewer topics. But research shows that students who work in groups develop an increased ability to solve problems and evidence greater understanding of the material. Some instructors assign additional homework or readings or distribute lecture notes to compensate for less material "covered" in class. (Source: Cooper and Associates, 1990)

Setting Up Study Teams

Tell students about the benefits of study teams. Study teams meet regularly outside of class to study together, read and review course material, complete course assignments, comment on each other's written work, prepare for tests and exams, and help each other with difficulties that are encountered in class. Study teams are guided by the notions that students can often do as a group what they cannot do by themselves and that students can benefit from peer teaching—explanations, comments, and instruction from their coursemates.

Explain how study teams work. Study teams can work in a number of ways. In one model, all students read the assignments but each member agrees to provide to the group in-depth coverage of a particular segment of the material and to answer as fully as possible whatever questions other members of the study team might raise. In this model, then, each member agrees to study all the material yet each also tries to become an "expert" in a certain area of the material.

In another model, the teams' activities vary from meeting to meeting. For example, at one meeting, teams might review class notes to see whether there is agreement on the most important points of the lecture or discussion. In another session, teams might go over a class quiz or test to ensure that all team members clearly understand each of the questions, especially those that were answered incorrectly by one or more members. Another session might be devoted to reviewing problem sets or exchanging drafts of written papers for peer editing.

In a third model, the main agenda for each study team session is a set of study questions. Early in the term, the study questions are provided by the professor or graduate student instructors. After three or four weeks, each team member must bring a study question related to the week's lecture material to the team meeting. The questions structure the discussion and are modified, discarded, or replaced by the group as the session proceeds. At the session's end, the study questions that the group chooses as the most valuable are turned in for review by the instructor. You can let students decide for themselves how to structure their study teams, or you can offer advice and suggestions. (Sources: Guskey, 1988; Johnson, Johnson, and Smith, 1991; Light, 1992; "Study Groups Pay Off," 1991)

If study teams are optional, offer students extra credit for participation. For example, students who are members of an official study team might get bonus points for each assignment, based on the average grade received by the individual group members. (Source: "Study Groups Pay Off," 1991)

Let students know what their responsibilities are as a study team member. Students who participate in study teams agree to do the following:

- Prepare before the study team meeting (for example, do all the required reading or problem sets)
- Complete any tasks that the group assigns to its members
- Attend all meetings and arrive on time
- Actively participate during the sessions in ways that further the work of the group
- Help promote one another's learning and success
- Provide assistance, support, and encouragement to group members

- Be involved in periodic self-assessments to determine whether the study team is working successfully (Is too much work being required? Is the time in study team meetings well spent?)

In addition, let students know that they can improve the effectiveness of their study teams by making sure each session has a clearly articulated agenda and purpose. They can also work more efficiently if all logistical arrangements are set for the semester: meeting time, length, location.

Help students locate meeting rooms. Arrange with your department or campus room scheduler to make available small meeting rooms for study teams. If appropriate, consider using group rooms in the residence halls.

Limit groups to no more than six students. Groups larger than six have several drawbacks: it is too easy for students to become passive observers rather than active participants; students may not get the opportunity to speak frequently since there are so many people; students' sense of community and responsibility may be less intense in larger groups.

Let students select their own study teams unless you have a large class. Since the groups are designed to last the term and will meet outside of class, give students the opportunity to form groups of three to six members. Arrange one or two open groups for students who do not know others in the class. If students will be selecting their own groups, offer several small group activities during the first three weeks of class and rotate the membership of these ad hoc groups so that students can get to know one another's interests and capabilities before forming study teams. See "Personalizing the Large Lecture," "Supplements and Alternatives to Lecturing," "Encouraging Student Participation in Discussion," and "The First Day of Class" for ideas on small group activities and how to help students get to know one another.

If your class is very large and letting students select their own groups seems too difficult, have students sign up for teams scheduled to meet at particular times. This means that students will form groups based solely on when they can regularly attend a study team meeting. Try to form the groups by sections rather than for the large lecture class overall. Students in the same section are more likely to know each other and feel a sense of responsibility for their study team. (Source: Walvoord, 1986)

Use a portion of class time for arranging study groups. Announce that study groups will be set up during the third or fourth week of the course. At that time, hand out a description of study teams and students' responsibilities, and let students talk among themselves to form groups or to sign up for scheduled time slots. Suggest that all members of the study team exchange phone numbers. Encourage the study teams to select one person as the convener who will let all members know where the group is to meet.

Devote a class session to study teams. Ask students to meet in their study teams to review course material or prepare for an upcoming exam or assignment. Use the time to check in with the groups to see how well they are operating. Some faculty regularly substitute study team meetings for lectures. To the extent possible, meet with a study team during an office hour or review the work of a study team sometime during the semester.

References

Beckman, M. "Collaborative Learning: Preparation for the Workplace and Democracy." *College Teaching*, 1990, *38*(4), 128–133.

Chickering, A. W., and Gamson, Z. F. (eds.), *Applying the Seven Principles for Good Practice in Undergraduate Education.* New Directions for Teaching and Learning, no. 47. San Francisco: Jossey-Bass, 1991.

Collier, K. G. "Peer-Group Learning in Higher Education: The Development of Higher-Order Skills." *Studies in Higher Education*, 1980, *5*(1), 55–62.

Connery, B. A. "Group Work and Collaborative Writing." *Teaching at Davis*, 1988, *14*(1), 2–4. (Publication of the Teaching Resources Center, University of California at Davis)

Cooper, J. "Cooperative Learning and College Teaching: Tips from the Trenches." *Teaching Professor*, 1990, *4*(5), 1–2.

Cooper, J., and Associates. *Cooperative Learning and College Instruction.* Long Beach: Institute for Teaching and Learning, California State University, 1990.

Fiechtner, S. B., and Davis, E. A. "Why Some Groups Fail: A Survey of Students' Experiences with Learning Groups." In A. Goodsell, M. Maher, V. Tinto, and Associates (eds.), *Collaborative Learning: A Sourcebook for Higher Education.* University Park: National Center on Postsecondary Teaching, Learning, and Assessment, Pennsylvania State University, 1992.

Goodsell, A., Maher, M., Tinto, V., and Associates (eds.). *Collaborative Learning: A Sourcebook for Higher Education.* University Park: National Center on Postsecondary Teaching, Learning, and Assessment, Pennsylvania State University, 1992.

Guskey, T. R. *Improving Student Learning in College Classrooms.* Springfield, Ill: Thomas, 1988.

Hendrickson, A. D. "Cooperative Group Test-Taking." *Focus*, 1990, *5*(2), 6. (Publication of the Office of Educational Development Programs, University of Minnesota)

Johnson, D. W., and Johnson, R. T. *Cooperation and Competition: Theory and Research*. Edina, Minn.: Interaction Books, 1989.

Johnson, D. W., Johnson, R. T., and Smith, K. A. *Cooperative Learning: Increasing College Faculty Instructional Productivity*. ASHE-ERIC Higher Education Report No. 4. Washington, D.C.: School of Education and Human Development, George Washington University, 1991.

Kohn, A. *No Contest: The Case Against Competition*. Boston: Houghton Mifflin, 1986.

Light, R. J. *The Harvard Assessment Seminars: Second Report*. Cambridge, Mass.: Harvard University, 1992.

McKeachie, W. J., Pintrich, P. R., Lin, Y.-G., and Smith, D.A.F. *Teaching and Learning in the College Classroom: A Review of the Research Literature*. Ann Arbor: National Center for Research to Improve Postsecondary Teaching and Learning, University of Michigan, 1986.

Rau, W., and Heyl, B. S. "Humanizing the College Classrooms: Collaborative Learning and Social Organization Among Students." *Teaching Sociology*, 1990, *18*(2), 141–155.

Sansalone, M. "Teaching Structural Engineering Through Case Studies and Competitions." *CUE*, 1989, *2*(2), 7. (Newsletter available from Cornell University, Ithaca, N.Y.)

Slavin, R. E. "Cooperative Learning." *Review of Educational Research*, 1980, *50*(2), 315–342.

Slavin, R. E. "When Does Cooperative Learning Increase Student Achievement?" *Psychological Bulletin*, 1983, *94*(3), 429–445.

Smith, K. A. "Cooperative Learning Groups." In S. F. Schmoberg (ed.), *Strategies for Active Teaching and Learning in University Classrooms*. Minneapolis: Office of Educational Development Programs, University of Minnesota, 1986.

"Study Groups Pay Off." *Teaching Professor*, 1991, *5*(7), 7.

Tiberius, R. G. *Small Group Teaching: A Trouble-Shooting Guide*. Toronto: Ontario Institute for Studies in Education Press, 1990.

Toppins, A. D. "Teaching by Testing: A Group Consensus Approach." *College Teaching*, 1989, *37*(3), 96–99.

Walvoord, B. F. *Helping Students Write Well: A Guide for Teachers in All Disciplines*. (2nd ed.) New York: Modern Language Association, 1986.

Whitman, N. A. *Peer Teaching: To Teach Is to Learn Twice*. Washington, D.C.: ASHE–ERIC Higher Education Report No. 4. Washington, D.C.: Association for the Study of Higher Education, 1988.

Role Playing and Case Studies

19

Role playing and case studies, which can be incorporated into almost any course, give students a chance to apply what they are learning.

In role-playing activities, you present to your students a realistic or hypothetical situation and a cast of characters. The students then improvise dialogue and actions to fit their views of the situation and the character they are playing. In a literature class, for example, students might be asked to play various characters responding to situations that occur after the end of a novel. In language classes, students can play the role of people in everyday situations such as someone ordering in a restaurant. In a city planning class, students might play the role of administrators and developers trying to resolve an issue about building on the waterfront.

The case study method originated in the teaching of law and medicine (Boehrer and Linsky, 1990) and has most often been extended to the teaching of business. Students are presented with a real-life problem that has been addressed by scholars, researchers, or practitioners. A good case study presents a realistic situation and includes the relevant background, facts, conflicts, and sequences of events—up to the point requiring a decision or action. As students analyze and discuss the case, they retrace and critique the steps taken by the key characters and try to deduce the outcome.

The following pointers show how role playing and case studies may be adapted for a wide variety of courses.

Role Playing

Begin informally. Divide the class into pairs and have all the pairs work simultaneously. For example, in a political science course ask all pairs to portray a petitioner seeking signatures on a proposition for district elections for the city council and a recalcitrant registered voter. As students become comfortable with role playing, have some students observe others.

Assign meaningful situations. Role playing works best when the situation involves some choice, decision, or conflict of motives. Draw situations from interpersonal conflicts, intergroup relations, moral conflicts, individual dilemmas, or historical or contemporary social problems (Fuhrmann and Grasha, 1983; McKeachie, 1986). For example, an architecture professor sets the context as follows:

> We have been talking about the responsibilities of architects, contractors, and owners. Let's look at a situation that involves all three. The setting is a retail store in a mall. The contractor is talking to the owner and the architect: "The drawings call for a special metal system for the display fixtures. The plumbing subcontractor says that since it is piping, it is her job to do it. The fixture subcontractor says that since it is not part of the shell, it is display, and it is his job to do. They are both unionized and threaten to walk off the project if they don't get that work." The architect responds, "It is not my responsibility to tell you how to get the work done." The owner announces, "I don't care who does it, but the store has to open next week, and I don't want to spend any more money." What happens next?

Students then assume the roles of architect, contractor, and owner to try to resolve the problem.

Brief the participants and observers. Inexperienced students need more detail and structure, but give all students some latitude in how they portray the characters. Cast roles against personality type. For example, consider asking a quiet student to play a dominating role. Also, consider asking people in adversary roles to switch places and play the role of the person they have been opposing. (Source: Christensen, Garvin, and Sweet, 1991)

Cut off the role play at a high point. If the situation does not call for consensus or a solution, stop the role playing before it languishes, even if students want to continue. This will make for livelier discussion. A typical role play might last five to ten minutes.

Plan a follow-up discussion to illuminate key issues raised by the role play. Here are some examples of general questions for analyzing a role play (adapted from Shannon, 1986, p. 35):

- How accurate were you at predicting the actions and reactions of the other players?

- What other approaches to resolving the situation could have been used?
- Would other approaches or decisions have been more effective? more satisfying? more realistic?
- How realistic was the situation as played? If it was not realistic or seemed over-simplified, what . . . [would have made it more accurate or true to life]?
- How did it feel to play this role?

Experiment with engaging the entire class in role playing. Frederick (1981) describes how to involve an entire class (up to thirty students) in role playing. As students walk into class, they find a card at their seat with the name of a historical or literary character. During the discussion that follows, they are to stay in character. In a large class, consider having groups of students simultaneously play the role of people in a particular situation (Erickson and Strommer, 1991). This approach involves more students in role playing, though it may complicate later discussion since everyone's experiences will be different. Another approach is to pose a particular problem and ask all students to assume essentially the same role, for example, the president's cabinet, a board of commissioners, or a group of consultants (Erickson and Strommer, 1991).

Case Studies

Prepare cases that are conducive to discussion. A good case poses a challenging problem. Cases can be detailed descriptions, running ten to twenty pages with supporting documentation, or they can be brief accounts of a specific problem in a paragraph or two. Cases can be gleaned from newspapers, magazine articles, journal reports, your experience, and the experiences of professionals and practitioners in your field. Long cases should be distributed in advance of the session in which they are discussed; short cases can be handed out at the beginning of class and read during the first few minutes. (Sources: Boehrer and Linsky, 1990; Erickson and Strommer, 1991; Olmstead, 1974)

Consult collections of case studies. Since preparing cases is time-consuming, you may want to begin by reviewing case studies developed by others to see if they are appropriate (adapted from Lang, 1986):

Christensen, C. R., and Hansen, A. J. *Teaching and the Case Method.* Boston: Harvard Business School, 1987. Cases related to teaching in colleges and universities.

Mandell, B. R., and Schram, B. *Human Services: An Introduction.* (2nd ed.) New York: Wiley, 1993. This text includes numerous cases.

Sasser, W. E., and others. *Cases in Operations Management: Analysis and Action.* Homewood, Ill.: Irwin, 1982. Business cases.

Silverman, R., and Welty, W. M. *Mainstreaming Exceptional Students: A Series of Cases.* New York: Center for Applied Research, Pace University, 1988. Cases related to educating students with disabilities.

HBS Case Services. Published by Harvard Business School, Boston, Mass., 02163. Cases in accounting, finance, general management, organizational behavior, marketing, and production and operations management.

Case Research Journal. Published by the North American Case Research Association, 1775 College Road, Columbus, Ohio, 43210. Business cases.

Kennedy School of Government, Harvard University. *Case Program Publication Series.* 79 John F. Kennedy Street, Cambridge, Mass., 02138. Cases in political analysis, policy analysis, and public management.

Select or prepare cases that are engaging. Research reported by Boehrer and Linsky (1990) and Lang (1986) has identified the features that characterize a good case study:

- Tells a "real" story
- Raises a thought-provoking issue
- Has elements of conflict
- Promotes empathy with the central characters
- Lacks an obvious or clear-cut right answer
- Encourages students to think and take a position
- Demands a decision
- Is relatively concise

True-to-life cases have an inherent appeal (this really occurred) and offer closure (this is finally what happened in the case), but hypothetical cases can also capture students' imagination and interest (Boehrer and Linsky, 1990). Hansen (1987b) offers practical advice on writing your own case studies. You can also engage students in writing cases. Zeakes (1989) describes such a procedure. He asks students to write up a medical case dealing with a parasite they have studied, emphasizing symptoms and pathology but not naming the parasite. Cases are exchanged and students try to identify the parasite described in each example.

Give students guidance on how to read and prepare to discuss a case. Experienced teachers recommend that you give students a list of study questions to guide them through the case. For example, you might ask students to examine the protagonist's actions up to the decision point, to identify the key events, or to specify what went wrong and why. Encourage students to form study groups to review the case before coming to class. Some teachers ask students to prepare a brief memo, due at the start of class, outlining their recommendations for action. You might also give students these tips on how to prepare for case discussions (adapted from Hansen, 1987a; McDaniel, n.d.):

- Skim the case quickly to get a general sense of the issues; then read the case carefully.
- Don't take everything in the case at face value. For example, just because the manager says communication is a problem does not necessarily mean that it is.
- Mentally prepare responses to the following questions: "Exactly what did Kady do?" "What might Kady have done, given what is practical and feasible?" "What will Kady do now?" "Why?" "What would you have done?" "What should have been done?"

(Sources: Boehrer and Linsky, 1990; Hansen, 1987a; McDaniel, n.d.)

Prepare yourself for leading a case study discussion. In addition to knowing the content of the case, plan how to get the discussion started, and draw up a set of questions you want to pose to students to highlight key points. Experienced teachers recommend these procedures for leading discussions on case studies:

- If the case has not been assigned in advance, hand out the case and instruct students to read it.
- Introduce the case (or ask a student to) by briefly summarizing the situation and reiterating the protagonist's dilemma. Do not at this point analyze the case or go beyond the facts presented.
- Ask: "Who would like to begin the analysis of the case by identifying one or two issues that it raises?" As students present their views, ask for clarification and reactions from other students. Keep a list on the board of all issues raised by the case for later, more in-depth discussion.

- If the discussion falters, ask appropriate questions: "What possibilities for action are there?" "What are the consequences of each?" "What should Mike do at the first decision point?" "How did Mike get into this predicament?" "If you were a friend of Mike's, what advice might you have given?" "What actions should be taken?" "What concepts, principles, or theories seem to follow from this analysis?"
- Consider asking groups of students to speak for different interests within the case.
- Consider staging a role-playing activity in which students assume the roles of various characters in the case study.
- Write noteworthy points on the board as the discussion progresses.
- If the case has a real-life conclusion, distribute the conclusion to students and hold a brief discussion on what transpired. Or encourage students to locate the original source to find out what happened. Compare the actual conclusion with the recommendations made during the discussion.
- At the conclusion of the discussion, summarize the key points and help students discuss how the content from the day's session relates to the rest of the course.

(Sources: Boehrer and Linsky, 1990; Hansen, 1987a; Lang, 1986; Olmstead, 1974; Welty, 1989)

Adopt a nondirective, facilitative role. In discussions of case studies, you will want to pose questions and guide the discussion toward points of major importance, but avoid lecturing or telling students the "right" answers. Use probes, questions, challenges, and rephrasing to help students analyze each case for themselves. As with other discussion activities, students should feel comfortable in openly speaking their mind. See "Leading a Discussion" and "Encouraging Student Participation in Discussion." (Sources: Boehrer and Linsky, 1990; Jacobson, 1984; Olmstead, 1974)

References

Boehrer, J., and Linsky, M. "Teaching with Cases: Learning to Question." In M. D. Svinicki (ed.), *The Changing Face of College Teaching*. New Directions for Teaching and Learning, no. 42. San Francisco: Jossey-Bass, 1990.

Christensen, C. R. "Teaching with Cases at the Harvard Business School." In C. R. Christensen and A. J. Hansen, *Teaching and the Case Method*. Boston: Harvard Business School, 1987.

Christensen, C. R., Garvin, D. A., and Sweet, A. (eds.) *Education for Judgment: The Artistry of Discussion Leadership.* Boston: Harvard Business School, 1991.

Erickson, B. L., and Strommer, D. W. *Teaching College Freshmen.* San Francisco: Jossey-Bass, 1991.

Frederick, P. "The Dreaded Discussion: Ten Ways to Start." *Improving College and University Teaching,* 1981, *29*(3), 109–114.

Fuhrmann, B. S., and Grasha, A. F. *A Practical Handbook for College Teachers.* Boston: Little, Brown, 1983.

Hansen, A. J. "Suggestions for Seminar Participants." In C. R. Christensen and A. J. Hansen, *Teaching and the Case Method.* Boston: Harvard Business School, 1987a.

Hansen, A. J. "Reflections of a Casewriter: Writing Teaching Cases." In C. R. Christensen and A. J. Hansen, *Teaching and the Case Method.* Boston: Harvard Business School, 1987b.

Jacobson, R. L. "College Teaching by the Case Method: Actively Involving Students Is the Aim." *Chronicle of Higher Education,* July 25, 1984, pp. 17, 20.

Lang, C. *Case Method Teaching in the Community Colleges.* Newton, Mass.: Education Development Center, 1986.

McDaniel, R. *Teaching with Cases.* Austin: Center for Teaching Effectiveness, University of Texas, n.d.

McKeachie, W. J. *Teaching Tips.* (8th ed.) Lexington, Mass.: Heath, 1986.

Olmstead, J. A. *Small-Group Instruction: Theory and Practice.* Alexandria, Va.: Human Resources Research Organization, 1974.

Shannon, T. M. "Introducing Simulation and Role-Play." In S. F. Schomberg (ed.), *Strategies for Active Teaching and Learning in University Classrooms.* Minneapolis: Office of Educational Development Programs, University of Minnesota, 1986.

Welty, W. M. "Discussion Method Teaching." *Change,* 1989, *21*(4), 40–49.

Zeakes, S. J. "Case Studies in Biology." *College Teaching,* 1989, *37*(1), 33–35.

20

Fieldwork

Field-based instruction combines academic inquiry with off-campus activities that enable students to learn by doing. Field-based instruction can take at least three forms (Wagner, n.d.): independent study in which students work on their own in a private or public organization, agency, or office; field-based academic courses that combine academic seminars with off-campus internships or research at designated field sites—typically students are assigned to different sites; and fieldwork assignments in which field exercises are incorporated into lecture or discussion courses. In all cases, students receive academic credit for their fieldwork.

Regardless of the form of field study, the goals are generally the same: to broaden, extend, and deepen the intellectual content of undergraduate instruction by integrating theory and practice in a particular subject area; to increase students' motivation to engage in academic work through the experience of applying knowledge; and to encourage students to develop their skills as independent scholars and researchers. Faculty who incorporate fieldwork into their courses report that this practice has enhanced their teaching experience and improved the quality of their instruction (Kendall and others, 1990).

A form of field studies, called service learning, emphasizes field projects that combine public service and academic studies; service and learning reinforce each other. While students are volunteering at a service agency or program, they study the historical, sociological, cultural, or political dimensions of the human needs that the agency addresses. For example, students working in a local food project might explore the economic, political, or social policies that contribute to or alleviate poverty and hunger. Service learning also emphasizes reciprocity between volunteers and agency clients, focusing on the insights each group has to offer the other. A two-volume work by Kendall and Associates (1990) offers an overview of service learning and practical advice for instructors. A growing number of universities and colleges are combining course work and community service to teach students about the responsibilities of citizenship (Mangan, 1992). Regardless of the type of field-based instruction you choose, the suggestions below are designed to help you address some of the administrative and logistical tasks associated with fieldwork and to help you plan experiences that will be worthwhile for your students.

General Strategies

Make learning the primary objective for any field experience. As Dewey (cited in Hutchings and Wutzdorff, 1988, p. 5) points out, "mere activity does not constitute experience." Nor does every experience promote educational growth. Field experiences are most likely to be academically and intellectually valid if they are carefully planned and monitored, structured to serve specific learning goals, and preceded by orientation and preparation. Students also need ongoing opportunities to reflect actively and critically on what they are learning from the field experience and to assess the results. (Source: Baker, 1991)

Become familiar with the field setting before placing or sending students. Learn enough about each setting to have a sense of what your students are likely to encounter. In addition, you will want to establish good contacts in each setting so that your students will be welcome in the future. Consult your campus career counseling office or community projects office for help in identifying field sites. National resources include the following:

- *National Directory of Internships* (1991), published by the National Society for Internships and Experiential Education (Raleigh, North Carolina), lists opportunities for placements in seventy-five academic fields in and outside the United States.
- *Volunteer USA* (1991), published by Fawcett Columbine, lists organizations that use volunteers.
- Campus Contact at Brown University is a consortium of two hundred colleges and universities engaged in linking community service to students' educational experiences.

Identify a specific project or set of activities for students to undertake. Do not simply turn students loose at a field site. Before assigning students to do extensive independent fieldwork or course-based fieldwork, meet with the agency or office representatives to determine the following:

- Their needs and objectives
- The products or outcomes that will result from the field experience
- Whether the project or activities fit your students' skills and academic needs and your learning goals
- Whether the project requires any funding and what the funding sources are
- What resources, if any, your department can provide (for example, photocopying)

For examples of student projects, see "Project Ideas for Combining Service and Learning for All Age Groups" (National Center for Service-Learning, 1990), which lists projects done by college students as part of their course work (for example, developing a system to help low-income people prepare tax returns; developing a plan to remove graffiti and stop vandalism at a high school). (Sources: Ramsay, 1990; Sand, 1986)

Plan projects or activities around the academic calendar. To avoid schedule conflicts, be sure that fieldwork experiences do not extend beyond the academic term or interfere with midterm breaks or final exams. (Source: Sand, 1986)

Draw up written agreements. Clarify the roles and responsibilities of both agency staff and your students. Written agreements might include guidelines on the agency's responsibilities to the students, including requirements for supervision and evaluation, and descriptions of the kind of work students will undertake. (Sources: Johnson Foundation, 1989; Sand, 1986)

Be aware of legal issues. Placing students in community settings has legal implications for the agency and the college or university. Goldstein (1990) describes the legal responsibilities of all parties and offers advice on topics such as liability for acts of students at field sites, liability for injuries, and legal implications for sponsoring organizations.

Students' Roles

Clarify the student's role. It is helpful for the student, faculty member, and field site personnel to have clear expectations of what the student will be doing at the field site. Written guidelines might include the following (Lipschutz and Long, 1983, p. 2):

- The learning objectives of the field study
- The responsibilities of the student (activities, observation, reports; number of hours)
- The means by which the student will integrate classroom learning and field experience
- Any requirements such as a fieldwork journal
- The means by which the field project will be evaluated and granted academic credit

Assess the knowledge and skills students bring to the project. As part of the preservice preparation, help students identify the skills that they will be bringing to their field placement. This self-assessment will help build students' confidence and help them identify weaknesses they need to work on to be effective in the field. (Source: Conrad and Hedin, 1990)

Ask students to keep a log or journal. The fieldwork journal should be both a record of daily activities and a compendium of reflection and ideas— an opportunity for students to write freely. Journals can also include a description or brief history of the agency, the role of different groups, the politics and economics of the situation, and other assigned topics (Lipschutz and Long, 1983). Examples of student logs are described in Wutzdorff and Hutchings (1988). Approaches to using journals are discussed in Zimmerman and others (1990).

Faculty Guidance of Student Fieldwork

Connect field experiences directly with academic inquiry. Develop explicit incremental tasks for students to complete in their field settings that will give them a chance to reflect critically on their experiences. For example, first ask students to record their detailed observations, then ask them to undertake structured interviews, and finally ask students to develop research designs to test theories or hypotheses.

Take the lead in organizing field projects, if needed. With large classes, tight schedules, or inexperienced students, you will need to provide more structure and guidance. Prepare a handout that describes the scope of the project, the purpose, the activities, the expectations of the agency, your expectations, and the deadlines. If time allows and your students have already done fieldwork, give student teams time to prepare a proposal for carrying out the project or activities. The amount of guidance you provide depends on the level of the students, the complexity of the activities, and the timetable. Some faculty recommend outlining for students the steps needed to carry out the project. (Source: Sand, 1986)

Give students explicit assignments. For example, if students are keeping a journal, ask them to focus on a particular issue for each week: list your learning goals; observe and describe the kind of clients your agency or organization seeks to serve; draw a map of the agency, indicating how the office layout encourages or inhibits various kinds of communication; describe what you did in your placement today and your reactions; reflect on your progress in achieving your learning goals.

Students in an introductory sociology course were assigned four questions for their fieldwork assignments (Office of Instructional Development, 1991, p. 1):

- How would you describe the culture of the agency, its employees, and the people it serves?
- What values seem important to the people who work in the organization, and how do they differ from those of the organization itself?
- Is there any relationship between participants' ethnicity or race and the roles they play in the organization?
- Analyze the role of your agency in promoting social change in the community and explain why you think it will or will not be successful in achieving its goals.

Here is another example of a journal exercise (Conrad and Hedin, 1990, p. 93):

- Describe an incident or situation in which you were not sure what to do or say.
- What's the first thing you thought of to do (or say)?
- List three other actions you might have taken (or things you might have said).
- Which of the above seems best to you now? Why?
- What do you think is the real problem in the situation? Why do you think it came up?

Provide students with the assistance they need to complete assignments. For example, if your students are going to write about their initial impressions of a field setting, direct them to the work of social scientists or novelists who have described other settings. If students are expected to conduct a series of interviews, give them information about the methodology of interviewing and a few examples of particularly effective interviews. (Source: Wagner, n.d.)

Provide students with ongoing opportunities for critical analysis of their field experiences. If field activities are part of a lecture class, devote some class time to discussing students' fieldwork. Ask students to present brief reports about their field activities, and encourage groups of students involved in similar placements to relate field observations to course topics. Group discussions are ideal opportunities for students to share their concerns, problems, accomplishments, and insights and learn from one another. (Sources: Johnson Foundation, 1989; Wagner, n.d.)

Familiarize the field supervisor with the aims and purposes of your course. In many ways field supervisors are second teachers for students engaged in field-based learning. Keep them informed about the course through phone calls or correspondence. As appropriate, invite field supervisors to class sessions, either as speakers or as guests. (Source: Wagner, n.d.)

Establish procedures for ongoing contact and review. Plan to meet with or telephone agency staff at key points during the term. If appropriate, provide or request written status reports.

Establish quality-control procedures. Remind students that they are seen as representatives of their college at the field site and that their projects and activities may be made public. Monitoring and review are essential to make sure that final products are up to classroom standards and appropriate for public distribution.

Develop contingency plans. If students encounter major difficulties, offer some alternatives: scaling down the tasks or scope of activities, for example. But don't let performance problems drag on. If a student persistently fails to meet deadlines, offers repeated excuses, or simply flakes off, terminate the student's involvement in the placement because such behavior hurts everyone's credibility. (Source: Sand, 1986)

Evaluation of Fieldwork Experiences

Evaluate the academic work that the student has produced in response to field experience, not the experience itself. Some students may expect to receive credit simply for having spent the required number of hours at the field site. However, the standard is not time spent but whether the student has developed an informed understanding as a result of the experience. Put another way, students are not getting credit for the field experience but for what they have learned as a result of that experience. (Source: Wagner, n.d.)

Evaluate students' journals. Criteria for evaluating or grading students' journals may include accuracy of entries, thoroughness, originality, and range of issues addressed (Zimmerman and others, 1990). It is helpful to let students know at the beginning of the term how their journals will be evaluated. You may also want to give students examples or models. For suggestions on how to respond to students' writing, see "Evaluating Students' Written Work."

Use a variety of ways to evaluate students' learning. For example, write exam questions that ask students to demonstrate familiarity with a body of literature or relate course readings to their field experiences. In class discussions, have students relate their understanding of the issues of the course to a critical analysis of their field experience. Ask students to write a "tip sheet" for students who may be placed in the same agency next semester. Or assign a report on a particular problem or issue facing the agency or service or a critical essay about the fieldwork. Term papers on fieldwork can be evaluated according to conventional academic criteria: Are the essential aspects of the topic related to the existing literature? Does the student's experience lead to an informed understanding of the theory? Is the focus of the paper appropriate to the observations on which it is based? (Sources: Conrad and Hedin, 1990; Wagner, n.d.)

Check in with field supervisors. After the fieldwork has ended, meet with representatives from the agency or office to discuss their response to your students' activities or projects. Ask for their comments on how to improve students'—and their own—experiences.

References

Baker, B. "Group Equates Service with Education and Experience." *National On-Campus Report*, 1991, *19*(16), 3.

Conrad, D., and Hedin, D. "Learning from Service: Experience Is the Best Teacher, or Is It?" In J. C. Kendall and Associates (eds.), *Combining Service and Learning: A Resource Book for Community and Public Service.*

Vol. 1. Raleigh, N.C.: National Society for Internships and Experiential Education, 1990.

Goldstein, M. B. "Legal Issues in Combining Service and Learning." In J. C. Kendall and Associates (eds.), *Combining Service and Learning: A Resource Book for Community and Public Service*. Vol. 2. Raleigh, N.C.: National Society for Internships and Experiential Education, 1990.

Hutchings, P., and Wutzdorff, A. "Experiential Learning Across the Curriculum: Assumptions and Principles." In P. Hutchings and A. Wutzdorff (eds.), *Knowing and Doing: Learning Through Experience*. New Directions for Teaching and Learning, no. 35. San Francisco: Jossey-Bass, 1988.

Johnson Foundation. *Principles of Good Practice for Combining Service and Learning*. Racine, Wis.: Johnson Foundation, 1989.

Kendall, J. C., and Associates (eds.). *Combining Service and Learning: A Resource Book for Community and Public Service*. 2 vols. Raleigh, N.C.: National Society for Internships and Experiential Education, 1990.

Kendall, J. C., and others. "Increasing Faculty Involvement." In J. C. Kendall and Associates (eds.), *Combining Service and Learning: A Resource Book for Community and Public Service*. Vol. 2. Raleigh, N.C.: National Society for Internships and Experiential Education, 1990.

Lipschutz, M., and Long, R. "The Field Studies Development Program at UCLA." *The TA at UCLA Newsletter*, Winter 1983, p. 10.

Mangan, K. S. "In Dallas' Inner City, SMU Students Live Out Their Book Learning." *Chronicle of Higher Education*, Nov. 4, 1992, p. A28.

National Center for Service-Learning. "Project Ideas for Combining Service and Learning for All Age Groups." In J. C. Kendall and Associates (eds.), *Combining Service and Learning: A Resource Book for Community and Public Service*. Vol. 2. Raleigh, N. C.: National Society for Internships and Experiential Education, 1990.

Office of Instructional Development. "Integrating Community Service into the Curriculum." *Notes on Teaching at UCLA*, 1991, *11*, 1–2.

Ramsay, W. R. "Establishing Agency Relations." In J. C. Kendall and Associates (eds.), *Combining Service and Learning: A Resource Book for Community and Public Service*. Vol. 2. Raleigh, N. C.: National Society for Internships and Experiential Education, 1990.

Sand, P. "Organizing Community Studies." In S. F. Schomberg (ed.), *Strategies for Active Teaching and Learning in University Classrooms*. Minneapolis: Office of Educational Development Programs, University of Minnesota, 1986.

Wagner, J. *Teaching Students to Learn from Field Experience: A Guide for Berkeley Faculty*. Berkeley: Field Studies Program, University of California, n.d.

Wutzdorff, A., and Hutchings, P. "An Integrating Seminar: Bringing Knowledge and Experience Together." In P. Hutchings and A. Wutzdorff (eds.), *Knowing and Doing: Learning Through Experience*. New Directions for Teaching and Learning, no. 35. San Francisco: Jossey-Bass, 1988.

Zimmerman, J., and others. "Journals: Diaries for Growth." In J. C. Kendall and Associates (eds.), *Combining Service and Learning: A Resource Book for Community and Public Service*. Vol. 2. Raleigh, N. C.: National Society for Internships and Experiential Education, 1990.

VI.

Enhancing Students' Learning and Motivation

Helping Students Learn

21

Researchers in cognitive and instructional psychology, learning, and motivation have proposed various hypotheses, models, and theories about learning, intellectual development, and information processing. This research is reshaping how we think about learning. Above all, learning is an active, constructive process that is contextual: new knowledge is acquired in relation to previous knowledge; information becomes meaningful when it is presented in some type of framework. In addition, the acquisition and application of knowledge benefit from social interaction. Questions about student learning can be grouped into four categories (Davidson and Ambrose):

1. How do students select, acquire, and construct knowledge?
2. How do students integrate and maintain knowledge?
3. How do students retrieve knowledge when they have to use it?
4. How do students develop effective learning skills?

The ideas presented below provide an overview of selected research findings and their application to improving instruction. See also "Motivating Students," "Explaining Clearly," "Learning Styles and Preferences," and the various tools on lecturing and discussion for additional ideas on ways to strengthen students' learning.

Promoting Students' Intellectual Development

Become familiar with models of intellectual development. William Perry (1970) has conceptualized college students' intellectual development as a series of nine stages commonly grouped into four substages. The earliest stages are dominated by either-or thinking (dualism). Students at these stages believe that there is a single right answer, that knowledge is a set of truths, that professors are authorities who know all the right answers, and that teaching consists of a professor giving authoritative explanations to students. Belenky, Clinchy, Goldberger, and Tarule (1986), in examining women's epistemological development, describe this situation as "received knowledge," a dependence upon authority. As Erickson and Strommer (1991) point out, students at these levels become uneasy when they are asked to think independently, draw their own conclusions, or state their own points of view. They are also uneasy when authorities disagree.

Gradually, students begin to revise their thinking as they encounter more areas of disagreement among authorities, compare different interpretations, and realize that on some topics no one has definitive answers. In these next stages (which Perry, 1970, calls multiplicity and Belenky, Clinchy, Goldberger, and Tarule, 1986, call subjective knowledge), knowledge no longer consists of right and wrong answers; knowledge becomes a matter of educated opinion. Faculty are now viewed as people with opinions, and students are also entitled to have opinions. All opinions are initially deemed equally valid. This mode of thinking is dominant among college students (Kurfiss, 1988).

Students' thinking begins to change again after faculty repeatedly ask them for evidence to support their points of view. As students learn to distinguish weak evidence from strong, they also come to see that knowledge is contextual and situational. What one "knows" is relative and affected by one's values, assumptions, and perspectives (relativism/procedural knowledge). Ambiguity is a part of life. Faculty are now viewed as experienced resources, who teach specialized procedures for reasoning and who can help students learn the skillful use of analytic methods to explore alternative points of view and make viable comparisons.

At the final positions, students begin to take their own stands on issues on the basis of their own analysis, which they realize reflects their values, experience, and knowledge. Perry calls this "commitment in relativism," reflecting the need to take a position and make a commitment. Belenky, Clinchy, Goldberger, and Tarule (1986) describe this level as constructed knowledge, integrating knowledge learned from others with knowledge learned from self-experience and self-reflection. (Sources: Belenky, Clinchy, Goldberger, and Tarule, 1986; Erickson and Strommer, 1991; Perry, 1970; Tiberius, 1990)

Gear your teaching to appropriate phases of intellectual development.
Students in introductory courses tend to need more structure; they are more likely to want the "right" answers and clear guidelines, and many may have little tolerance for open-ended discussions. When you assign grades to

student essays or papers, be explicit about your criteria so students do not view them as simply "your opinion." (Sources: Erickson and Strommer, 1991; Tiberius, 1990)

Plan activities that will help students move to higher levels of cognitive development. For example, if your freshman students complain about your refusal to give simple yes-or-no answers to complex problems or if they are uneasy about assignments that require independent thought, try to help them see beyond "the right answer."

Here are some suggestions, keyed to Perry's (1970) model (adapted from Schmidt and Davidson, 1983, and cited in Tiberius, 1990, pp. 44–47):

- *To help students appreciate other points of view*: challenge students' clichés; require them to provide evidence in support of their opinions; reinforce the value of entertaining competing points of view; support students in their growing awareness that it is all right to change their minds on the basis of rational arguments.
- *To help students evaluate different points of view*: encourage students to appreciate why some points of view are logically stronger than others; help students appreciate why authorities disagree; identify criteria for judging between conflicting points of view; divide arguments into component parts; emphasize that not all evidence is equally valid.
- *To help students understand the process of making judgments*: encourage students to rethink their decisions whenever conditions change and new information comes to light; discuss how to make decisions when information is uncertain; explain reasoned judgment; encourage probabilistic statements.

Create assignments that entail the development of alternative perspectives. To prod students beyond the either-or stage, a professor of biology asks his students to complete worksheets based on the assigned readings and has his class discuss the worksheets in small groups (five to seven students). Each worksheet asks students to (a) summarize the author's overall argument and list each of the major points, (b) list the criteria that should be used to evaluate the adequacy of the author's arguments, (c) evaluate the overall argument and the major points against the list of criteria, and (d) decide whether to accept, reject, or withhold judgment on the adequacy of each major point and the overall argument. (Source: Grasha, 1990)

Include real-world experiences in your courses. Internships, fieldwork, and hands-on activities provide a bridge between abstract and concrete learning and can free some students from strongly held or simplistic positions. (Source: Kurfiss, 1988)

Be sensitive to students' struggles. Students may need guidance, empathy, and understanding as they face the anxiety of appreciating multiple points of views, making wrong decisions, and dealing with uncertainties that lie beyond either-or thinking. (Sources: Kurfiss, 1988; Schmidt and Davidson, 1983; Tiberius, 1990)

Helping Students Contextualize New Information

Allow for the fact that different students learn, think, and process information in different ways. Because learning is a highly individual process, based on personal constructions of meaning, students vary in how they learn—and how long they take to learn—something. These differences are more noticeable when the new information is abstract and complex rather than simple and concrete. Moreover, learners do not make uniform progress. Sometimes students reach plateaus and their rate of learning slows down. Research also suggests that men and women may differ in "ways of knowing" and that women may respond better to certain types of learning strategies, such as small group discussion and experiential learning activities. (Sources: American Psychological Association, 1992; Belenky, Clinchy, Goldberger, and Tarule, 1986; Eble, 1988; Lowman, 1984; McCombs, 1991)

Let students know what they are expected to learn. Alert your students to the key concepts of the course and to the most important points in a session ("Now, this is really critical").

Give students a framework within which to fit new facts. Students need a meaningful structure for organizing core concepts and acquiring and integrating knowledge. Use outlines, study questions, or study guides to provide a broad conceptual framework or structure for related concepts. When you are lecturing, write an outline on the board or prepare a handout. (Sources: American Psychological Association, 1992; McKeachie, 1986; McKeachie, Pintrich, Lin, and Smith, 1986; Svinicki, 1991)

Remember that students' previous knowledge exerts a powerful influence on what they will learn in your course. When learners encounter new material, they place it in the framework of what they already know about the subject. This framework also affects which aspects of the new material they pay attention to and how they organize that new material. If material in your course conflicts with students' earlier understandings or firmly held assumptions, they may distort the new information so that it will fit into their old framework. (Sources: American Psychological Association, 1992; Pintrich, 1988)

Present material in ways that are meaningful to students. If you can relate what you are teaching to something already meaningful, relevant, or important to students, they are more likely to understand and remember the new material. In small classes you may be able to tailor your examples to your students' interests and backgrounds. In all courses, you can encourage students to draw connections between what they already know and what they are learning. (Sources: American Psychological Association, 1992; Erickson and Strommer, 1991; Lowman, 1984; McKeachie, 1986; Svinicki, 1991)

Limit the amount of information you present. Students can absorb only a small amount of new information at a time. So try to limit the number of new points you make in any single presentation to three or four.

Stress concepts, not facts. Broad concepts are more easily understood and remembered and are more meaningful than facts or details. If you stress the key concepts and forgo bits of data and information, your students won't feel overwhelmed by details. (Source: Ericksen, 1969)

Helping Students Retain and Retrieve New Information

Provide opportunities for active learning. Students learn best by doing, writing, discussing, or taking action, because active learning situations provide opportunities for students to test out what they have learned and how thoroughly they understand it. For example, discussions give students a chance to check their thinking with each other and to articulate their ideas clearly enough to prevent being misunderstood. Provide frequent opportunities for students to actively restate or apply key concepts. The more frequently students apply new concepts to different situations, the better they will be able to remember and use those new concepts. So, don't tell students when you can show them, and don't show them when they can do it themselves. Let students summarize, paraphrase, or generalize about the important ideas in your class through group discussions, skits, role playing, simulations, case studies, and written assignments. (Sources: American Psychological Association, 1992; Lowman, 1984; McKeachie, 1986)

Encourage cooperation and group work: students teaching students.
Learning is enhanced by social interaction. In fact, explaining material to
another student helps reinforce the explainer's learning. Collaborative team-
work and projects undertaken by heterogeneous groups encourage higher-
order thinking and problem solving. (Sources: American Psychological
Association, 1992; McCombs, 1991)

**Present material in class in ways that encourage students to take
notes.** Note taking increases students' attention in class, and reviewing
notes increases students' performance on tests. Present material in class in
ways that encourage students to take detailed notes: speak slowly to give
students time to write; provide general outlines so students do not have to
figure out the organizational pattern while they're taking notes. Give students specific suggestions on how to take notes in your class. For example, let
students know what the important points are ("Be sure to underline this
concept"). Tell students how to decide what to record from your board work.
(See "Chalkboards".) Provide students opportunities to review their notes:
"Remember when we discussed the Grand Unification Theory? You should
have that in your notes. What do you have written down?" Or stop five
minutes before the session ends and ask students to review their notes and
highlight or underline key concepts. (Sources: Carrier, 1983; Kiewra, 1987;
"Note-Taking Behaviors Prescribe Note-Giving Practices," 1987)

**Give students specific pointers about what they are doing well and
what they are doing poorly.** Frequent, immediate, and specific feedback
helps students learn. Focus your comments on one or two items at a time.
Constructive criticism and evidence of progress help sustain students' motivation to learn and to struggle onward on a task. In addition to making
comments to individual students, you can photocopy examples of good
papers or hand out solutions to problem sets so that students can compare
their performance to a standard. Most students tend to increase their effort
in response to praise and encouragement rather than reprimands. (Sources:
American Psychological Association, 1992; Lowman, 1984)

Helping Students Develop Effective Learning Skills

Teach students how to select effective learning strategies. Students
who understand the demands of a given learning task and who consciously
select appropriate learning strategies learn more effectively. Research shows
that learning strategies can be taught to students (McKeachie, Pintrich, Lin,
and Smith, 1986). You can help your students become more self-reflective

and self-regulated learners by coaching them on how to improve their reading comprehension and retention, how to take notes, how to participate in class discussions, and how to study for tests. Davidson and Ambrose offer the following advice to faculty who want to help students develop effective learning strategies:

- Give students opportunities to rehearse new information through repetition.
- Help students set goals for the amount of material to be studied.
- Explain the value of skimming prior to careful reading.
- Stress the importance of generating questions about the material both to focus study efforts and to identify what is known and not known.
- Give students guidelines for when to seek help from teachers, tutors, and other students.

References

American Psychological Association. *Learner-Centered Psychological Principles: Guidelines for School Redesign and Reform.* Washington D.C.: American Psychological Association, 1992.

Belenky, M. F., Clinchy, B. M., Goldberger, N. R., and Tarule, J. M. *Women's Ways of Knowing: The Development of Self, Body, and Mind.* New York: Basic Books, 1986.

Carrier, C. A. "Note-Taking Research: Implications for the Classroom." *Journal of Instructional Development*, 1983, 6(3), 19–26.

Davidson, C. I., and Ambrose, S. A. "An Introductory Guide to Teaching and Research." Unpublished manuscript.

Eble, K. E. *The Craft of Teaching.* (2nd ed.) San Francisco: Jossey-Bass, 1988.

Ericksen, S. C. "Learning Theory and the Teacher." *Memo to the Faculty*, no. 33. Ann Arbor: Center for Research on Learning and Teaching, University of Michigan, 1969.

Erickson, B. L., and Strommer, D. W. *Teaching College Freshmen.* San Francisco: Jossey-Bass, 1991.

Grasha, T. "The Naturalistic Approach to Learning Styles." *College Teaching*, 1990, 38(3), 106–113.

Kiewra, K. A. "Notetaking and Review: The Research and Its Implications." *Instructional Science*, 1987, 16(3), 233–249.

Kurfiss, J. G. *Critical Thinking*. ASHE-ERIC Higher Education Report No. 2. Washington, D.C.: Association for the Study of Higher Education, 1988.

Lowman, J. *Mastering the Techniques of Teaching*. San Francisco: Jossey-Bass, 1984.

McCombs, B. L. "Motivation and Lifelong Learning." *Educational Psychologist*, 1991, *26*(2), 117–127.

McKeachie, W. J. *Teaching Tips*. (8th ed.) Lexington, Mass.: Heath, 1986.

McKeachie, W. J., Pintrich, P. R., Lin, Y.-G., and Smith, D.A.F. *Teaching and Learning in the College Classroom: A Review of the Research Literature*. Ann Arbor: National Center for Research to Improve Postsecondary Teaching and Learning, University of Michigan, 1986.

"Note-Taking Behaviors Prescribe Note-Giving Practices." *Teaching Professor*, 1987, *1*(7), 6.

Perry, W. G., Jr. *Forms of Intellectual and Ethical Development in the College Years*. New York: Holt, Rinehart & Winston, 1970.

Pintrich, P. R. "Student Learning and College Teaching." In R. E. Young and K. E. Eble (eds.), *College Teaching and Learning: Preparing for New Commitments*. New Directions for Teaching and Learning, no. 33. San Francisco: Jossey-Bass, 1988.

Schmidt, J. A., and Davidson, M. L. "Helping Students Think." *Personnel and Guidance Journal*, 1983, *61*(9), 563–569.

Svinicki, M. D. "Practical Implications of Cognitive Theories." In R. J. Menges and M. D. Svinicki (eds.), *College Teaching: From Theory to Practice*. New Directions for Teaching and Learning, no. 45. San Francisco: Jossey-Bass, 1991.

Tiberius, R. G. *Small Group Teaching: A Trouble-Shooting Guide*. Toronto: Ontario Institute for Studies in Education Press, 1990.

Learning Styles and Preferences

22

The term *learning styles* refers to individuals' characteristic and preferred ways of gathering, interpreting, organizing, and thinking about information. Some students prefer to work independently, while others do better in groups. Some students prefer to absorb information by reading, others by active manipulation. No one style of learning has been shown to be better than any other, and no single style leads to better learning. For college instructors, understanding learning styles is useful for three reasons. First, knowing about learning styles may help you understand and explain the differences you observe among students. Second, you may want to develop a range of teaching strategies to build on the different strengths individual students bring to the classroom. Third, knowing how students differ may help you help your students expand their repertoire of learning strategies.

Researchers Claxton and Murrell (1987) have grouped various models of learning styles into four general categories. *Personality models* refer to basic personality characteristics (for example, extrovert versus introvert). *Information-processing* models reflect how people take in and process information (for example, holistic manner—seeking overall understanding—versus serial manner—adopting a step-by-step approach). *Social-interaction models* focus on how students interact and behave in the classroom (for example, learning oriented versus grade oriented). *Instructional preference models* focus on the medium in which learning occurs (for example, listening, reading, direct experience). At least sixteen models of learning styles (Claxton and Murrell, 1987) and twenty cognitive dimensions (Messick and Associates, 1976; Grasha, 1984) have been postulated—well beyond the scope of this tool to discuss in detail. Instead, the focus here is on two of the better-researched models and their applications to improving instruction.

An understanding of learning styles and orientations may enhance your teaching effectiveness: students may be more satisfied and more productive if they are studying with methods compatible with their styles (Cross, 1976; Matthews, 1991). However, as Wilson (1981) points out, instructors should observe several cautions in making use of information about learning styles. First, be careful not to categorize a student as one specific type of learner. Researchers describe learners' consistent tendencies to use particular strategies but also note that learners may move from one style or orientation to another, depending on the situation (McKeachie, Pintrich, Lin, and Smith, 1986; Ramsden, 1988). Second, don't worry about matching your teaching to your students' learning style: that is both counterproductive and nearly impossible to do. Instead, use a variety of teaching activities and strategies to meet a broad range of student learning styles. Third, research on cognition reported by Pintrich (1988) suggests that it may be more relevant for you to focus on the cognitive processes students actually use when trying to learn, remember, and understand course material than for you to use personality or style variables.

Models of Learning Styles

Witkin's field independence and field sensitivity (a personality model). From experiments in visual pattern detection, researchers have described two broad categories of learners. *Field-independent* viewers are not distracted by the global complexities of a pattern in their effort to detect within that pattern a given geometric figure. *Field-sensitive* (formerly called field-dependent but renamed by Claxton and Murrell, 1987) viewers have more difficulty finding the geometric figure because they do not so easily ignore the visual "static" in the complex pattern. Using this distinction, researchers have generalized that field-independent learners tend to approach learning tasks analytically, looking at pieces of the whole or particular aspects of a concept or idea. They often prefer working alone. Field-sensitive learners tend to approach learning tasks more globally, viewing ideas in a larger context. These learners prefer small group work and discussion. As reported by Wilson (1981) and McKeachie, Pintrich, Lin, and Smith (1986), the entire concept of field independence has been criticized by researchers who argue that this model may be simply a measure of spatial ability under a new name. (Sources: Claxton and Murrell, 1987; Erickson and Strommer, 1991)

Kolb's learning cycle (an information-processing model). Kolb (1984) has identified four phases of learning, each of which entails different processes and abilities in acquiring new information or skills:

- *Concrete experience* (feeling): becoming fully involved in a new activity in order to understand it firsthand

- *Reflective observation* (watching): viewing experiences impartially or from many different perspectives
- *Abstract conceptualization* (thinking): creating concepts that integrate observations and experiences into theories and developing generalizable explanations or hypotheses
- *Active experimentation* (doing): using theories to make decisions and solve problems and testing and elaborating generalizations in different situations

Kolb maintains that new information is more meaningful and is retained longer when students work through all four phases of the learning cycle for each major concept or idea. Svinicki and Dixon (1987) suggest activities for each phase: Concrete experience is offered by films, games, fieldwork, lab work, and observation. Reflective observation can be achieved through journals, discussion, and questioning. Abstract conceptualization is developed from building models, writing papers, and creating analogies. Active experimentation includes case studies, projects, and simulations. Smith and Kolb (1986) describe a writing assignment that helps students move through the cycle by asking them to select an experience, either in or out of the classroom, and to do the following:

- Chronicle the details of the experience as it unfolds
- Reflect on their thoughts and feelings about the experience
- Develop a concept or "theory" to make sense of the experience or provide some insight
- Create an action plan based on their learning from the experience

By extending these four phases, Kolb (1984) identifies four learning styles: *Convergers* rely on abstract conceptualization and active experimentation; they like to find concrete answers and move quickly to find solutions to problems; they are good at defining problems and making decisions. *Divergers* use concrete experience and reflective observation to generate a range of ideas; they excel at brainstorming and imagining alternatives. *Assimilators* rely on abstract conceptualization and reflective observation; they like to assimilate a wide range of information and recast it into a concise logical form; they are good at planning, developing theories, and creating models. *Accommodators* are best at concrete experience and active experimentation; they often use trial-and-error or intuitive strategies to solve problems; they tend to take risks and plunge into problems.

In terms of classroom activities, convergers tend to prefer solving problems that have definite answers. Divergers may benefit more from discussion groups and working collaboratively on projects. Assimilators would feel most comfortable observing, watching role plays and simulations in class, and then generating concepts. Accommodators may prefer hands-on activities. (Sources: Claxton and Murrell, 1987; Erickson and Strommer, 1991; Fuhrmann and Grasha, 1983)

Helping Students Recognize Their Learning Styles

Ask students to observe their own learning styles and preferences. When students are trying to learn something new (for example, new computer software), ask them to notice what actions they take to acquire new information and skills. Encourage them to think about what kinds of activities they find most comfortable and most productive, or at the beginning of the term, ask students to write a brief essay about their most rewarding learning experience. (Sources: Fuhrmann and Grasha, 1983; Grasha, 1984, 1990)

Administer a short survey that students can score themselves. Fuhrmann and Grasha (1983, pp. 105–106) present an exercise and scoring key for determining field independence and field sensitivity. Kolb (1985) has developed a learning style inventory as a paper-and-pencil test that can be self-scored by students. Let students know that these questionnaires are not intended to typecast them but to help them become more aware of how they learn. (Sources: Bonham, 1989; Fuhrmann and Grasha, 1983; Grasha, 1984; Kolb, 1985)

Administer a checklist. Researchers have developed checklists that students can complete to help them understand how they have learned a specific skill or domain of knowledge. Items on the checklists include amount of time spent on learning; motivation for learning; learning processes employed — doing, observing, practicing; and cognitive processes used — analyzing information, using rules to guide thinking, forming principles. (Source: Grasha, 1990)

Have students interview each other about their learning processes. Suggest such questions as: How do you go about reading the assignments and preparing for class? How do you study for exams? How would you describe the learning that takes place in class? What is particularly helpful or not helpful to your learning the material? (Source: Katz, 1989)

Pose a problem for students to solve in a group. For example, the "Stuck Truck" is a small group exercise developed by Baker and Kolb (1980) in which students must figure out a quick and safe way to get a truck carrying hazardous waste material unstuck from under a highway overpass. Groups are given a list of items that could be used (for example, CB radio, tire jack) and are asked to rank order the items by their importance to solving the problem. Information is provided to instructors on how the exercise can be used to identify various learning styles and relate learning styles to problem solving. (Source: Baker and Kolb, 1980)

Use metaphors to help students identify their learning styles. Grasha (1990) asks students to think about a recent course that was effective or ineffective. Then students are asked to list the words, images, and feelings that they had about the course. Here are some examples of students' responses to ineffective courses (p. 112): *words*: repetitive, uninformative, boring, confusing; *images*: living in a foreign country, Mafia, jail; *feelings*: bored, frustrated, angry, stressful. Next, students develop a "guiding metaphor" that summarizes the words, images, and feelings. For ineffective courses, students generated these metaphors: "a bike without wheels," "a train on a circular track going nowhere," "a foreign movie without subtitles." Students next list specific classroom practices associated with the guiding metaphors. For example: "rambling style of presentation," "lectured without asking questions," "instructor talked over students' head." Finally, students are asked to list changes they would like to see in the course and the instructional implications of those changes. Example: "instructor ensures that students understand," "teacher solicits questions," "teacher explains concepts clearly." (Source: Grasha, 1990)

Accommodating Different Learning Styles

Recognize your own style and how it influences the way you teach. Teachers with more analytic styles may want to make an effort to develop explanations that will be clear to students whose styles are more intuitive and inductive. Teachers with strongly intuitive styles may want to develop course materials that draw on their analytic students' needs for definition and structure. (Source: "The Business of the Business," 1989)

But don't try to match your teaching methods to students' learning styles. There is no consensus in the research about whether matching teaching methods to learning styles increases learning; some research shows no measurable gains in matching instruction to students' learning preference. Further, it is frequently found that students with one style outperform others in a given course regardless of which teaching method is used. (Sources: Bonham, 1989; Grasha, 1984; O'Neil, 1990)

Be sensitive to the relationships of learning style, ethnicity, and gender. Some research suggests that there may be relationships between culture, conceptual systems, and learning styles (Anderson, 1988; Anderson and Adams, 1992; Chism, Cano, and Pruitt, 1989; Claxton and Murrell, 1987; Gordon, 1991). In addition, a student's previous educational experiences, family relationships, socioeconomic class, and academic environment all contribute to his or her learning style (Anderson, 1988). Research is sketchy and inconclusive, in part because most studies on learning styles have been done from a Western, white, middle-class perspective. Some researchers argue against linking style and culture because it could result in discriminatory treatment and lead to reinforcing stereotypes (O'Neil, 1990).

Vary your teaching strategies, assignments, and learning activities. For example, give students opportunities to do group work as well as to work alone. Provide options for assignments: written papers, oral reports, and videotapes. Present the same information in several modes (lecture, reading, audiovisual materials, and hands-on activities). (Sources: American Psychological Association, 1992; Chism, Cano, and Pruitt, 1989)

Give exams that call on students to think in different ways. Questions that ask students to give specific information or select the correct answer from alternatives call for convergent thinking. Open-ended essay questions call on students to generate solutions to problems and think in divergent ways. Questions that ask students to compare and contrast test assimilative thinking. Questions calling for practical application of theoretical principles support accommodative thinking. (Source: Claxton and Murrell, 1987)

Encourage students to value different learning styles and orientations. Students may prefer to work with people whose learning styles are similar to their own, but some research suggests that although students with the same style enjoy working together, they learn less effectively because they reinforce one another's weaknesses. Suggest to students that they can enrich their learning experiences and develop new strengths by working with a variety of learners. (Source: Bonham, 1989)

References

American Psychological Association. *Learner-Centered Psychological Principles: Guidelines for School Redesign and Reform.* Washington D.C.: American Psychological Association, 1992.

Anderson, J. A. "Cognitive Styles and Multicultural Populations." *Journal of Teacher Education*, 1988, *39*(1), 2–9.

Anderson, J. A., and Adams, M. "Acknowledging the Learning Styles of Diverse Student Populations: Implications for Instructional Design." In L.L.B. Border and N.V.N. Chism (eds.), *Teaching for Diversity*. New Directions for Teaching and Learning, no. 49. San Francisco: Jossey-Bass, 1992.

Baker, R. J., and Kolb, D. A. *The Stuck Truck*. Boston: McBer, 1980.

Bonham, L. A. "Using Learning Style Information, Too." In E. Hayes (ed.), *Effective Teaching Styles*. New Directions for Continuing Education, no. 43. San Francisco: Jossey-Bass, 1989.

"The Business of the Business." *Policy Perspectives*, 1989 *1*(entire issue 3). (Newsletter of the Higher Education Research Program, sponsored by the Pew Charitable Trusts)

Chism, N.V.N., Cano, J., and Pruitt, A. S. "Teaching in a Diverse Environment: Knowledge and Skills Needed by TAs." In J. D. Nyquist, R. D. Abbott, and D. H. Wulff (eds.), *Teaching Assistant Training in the 1990s*. New Directions for Teaching and Learning, no. 39. San Francisco: Jossey-Bass, 1989.

Claxton, C. S., and Murrell, P. H. *Learning Styles: Implications for Improving Educational Practices*. ASHE-ERIC Higher Education Report No. 4. Washington, D. C.: Association for the Study of Higher Education, 1987.

Cross, K. P. *Accent on Learning*. San Francisco: Jossey-Bass, 1976.

Erickson, B. L., and Strommer, D. W. *Teaching College Freshmen*. San Francisco: Jossey-Bass, 1991.

Fuhrmann, B. S., and Grasha, A. F. *A Practical Handbook for College Teachers*. Boston: Little, Brown, 1983.

Gordon, E. W. "Human Diversity and Pluralism." *Educational Psychologist*, 1991, *26*(2), 99–108.

Grasha, A. F. "Learning Styles: The Journey from Greenwich Observatory (1796) to the College Classroom (1984)." *Improving College and University Teaching*, 1984, *32*(1), 46–53.

Grasha, T. "The Naturalistic Approach to Learning Styles." *College Teaching*, 1990, *38*(3), 106–113.

Green, M. F. (ed.). *Minorities on Campus: A Handbook for Enriching Diversity*. Washington, D.C.: American Council on Education, 1989.

Katz, J. "Helping Faculty to Help Their Students Learn." In A. F. Lucas (ed.), *The Department Chairperson's Role in Enhancing College Teaching*. New Directions for Teaching and Learning, no. 37. San Francisco: Jossey-Bass, 1989.

Kolb, D. A. *Experiential Learning: Experiences as a Source of Learning and Development*. Englewood Cliffs: N. J.: Prentice-Hall, 1984.

Kolb, D. A. *Learning Style Inventory*. Boston: McBer, 1985.

McKeachie, W. J., Pintrich, P. R., Lin, Y.-G., and Smith, D.A.F. *Teaching and Learning in the College Classroom: A Review of the Research Literature*. Ann Arbor: National Center for Research to Improve Postsecondary Teaching and Learning, University of Michigan, 1986.

Matthews, D. B. "The Effects of Learning Style on Grades of First-Year College Students." *Research in Higher Education*, 1991, *32*(3), 253–268.

Messick, S., and Associates. *Individuality in Learning*. San Francisco: Jossey-Bass, 1976.

O'Neil, J. "Making Sense of Style." *Educational Leadership*, 1990, *48*(2), 4–9.

Pintrich, P. R. "Student Learning and College Teaching." In R. E. Young and K. E. Eble (eds.), *College Teaching and Learning: Preparing for New Commitments*. New Directions for Teaching and Learning, no. 33. San Francisco: Jossey-Bass, 1988.

Ramsden, P. "Context and Strategy: Situational Influences on Learning." In R. R. Schmeck (ed.), *Learning Strategies and Learning Styles*. New York: Plenum, 1988.

Smith, D. M., and Kolb, D. A. *User's Guide for the Learning Style Inventory*. Boston: McBer, 1986.

Svinicki, M. D., and Dixon, N. M. "Kolb Model Modified for Classroom Activities." *College Teaching*, 1987, *35*(4), 141–146.

Wilson, J. D. *Student Learning in Higher Education*. New York: Wiley, 1981.

Motivating Students

23

Some students seem naturally enthusiastic about learning, but many need — or expect — their instructors to inspire, challenge, and stimulate them: "Effective learning in the classroom depends on the teacher's ability . . . to maintain the interest that brought students to the course in the first place" (Ericksen, 1978, p. 3). Whatever level of motivation your students bring to the classroom will be transformed, for better or worse, by what happens in that classroom.

Unfortunately, there is no single magical formula for motivating students. Many factors affect a given student's motivation to work and to learn (Bligh, 1971; Sass, 1989): interest in the subject matter, perception of its usefulness, general desire to achieve, self-confidence and self-esteem, as well as patience and persistence. And, of course, not all students are motivated by the same values, needs, desires, or wants. Some of your students will be motivated by the approval of others, some by overcoming challenges.

Researchers have begun to identify those aspects of the teaching situation that enhance students' self-motivation (Lowman, 1984; Lucas, 1990; Weinert and Kluwe, 1987; Bligh, 1971). To encourage students to become self-motivated independent learners, instructors can do the following:

- Give frequent, early, positive feedback that supports students' beliefs that they can do well.
- Ensure opportunities for students' success by assigning tasks that are neither too easy nor too difficult.
- Help students find personal meaning and value in the material.
- Create an atmosphere that is open and positive.
- Help students feel that they are valued members of a learning community.

Research has also shown that good everyday teaching practices can do more to counter student apathy than special efforts to attack motivation directly

(Ericksen, 1978). Most students respond positively to a well-organized course taught by an enthusiastic instructor who has a genuine interest in students and what they learn. Thus activities you undertake to promote learning will also enhance students' motivation.

General Strategies

Capitalize on students' existing needs. Students learn best when incentives for learning in a classroom satisfy their own motives for enrolling in the course. Some of the needs your students may bring to the classroom are the need to learn something in order to complete a particular task or activity, the need to seek new experiences, the need to perfect skills, the need to overcome challenges, the need to become competent, the need to succeed and do well, the need to feel involved and to interact with other people. Satisfying such needs is rewarding in itself, and such rewards sustain learning more effectively than do grades. Design assignments, in-class activities, and discussion questions to address these kinds of needs. (Source: McMillan and Forsyth, 1991)

Make students active participants in learning. Students learn by doing, making, writing, designing, creating, solving. Passivity dampens students' motivation and curiosity. Pose questions. Don't tell students something when you can ask them. Encourage students to suggest approaches to a problem or to guess the results of an experiment. Use small group work. See "Leading a Discussion," "Supplements and Alternatives to Lecturing," and "Collaborative Learning" for methods that stress active participation. (Source: Lucas, 1990)

Ask students to analyze what makes their classes more or less "motivating." Sass (1989) asks his classes to recall two recent class periods, one in which they were highly motivated and one in which their motivation was low. Each student makes a list of specific aspects of the two classes that influenced his or her level of motivation, and students then meet in small groups to reach consensus on characteristics that contribute to high and low motivation. In over twenty courses, Sass reports, the same eight characteristics emerge as major contributors to student motivation:

- Instructor's enthusiasm
- Relevance of the material
- Organization of the course
- Appropriate difficulty level of the material

- Active involvement of students
- Variety
- Rapport between teacher and students
- Use of appropriate, concrete, and understandable examples

Incorporating Instructional Behaviors That Motivate Students

Hold high but realistic expectations for your students. Research has shown that a teacher's expectations have a powerful effect on a student's performance. If you act as though you expect your students to be motivated, hardworking, and interested in the course, they are more likely to be so. Set realistic expectations for students when you make assignments, give presentations, conduct discussions, and grade examinations. "Realistic" in this context means that your standards are high enough to motivate students to do their best work but not so high that students will inevitably be frustrated in trying to meet those expectations. To develop the drive to achieve, students need to believe that achievement is possible—which means that you need to provide early opportunities for success. (Sources: American Psychological Association, 1992; Bligh, 1971; Forsyth and McMillan, 1991; Lowman, 1984)

Help students set achievable goals for themselves. Failure to attain unrealistic goals can disappoint and frustrate students. Encourage students to focus on their continued improvement, not just on their grade on any one test or assignment. Help students evaluate their progress by encouraging them to critique their own work, analyze their strengths, and work on their weaknesses. For example, consider asking students to submit self-evaluation forms with one or two assignments. (Sources: Cashin, 1979; Forsyth and McMillan, 1991)

Tell students what they need to do to succeed in your course. Don't let your students struggle to figure out what is expected of them. Reassure students that they can do well in your course, and tell them exactly what they must do to succeed. Say something to the effect that "If you can handle the examples on these problem sheets, you can pass the exam. People who have trouble with these examples can ask me for extra help." Or instead of saying, "You're way behind," tell the student, "Here is one way you could go about learning the material. How can I help you?" (Sources: Cashin, 1979; Tiberius, 1990)

Strengthen students' self-motivation. Avoid messages that reinforce your power as an instructor or that emphasize extrinsic rewards. Instead of saying, "I require," "you must," or "you should," stress "I think you will find . . . ," or "I will be interested in your reaction." (Source: Lowman, 1990)

Avoid creating intense competition among students. Competition produces anxiety, which can interfere with learning. Reduce students' tendencies to compare themselves to one another. Bligh (1971) reports that students are more attentive, display better comprehension, produce more work, and are more favorable to the teaching method when they work cooperatively in groups rather than compete as individuals. Refrain from public criticisms of students' performance and from comments or activities that pit students against each other. (Sources: Eble, 1988; Forsyth and McMillan, 1991)

Be enthusiastic about your subject. An instructor's enthusiasm is a crucial factor in student motivation. If you become bored or apathetic, students will too. Typically, an instructor's enthusiasm comes from confidence, excitement about the content, and genuine pleasure in teaching. If you find yourself uninterested in the material, think back to what attracted you to the field and bring those aspects of the subject matter to life for your students. Or challenge yourself to devise the most exciting way to present the material, however dull the material itself may seem to you.

Structuring the Course to Motivate Students

Work from students' strengths and interests. Find out why students are enrolled in your course, how they feel about the subject matter, and what their expectations are. Then try to devise examples, case studies, or assignments that relate the course content to students' interests and experiences. For instance, a chemistry professor might devote some lecture time to examining the contributions of chemistry to resolving environmental problems. Explain how the content and objectives of your course will help students achieve their educational, professional, or personal goals. (Sources: Brock, 1976; Cashin, 1979; Lucas, 1990)

When possible, let students have some say in choosing what will be studied. Give students options on term papers or other assignments (but not on tests). Let students decide between two locations for the field trip, or have them select which topics to explore in greater depth. If possible, include optional or alternative units in the course. (Sources: Ames and Ames, 1990; Cashin, 1979; Forsyth and McMillan, 1991; Lowman, 1984)

Increase the difficulty of the material as the semester progresses. Give students opportunities to succeed at the beginning of the semester. Once students feel they can succeed, you can gradually increase the difficulty level. If assignments and exams include easier and harder questions, every student will have a chance to experience success as well as challenge. (Source: Cashin, 1979)

Vary your teaching methods. Variety reawakens students' involvement in the course and their motivation. Break the routine by incorporating a variety of teaching activities and methods in your course: role playing, debates, brainstorming, discussion, demonstrations, case studies, audiovisual presentations, guest speakers, or small group work. (Source: Forsyth and McMillan, 1991)

De-emphasizing Grades

Emphasize mastery and learning rather than grades. Ames and Ames (1990) report on two secondary school math teachers. One teacher graded every homework assignment and counted homework as 30 percent of a student's final grade. The second teacher told students to spend a fixed amount of time on their homework (thirty minutes a night) and to bring questions to class about problems they could not complete. This teacher graded homework as satisfactory or unsatisfactory, gave students the opportunity to redo their assignments, and counted homework as 10 percent of the final grade. Although homework was a smaller part of the course grade, this second teacher was more successful in motivating students to turn in their homework. In the first class, some students gave up rather than risk low evaluations of their abilities. In the second class, students were not risking their self-worth each time they did their homework but rather were attempting to learn. Mistakes were viewed as acceptable and something to learn from.

Researchers recommend de-emphasizing grading by eliminating complex systems of credit points; they also advise against trying to use grades to control nonacademic behavior (for example, lowering grades for missed classes) (Forsyth and McMillan, 1991; Lowman 1990). Instead, assign ungraded written work, stress the personal satisfaction of doing assignments, and help students measure their progress.

Design tests that encourage the kind of learning you want students to achieve. Many students will learn whatever is necessary to get the grades they desire. If you base your tests on memorizing details, students will focus on memorizing facts. If your tests stress the synthesis and evaluation of information, students will be motivated to practice those skills when they study. (Source: McKeachie, 1986)

Avoid using grades as threats. As McKeachie (1986) points out, the threat of low grades may prompt some students to work hard, but other students may resort to academic dishonesty, excuses for late work, and other counter-productive behavior.

Motivating Students by Responding to Their Work

Give students feedback as quickly as possible. Return tests and papers promptly, and reward success publicly and immediately. Give students some indication of how well they have done and how to improve. Rewards can be as simple as saying a student's response was good, with an indication of why it was good, or mentioning the names of contributors: "Cherry's point about pollution really synthesized the ideas we had been discussing." (Source: Cashin, 1979)

Reward success. Both positive and negative comments influence motivation, but research consistently indicates that students are more affected by positive feedback and success. Praise builds students' self-confidence, competence, and self-esteem. Recognize sincere efforts even if the product is less than stellar. If a student's performance is weak, let the student know that you believe he or she can improve and succeed over time. (Sources: Cashin, 1979; Lucas, 1990)

Introduce students to the good work done by their peers. Share the ideas, knowledge, and accomplishments of individual students with the class as a whole:

- Pass out a list of research topics chosen by students so they will know whether others are writing papers of interest to them.
- Make available copies of the best papers and essay exams.
- Provide class time for students to read papers or assignments submitted by classmates.
- Have students write a brief critique of a classmate's paper.
- Schedule a brief talk by a student who has experience or who is doing a research paper on a topic relevant to your lecture.

Be specific when giving negative feedback. Negative feedback is very powerful and can lead to a negative class atmosphere. Whenever you identify a student's weakness, make it clear that your comments relate to a particular task or performance, not to the student as a person. Try to cushion negative comments with a compliment about aspects of the task in which the student succeeded. (Source: Cashin, 1979)

Avoid demeaning comments. Many students in your class may be anxious about their performance and abilities. Be sensitive to how you phrase your comments and avoid offhand remarks that might prick their feelings of inadequacy.

Avoid giving in to students' pleas for "the answer" to homework problems. When you simply give struggling students the solution, you rob them of the chance to think for themselves. Use a more productive approach (adapted from Fiore, 1985):

- Ask the students for one possible approach to the problem.
- Gently brush aside students' anxiety about not getting the answer by refocusing their attention on the problem at hand.
- Ask the students to build on what they do know about the problem.
- Resist answering the question "Is this right?" Suggest to the students a way to check the answer for themselves.
- Praise the students for small, independent steps.

If you follow these steps, your students will learn that it is all right not to have an instant answer. They will also learn to develop greater patience and to work at their own pace. And by working through the problem, students will experience a sense of achievement and confidence that will increase their motivation to learn.

Motivating Students to Do the Reading

Assign the reading at least two sessions before it will be discussed. Give students ample time to prepare and try to pique their curiosity about the reading: "This article is one of my favorites, and I'll be interested to see what you think about it." (Sources: Lowman, 1984; "When They Don't Do the Reading," 1989)

Assign study questions. Hand out study questions that alert students to the key points of the reading assignment. To provide extra incentive for students, tell them you will base exam questions on the study questions. (Source: "When They Don't Do the Reading," 1989)

If your class is small, have students turn in brief notes on the day's reading that they can use during exams. At the start of each class, a professor in the physical sciences asks students to submit a 3″ × 5″ card with an outline, definitions, key ideas, or other material from the day's assigned reading. After class, he checks the cards and stamps them with his name. He returns the cards to students at a class session prior to the midterm. Students can then add any material they would like to the cards but cannot submit additional cards. The cards are again returned to the faculty member who distributes them to students during the test. This faculty member reports that the number of students completing the reading jumped from 10 percent to 90 percent and that students especially valued these "survival cards." (Source: Daniel, 1988)

Ask students to write a one-word journal or one-word sentence. Angelo (1991) describes the one-word journal as follows: students are asked to choose a single word that best summarizes the reading and then write a page or less explaining or justifying their word choice. This assignment can then be used as a basis for class discussion. A variation reported by Erickson and Strommer (1991) is to ask students to write one complex sentence in answer to a question you pose about the readings and provide three sources of supporting evidence: "In one sentence, identify the type of ethical reasoning Singer uses in his article 'Famine, Affluence, and Morality.' Quote three passages that reveal this type of ethical reasoning" (p. 125).

Ask nonthreatening questions about the reading. Initially pose general questions that do not create tension or feelings of resistance: "Can you give me one or two items from the chapter that seem important?" "What section of the reading do you think we should review?" "What item in the reading surprised you?" "What topics in the chapter can you apply to your own experience?" (Source: "When They Don't Do the Reading," 1989)

Use class time as a reading period. If you are trying to lead a discussion and find that few students have completed the reading assignment, consider asking students to read the material for the remainder of class time. Have them read silently or call on students to read aloud and discuss the key points. Make it clear to students that you are reluctantly taking this unusual step because they have not completed the assignment.

Prepare an exam question on undiscussed readings. One faculty member asks her class whether they have done the reading. If the answer is no, she says, "You'll have to read the material on your own. Expect a question on the next exam covering the reading." The next time she assigns reading, she reminds the class of what happened the last time, and the students come to class prepared. (Source: "When They Don't Do the Reading," 1989)

Give a written assignment to those students who have not done the reading. Some faculty ask at the beginning of the class who has completed the reading. Students who have not read the material are given a written assignment and dismissed. Those who have read the material stay and participate in class discussion. The written assignment is not graded but merely acknowledged. This technique should not be used more than once a term. (Source: "When They Don't Do the Reading," 1989)

References

American Psychological Association. *Learner-Centered Psychological Principles: Guidelines for School Redesign and Reform.* Washington, D.C.: American Psychological Association, 1992.

Ames, R., and Ames, C. "Motivation and Effective Teaching." In B. F. Jones and L. Idol (eds.), *Dimensions of Thinking and Cognitive Instruction.* Hillsdale, N. J.: Erlbaum, 1990.

Angelo, T. A. "Ten Easy Pieces: Assessing Higher Learning in Four Dimensions." In T. A. Angelo (ed.), *Classroom Research: Early Lessons from Success.* New Directions for Teaching and Learning, no. 46. San Francisco: Jossey-Bass, 1991.

Bligh, D. A. *What's the Use of Lecturing?* Devon, England: Teaching Services Centre, University of Exeter, 1971.

Brock, S. C. *Practitioners' Views on Teaching the Large Introductory College Course.* Manhattan: Center for Faculty Evaluation and Development, Kansas State University, 1976.

Cashin, W. E. "Motivating Students." *Idea Paper*, no. 1. Manhattan: Center for Faculty Evaluation and Development in Higher Education, Kansas State University, 1979.

Daniel, J. W. "Survival Cards in Math." *College Teaching*, 1988, *36*(3), 110.

Eble, K. E. *The Craft of Teaching.* (2nd ed.) San Francisco: Jossey-Bass, 1988.

Ericksen, S. C. "The Lecture." *Memo to the Faculty*, no. 60. Ann Arbor: Center for Research on Teaching and Learning, University of Michigan, 1978.

Erickson, B. L., and Strommer, D. W. *Teaching College Freshmen.* San Francisco: Jossey-Bass, 1991.

Fiore, N. "On Not Doing a Student's Homework." *Chemistry TA Handbook.* Berkeley: Chemistry Department, University of California, 1985.

Forsyth, D. R., and McMillan, J. H. "Practical Proposals for Motivating Students." In R. J. Menges and M. D. Svinicki (eds.), *College Teaching: From Theory to Practice*. New Directions in Teaching and Learning, no. 45. San Francisco: Jossey-Bass, 1991.

Lowman, J. *Mastering the Techniques of Teaching*. San Francisco: Jossey-Bass, 1984.

Lowman, J. "Promoting Motivation and Learning." *College Teaching*, 1990, *38*(4), 136–39.

Lucas, A. F. "Using Psychological Models to Understand Student Motivation." In M. D. Svinicki (ed.), *The Changing Face of College Teaching*. New Directions for Teaching and Learning, no. 42. San Francisco: Jossey-Bass, 1990.

McKeachie, W. J. *Teaching Tips*. (8th ed.) Lexington, Mass.: Heath, 1986.

McMillan, J. H., and Forsyth, D. R. "What Theories of Motivation Say About Why Learners Learn." In R. J. Menges and M. D. Svinicki (eds.), *College Teaching: From Theory to Practice*. New Directions for Teaching and Learning, no. 45. San Francisco: Jossey-Bass, 1991.

Sass, E. J. "Motivation in the College Classroom: What Students Tell Us." *Teaching of Psychology*, 1989, *16*(2), 86–88.

Tiberius, R. G. *Small Group Teaching: A Trouble-Shooting Guide*. Toronto: Ontario Institute for Studies in Education Press, 1990.

Weinert, F. E., and Kluwe, R. H. *Metacognition, Motivation and Understanding*. Hillsdale, N.J.: Erlbaum, 1987.

"When They Don't Do the Reading." *Teaching Professor*, 1989, *3*(10), 3–4.

VII.

Writing Skills and Homework Assignments

Helping Students Write Better in All Courses

24

Few faculty would deny the importance of writing in their academic discipline or the role writing plays in mastering material, shaping ideas, and developing critical thinking skills. Writing helps students learn the subject matter: they understand and retain course material much better when they write about it.

You don't have to be a writing specialist—or even an accomplished writer—to improve your students' writing skills, and you don't have to sacrifice hours of class time or grading time. The ideas that follow are designed to make writing more integral to your courses and less onerous to you and your students.

General Strategies

View the improvement of students' writing as your responsibility. Many faculty erroneously believe that teaching writing is the job of the English department or composition program alone. Not true! Writing is an essential tool for learning a discipline. Helping students improve their writing skills is therefore the responsibility of all faculty.

Let students know that you value good writing. Stress the importance of clear, thoughtful writing. As Elbow (1987) has noted, you can require competent writing without knowing how to teach composition. In general, faculty who tell students that good writing will be rewarded and poor writing will be penalized receive better essays than instructors who don't make such demands. In the syllabus, on the first day of class, and throughout the term, remind students that they must make their best efforts in expressing themselves on paper. Back up your statements with comments on early assignments that show you really mean it, and students will respond. (Source: Elbow, 1987)

Regularly assign brief writing exercises in your classes. Writing is a complex set of skills that requires continuous practice. You need not assign weekly papers to give students experience in writing. To vary the pace of a lecture course, ask students to write for a few minutes during class. Some mixture of in-class writing, outside writing assignments, and exams with open-ended questions will give students the practice they need to improve their skills. (Source: Tollefson, 1988)

Provide guidance throughout the writing process. After you have made an assignment, discuss the value of outlines and notes, explain how to select and narrow a topic, and critique first drafts. Define plagiarism as well; see "Preventing Academic Dishonesty." (Source: Tollefson, 1988)

Don't feel as though you have to read and grade every piece of your students' writing. Since students are writing primarily to learn a subject, it is better to have them write than not write, even if you cannot evaluate each piece of writing. Ask students to analyze each other's work during class, or ask them to critique their work in small groups. Or simply have students write for their own purposes, without any feedback. Students will learn that they are writing in order to think more clearly, not to obtain a grade. Keep in mind, too, that you can collect students' papers and skim their work. (Source: Watkins, 1990)

Find other faculty members who are trying to use writing more effectively in their courses. Share the writing assignments you have developed and discuss how students did on the assignments. Pool ideas about ways in which writing can help students learn more about the subject matter. See if there is sufficient interest to warrant drawing up writing guidelines for your discipline. Students welcome handouts that give them specific instructions on how to write papers for a particular course or in a particular subject area.

Teaching Writing When You Are Not an English Teacher

Remind students that writing is a process that helps us clarify ideas. Tell them that writing is a way of learning, not an end in itself. Let students know that none of us knows exactly what we think about a topic or issue until we put our views on paper. Also let students know that writing is a complicated, messy, nonlinear process filled with false starts. Help them identify the writer's key activities:

- Developing ideas
- Finding a focus and a thesis

- Composing a draft
- Getting feedback and comments from others
- Revising the draft by expanding ideas, clarifying meaning, reorganizing
- Editing
- Presenting the finished work to readers

Explain that writing is hard work. Share with your class your own struggles in grappling with difficult topics. If they know that writing takes effort, they won't be discouraged by their pace or progress. One faculty member shares with students a notebook that contains the chronology of one of his published articles: first ideas, successive drafts, submitted manuscript, reviewers' suggested changes, revised version, galley proofs, and published article (Professional and Organizational Development Network in Higher Education, 1989).

Give students opportunities to talk about their writing. Students need to talk about papers in progress so that they can formulate their thoughts, generate ideas, and focus their topics. It is also important for students to hear what their peers have written. Take five or ten minutes of class time for students to read their writing to each other in small groups or pairs or to talk about what they plan to write.

Encourage students to revise their work. Provide formal steps for revision. For example, ask students to submit first drafts of papers for your review or for peer critique. Or give students the option of revising and rewriting one assignment during the term for a higher grade. Faculty who extend this invitation to their students report that 10 to 40 percent of the students take advantage of it. (Source: Lowman, 1984)

Explain thesis statements. A thesis statement makes an assertion about some issue: "The savings and loan crisis resulted from the relaxation of government regulations." A common student problem is to write papers that have a diffuse thesis statement ("The savings and loan crisis has caused major problems") or papers that present overviews of facts with no thesis statement.

Stress clarity and specificity. Let students know that the more abstract and difficult the topic, the more concrete their language should be (Tollefson, 1988). Tell students that inflated language and academic jargon camouflage rather than clarify their point.

Explain the importance of grammar and sentence structure, as well as content. Don't let students fall back on the rationalization that only English teachers should be judges of grammar and style. Tell students you will be looking at both the quality of their writing and the content.

Distribute bibliographies and tip sheets on good writing practices. Check with your English department, composition program, or writing center to identify materials that can easily be distributed to students. Consider giving students a bibliography of writing guides, for example:

Crews, F. C. *Random House Handbook.* (6th ed.) New York: McGraw-Hill, 1992. A classic comprehensive textbook for college students. Well written and well worth reading.

Lanham, R. A. *Revising Prose.* (3rd ed.) New York: Scribner's, 1991. Techniques for eliminating bureaucratese and restoring energy to tired prose.

Tollefson, S. K. *Grammar Grams* and *Grammar Grams II.* New York: HarperCollins, 1989, 1992. Two short, witty guides that answer common questions about grammar, style, and usage. Both are fun to read.

Discipline-specific guides may also be useful. Petersen (1982) has a dated but good bibliography on writing in particular content areas. Other publications follow.

Science and Engineering

Barrass, R. *Scientists Must Write.* New York: Chapman and Hall, 1978.

Biddle, A. W., and Bean, D. J. *Writer's Guide: Life Sciences.* Lexington, Mass.: Heath, 1987.

Connolly, P., and Vilvardi, T. (eds.). *Writing to Learn Mathematics and Science.* New York: Teachers College Press, 1989.

Day, R. A. *How to Write and Publish a Scientific Paper.* (3rd ed.) Philadelphia: ISI Press, 1988.

Maimon, E. P., and others. *Writing in the Arts and Sciences.* Boston: Little, Brown, 1981.

Michaelson, R. *How to Write and Publish Engineering Papers and Reports.* Philadelphia: ISI Press, 1990.

Arts and Humanities

Barnet, S. *A Short Guide to Writing About Art.* Boston: Little, Brown, 1989.

Biddle, A. W., Steffens, H. J., Dickerson, M. J., and Fulwiler, T. *Writer's Guide: History.* Lexington, Mass.: Heath, 1987.

Goldman, B. *Reading and Writing in the Arts.* Detroit: Wayne State University Press, 1978.

Social Sciences

Biddle, A. W., Fulwiler, T., and Holland, K. M. *Writer's Guide: Psychology.* Lexington, Mass.: Heath, 1987.

Biddle, A. W., Holland, K. M., and Fulwiler, T. *Writer's Guide: Political Science.* Lexington, Mass.: Heath, 1987.

Lanham, R. A. *Revising Business Prose.* (3rd ed.) New York: Scribner's, 1991.

McCloskey, D. N. *The Writing of Economics.* New York: Macmillan, 1987.

Steward, J. S., and Smelstor, M. *Writing in the Social Sciences.* Glenview, Ill.: Scott, Foresman, 1984.

Tallent, N. *Psychological Report Writing.* (4th ed.) Englewood Cliffs, N.J.: Prentice-Hall, 1992.

Ask a composition instructor to give a presentation to your students. Invite a guest speaker to talk to your class about effective writing and common writing problems. Faculty who have invited experts from composition departments or student learning centers report that such presentations reinforce the values of the importance of writing.

Let students know about available tutoring services. Most campuses offer individual or group tutoring in writing. Distribute brochures or ask someone from the tutoring center to give a demonstration in your class.

Use computers to help students write better. Faculty are beginning to use commercially available and locally developed software to help students plan, write, and revise their written work. Some software lets instructors monitor students' work in progress and lets students collaborate with their classmates. Holdstein and Selfe (1990) and Hawisher and Selfe (1989) discuss computers and composition.

Assigning In-Class Writing Activities

Ask students to write what they know about a topic before you discuss it. Before discussing a topic or lecturing on it, ask students to write a brief account of what they already know about the subject or what opinions they hold. You need not collect these; the purpose is to focus students' attention. (Source: Tollefson, 1988)

Ask students to respond in writing to questions you pose during class. For example, at the beginning of a class, list two or three short-answer questions on the board and ask students to write their responses. The questions might call for a review of material previously covered or test students' recall of the assigned readings. Asking students to write down their responses also helps generate more lively discussion because students will have a chance to think about the material. (Source: Tollefson, 1988)

Ask students to write from a pro or con position. When an argument has been presented in class, stop for a few minutes and ask students to write down all the reasons and evidence they can think of that supports one side or the other. Use these statements as the basis for discussion. (Source: Walvoord, 1986)

During class, pause for a three-minute write. Periodically ask students to write for three minutes on a specific question or topic. Tell students to write freely, whatever pops into their minds without worrying about grammar, spelling, phrasing, or organization. Writing experts believe that this kind of free writing helps students synthesize diverse ideas and identify points they don't understand. You need not collect these exercises. (Source: Tollefson, 1988)

Have students write a brief summary at the end of class. Give students two or three minutes to jot down the key themes, major points, or general principles of the day's discussion. If you give students index cards to write on, you can easily collect and review them to see whether your class understood the discussion.

Have one student keep minutes to be read at the next class meeting. Taking minutes gives students a chance to develop their listening, synthesizing, and writing skills. Boris (1983) suggests the following procedure:

- Prepare your students by having everyone in class take careful notes for a period, rework them at home as minutes, and hand them in for comments. Leave it to students' discretion whether the minutes are in outline or narrative form.
- Select one or two good models to read or distribute to the class.
- At the start of each of the following classes, assign one student to take the minutes for the day.
- Give the person who takes the minutes a piece of carbon paper so that you can have a carbon copy of the rough minutes. This person then takes home the original and revises it in time to read it aloud at the next class meeting.
- After the student has read the minutes, ask the class to comment on their accuracy and quality. The student then revises the minutes, if

necessary, and turns in two copies, one for grading and one for your files.

Structure small group discussion around a writing task. For example, ask each student to pick three words of major importance to the day's session. Then ask the class to write freely for two or three minutes on one of the words. Next, give the students five to ten minutes to meet in groups of three, sharing what they have written and generating questions to ask in class.

Use peer response groups. Divide the class into groups of three or four students, no larger. Tell your students to bring to class enough copies of a rough draft of a paper for each member of their group. Give students guidelines for critiquing the drafts. The most important step in any response task is for the reader to note the part of the paper that is the strongest and describe to the writer why it worked well. Readers can also be given the following instructions (adapted from Walvoord, 1986, p. 113):

- State the main point of the paper in a single sentence.
- List the major subtopics.
- Identify confusing sections of the paper.
- Decide whether each section of the paper has enough detail, evidence, and information.
- Indicate whether the paper's points follow one another in sequence.
- Judge the appropriateness of the opening and concluding paragraphs.
- Identify the strengths of the paper.

The critiques may be done during class time, but written critiques done as homework are likely to be more thoughtful. Use class time for the groups to discuss each paper and critique. Students then revise their drafts for submission.

Use read-around groups. Read-around groups allow everyone to read everyone else's paper. The technique works best for short assignments (two to four pages). Divide the class into groups of four students, no larger, and divide the papers (coded for anonymity) into as many sets as there are groups. Give each group a set and ask students to read each paper silently and select the best paper in the set. Each group discusses their choices and comes to consensus on the best paper. The paper's code number is recorded by the group, and the process is repeated with a new set of papers. After all the sets have been read by all the groups, someone from each group writes on the board the code number of the best paper in each set. Recurring numbers are circled. Typically, one to three papers stand out. (Source: Pytlik, 1989)

Ask students to identify the characteristics of effective writing. After students have completed the read-around activity, ask them to reconsider those papers voted as excellent by the entire class and to jot down features that made each paper outstanding. Record their comments on the board, asking for elaboration and probing vague generalities (for example, "The paper was interesting." "What made the paper interesting?"). In pairs, students discuss the comments on the board and try to place them in categories such as organization, awareness of audience, thoroughness of detail, and so on. You may need to help the students arrange the characteristics into meaningful categories. (Source: Pytlik, 1989)

References

Boris, E. Z. "Classroom Minutes: A Valuable Teaching Device." *Improving College and University Teaching*, 1983, *31*(2), 70–73.

Elbow, P. "Using Writing to Teach Something Else." Unpublished paper, 1987.

Hawisher, G. E., and Selfe, C. L. (eds.). *Critical Perspectives on Computers and Composition Instruction*. New York: Teachers College Press, 1989.

Holdstein, D. H., and Selfe, C. L. (eds.). *Computers and Writing: Theory, Research, Practice*. New York: Modern Language Association, 1990.

Lowman, J. *Mastering the Techniques of Teaching*. San Francisco: Jossey-Bass, 1984.

Petersen, B. T. "Additional Resources in the Practice of Writing Across the Disciplines." In C. W. Griffin (ed.), *Teaching Writing in All Disciplines*. New Directions in Teaching and Learning, no. 12. San Francisco: Jossey-Bass, 1982.

Professional and Organizational Development Network in Higher Education. *Bright Idea Network*, 1989. (For information contact David Graf, Iowa State University, Ames.)

Pytlik, B. P. "Teaching Teachers of Writing: Workshops on Writing as a Collaborative Process." *College Teaching*, 1989, *37*(1), 12–14.

Tollefson, S. K. *Encouraging Student Writing*. Berkeley: Office of Educational Development, University of California, 1988.

Walvoord, B. F. *Helping Students Write Well: A Guide for Teachers in All Disciplines*. (2nd ed.) New York: Modern Language Association, 1986.

Watkins, B. T. "More and More Professors in Many Academic Disciplines Routinely Require Students to Do Extensive Writing." *Chronicle of Higher Education*, 1990, *36*(44), pp. A13–14, A16.

Designing Effective Writing Assignments

25

Your very best students may be able to write strong papers no matter how the assignment is worded, but most students need clear, specific instructions regarding the topic, approach, and format of their papers. The suggestions below are designed to help you prepare assignments that challenge and teach students without intimidating or frustrating them.

General Strategies

Assign several short papers. Early short assignments allow you to identify students whose writing skills are weak and to refer them to the tutoring center for help. Such assignments also give all students the benefit of your comments and suggestions for improvement before they tackle a long paper, if you assign one. Finally, short assignments can be more motivating to students. They know that you are interested in their progress and improvement and not just in a final product.

Occasionally test out the assignment by pretending to be a student and completing it yourself. By doing the assignment, you may discover changes that need to be made, and you will be better able to advise students on the steps required to complete the assignment. Or ask your graduate student instructor, if you have one, to complete the assignment, and use that response to double-check the assignment's clarity, focus, and completeness.

Keep copies of good papers in a department or library file. Students appreciate seeing samples of the type of writing you expect in your course. You might also distribute copies of model papers and discuss them in class.

Keep notes on the success and pitfalls of each assignment. Try to keep a running list of problems as you grade papers, and use these notes to modify future versions of an assignment.

The Assignment

State the topic. You might think that giving students the opportunity to select their own topic will lead to better papers, but most students will then spend a great deal of time searching for a suitable topic rather than actually writing. In lower-division classes, especially, you should supply the topic.

Define the task. Simply stating a topic ("Discuss the ethics of laboratory experiments on animals") does not give students a clear sense of how to proceed. Some students will begin to string together summaries of newspaper and magazine articles on the topic; others will compose off-the-top-of-their-head diatribes or sermons. Instead, propose a task for them. In defining the task, try to avoid vague verbs such as *discuss*, *tell*, and *explore*.

> *Vague:* Much has been written lately about the use of animals in laboratory experiments. Explore these views and draw some conclusions about the moral considerations inherent in this debate.
>
> *Better:* Animal rights activists believe that laboratory experiments on animals should be curtailed severely and monitored rigorously. Write an essay supporting their point of view. OR
> Animal rights activists, scientists, and agencies funding research are engaged in a lively debate on the use of animals in laboratory experiments. Define your own position in this debate and defend that position in your essay [Simon, 1988, p. 6].
>
> *Vague:* What does a carefully developed analysis of the contrasts between the gods Yahweh and Zeus and the men Moses and Socrates tell us about the ways in which the cultural assumptions of ancient Israel and ancient Greece were fundamentally different from one another?
>
> *Better:* Compare and contrast the cultural assumptions of ancient Israel and ancient Greece in terms of the gods Yahweh and Zeus and the men Moses and Socrates. [Strenski, 1984, p. 4].

Create realistic writing situations. Ask students to communicate with a real audience that has a genuine need for information. For example, an instructor who wanted the class to write about standards of architectural excellence composed the following assignment:

> What makes excellent architecture? In an attempt to recognize, reward, and publicize excellent architecture, a philanthropic patron of the arts has decided to initiate the John Beresford Tipton Award for Excellence in Public Buildings. Mr. Tipton has asked you to help prepare the guidelines for the judging of this annual award.

Write a concise memo (500 words; typed double-spaced) to Mr. Tipton that addresses such issues as the following:

- What is the definition of excellent architecture? What criteria will be used to judge buildings?
- What evidence is appropriate to document architectural excellence?
- Who should judge excellence?
- What procedures are best used to determine excellence?

You should propose your own definition of excellence, but you must support your views by citing published sources. For example, if you feel that social factors are important, refer Mr. Tipton to several key works in the literature on social factors in architecture.

Or, consider this example from a business class. To elicit a short essay describing what certified public accountants (CPAs) do, the instructor devised this assignment:

You are a CPA in a large, prestigious, and highly respected firm of accountants and business consultants. You have been called to superior court to testify as an expert witness in a divorce case. To establish a fair property settlement between husband and wife, it is necessary for the court to determine the value of their restaurant. You have examined the restaurant's accounts. But before you give your financial analysis, the judge who is hearing the case asks you to establish your authority by explaining briefly how CPAs are trained and accredited and what domains their expertise and responsibilities encompass.

For first-year students, turn each step of a large assignment into a smaller assignment. For example, ask students to turn in an outline, then a bibliography, and then a first draft. Even if your students are experienced writers, construct a series of assignments, such as the following, leading up to the final paper (Persky and Raimes, 1981, p. 32):

- A description of one experiment, research project, or theory
- A description of a second experiment, research project, or theory
- A comparison and contrast of the two

- An analysis of the effect of such experiments, projects, or theories on the field being studied
- A final paper integrating all of the above

By making cumulative assignments, you help students work through the process of composing a long paper and help them better manage their time.

Distribute a handout for each written assignment. Preparing the handout allows you to check on the completeness of your instructions and also precludes misunderstandings and arguments over length, task, deadlines, and so on. The handout should list all the essential information about the assignment:

- The specific task (for example, summarize, draw inferences, compare and contrast, select evidence to support a thesis)
- The genre of paper you expect (for example, memo, report, essay, outline)
- The audience for the assignment (to help students make decisions about tone, language, and organization)
- Your expectations of what should be included in the finished product (for example, a definition of family and the varieties of family life-styles; relate the variation in family life-styles to broader cultural, social, psychological, and economic contexts)
- The approximate length, in number of words, not pages
- The physical format of the paper (double-spaced copy, margins, no onionskin paper, stapled)
- Guidelines about types and number of sources if you are asking for research, and format for citations, footnotes, or bibliography
- A reminder to retain all drafts and notes (should issues of plagiarism arise) and a copy of the completed paper (should a submitted paper become lost)
- An explanation of how the paper will be graded and what criteria you will use
- An indication of any opportunities to revise and rewrite papers for higher grades, and the schedule for doing so
- The due date and policies regarding late papers

After you distribute the handout, take five or ten minutes to review the assignment and answer questions. Mention problems students might encounter and suggest how to avoid them. Provide materials on how to complete the assignment successfully or refer students to appropriate composition textbooks.

Discuss the assignment in class. After presenting an assignment, take some class time for small group discussion. Ask students to free associate words, facts, ideas, and questions and to begin to formulate theses.

Ask students to select someone to read their first draft. Make this part of the assignment. Provide students with a checklist for reviewing papers, perhaps developed in class, and require that the checklist be completed and signed by an outside reviewer selected by the student.

Alternatives to Typical Research and Term Paper Assignments

Article for a professional journal. Ask students to write as though they were going to submit their work to a professional journal. Give them the author's guidelines for a particular journal, and evaluate their papers as a journal referee would. The specification of an audience makes written assignments more challenging and realistic. (Source: Tollefson, 1988)

Abstract for a professional journal. Distribute an article in your field with the abstract removed. Ask students to write the abstract. Then have students compare what they have written. Distribute the published abstract and ask students to write a short comparison of their version and the author's. (Sources: Cullen, 1984; Light, 1992)

Book review for a professional journal. Provide sample book reviews from journals in your field and discuss particular features that make them effective. Then ask students to select a book from a reading list and prepare a book review suitable for publication. (Source: Tollefson, 1988)

Office report. Help students practice writing for professionals in other fields by structuring an assignment as a report, memo, or briefing for a professional audience unfamiliar with the field. For example, architecture students can write a report for bankers and other financial backers. (Source: Tollefson, 1988)

Memo recommending action. Pose a controversial issue or perplexing problem and ask students to prepare a brief memo outlining a course of action and identifying their reasons for selecting that strategy. (Source: Tollefson, 1988)

Letter to a public official or company officer. Ask students to write a persuasive or argumentative letter for or against a particular policy or decision. In your instructions stress the need to present evidence and respond to anticipated counterarguments. (Source: Tollefson, 1988)

Letter to the editor, op-ed piece. To give students a chance to explain technical, abstract, or highly specialized material to an audience of laypeople, have them write a letter to the editor on a topic relevant to the course material. Or have them respond to an editorial by taking the opposite position. (Sources: Erickson and Strommer, 1991; Tollefson, 1988)

Update of the readings. Ask students to select a section of the text or readings and prepare a two-page update that stresses new research or references that were unavailable to the original authors. (Source: Brooks, 1988)

Letter of critique to the author of the textbook. Have students write a letter to the author(s) of the course textbook assessing the book's strengths and weaknesses. (Source: "Simple Ways to Incorporate More Writing into Your Courses," 1990)

Think piece. Assign short exploratory think pieces that call for one intellectual task: compare two approaches, analyze reasons for behavior, and so on. Grade the think pieces OK/no. (Source: Elbow, 1987)

Microtheme. A microtheme is a very brief essay, two hundred words or less, in response to a narrowly focused question (Bean, Drenk, and Lee, 1982). Examples: "From the data in Table 1 (birthrates by ethnicity) extrapolate the significant changes that have occurred in the last 20 years and speculate on the causes of these changes." "Suppose you put a big block of ice in a bucket and then fill the bucket with water until the water level is exactly even with the edge of the bucket. After several hours the ice has melted. Which of the following will happen? (a) The water level in the bucket will remain exactly the same; (b) the water level in the bucket will drop; (c) some water will overflow the sides of the bucket. Decide on your response and write a brief explanation to a classmate who doesn't understand flotation" (Bean, Drenk, and Lee, 1982, p. 36).

Biographical or historical sketch. Ask students to write a brief description of a particular individual or an event in their own lives. Be sure to give students specific instructions on the scope and purpose of the writing assignment and relate it to the course material. For example, in a sociology class, ask students to write about an incident from their own lives that illustrates social stratification. In a psychology class ask students to describe an episode of gender stereotyping. (Sources: Angelo and Cross, 1993; Tollefson, 1988)

Notebook, journal, or learning log. Ask students to keep a journal of ideas, questions, or comments they have as they attend class and do the readings. Or have students daily write a half-page about their lives and activities. Collect the notebooks two or three times a semester. (Sources: Ehrhart, 1991; Leahy, 1985; Tollefson, 1988)

Invented dialogue. Ask students to write conversations between real or imagined individuals in the same or different time periods (for example, Napoleon and Caesar discussing the difference between the leadership skills needed to conquer an empire and those needed to maintain one). (Source: Angelo and Cross, 1993)

In-class poster session. Students prepare and present a project to their classmates in a poster session format similar to sessions at professional and scientific conferences. Poster sessions are held on sequential days so students get a chance to present their projects and to view the work of other students. Projects, which must be approved in advance, can be traditional papers, research studies, or artistic presentations. (Source: Baird, 1991)

Interview. Have students interview another faculty member, professional, or other individual related to the content of the course. Give students guidelines on how to conduct and write up interviews.

Research and Term Papers

Clarify what skills you expect students to develop as they complete the term paper assignment. For example, do you want students to gain experience in using the library? In locating and evaluating information needed to support a thesis? In synthesizing disparate material? Make it clear to students whether they can use popular and scholarly sources, primary and secondary sources, and so on. (Source: Fink, 1988)

Check with your library to make sure it can support your research requirements. Librarians recommend that instructors avoid assigning topics that are too specialized or beyond the scope of the university's collection. Librarians also urge instructors to avoid topics that require very recent articles or books—it generally takes months before materials are catalogued and shelved, and browsing in current periodicals is often frustrating for students. (Source: Fink, 1988)

Invite a librarian to make a presentation to your students. Most campus librarians are eager to make presentations on library skills, resources, and search strategies. Also, encourage students to ask for assistance at the library's reference desk and to take advantage of library tours, instructional workshops, and tip sheets.

Do not send an entire class in search of the same information. If you want all your students to read an article, place several copies on reserve at the library or in your office or arrange for it to be duplicated for purchase. To send a roomful of students to compete for one copy of an article frustrates both the students and the library staff. (Source: Fink, 1988)

Break the term paper assignment into manageable chunks. Assignments made early in the semester and never referred to again inevitably create last-minute panic. Interim due dates help students structure the research process and learn from each step. For example, set deadlines for the following steps:

- Identifying a topic
- Preparing a prospectus that states the paper's title, purpose, intended audience, major points, and a schedule of tasks
- Gathering sources, data, references
- Developing an outline
- Writing a first draft
- Rewriting

Consider asking students to indicate, at each step, their biggest concerns or questions at that point. If your schedule permits, meet with the students to provide guidance and advice. (Sources: Angelo and Cross, 1993; Fink, 1988; McKeachie, 1986)

Specify a style manual. If the assignment calls for in-text citations, footnotes, or bibliographies, distribute a handout showing the format for these or refer students to a style manual. Select the style of your professional association or ask students to follow the guidelines in a particular composition handbook or those in Kate L. Turabian, *Student's Guide for Writing College Papers*, 3rd ed. (Chicago: University of Chicago Press, 1976).

References

Angelo, T. A., and Cross, K. P. *Classroom Assessment Techniques: A Handbook for College Teachers.* (2nd ed.) San Francisco: Jossey-Bass, 1993.

Baird, B. N. "In-Class Poster Sessions." *Teaching of Psychology*, 1991, *18*(1), 27–29.

Bean, J. C., Drenk, D., and Lee, F. D. "Microtheme Strategies for Developing Cognitive Skills." In C. W. Griffin (ed.), *Teaching Writing in All Disciplines*. New Directions for Teaching and Learning, no. 12. San Francisco: Jossey-Bass, 1982.

Brooks, M. "Medical Students Rewrite the Book." *VCU Teaching*, 1988, *1*(1), 5–7.

Cullen, R. "How to Use Writing Assignments Without Grading Papers." *The TA at UCLA Newsletter*, 1984, *12*, 11.

Ehrhart, M. J. "Dear Journal." *College Teaching*, 1991, *39*(2), 55–56.

Elbow, P. "Using Writing to Teach Something Else." Unpublished paper, 1987.

Erickson, B. L., and Strommer, D. W. *Teaching College Freshmen*. San Francisco: Jossey-Bass, 1991.

Fink, D. "What You Ask for Is What You Get. . ." *The Tutor*, 1988, *4*(1), 1–2. (Publication of the Faculty Teaching Excellence Program, University of Colorado at Boulder)

Leahy, R. "The Power of the Student Journal." *College Teaching*, 1985, *33*(3), 108–112.

Light, R. J. *The Harvard Assessment Seminars. Second Report.* Cambridge, Mass.: School of Education, Harvard University, 1992.

McKeachie, W. J. *Teaching Tips.* (8th ed.) Lexington, Mass.: Heath, 1986.

Persky, C., and Raimes, A. *Learning Through Writing*. New York: Hunter College, 1981.

Simon, L. "The Papers We Want to Read." *College Teaching*, 1988, *36*(1), 6–8.

"Simple Ways to Incorporate More Writing into Your Courses." *UC Ideas.* Irvine: Instructional Development Service, University of California, Jan. 1990.

Strenski, E. "Design Principles for Good Essay and Paper Topics." *The TA at UCLA Newsletter*, 1984, *12*, 4.

Tollefson, S. K. *Encouraging Student Writing*. Berkeley: Office of Educational Development, University of California, 1988.

26 Evaluating Students' Written Work

Try to use the occasion of grading papers to reinforce each student's strengths and to identify areas needing improvement so that your students will know what they are doing right and what is impeding their efforts to communicate. Make your suggestions as tactful and specific as you can—no one benefits from sharp remarks or vague hints. The following pointers will help you evaluate papers efficiently, fairly, and constructively.

General Strategies

Give yourself time to read the papers. While your goal is to return papers promptly, avoid, if you can, reading a large number of papers in a single sitting. It is hard to maintain your concentration, and some papers may be unfairly assessed. It is better to read a few papers at a time (three to five, depending upon length), with ample breaks. When you start reading again, review the last paper or two to make sure you weren't overly lax or overly harsh because you were tired.

Get a general sense of the entire set of papers before grading any papers. Some faculty read through all the papers quickly, sorting them into three or four piles according to a quick assessment of their quality. Once you have a general sense of how well students handled the assignment, you are less likely to overestimate an average paper or to wait expectantly for an outstanding one. From these piles, you can select "anchor papers" (A, B, C, D) against which you can compare all other papers. (Sources: Lowman, 1984; Morris and Tucker, 1985)

Write legibly. If your handwriting is difficult to read, encourage students to ask you to decipher it. Remind graduate student instructors and readers (if you have them) to write clearly and to avoid felt marking pens that are too thick to be legible. Some teachers type their end comments on the computer. That way the comments are legible, and the teacher can keep them for reference.

Have students complete a self-evaluation form. One faculty member asks students to complete a brief form indicating the extent to which they felt they followed good writing practices:

- An opening that catches the reader's attention
- A strong thesis
- A balance of fact and opinion
- Selectively chosen examples
- A conclusion that leaves the reader with a clear understanding of the writer's point of view

Students need not turn in these forms but can compare them to the instructor's comments on graded papers. A variation is for the instructor to read the students' assessments.

Grading

Develop a brief checklist of your grading criteria, but grade the essay holistically. Use criteria generated through in-class activities or adapt criteria developed by others. The criteria given below are adapted from McKeachie (1986, pp. 132–134) and Morris and Tucker (1985, p. 6):

- *Focus:* Is the problem chosen focused enough to be covered adequately within the space of the paper?
- *Organization:* Is the paper's structure apparent and easy to follow?
- *Development:* Does the paper adequately introduce the topic, present convincing evidence to support the writer's position, summarize findings, and offer a reasonable conclusion?
- *Sentence structure:* Are sentences well formed, appropriately varied in length and style, and used for different effects?
- *Mechanics:* Is the paper generally free of spelling, typographical, and grammatical errors?

Greenberg (1988, p. 49) has developed a ten-point checklist based on the tasks involved in composing:

- Limit a subject.
- Clarify ideas.
- Organize ideas.
- Coherently develop ideas.

- Provide and effectively synthesize supporting material.
- Create and evaluate rhetorical structures appropriate to subject and readers.
- Make sure syntax is suited to intended purpose and readers.
- Make sure diction is suited to intended purpose and readers.
- Make writing conform to conventions of academic use and mechanics.
- Document citations, with the help of an appropriate style manual.

When you assign a paper, discuss your set of criteria in class. As you are commenting on submitted papers, phrase your remarks in terms of these criteria. But refrain from assigning a certain number of points for each criterion. Instead, approach the essay holistically, judging its overall quality.

Resist the temptation to assign split grades (one for content, one for writing). Split grades tend to reinforce the false notion that content can be divorced from the clarity and precision with which the ideas are expressed. (Source: Tollefson, 1988)

Explain your grade. Students often believe that grading essay papers and assignments is purely subjective. Debunk this myth by clearly explaining to students the reason for their grade. Tollefson (1988, p. 11) offers the following example for a B paper: "While the sections in which you discuss X and Y are well reasoned, your discussion of Z is rather sketchy. That section, more than anything else, keeps this from being an A paper." Some faculty find it useful to distribute to students at the beginning of class their notions of good and poor papers. The following example is adapted from Crews (1983, p. 14) and Tollefson (1988, p. 12):

A: Excellent in all or nearly all aspects. The interest of the reader is engaged by the ideas and presentation. Style and organization seem natural and easy. Paper marked by originality of ideas.

B: Technically competent, with a lapse here and there. The thesis is clear, properly limited, and reasonable, and the prose is generally effective without rising to sustained distinction.

C: A competent piece of work but not yet good. C papers are more or less adequately organized along obvious lines, and the thesis tends to be oversimple or imprudent without being wildly implausible. Monotony of sentence structure is apparent, and errors are sprinkled throughout. In some C papers, excellent ideas are marred by poor presentation—either development, organization, or technical errors. In other C papers, the organization, structure, and grammar are not flawed, but the ideas and how they are developed need work. In yet other C papers, there are only a few technical errors and the organization and ideas are adequate but not noteworthy.

D: A piece of work that demonstrates some effort on the author's part but that is too marred by technical problems or flaws in thinking and development of ideas to be considered competent work.

F: This is a failing grade, usually reserved for pieces of work that demonstrate minimal effort on the author's part. The writer has drastically misinterpreted the assignment and written half as many words as requested. Paragraph breaks are random; subjects and verbs, pronouns and antecedents turn against one another in wild discord.

Responding to Students' Writing

Begin by reading the paper once through. Identify strengths and note, but do not correct, problem areas. Read the paper for an overall impression, noting features that interfere with your ability to follow the author's train of thought.

Avoid overmarking. Do not feel that you must correct every grammatical error, respond to every idea, or propose alternatives for each section. Overmarking overwhelms students and diverts their attention from key problems. It is best to focus on only one or two major problems and to look for patterns of errors rather than noting every flaw. Some faculty circle all misspellings and grammatical errors, but others circle them on the first few pages only and make a general note at the end of the paper: "Try to pay more attention to punctuation; your errors detract from your good ideas."

Avoid undermarking. Placing only one or two general comments on a paper and then assigning a grade, even an A, is not very helpful to students. Students want to know what you thought about their work. Praise the paper's strengths and offer constructive criticism on its weaknesses.

Respond to the paper as an interested reader or reviewer would. Set yourself three goals: to tell the student what he or she has done well (to build confidence), to make the student aware of errors and weaknesses that need correction, and to inform the student of ways to improve (Persky and Raimes, 1981). Some tips:

- Phrase criticisms as questions: "Are you saying that decision makers use data in a logical way? What about political pressures and financial constraints affecting the decision-making process?"
- Phrase criticisms as suggestions for revising the paper: not "This point was not explained fully enough," but "Explain further."
- Indicate major errors of logic, confusion, or organization but refrain from arguing with every point ("Your third argument is barely supported by any evidence").
- Make two or three suggestions for improvement.
- Avoid sarcastic, impatient, or punitive comments.

Experienced writing teachers believe that students benefit most from a mix of marginal notations and a longer overall comment at the end of the paper. The overall comment should match the grade you assign to the paper. It is also helpful if your comments guide students to rethink their ideas and prepare them to improve on the next assignment. If you have students turn in a folder with all their papers to date, you can monitor their progress and check whether they are incorporating earlier comments and recommendations and whether they are repeating the same mistakes and errors. Some faculty members use a computer to write each student a memo about his or her paper, "recycling" comments (through block and copy) on style or organization (Lidicker, 1991). If you use this strategy, be sure to personalize the comments whenever possible; do not simply rely on canned remarks. If you are assigning several papers during the term, save all the memos on disk so that you can monitor each student's progress. (Sources: Morris and Tucker, 1985; Persky and Raimes, 1981; Tollefson, 1988)

Don't rewrite students' papers. Indicate the major problems with a segment of the paper and perhaps rewrite one weak paragraph as an example, but leave the bulk of the revising to students. If you do all their rewriting for them, the main thing they will learn is that you are a better writer than they are. (Sources: Light, 1992; Tollefson, 1988)

Comment on the quality of the writing. Reinforce strengths and point out areas of grammar, style, and usage that need improvement. Tollefson (1988, p. 11) suggests you write something like, "The variety in sentence length and structure makes for lively reading, but your overreliance on the passive voice produces some wordy and confusing patches." If students have writing problems, say so: "I hate to see your good ideas expressed so carelessly. Be sure to run the spell checker on your word processor and consult a reference text for the correct use of apostrophes."

Use marking symbols. Making symbols will save you time in correcting students' papers and will help students think about common writing errors. Adopt the symbols used in any standard composition textbook, or ask for handouts from your campus English department or writing center. For example:

AGR Subject-verb or pronoun-antecedent agreement
Incorrect: Each of these studies have problems.
Correct: Each of these studies has problems.

FRAG Sentence fragment (incomplete sentence)
Incorrect: The strike was bitter. But without violence.
Correct: The strike was bitter but without violence.

RTS Run-together (run-on) sentence
Incorrect: The Scopes trial was a farce, however, it had a great impact.
Correct: The Scopes trial was a farce; however, it had a great impact.

If these symbols seem too burdensome, develop your own system. For example, use straight lines under or alongside strong passages and wavy lines under and alongside problem sections (Elbow, 1987).

Use concrete, specific language. Comments such as "awkward," "unclear," and "vague" are not particularly helpful to students since they may refer to organization, content, or mechanics. Be more specific in how you respond to fuzzy passages: "How else would you describe this?" "Why is this so?" "Are you saying this is necessary?" Don't hesitate to write, "I don't understand this sentence." It is also helpful to suggest specific strategies or writing exercises students can use to revise their papers. For example Light (1992) recommends that students check the organization of a paper by writing an outline that consists of a single summary sentence for each paragraph. To identify awkward phrases or words, students can read the paper aloud or have someone read it to them.

Avoid overly prescriptive suggestions. Rather than instructing students to do this or that, help them see the effect of what they have written. For example, write, "I think you are saying that affordable housing costs more than market rate housing. If this is different from what you want the reader to think, what can you do to help the reader see what you mean?" (Source: Smit, 1991)

Focus on errors that indicate cognitive confusion. Most mechanical errors do not reflect fuzzy or illogical thinking, and you can simply circle these errors. But do call students' attention to sentences in which the writing confuses the reader or indicates the writer's own confusion. For example, call out absent, vague, or incorrect referents; errors in tense (switching between present and future); overreliance on the passive voice; and weak predications or predication errors, illogical subject-verb complement (for example, "Redistricting is when you redo the boundary lines for representation"). (Source: Tollefson, 1988)

Balance positive and negative comments. Try to write specific positive feedback on every paper, both to encourage students and to reinforce what they are doing well. (Source: "Make the Most of Written Feedback," 1991)

Returning Students' Assignments

Give students an overall sense of the class's performance. When you hand back papers, comment on the set as a whole. If several students made the same kinds of errors, prepare a handout on the problem. It is also helpful to take time to read a particularly strong paper. Invite students who want to discuss their papers with you to meet with you during your office hours.

Reinforce your expectations of good writing. Let students know what they did well, what they need to improve, and what you would like to see in future assignments. Use the occasion to reinforce the importance of writing as a way of learning the subject matter.

Ask students to comment on the assignment. Inquire about the difficulties students had with the assignment and their suggestions for improving it.

References

Crews, F. *English 1A-1B Instructor's Manual.* Berkeley: Department of English, University of California, 1983.

Elbow, P. "Using Writing to Teach Something Else." Unpublished paper, 1987.

Greenberg, K. L. "Assessing Writing: Theory and Practice." In J. H. McMillan (ed.), *Assessing Students' Learning.* New Directions for Teaching and Learning, no. 34. San Francisco: Jossey-Bass, 1988.

Lidicker, R. "Computer Techniques for Giving Students Feedback." *Teaching Professor,* 1991, 5(10), 2.

Light, R. J. *The Harvard Assessment Seminars. Second Report.* Cambridge, Mass.: School of Education, Harvard University, 1992.

Lowman, J. *Mastering the Techniques of Teaching.* San Francisco: Jossey-Bass, 1984.

McKeachie, W. J. *Teaching Tips.* (8th ed.) Lexington, Mass.: Heath, 1986.

"Make the Most of Written Feedback." *Teaching Professor*, 1991, *5*(7), 1–2.

Morris, L. A., and Tucker, S. "Evaluating Student Writing." *Teaching at Davis Newsletter*, 1985, *10*(2), 1, 6.

Persky, C., and Raimes, A. *Learning Through Writing.* New York: Hunter College, 1981.

Smit, D. W. "Improving Student Writing." *Idea Paper*, no. 25. Manhattan: Center for Faculty Evaluation and Development in Higher Education, September, Kansas State University, 1991.

Tollefson, S. K. *Encouraging Student Writing.* Berkeley: Office of Educational Development, University of California, 1988.

27

Homework: Problem Sets

Most colleges tell students to expect to spend two or three hours studying outside of class for each hour of lecture or discussion. This means that students will spend at least two-thirds of the time they devote to your course on homework: reading assignments, problem sets, projects, papers, and so on. Your out-of-class assignments, therefore, should be as well conceived and well prepared as your in-class lectures and demonstrations. In addition to the suggestions below on preparing and making effective use of problem sets, see "Helping Students Write Better in All Courses," "Designing Effective Writing Assignments," and "Evaluating Students' Written Work" for helpful hints on preparing and grading written assignments.

General Strategies

Decide when you want to announce and hand out homework assignments. Some faculty distribute the entire set of assignments for the term on the first day of class so that students can plan their time and know what the course will require of them. Other faculty give students one assignment at a time, which allows for modifications in assignments to meet the pace and ability of the class. Still others list the due dates for assignments in the syllabus but make the specific assignments as the term proceeds. You should also decide whether you prefer making assignments at the beginning of the class meetings or close to the end. Whatever you decide, make it clear to students when assignments will be distributed, when they will be due, and what they will entail.

Coordinate problem sets with lecture topics. Do not confuse or frustrate your students by making assignments that require information, skills, or techniques they have not yet acquired in class. If the lectures and homework diverge, explain your rationale to the class. (Source: Marincovich and Rusk, 1987)

Distribute the work load evenly throughout the term. Try to pace the assignments so that students do not have a massive chunk of homework during the last weeks of the term.

Give frequent assignments. Asking students to turn in frequent short assignments has a number of advantages (Committee on the Teaching of Undergraduate Mathematics, 1979):

- You have continual opportunities to see how your students are doing.
- Students become accustomed to regular and systematic study and tend to procrastinate less.
- Students acquire a clear idea of what sorts of problems or assignments they should be able to do.

You need not grade every assignment. Instead, grade one or two problems without telling the students in advance which ones those will be. Or collect two or three problems a week for grading. Some faculty ask their students to accumulate homework in a notebook, which is called in for checking from time to time, or they give short quizzes on the problem sets and grade those. For assignments you do not grade, distribute an answer sheet on the day the homework is due so that students can check their work. (Source: Committee on the Teaching of Undergraduate Mathematics, 1979)

Give students tips on how to solve problems. According to Whitman (1983), research shows that the key difference between novice and experienced problem solvers is that experts have more immediate access to a wider repertory of skills. Novice problem solvers take longer to locate appropriate strategies and proceed in slow, step-by-step fashion. Help students figure out how to approach an unfamiliar or difficult problem. Here are some suggestions (adapted from Andrews, 1989; Brown and Atkins, 1988, p. 185):

- Write out the information specifically requested by the problem.
- List all the givens, both explicit and implicit.
- Distinguish the key points.
- Try to explain the problem to someone else.
- Make a flowchart with yes/no options, draw a diagram, or represent the problem graphically or mathematically.
- Think of similar problems you have solved successfully.
- Break the problem into smaller parts.
- Do the easiest parts or steps first.
- Make a rough approximation of what the solution should look like.
- Work backward from the goal.
- Work backward and forward from the midpoint.
- Systematically use trial and error.

- After you have solved the problem:
  Verbally summarize the solution to reinforce what you have learned.
  Check to see whether there is a simpler or alternative method.
  Keep a log of problems you found difficult; see whether there are any commonalities in these problems, and use this information to identify areas you need to work on.

Raise the issue with your students to see what other strategies they use to become unstuck when they cannot solve a problem.

Preparing Assignments

Make the first assignment a review. Have the first assignment include material that students should have learned in prerequisite courses. Use the assignment to determine whether each student has the skills, knowledge, and background information to succeed in your course. Ask inadequately prepared students to delay entry into your course or recommend ways that they can address gaps in their knowledge.

Cull assignments from a variety of sources. Look through textbooks in the subject area and exchange assignments with colleagues at other institutions. Some faculty members also ask students to submit problems for future assignments. (Source: Marincovich and Rusk, 1987)

Be imaginative in creating assignments. For example, tie assignments to real-life situations, if possible. Students approach homework with more interest if they can see the assignment's applicability and relevance. Or think of new ways of using problems. An instructor in computer science prints out a program about thirty statements long that performs an interesting task. He then cuts the printout into one-statement strips, gives a packet of strips to each small group of students, and asks them to put the puzzle together.

Choose homework problems selectively. Include a reasonable mix of routine exercises and more challenging problems. But avoid excessively tricky problems. Also, cover a particular topic in at least two assignments to reinforce students' learning. (Source: Committee on the Teaching of Undergraduate Mathematics, 1979)

Divide homework into hand-in and "also-do" problems. Grade the hand-in problems, but let students know that the "also-do" problems are candidates for midterms and the final exam. (Source: Reznick, 1985)

Ask students to describe how they solved one of their homework problems. A mathematics professor gives students the following assignment: "Choose any one of the problems you have already solved, and explain in complete sentences, step-by-step, exactly how you solved the problem." This technique will help you see your students' thinking processes and problem-solving strategies. (Source: Angelo, 1991)

Do all the problems yourself before giving them to students. By doing the assignment yourself, you can see what is required to complete the problem sets and what difficulties students might have. You will also be able to catch any errors in the instructions, problems, and data. Try to work on the problem sets a week or two before your students do. If you complete all the assignments before the course starts, you probably won't remember the problems well enough to advise students.

Giving and Collecting Homework

Ask students to submit all assignments on time and in organized, legible form. Set high standards and enforce them. Some faculty penalize late work by a set number of points for each day that the work is late. Remember, though, that students may have compelling reasons for missing a deadline. One faculty member who gives weekly assignments announces that the two worst grades will not be counted, which means in effect that students can skip two assignments. Another faculty member gives students a two-day grace period that they can use to turn in one assignment two days late or two assignments each a day late (Marincovich and Rusk, 1987).

Collect homework at the beginning of class. If you accept papers up to the end of the period, students may come late to class.

Making Effective Use of Homework Assignments

Encourage students to work collaboratively on their homework. Students can learn from each other by working together. Some faculty hope to minimize dishonest copying by forbidding collaborative work; but such a policy will not discourage cheating, and it deprives students of the benefits of peer learning. Some faculty allow any amount of discussion among students, but they require students to write up their work independently. (Sources: Marincovich and Rusk, 1987; Reznick, 1985)

Limit the amount of class time devoted to reviewing homework. Going over homework problems may be a waste of time for many students and may discourage students from doing difficult parts of the assignment on their own.

Vary the type of homework you assign. For example, two or three times during the semester, give students the assignment of summarizing the key concepts, principles, or formulas in the course up to that point. Summaries help students synthesize course material, focus on the larger context of the course, and distinguish between important and less important material.

Grade and comment on students' problem sets as you would on their writing. Check a student's method as well as his or her answer. Briefly point out what is especially good. If the solution is incorrect, identify the error or give the student guidance on how to approach the problem. If a student solves a problem with a method different from the one you would have chosen, be certain that a "right answer" does not hide conceptual or logical errors. Alternatively, a wrong answer does not necessarily mean the student's method was incorrect. Some students may come up with creative or inventive solutions. Even when a student's method is acceptable, make a comment about simpler or more powerful methods. Posting or distributing solutions is not an adequate substitute for at least occasional comments on the work of individual students. (Source: Committee on Teaching Assistants, 1978)

Be fair and consistent in how you grade. Decide how you will credit answers that are partially correct. Try to reward students who made genuine progress toward the right answer by giving them credit for correct concepts or methods, even if they committed errors in their calculations. (Source: Committee on Teaching Assistants, 1978)

Return homework promptly. Try to return homework by the next class session so students will have a current sense of what they have not yet mastered. (Source: Reznick, 1985)

Ask students how long the homework is taking. Overly time-consuming homework may lead students to consider dishonest shortcuts. (Source: Marincovich and Rusk, 1987)

References

Andrews, J. *Problem Solving Brainstorm List.* San Diego: TA Development Program, University of California, 1989.

Angelo, T. A. "Ten Easy Pieces: Assessing Higher Learning in Four Dimensions." In T. A. Angelo (ed.), *Classroom Research: Early Lessons from*

Success. New Directions for Teaching and Learning, no. 46. San Francisco: Jossey-Bass, 1991.

Brown, G., and Atkins, M. *Effective Teaching in Higher Education.* London: Methuen, 1988.

Committee on Teaching Assistants. *Chemistry TA Handbook.* Berkeley: Chemistry Department, University of California, Berkeley, 1978.

Committee on the Teaching of Undergraduate Mathematics. *College Mathematics: Suggestions on How to Teach It.* Washington, D.C.: Mathematical Association of America, 1979.

Marincovich, M., and Rusk, L. *Excellence in Teaching Electrical Engineering.* Stanford, Calif.: Center for Teaching and Learning, Stanford University, 1987.

Reznick, B. A. *Chalking It Up: Advice to a New TA.* New York: Random House, 1985.

Whitman, N. "Teaching Problem-Solving and Creativity in College Courses." *AAHE Bulletin,* 1983, *35*(6), 9–13.

VIII.

Testing and Grading

Quizzes, Tests, and Exams

28

Many teachers dislike preparing and grading exams, and most students dread taking them. Yet tests are powerful educational tools that serve at least four functions. First, tests help you evaluate students and assess whether they are learning what you are expecting them to learn. Second, well-designed tests serve to motivate and help students structure their academic efforts. Crooks (1988), McKeachie (1986), and Wergin (1988) report that students study in ways that reflect how they think they will be tested. If they expect an exam focused on facts, they will memorize details; if they expect a test that will require problem solving or integrating knowledge, they will work toward understanding and applying information. Third, tests can help you understand how successfully you are presenting the material. Finally, tests can reinforce learning by providing students with indicators of what topics or skills they have not yet mastered and should concentrate on. Despite these benefits, testing is also emotionally charged and anxiety producing. The following suggestions can enhance your ability to design tests that are effective in motivating, measuring, and reinforcing learning.

A note on terminology: instructors often use the terms *tests*, *exams*, and even *quizzes* interchangeably. Test experts Jacobs and Chase (1992), however, make distinctions among them based on the scope of content covered and their weight or importance in calculating the final grade for the course. An examination is the most comprehensive form of testing, typically given at the end of the term (as a final) and one or two times during the semester (as midterms). A test is more limited in scope, focusing on particular aspects of the course material. A course might have three or four tests. A quiz is even more limited and usually is administered in fifteen minutes or less. Though these distinctions are useful, the terms *test* and *exam* will be used interchangeably throughout the rest of this section because the principles in planning, constructing, and administering them are similar.

General Strategies

Spend adequate amounts of time developing your tests. As you prepare a test, think carefully about the learning outcomes you wish to measure, the type of items best suited to those outcomes, the range of difficulty of items, the length and time limits for the test, the format and layout of the exam, and your scoring procedures.

Match your tests to the content you are teaching. Ideally, the tests you give will measure students' achievement of your educational goals for the course. Test items should be based on the content and skills that are most important for your students to learn. To keep track of how well your tests reflect your objectives, you can construct a grid, listing your course objectives along the side of the page and content areas along the top. For each test item, check off the objective and content it covers. (Sources: Ericksen, 1969; Jacobs and Chase, 1992; Svinicki and Woodward, 1982)

Try to make your tests valid, reliable, and balanced. A test is *valid* if its results are appropriate and useful for making decisions about an aspect of students' achievement (Gronlund and Linn, 1990). Technically, validity refers to the appropriateness of the interpretation of the *results* and not to the test itself, though colloquially we speak about a test being valid. Validity is a matter of degree and considered in relation to specific use or interpretation (Gronlund and Linn, 1990). For example, the results of a writing test may have a high degree of validity for indicating the level of a student's composition skills, a moderate degree of validity for predicting success in later composition courses, and essentially no validity for predicting success in mathematics or physics. Validity can be difficult to determine. A practical approach is to focus on *content validity*, the extent to which the content of the test represents an adequate sampling of the knowledge and skills taught in the course. If you design the test to cover information in lectures and readings in proportion to their importance in the course, then the interpretations of test scores are likely to have greater validity. An exam that consists of only a few difficult items, however, will not yield valid interpretations of what students know.

A test is *reliable* if it accurately and consistently evaluates a student's performance. The purest measure of reliability would entail having a group of students take the same test twice and get the same scores (assuming that we could erase their memories of test items from the first administration). This is impractical, of course, but there are technical procedures for determining reliability. In general, ambiguous questions, unclear directions, and vague scoring criteria threaten reliability. Very short tests are also unlikely to be highly reliable. It is also important for a test to be balanced: to cover most of the main ideas and important concepts in proportion to the emphasis they received in class.

If you are interested in learning more about psychometric concepts and the technical properties of tests, here are some books you might review:

Ebel, R. L., and Frisbie, D. A. *Essentials of Educational Measurement.* (5th ed.) Englewood Cliffs, N.J.: Prentice-Hall, 1990.

Gronlund, N. E., and Linn, R. *Measurement and Evaluation in Teaching.* (6th ed.) New York: Macmillan, 1990.

Mehrens, W. A., and Lehmann, I. J. *Measurement and Evaluation in Education and Psychology.* (4th ed.) New York: Holt, Rinehart & Winston, 1991.

Use a variety of testing methods. Research shows that students vary in their preferences for different formats, so using a variety of methods will help students do their best (Jacobs and Chase, 1992). Multiple-choice or short-answer questions are appropriate for assessing students' mastery of details and specific knowledge, while essay questions assess comprehension, the ability to integrate and synthesize, and the ability to apply information to new situations. A single test can have several formats. Try to avoid introducing a new format on the final exam: if you have given all multiple-choice quizzes or midterms, don't ask students to write an all-essay final. (Sources: Jacobs and Chase, 1992; Lowman, 1984; McKeachie, 1986; Svinicki, 1987)

Write questions that test skills other than recall. Research shows that most tests administered by faculty rely too heavily on students' recall of information (Milton, Pollio, and Eison, 1986). Bloom (1956) argues that it is important for tests to measure higher-learning as well. Fuhrmann and Grasha (1983, p. 170) have adapted Bloom's taxonomy for test development. Here is a condensation of their list:

To measure *knowledge* (common terms, facts, principles, procedures), ask these kinds of questions: Define, Describe, Identify, Label, List, Match, Name, Outline, Reproduce, Select, State. Example: "List the steps involved in titration."

To measure *comprehension* (understanding of facts and principles, interpretation of material), ask these kinds of questions: Convert, Defend,

Distinguish, Estimate, Explain, Extend, Generalize, Give examples, Infer, Predict, Summarize. Example: "Summarize the basic tenets of deconstructionism."

To measure *application* (solving problems, applying concepts and principles to new situations), ask these kinds of questions: Demonstrate, Modify, Operate, Prepare, Produce, Relate, Show, Solve, Use. Example: "Calculate the deflection of a beam under uniform loading."

To measure *analysis* (recognition of unstated assumptions or logical fallacies, ability to distinguish between facts and inferences), ask these kinds of questions: Diagram, Differentiate, Distinguish, Illustrate, Infer, Point out, Relate, Select, Separate, Subdivide. Example: "In the president's State of the Union Address, which statements are based on facts and which are based on assumptions?"

To measure *synthesis* (integrate learning from different areas or solve problems by creative thinking), ask these kinds of questions: Categorize, Combine, Compile, Devise, Design, Explain, Generate, Organize, Plan, Rearrange, Reconstruct, Revise, Tell. Example: "How would you restructure the school day to reflect children's developmental needs?"

To measure *evaluation* (judging and assessing), ask these kinds of questions: Appraise, Compare, Conclude, Contrast, Criticize, Describe, Discriminate, Explain, Justify, Interpret, Support. Example: "Why is Bach's Mass in B Minor acknowledged as a classic?"

Many faculty members have found it difficult to apply this six-level taxonomy, and some educators have simplified and collapsed the taxonomy into three general levels (Crooks, 1988): The first category is knowledge (recall or recognition of specific information). The second category combines comprehension and application. The third category is described as "problem solving," transferring existing knowledge and skills to new situations.

If your course has graduate student instructors (GSIs), involve them in designing exams. At the least, ask your GSIs to read your draft of the exam and comment on it. Better still, involve them in creating the exam. Not only will they have useful suggestions, but their participation in designing an exam will help them grade the exam.

Take precautions to avoid cheating. See "Preventing Academic Dishonesty."

Types of Tests

Multiple-choice tests. Multiple-choice items can be used to measure both simple knowledge and complex concepts. Since multiple-choice questions can be answered quickly, you can assess students' mastery of many topics on an hour exam. In addition, the items can be easily and reliably scored. Good multiple-choice questions are difficult to write — see "Multiple-Choice and Matching Tests" for guidance on how to develop and administer this type of test.

True-false tests. Because random guessing will produce the correct answer half the time, true-false tests are less reliable than other types of exams. However, these items are appropriate for occasional use. Some faculty who use true-false questions add an "explain" column in which students write one or two sentences justifying their response.

Matching tests. The matching format is an effective way to test students' recognition of the relationships between words and definitions, events and dates, categories and examples, and so on. See "Multiple-Choice and Matching Tests" for suggestions about developing this type of test.

Essay tests. Essay tests enable you to judge students' abilities to organize, integrate, interpret material, and express themselves in their own words. Research indicates that students study more efficiently for essay-type examinations than for selection (multiple-choice) tests: students preparing for essay tests focus on broad issues, general concepts, and interrelationships rather than on specific details, and this studying results in somewhat better student performance regardless of the type of exam they are given (McKeachie, 1986). Essay tests also give you an opportunity to comment on students' progress, the quality of their thinking, the depth of their understanding, and the difficulties they may be having. However, because essay tests pose only a few questions, their content validity may be low. In addition, the reliability of essay tests is compromised by subjectivity or inconsistencies in grading. For specific advice, see "Short-Answer and Essay Tests." (Sources: Ericksen, 1969; McKeachie, 1986)

A variation of an essay test asks students to correct mock answers. One faculty member prepares a test that requires students to correct, expand, or refute mock essays. Two weeks before the exam date, he distributes ten to twelve essay questions, which he discusses with students in class. For the actual exam, he selects four of the questions and prepares well-written but intellectually flawed answers for the students to edit, correct, expand, and refute. The mock essays contain common misunderstandings, correct but incomplete responses, or absurd notions; in some cases the answer has only one or two flaws. He reports that students seem to enjoy this type of test more than traditional examinations.

Short-answer tests. Depending on your objectives, short-answer questions can call for one or two sentences or a long paragraph. Short-answer tests are easier to write, though they take longer to score, than multiple-choice tests. They also give you some opportunity to see how well students can express their thoughts, though they are not as useful as longer essay responses for this purpose. See "Short-Answer and Essay Tests" for detailed guidelines.

Problem sets. In courses in mathematics and the sciences, your tests can include problem sets. As a rule of thumb, allow students ten minutes to solve a problem you can do in two minutes. See "Homework: Problem Sets" for advice on creating and grading problem sets.

Oral exams. Though common at the graduate level, oral exams are rarely used for undergraduates except in foreign language classes. In other classes they are usually time-consuming, too anxiety provoking for students, and difficult to score unless the instructor tape-records the answers. However, a math professor has experimented with individual thirty-minute oral tests in a small seminar class. Students receive the questions in advance and are allowed to drop one of their choosing. During the oral exam, the professor probes students' level of understanding of the theory and principles behind the theorems. He reports that about eight students per day can be tested.

Performance tests. Performance tests ask students to demonstrate proficiency in conducting an experiment, executing a series of steps in a reasonable amount of time, following instructions, creating drawings, manipulating materials or equipment, or reacting to real or simulated situations. Performance tests can be administered individually or in groups. They are seldom used in colleges and universities because they are logistically difficult to set up, hard to score, and the content of most courses does not necessarily lend itself to this type of testing. However, performance tests can be useful in classes that require students to demonstrate their skills (for example, health fields, the sciences, education). If you use performance tests, Anderson (1987, p. 43) recommends that you do the following (I have slightly modified her list):

- Specify the criteria to be used for rating or scoring (for example, the level of accuracy in performing the steps in sequence or completing the task within a specified time limit).

- State the problem so that students know exactly what they are supposed to do (if possible, conditions of a performance test should mirror a real-life situation).
- Give students a chance to perform the task more than once or to perform several task samples.

"Create-a-game" exams. For one midterm, ask students to create either a board game, word game, or trivia game that covers the range of information relevant to your course. Students must include the rules, game board, game pieces, and whatever else is needed to play. For example, students in a history of psychology class created "Freud's Inner Circle," in which students move tokens such as small cigars and toilet seats around a board each time they answer a question correctly, and "Psychogories," a card game in which players select and discard cards until they have a full hand of theoretically compatible psychological theories, beliefs, or assumptions. (Source: Berrenberg and Prosser, 1991)

Alternative Testing Modes

Take-home tests. Take-home tests allow students to work at their own pace with access to books and materials. Take-home tests also permit longer and more involved questions, without sacrificing valuable class time for exams. Problem sets, short answers, and essays are the most appropriate kinds of take-home exams. Be wary, though, of designing a take-home exam that is too difficult or an exam that does not include limits on the number of words or time spent (Jedrey, 1984). Also, be sure to give students explicit instructions on what they can and cannot do: for example, are they allowed to talk to other students about their answers? A variation of a take-home test is to give the topics in advance but ask the students to write their answers in class. Some faculty hand out ten or twelve questions the week before an exam and announce that three of those questions will appear on the exam.

Open-book tests. Open-book tests simulate the situations professionals face every day, when they use resources to solve problems, prepare reports, or write memos. Open-book tests tend to be inappropriate in introductory courses in which facts must be learned or skills thoroughly mastered if the student is to progress to more complicated concepts and techniques in advanced courses. On an open-book test, students who are lacking basic knowledge may waste too much of their time consulting their references rather than writing. Open-book tests appear to reduce stress (Boniface,

1985; Liska and Simonson, 1991), but research shows that students do not necessarily perform significantly better on open-book tests (Clift and Imrie, 1981; Crooks, 1988). Further, open-book tests seem to reduce students' motivation to study. A compromise between open- and closed-book testing is to let students bring an index card or one page of notes to the exam or to distribute appropriate reference material such as equations or formulas as part of the test.

Group exams. Some faculty have successfully experimented with group exams, either in class or as take-home projects. Faculty report that groups outperform individuals and that students respond positively to group exams (Geiger, 1991; Hendrickson, 1990; Keyworth, 1989; Toppins, 1989). For example, for a fifty-minute in-class exam, use a multiple-choice test of about twenty to twenty-five items. For the first test, the groups can be randomly divided. Groups of three to five students seem to work best. For subsequent tests, you may want to assign students to groups in ways that minimize differences between group scores and balance talkative and quiet students. Or you might want to group students who are performing at or near the same level (based on students' performance on individual tests). Some faculty have students complete the test individually before meeting as a group. Others just let the groups discuss the test, item by item. In the first case, if the group score is higher than the individual score of any member, bonus points are added to each individual's score. In the second case, each student receives the score of the group. Faculty who use group exams offer the following tips:

- Ask students to discuss each question fully and weigh the merits of each answer rather than simply vote on an answer.
- If you assign problems, have each student work a problem and then compare results.
- If you want students to take the exam individually first, consider devoting two class periods to tests; one for individual work and the other for group.
- Show students the distribution of their scores as individuals and as groups; in most cases group scores will be higher than any single individual score.

A variation of this idea is to have students first work on an exam in groups outside of class. Students then complete the exam individually during class time and receive their own score. Some portion of the test items are derived from the group exam. The rest are new questions. Or let students know in advance you will be asking them to justify a few of their responses; this will keep students from blithely relying on their work group for all the answers. (Sources: Geiger, 1991; Hendrickson, 1990; Keyworth, 1989; Murray, 1990; Toppins, 1989)

Paired testing. For paired exams, pairs of students work on a single essay exam, and the two students turn in one paper. Some students may be reluctant to share a grade, but good students will most likely earn the same grade they would have working alone. Pairs can be self-selected or assigned. For example, pairing a student who is doing well in the course with one not doing well allows for some peer teaching. A variation is to have students work in teams but submit individual answer sheets. (Source: Murray, 1990)

Portfolios. A portfolio is not a specific test but rather a cumulative collection of a student's work. Students decide what examples to include that characterize their growth and accomplishment over the term. While most common in composition classes, portfolios are beginning to be used in other disciplines to provide a fuller picture of students' achievements. A student's portfolio might include sample papers (first drafts and revisions), journal entries, essay exams, and other work representative of the student's progress. You can assign portfolios a letter grade or a pass/not pass. If you do grade portfolios, you will need to establish clear criteria. (Source: Jacobs and Chase, 1992)

Construction of Effective Exams

Prepare new exams each time you teach a course. Though it is time-consuming to develop tests, a past exam may not reflect changes in how you have presented the material or which topics you have emphasized in the course. If you do write a new exam, you can make copies of the old exam available to students.

Make up test items throughout the term. Don't wait until a week or so before the exam. One way to make sure the exam reflects the topics emphasized in the course is to write test questions at the end of each class session and place them on index cards or computer files for later sorting. Software that allows you to create test banks of items and generate exams from the pool is now available.

Ask students to submit test questions. Faculty who use this technique limit the number of items a student can submit and receive credit for. Here is an example (adapted from Buchanan and Rogers, 1990, p. 72):

You can submit up to two questions per exam. Each question must be typed or legibly printed on a separate 5″ × 8″ card. The correct answer and the source (that is, page of the text, date of lecture, and so on) must be provided for each question. Questions can be of the short-answer, multiple-choice, or essay type.

Students receive a few points of additional credit for each question they submit that is judged appropriate. Not all students will take advantage of this opportunity. You can select or adapt students' test items for the exam. If you have a large lecture class, tell your students that you might not review all items but will draw randomly from the pool until you have enough questions for the exam. (Sources: Buchanan and Rogers, 1990; Fuhrmann and Grasha, 1983)

Cull items from colleagues' exams. Ask colleagues at other institutions for copies of their exams. Be careful, though, about using items from tests given by colleagues on your own campus. Some of your students may have previously seen those tests.

Consider making your tests cumulative. Cumulative tests require students to review material they have already studied, thus reinforcing what they have learned. Cumulative tests also give students a chance to integrate and synthesize course content. (Sources: Crooks, 1988; Jacobs and Chase, 1992; Svinicki, 1987)

Prepare clear instructions. Test your instructions by asking a colleague (or one of your graduate student instructors) to read them.

Include a few words of advice and encouragement on the exam. For example, give students advice on how much time to spend on each section or offer a hint at the beginning of an essay question or wish students good luck. (Source: "Exams: Alternative Ideas and Approaches," 1989)

Put some easy items first. Place several questions all your students can answer near the beginning of the exam. Answering easier questions helps students overcome their nervousness and may help them feel confident that they can succeed on the exam. You can also use the first few questions to identify students in serious academic difficulty. (Source: Savitz, 1985)

Challenge your best students. Some instructors like to include at least one very difficult question—though not a trick question or a trivial one—to challenge the interest of the best students. They place that question at or near the end of the exam.

Try out the timing. No purpose is served by creating a test too long for even well-prepared students to finish and review before turning it in. As a rule of thumb, allow about one-half minute per item for true-false tests, one minute per item for multiple-choice tests, two minutes per short-answer requiring a few sentences, ten or fifteen minutes for a limited essay question, and about thirty minutes for a broader essay question. Allow another five or ten minutes for students to review their work, and factor in time to distribute and collect the tests. Another rule of thumb is to allow students about four times as long as it takes you (or a graduate student instructor) to complete the test. (Source: McKeachie, 1986)

Give some thought to the layout of the test. Use margins and line spacing that make the test easy to read. If items are worth different numbers of points, indicate the point value next to each item. Group similar types of items, such as all true-false questions, together. Keep in mind that the amount of space you leave for short-answer questions often signifies to the students the length of the answer expected of them. If students are to write on the exam rather than in a blue book, leave space at the top of each page for the student's name (and section, if appropriate). If each page is identified, the exams can be separated so that each graduate student instructor can grade the same questions on every test paper, for courses that have GSIs.

References

Anderson, S. B. "The Role of the Teacher-Made Test in Higher Education." In D. Bray and M. J. Blecher (eds.), *Issues in Student Assessment.* New Directions for Community Colleges, no. 59. San Francisco: Jossey-Bass, 1987.

Berrenberg, J. L., and Prosser, A. "The Create-a-Game Exam: A Method to Facilitate Student Interest and Learning." *Teaching of Psychology*, 1991, *18*(3), 167–169.

Bloom, B. S. (ed.). *Taxonomy of Educational Objectives. Vol. I: Cognitive Domain.* New York: McKay, 1956.

Boniface, D. "Candidates' Use of Notes and Textbooks During an Open Book Examination." *Educational Research*, 1985, *27*(3), 201–209.

Brown, I. W. "To Learn Is to Teach Is to Create the Final Exam." *College Teaching*, 1991, *39*(4), 150–153.

Buchanan, R. W., and Rogers, M. "Innovative Assessment in Large Classes." *College Teaching*, 1990, *38*(2), 69–73.

Clift, J. C., and Imrie, B. W. *Assessing Students, Appraising Teaching.* New York: Wiley, 1981.

Crooks, T. J. "The Impact of Classroom Evaluation Practices on Students." *Review of Educational Research*, 1988, *58*(4), 438–481.

Ericksen, S. C. "The Teacher-Made Test." *Memo to the Faculty*, no. 35. Ann Arbor: Center for Research on Learning and Teaching, University of Michigan, 1969.

"Exams: Alternative Ideas and Approaches." *Teaching Professor*, 1989, *3*(8), 3–4.

Fuhrmann, B. S., and Grasha, A. F. *A Practical Handbook for College Teachers*. Boston: Little, Brown, 1983.

Geiger, T. "Test Partners: A Formula for Success." *Innovation Abstracts*, 1991, *13*(11). (Newsletter published by College of Education, University of Texas at Austin)

Gronlund, N. E., and Linn, R. *Measurement and Evaluation in Teaching*. (6th ed.) New York: Macmillan, 1990.

Hendrickson, A. D. "Cooperative Group Test-Taking." *Focus*, 1990, *5*(2), 6. (Publication of the Office of Educational Development Programs, University of Minnesota)

Jacobs, L. C., and Chase, C. I. *Developing and Using Tests Effectively: A Guide for Faculty*. San Francisco: Jossey-Bass, 1992.

Jedrey, C. M. "Grading and Evaluation." In M. M. Gullette (ed.), *The Art and Craft of Teaching*. Cambridge, Mass.: Harvard University Press, 1984.

Keyworth, D. R. "The Group Exam." *Teaching Professor*, 1989, *3*(8), 5.

Liska, T., and Simonson, J. "Open-Text and Open-Note Exams." *Teaching Professor*, 1991, *5*(5), 1–2.

Lowman, J. *Mastering the Techniques of Teaching*. San Francisco: Jossey-Bass, 1984.

McKeachie, W. J. *Teaching Tips*. (8th ed.) Lexington, Mass.: Heath, 1986.

Milton, O., Pollio, H. R., and Eison, J. A. *Making Sense of College Grades: Why the Grading System Does Not Work and What Can Be Done About It*. San Francisco: Jossey-Bass, 1986.

Murray, J. P. "Better Testing for Better Learning." *College Teaching*, 1990, *38*(4), 148–152.

Savitz, F. "Effects of Easy Examination Questions Placed at the Beginning of Science Multiple-Choice Examinations." *Journal of Instructional Psychology*, 1985, *12*(1), 6–10.

Svinicki, M. D. "Comprehensive Finals." *Newsletter*, 1987, *9*(2), 1–2. (Publication of the Center for Teaching Effectiveness, University of Texas at Austin)

Svinicki, M. D., and Woodward, P. J. "Writing Higher-Level Objective Test Items." In K. G. Lewis (ed.), *Taming the Pedagogical Monster*. Austin: Center for Teaching Effectiveness, University of Texas, 1982.

Toppins, A. D. "Teaching by Testing: A Group Consensus Approach." *College Teaching*, 1989, *37*(3), 96–99.

Wergin, J. F. "Basic Issues and Principles in Classroom Assessment." In J. H. McMillan (ed.), *Assessing Students' Learning*. New Directions for Teaching and Learning, no. 34. San Francisco: Jossey-Bass, 1988.

29 Allaying Students' Anxieties About Tests

Anxiety can interfere with students' performance on tests. You can reduce students' anxiety and enhance their performance by taking care in how you prepare students for an exam, how you administer and return the test, and how you handle makeup tests. All students, but especially freshmen and sophomores, can benefit from knowing what they will be asked to do on an exam and under what conditions. Students will also feel more relaxed and less intimidated if you provide reassurance and encouragement rather than dire warnings about a test's difficulty. The suggestions below are designed to help you prepare your students to do their best on tests.

General Strategies

Make the first exam relatively easy. Research on motivation indicates that early success in a course increases students' motivation and confidence (Lucas, 1990). In particular, students who do well on the first test generally improve their grades on subsequent tests (Guskey, 1988).

Give more than one examination. The length of the school term, the difficulty level of the course, and the amount of course material all determine the number of exams an instructor gives. Periodic testing during the term has been shown to improve students' performance on the final exam (Lowman, 1984). Giving two or more midterm exams also spreads out the pressure, allows students to concentrate on one chunk of material at a time, and allows students and instructors to monitor progress.

Avoid "pop" quizzes. Unannounced or surprise quizzes may penalize students who are unable to prepare for every single class meeting. (Source: Jacobs and Chase, 1992)

Give students advice on how to study. Help students develop appropriate study strategies to organize and understand information from the assigned readings and class notes. Consult with your student learning center for information. Also see "Helping Students Learn." (Source: Mealey and Host, 1992)

Encourage students to study in groups. According to researchers, students who study in groups recall more information than students working alone and are able to overcome their feelings of academic inadequacy and isolation (Mealey and Host, 1992).

Schedule extra office hours before a test. Some instructors schedule extra office hours for the week or so before an exam to give students a chance to ask questions and go over difficult aspects of the material. They especially encourage study groups to visit during office hours.

Schedule review sessions before major exams. See "The Last Days of Class" for advice on how to structure a review session.

Ask students how you can help them feel less anxious. Students often make requests that faculty can easily accommodate, such as providing information about the test format, offering a review session, or refraining from walking around during the exam. (Source: Mealey and Host, 1992)

Preparing Students for an Exam

Give a diagnostic test early in the term. An early diagnostic test alerts students to the prerequisite skills and knowledge they need to succeed in your class. Some faculty give diagnostic tests throughout the term to identify which students are keeping up and which need help and to enable all students to identify the areas they need to work on. These diagnostic tests provide students with quick and frequent feedback and typically do not count heavily in the final grade. (Sources: Ericksen, 1969; Svinicki, 1976)

Attach a pool of final exam questions to the course syllabus and distribute both on the first day of class. A faculty member who uses this technique attaches to the syllabus fifty essay questions, all of which the class discusses during the term. The final exam is composed of five essay questions from the list. Under this system, students need not spend the semester worrying about what will be on the final. If the exam is too long to be attached to the syllabus, bind it to the course reader so that every student has a copy at a small additional cost. (Source: "Exams: Alternative Ideas and Approaches," 1989)

Put old exams on file in the department office or library. Reviewing past exams gives students clues about what to study. Students can analyze old exams for format (length of test, number of points for each type of question), types of questions, and level of difficulty. If your campus is networked, you can enter exams onto a file server and students can retrieve them whenever they want.

Distribute practice exams. Practice tests with answers help students gauge what is expected of them. You can use practice exams as the basis for review sessions or student study groups. If you will be administering a multiple-choice test, you could distribute the stems of multiple-choice questions but not the response choices; for example, "Which of the following statements best characterizes Melanie Klein's view of the first year of life?" (Source: Erickson and Strommer, 1991)

Before an exam, explain the format to students. Let students know the number of questions, whether the test will be multiple-choice or essay and open or closed book, and whether they can bring in notes.

Give students advice on how to prepare for an exam. For example, remind them to allocate their study time in proportion to the relative importance of various topics. See "Multiple-Choice and Matching Tests" and "Short-Answer and Essay Tests" for suggestions to give students for those types of exams. To lessen students' tension before a test, give the following recommendations:

- Avoid cramming by spreading studying over several weeks.
- Eat sensibly the night before a test and get a good night's sleep.
- Arrive early for the test.
- Take deep relaxing breaths as the test starts.

Administering Tests

Duplicate extra copies of the exam. Have extra copies on hand to replace copies that have blank pages or are collated incorrectly. (Source: McKeachie, 1986)

Administer the test yourself. You will want to be present to announce any corrections (of typographical errors, for example) or changes in the exam. Your presence can also motivate and reassure students and signal to them the importance of the test. Arrive early on the day of the test to answer questions and stay late to talk with students. (Sources: Jacobs and Chase, 1992; Lowman, 1984)

Read the instructions aloud at the beginning of class. Even if you write the clearest of instructions, it is helpful to read them aloud to the class. Ask students whether they have any questions about what they are supposed to do. Be brief, however, since students want to use their time to show you what they know.

Plan for "what ifs." Decide how you will respond to questions such as "What if we don't finish?" or "What if we think two answers are correct?"

Minimize temptations for cheating. Actively proctor exams, unless your institution is on the honor system. See "Preventing Academic Dishonesty" for advice on ways to reduce cheating during exams.

Don't hover over the class. Bring a book or work that will occupy you so that you will not be looking over students' shoulders. But be watchful to discourage cheating. (Source: Mealey and Host, 1992)

If there is no clock in the room, keep students apprised of the time. At the start of the exam write on the board the beginning time, the finishing time, and the time remaining. Once or twice update the time remaining and announce the last segment ("You have five minutes left."). Some faculty give students prompts during the test ("If you are not yet on question 5, you need to work a little more quickly"). Keep to the finishing time—it is unfair to allow some students to go on working when others must leave to go to another class.

Devote part of the session to reviewing the answers with students. One faculty member gives a thirty-minute midterm in a fifty-minute class. Students turn in their answer sheets after thirty minutes, but they keep the question sheet. The remaining class time is devoted to going over the correct answers and answering questions (Friedman, 1987). A variation on this technique is to divide the class into small groups and have them review answers and then reconvene as a class to discuss areas of disagreement or confusion. Another option is to ask for student volunteers who will meet with you immediately after the test to identify any specific problems with the exam. Or you could set up a student exam review committee. See "Preparing to Teach the Large Lecture Course."

Make one copy of the answer sheet available at the end of the test period. One faculty member described by Jacobs and Chase (1992) places a corrected test copy (multiple-choice items) on his desk so that students can review it after they have turned in their own exam. This is only possible, of course, in small classes.

Letting Students Show What They Know

Give students the opportunity to comment on the test. Researchers report that giving students space on the test itself to explain their responses to multiple-choice items helped relieve students' anxiety and reduced posttest complaints from students. Students were directed to write a short justification for any answer they felt needed more explanation or for questions they perceived to be tricky. The researchers noted that students averaged less than one explanation per test over four tests. The instructors added a point for a "good explanation of a wrong answer" and subtracted a point for "a bad explanation of a right answer" (Dodd and Leal, 1988; Nield and Wintre, 1986). Or you can ignore the comments on those items for which a student selected the correct multiple-choice option. Some faculty offer students extra credit for rewriting multiple-choice items (limit two items per test).

Include a blank question on the exam. Ask students to write a question or pose a problem that they were well prepared to answer. Grade students on the quality of the question (level of difficulty, appropriateness) and their answer. (Source: "Exams: Alternative Ideas and Approaches," 1989)

Include one or more extra-credit questions on the exam. Give students the opportunity to answer additional questions for extra credit at the end of the test. Add these points to their scores and to offset items they answered incorrectly.

Let students "buy" information from you during the exam. Tell students that midway through the exam (say, between twenty and thirty minutes of a sixty-minute test) they can ask you questions for a price. The price is losing points from their total score. For example, a student might ask whether an answer is right or wrong at a cost of one penalty point; an equation or formula may cost two penalty points; a diagram setup, four penalty points; and so on. A faculty member in mathematics who uses this technique reports that half of a typical class takes advantage of this approach to help them "unfreeze" on difficult problems. A chemistry professor uses a similar strategy but makes the option available to all students. He distributes a "test insurance page," in a lottery scratch-off format, to students along with their exams. The page contains clues to answers; each time students scratch off a clue, points are deducted from their total score. (Sources: Ellis, 1992; Gordon, 1988)

Let students bring in "crib sheets." As reported in "Exams: Alternative Ideas and Approaches" (1989) and Janick (1990), some faculty have had success by asking students to prepare one $5'' \times 8''$ index card that they can consult during the exam. According to the faculty, this technique helps students make decisions about what material is most important, and it can alleviate pretest anxiety. Vessey and Woodbury (1992) report negative effects of using crib sheets. Students, they believe, become "crib sheet focused"; they fail to answer the exam questions appropriately and instead look for key words on the test question that they can match to key terms on their crib sheet. When a match is found, students simply end up transcribing their crib sheet to their test.

Encourage students to evaluate the exam. If you want a sense of how students felt about the exam, ask them to complete an unsigned evaluation form that poses questions such as the following (adapted from "Let Students Grade the Exam," 1987):

- Did the content you expected to see appear on this exam?
- Identify the questions you never expected to see.
- Were the questions clear enough that, even though you may not have known the answer, you knew what was being asked?
- What questions confused you?

Or ask students to give a letter grade to the content, format, and fairness of the test.

Give students "a second chance to learn." After students turn in their in-class, closed-book exam, they receive a second copy to take home and complete as an open-book exam. Both exams are scored, and students can earn back up to one-half of the points lost on the in-class exam. A variation is not to give students a take-home test but instead to schedule, some days later, a repeat test containing equivalent items. Grading is handled by weighting the two exams differently: the lower score counts 25 percent and the higher score 75 percent. (Sources: Davidson, House, and Boyd, 1984; Murray, 1990)

Returning Examinations

Return test papers promptly. Most students are anxious to know how they have done, and a quick turnaround also encourages relearning or corrective learning. Most experts recommend that tests be returned within five days. Laws governing the privacy and confidentiality of student records forbid the posting of grades by name, initials, or student numbers; confidentiality and concerns about security also dictate that exams not be left in a pile in the department office for students to pick up. If you cannot return papers to your students during class or office hours (using photo IDs if necessary), arrange for a staff member in the department to return the tests. For example, let students know that they can pick up their own test from the department secretary between 3 and 5 P.M. in the department office. (Sources: Lowman, 1984; Unruh, 1990)

Use some class time to discuss the overall results. After making some general comments on how the class performed as a whole, you can show the general distribution of scores, note items missed by many people, and correct widespread misunderstandings. For essay tests, describe what you expected in a good answer and the most common problems. Some faculty read or distribute unsigned excerpts from outstanding papers. Smith (1992) returns graded multiple-choice exams to students and then divides them into groups to discuss the answers among themselves. "Questionable" questions are referred to the instructor for discussion by the entire class. She reports that having students review exams in groups often takes less time than her own reviews and students report enjoying it more. (Source: McKeachie, 1986; Smith, 1992)

Schedule extra office hours after returning a test. Students who come to see you may be angry or may try to have their grades changed.

- Request that students wait twenty-four hours before coming to see you. This gives them a chance to reread the exam, cool down, and prepare specific questions.
- Let students know that if they request a review of the grading of their test, you reserve the right to change the grade either positively or negatively.
- Ask students to come with specific questions (*not* "Why is my grade so low?"). Some faculty request that students prepare a brief paragraph expressing their complaint and justifying the correctness of their answer.
- When a student comes to see you, listen carefully. Do not interrupt the student to rebut each point.
- Try to shift the focus of the discussion from grades to problemsolving. Ask, "What can we do to help you do better next time?" Help the student shift his or her attitude from blaming you or the test toward gaining motivation to work more effectively.

- Don't change a grade out of sympathy or compassion but only because you have made a clerical error or mistakenly evaluated a response.

(Sources: Jacobs and Chase, 1992; Jedrey, 1984, McKeachie, 1986)

Arranging Makeup Tests

Avoid the need to arrange for makeup tests by giving frequent exams. Makeup tests are problematic. If you devise a new test, it might not be comparable to the original test. But if you use the same test, some students may have talked to others who took the original test. Scheduling a makeup test also poses logistical problems. One way to avoid using makeup tests is to give four exams, for example, and count the grades of only three. Students who take all four tests can drop their lowest score. Students who miss an exam will be graded on the three they have taken. Some faculty who give two midterms give double weight to one if a student misses the other. (Source: McKeachie, 1986)

Give students options on the number of tests they take. Buchanan and Rogers (1990) offer students the following options: (1) four multiple-choice tests, (2) four multiple-choice tests and a final, or (3) three multiple-choice tests and a final. In options one and three, each test is worth 25 percent of the course grade; in option two, each test is worth 20 percent. Students who miss one of the multiple-choice tests must elect option three. Students who miss two tests are handled on a case-by-case basis. The researchers report that about 5 percent of the students elect to miss any given test.

Give an additional exam for the entire class at the end of the semester. The grade on this extra test can replace a missed exam or replace a lower grade. This procedure frees you from policing excuses and illness on exam days. This option also helps out the student who has an off day on a test. (Source: Shea, 1990)

Hand out essay questions in advance. If you distribute in advance a list of essay questions from which the midterm questions will be taken, you will not have to write a makeup test. (Source: Lewis, 1982)

Give a two-hour rather than a three-hour final exam and use the last hour for makeup tests. By administering makeup tests during the time block reserved for the final exam, you can avoid the complexities of special scheduling.

Give an oral exam as a substitute. Oral exams are a practical alternative only in small classes and are more effective in advanced courses, where higher levels of learning can be assessed. Oral exams typically cover less material, but in more depth, than written exams.

References

Buchanan, R. W., and Rogers, M. "Innovative Assessment in Large Classes." *College Teaching*, 1990, *38*(2), 69–73.

Davidson, W. B., House, W. J., and Boyd, T. L. "A Test-Retest Policy for Introductory Psychology Courses." *Teaching of Psychology*, 1984, *11*(3), 182–184.

Dodd, D. K., and Leal, L. "Answer Justification: Removing the 'Trick' from Multi-Choice Questions." *Teaching of Psychology*, 1988, *15*(1), 37–38.

Ellis, A. "Scratching for Grades." *National Teaching and Learning Forum*, 1992, *1*(5), 4–5.

Ericksen, S. C. "The Teacher-Made Test." *Memo to the Faculty*, no. 35. Ann Arbor: Center for Research on Learning and Teaching, University of Michigan, 1969.

Erickson, B. L., and Strommer, D. W. *Teaching College Freshmen*. San Francisco: Jossey-Bass, 1991.

"Exams: Alternative Ideas and Approaches." *Teaching Professor*, 1989, *3*(8), 3–4.

Friedman, H. "Immediate Feedback, No Return Test Procedure for Introductory Courses." *Teaching of Psychology*, 1987, *14*(4), 244.

Gordon, L. "Cost-Benefit Testing." *Academic Leader*, 1988, *4*(4), 1–2.

Guskey, T. R. *Improving Student Learning in College Classrooms*. Springfield, Ill.: Thomas, 1988.

Jacobs, L. C., and Chase, C. I. *Developing and Using Tests Effectively: A Guide for Faculty*. San Francisco: Jossey-Bass, 1992.

Janick, J. "Crib Sheets." *Teaching Professor*, 1990, *4*(6), 2.

Jedrey, C. M. "Grading and Evaluation." In M. M. Gullette (ed.), *The Art and Craft of Teaching*. Cambridge, Mass.: Harvard University Press, 1984.

"Let Students Grade the Exam." *Teaching Professor*, 1987, *1*(5), 4.

Lewis, K. G. *Taming the Pedagogical Monster*. Austin: Center for Teaching Effectiveness, University of Texas, 1982.

Lowman, J. *Mastering the Techniques of Teaching*. San Francisco: Jossey-Bass, 1984.

Lucas, A. F. "Using Psychological Models to Understand Student Motivation." In M. D. Svinicki (ed.), *The Changing Face of College Teaching.* New Directions for Teaching and Learning, no. 42. San Francisco: Jossey-Bass, 1990.

McKeachie, W. J. *Teaching Tips.* (8th ed.) Lexington, Mass: Heath, 1986.

Mealey, D. L., and Host, T. R, "Coping with Test Anxiety." *College Teaching,* 1992, *40*(4), 147–150.

Murray, J. P. "Better Testing for Better Learning." *College Teaching,* 1990, *38*(4), 148–152.

Nield, A. F., and Wintre, M. "Multiple Choice Questions with an Option to Comment: Students' Attitude and Use." *Teaching of Psychology,* 1986, *13*(4), 196–199.

Shea, M. A. *Compendium of Good Ideas on Teaching and Learning.* Boulder: Faculty Teaching Excellence Program, University of Colorado, 1990.

Smith, M. A. "How to Make the Most of the 'Test Post-Mortem.'" *Teaching Professor,* 1992, *6*(5), 5–6.

Svinicki, M. D. "The Test: Uses, Construction and Evaluation." *Engineering Education,* 1976, *66*(5), 408–411.

Unruh, D. *The Teacher's Guide.* Los Angeles: Office of Instructional Development, University of California, 1990.

Vessey, J. K., and Woodbury, W. "Crib Sheets: Use with Caution." *Teaching Professor,* 1992, *6*(7), 6–7.

30

Multiple-Choice and Matching Tests

Forced-choice test items require students to select a choice from the alternatives given; students don't compose the answers but instead choose the one they think is best. The most common forced-choice format is multiple choice. On a multiple-choice test item, students are presented with a question or incomplete statement (a stem) and four or five suggested answers or completions, one of which is best (the key); the incorrect choices are called distractors or foils. On matching test items, students are asked to match a set of premises or stimuli with a list of response choices.

Use multiple-choice or matching tests when you want to test the breadth of students' learning (a forced-choice test can cover more topics than an essay test), when you want to test a variety of levels of learning (from recall of factual information to problem solving), or when you have more time to prepare an exam than to score it (Clegg and Cashin, 1986). Multiple-choice and matching tests have been criticized as measuring only recall of basic facts or rote memorization. However, with some time and skill, you can develop tests that assess whether students have mastered complex concepts and ideas.

General Strategies

Make sure that at least some test items require higher-level learning. Use Bloom's taxonomy (described in "Quizzes, Tests, and Exams") to help you develop forced-choice items that address higher-order learning such as understanding, application, and synthesis. For example, write a question that requires students to predict the outcome of a situation rather than simply label a phenomenon or provide an abstraction or principle and ask for examples ("What are the key symptoms of paranoia?") Or give examples and ask for the principle or theory the examples illustrate. (Source: McKeachie, 1986)

Here are three examples of multiple-choice items that cover a range of learning outcomes (adapted from Welsh, 1978, pp. 204–206)

1. Which of the following has contributed most to long-term economic growth in the United States?
   a. Increasing personal income tax rates
   b. Reducing hours worked per week to spread employment among more people
   c. Increasing tariffs on imported goods that compete with domestically produced goods
   d. Increasing levels of education and technological improvement

[This question tests whether students can recognize ideas in somewhat different language from that used in the textbook and whether students can make comparative generalizations.]

2. A large city is investigating the elimination of rent controls on housing at a time when the vacancy rate is extremely low — only 1 percent of all apartments in the city are vacant. Which of the following is most likely to occur if rent controls are eliminated?
   a. An increase in the demand for housing, followed by a decrease in the supply of housing
   b. An increase in rents, followed by an increase in the supply of housing
   c. A decrease in rents and a decrease in the supply of housing
   d. No change in rents because price controls are usually set where supply and demand intersect

[This question asks students to apply supply and demand principles to explain a specific situation.]

3. Because of rapidly rising national defense expenditures, the country of Parador will experience price inflation unless measures are taken to restrict the growth of aggregate private demand. If Parador wishes to minimize the adverse effects of anti-inflationary policies on economic growth, it should implement
   a. a tight monetary policy because it would restrict consumption expenditures more than investment.
   b. a tight monetary policy because the tax increase would restrict consumption expenditures.
   c. an increase in personal income taxes because it would restrict consumption expenditures more than investment.
   d. either a tight monetary policy or an increase in personal income taxes because both depress investment equally.

[This question requires students to analyze the information presented, select the most appropriate policy, and predict the expected effects of the policy.]

Write test items throughout the term. Good test items are difficult to create, and you will find the task easier if you spread out the work. Set yourself a goal of writing three to five items each week. If you keep the items on index cards or on a computer, you can easily sort through them when you are putting together the test. Observers note that most professional item writers can only manage three or four per day; it is simply not possible to write a good multiple-choice exam the night before the test at the last minute (Jacobs and Chase, 1992).

Take precautions to minimize cheating during tests. See "Preventing Academic Dishonesty" for suggestions on how to create and administer tests in ways that minimize opportunities for cheating.

Give students advice on how to take a multiple-choice or matching test. Some faculty give students tips such as these on test taking (adapted from McKeachie, 1986, pp. 95–96):

- Go through the test once and answer all the questions you can.
- Go through the test again; spend a reasonable amount of time on each problem but move on if you get stuck.
- Save some time at the end to double-check your answers and make sure you haven't made any clerical errors.
- Change your answers if you wish; research shows that most students gain more than they lose on changed answers.

Multiple-Choice Test Items

In the directions, instruct students to select the "best answer" rather than the "correct answer." Asking for the correct answer is more likely to invite arguments from contentious students that their selections are correct as well. If you ask for the best answer, you can acknowledge that other responses have some element of truth or accuracy but that the keyed response is the best. (Source: Jacobs and Chase, 1992)

In the directions, let students know whether they can guess. Observers recommend that you encourage students to answer every item, even when they are unsure about the correct answer (Jacobs and Chase, 1992). Help students recognize that they can use their partial knowledge of the topic to figure out a response and make an informed guess. In scoring the test, don't penalize students for guessing.

Express the full problem in the stem. Make sure that students can understand the problem before reading the alternative answers. Usually, direct questions are clearer than sentence completions, though you may use either. Keep in mind that the stem can also consist of a map, diagram, picture, or graph.

Here is an example of a poor item and a better version:

Poor: Grading is
a. most often used to distinguish between students.
b. a way of reporting students' progress.
c. the only reason students study.
d. something teachers put off if they can.

Better: The main reason most universities use the letter-grading system is its convenience for
a. reporting students' progress.
b. keeping permanent records.
c. distinguishing among students.
d. motivating students to learn.

Put all relevant material in the stem. Do not repeat phrases in the options if the phrase can be stated in the stem. Forcing students to reread a phrase wastes time they could put to better use selecting an answer.

Here is an example of a poor item and a better version (Ory, 1985, p. 8):

Poor: In national elections in the United States the president is officially
a. chosen by the people.
b. chosen by members of Congress.
c. chosen by the House of Representatives.
d. chosen by the Electoral College.

Better: In national elections in the United States the President is officially chosen by
a. the people.
b. members of Congress.
c. the House of Representatives.
d. the Electoral College.

Keep the stem short. Unnecessary information confuses students and wastes their time. Compare the following (Welsh 1978, p. 198):

Poor: Monetary and fiscal policies are commonly used in the U. S. for stabilization purposes. Leaving aside fiscal policies for the moment, which of the following monetary policies would be most effective in combating inflation?

Better: Which of the following monetary policies would be most effective in combating inflation?

Limit the number of response alternatives. According to McKeachie (1986, p. 92), research shows that three-choice items are about as effective as four-choice items. A four-response (including the correct answer) format is the most popular. In any event, never give students more than five alternatives.

Make the distractors appealing and plausible. The most challenging aspect of creating multiple-choice items is designing plausible distractors. If the distractors are farfetched, students will too easily locate the correct answer. Distractors should represent errors commonly made by students. The best distractors are statements that are too general or too specific for the requirements of the problem, statements that are accurate but do not fully meet the requirements of the problem, and incorrect statements that seem right to the poorly prepared student. On rare occasion an implausible distractor can relieve tension among students.

In the following example (Welsh, 1978, p. 199), the last alternative is implausible:

1. The demand for a factor of production depends largely on
    a. the supply of the factor.
    b. the supply of other factors of production.
    c. the demand for the product or products that it helps produce.
    d. the considered judgment of the Federal Reserve System.

A better alternative would be the demand for other factors of production. (Sources: Clegg and Cashin, 1986; McKeachie, 1986; Welsh, 1978)

Make all choices equal in length and parallel in structure. Do not give away the best choice by making it longer, more detailed, or filled with more qualifiers than the alternatives. (Source: Clegg and Cashin, 1986)

Avoid trick questions or negative wording. Negative wording often confuses students and makes items unnecessarily complex. If you do use negatives, underline or capitalize them or put them in bold so students don't overlook them. Always avoid having negatives in both the stem and the options. For example:

Poor: Which of the following is not a characteristic of Fauvism?

Better: Which of the following best distinguishes Fauvism from other art movements?

(Source: Clegg and Cashin, 1986)

Refrain from using words such as *always, never, all,* or *none.* Savvy students know that few ideas or situations are absolute or universally true. (Source: Clegg and Cashin, 1986)

Place the choices in some meaningful order. As appropriate, order the responses logically, chronologically, numerically, or conceptually.

Make the choices grammatically consistent with the stem. Read the stem and each of the choices aloud to be sure that each is correct in the use of *a* or *an*, singular and plural, and subject-verb agreement. Here is an example in which two of the choices need to be reworded (Welsh, 1978, p. 200):

1. The functions of the Federal Reserve are to provide the nation with an elastic money supply and to
   a. help stabilize the economy.
   b. correction of national income statistics.
   c. correction of tax laws.
   d. help levy property taxes.

Avoid giving "all of the above" or "none of the above" as choices. These items do not discriminate well among students with differing knowledge. Students need only compare two choices: if both are acceptable, then "all of the above" is the logical answer, even if the student is unsure about a third choice. (Sources: Jacobs and Chase, 1992; Lowman, 1984; McKeachie, 1986)

Vary the position of the best answer. Research shows that faculty tend to locate the best answer in the *b* or *c* position (McKeachie, 1986). (Perhaps it seems too obvious to put the answer first or last.) Instead, use a deck of cards to locate correct responses randomly (for example, hearts = first position, spades = second position, and so on) unless you are arranging the choices in some meaningful order (for example, numerical, chronological, or conceptual). (Source: McKeachie, 1986)

Keep the test length manageable. Students can complete between one and two multiple-choice items per minute. (Source: Lowman, 1984)

Take advantage of machine scoring capabilities. Many campuses have optical scanning equipment that can quickly score multiple-choice exams. Special answer forms and number two pencils are necessary. Check with your campus testing service to see whether machine scoring is available.

Matching Test Items

Give clear instructions. Let students know the basis on which items are to be matched, where to write answers, and whether a response may be used more than once. For example: "Next to each architectural concept in Column 1, write the letter of the project in Column 2 that best exemplifies that concept. You may use each project in Column 2 more than once or not at all." (Sources: Fuhrmann and Grasha, 1983; Ory, 1985)

Keep the two sets of items homogeneous. For example, Column 1 may list events and Column 2 may list dates; do not combine events, dates, and names in one column. (Source: Fuhrmann and Grasha, 1983)

Try to order the responses. If you order the items in Column 2 alphabetically, chronologically, or conceptually, students will be able to read the series quickly and locate answers rapidly. (Source: Ory, 1985)

Create more responses than premises. In general, give students five to ten alternatives in Column 2. If you include distractors in Column 2, let students know that some of the entries in Column 2 do not apply. (Source: Ory, 1985)

Be conscious of layout and format. Always keep both columns on the same page so that students don't have to flip back and forth. Place answer blanks to the left of each entry in Column 1. Place Column 2 on the right-hand side of the page. Use capital letters for the responses (they are easier to discern than lowercase letters) and numbers for the premises (for later discussion). (Source: Fuhrmann and Grasha, 1983)

After the Test: Item Analysis

After you have scored the exams, evaluate the test items. An item analysis can help you improve your tests by showing you which items are too easy or too hard and how well an item distinguishes between students at the top and bottom. Your campus may have a testing office that can help you with this type of analysis.

Look at the difficulty of each item. By hand or with computer software, calculate the percentage of students answering each item correctly. The goal is to construct a test that contains only a few items that more than 90 percent or less than 30 percent of students answer correctly. Optimally, difficult items are those that about 50 to 75 percent of the class answer correctly. Items are considered moderately difficult if between 70 and 85 percent of the students get the correct response. Jacobs and Chase (1992) point out that an item may be difficult for a variety of reasons: it may be unclearly written; the content may be challenging; or the students may be unprepared. In interpreting item difficulty indices, consider all three possibilities. (Sources: Jacobs and Chase, 1992; Lowman, 1984; Wergin, 1988)

Look at how well each item discriminates between high and low scorers. The statistical technique called *item discrimination* lets you know whether individual test items discriminate between top and bottom students. If you do not have access to a computer program that calculates correlation coefficients, you can determine discrimination levels by hand. Svinicki (1976) recommends the following procedure:

1. Identify the ten highest-scoring exams and the ten lowest-scoring exams.
2. For each question, identify the number of students in the top group of ten who answered correctly. Do the same for the bottom group of ten students.
3. Compute the *discrimination ratio* by subtracting the number of students in the bottom group who answered correctly from the number of students in the top group who answered correctly and dividing by ten (the number of students in each group).

For example, if nine of ten of the highest-scoring group and three of ten of the lowest-scoring group answered the eighth item correctly, the discrimination ratio for that item is .6 (9 − 3 / 10). The discrimination ratio will fall between − 1.0 and + 1.0. The closer the ratio is to + 1.0, the more effectively that question distinguishes students who know the material (the top group) from those who don't (the bottom group). Ideally, each item will have a ratio of at least + .5. Items with discrimination ratios of 0.0 do not distinguish among students very well, but you may wish to retain those items on future tests if the material is important or if you want to assure that the test has a few items that everyone answers correctly. If few students in the top group achieved a correct score on the item, take a look at the structure of the item and the distractors to see whether they may be causing problems. (Sources: Lowman, 1986; Svinicki, 1976)

Use the results to improve your tests. Use both the difficulty level and discrimination ratio to drop or revise items. Seyer (1981) recommends these rules of thumb: items with a difficulty level of between 30 percent and 70 percent can be expected to have an acceptable discrimination ratio, that is, at least + .3 or above. Items with difficulty levels below 30 percent or above 70 percent cannot be expected to have high discrimination ratios. If an item has a high difficulty level and a low discrimination ratio (below + .3), the item needs to be revised. You may find that many items fall on the borderline: discrimination ratios just under + .3 and difficulty levels of between 30 percent and 70 percent. Those items do not necessarily need revision. Seyer (1981, W–10) offers the following advice to help you decide which items to revise:

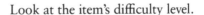

Look at the item's difficulty level.

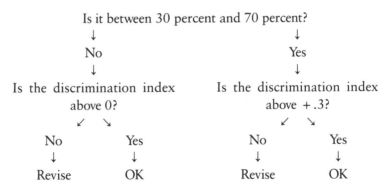

Is it between 30 percent and 70 percent?

    ↓   ↓

  No   Yes

  ↓   ↓

Is the discrimination index   Is the discrimination index

above 0?   above + .3?

No   Yes   No   Yes

↓   ↓   ↓   ↓

Revise   OK   Revise   OK

Solicit students' comments about the test. See "Allaying Students' Anxieties About Tests."

References

Clegg, V. L., and Cashin, W. E. "Improving Multiple-Choice Tests." *Idea Paper*, no. 16. Manhattan: Center for Faculty Evaluation and Development in Higher Education, Kansas State University, 1986.

Fuhrmann, B. S., and Grasha, A. F. *A Practical Handbook for College Teachers*. Boston: Little, Brown, 1983.

Jacobs, L. C., and Chase, C. I. *Developing and Using Tests Effectively: A Guide for Faculty*. San Francisco: Jossey-Bass, 1992.

Lowman, J. *Mastering the Techniques of Teaching*. San Francisco: Jossey-Bass, 1984.

McKeachie, W. J. *Teaching Tips*. (8th ed.) Lexington, Mass.: Heath, 1986.

Ory, J. C. *Improving Your Test Questions*. Urbana: Office of Instructional Resources, University of Illinois, 1985.

Seyer, P. C. *Item Analysis*. San Jose, Calif.: Faculty and Instructional Development Office, San Jose State University, 1981.

Svinicki, M. D. "The Test: Uses, Construction and Evaluation." *Engineering Education*, 1976, 66(5), 408–411.

Welsh, A. L. "Multiple Choice Objective Tests." In P. Saunders, A. L. Welsh, and W. L. Hansen (eds.), *Resource Manual for Teaching Training Programs in Economics*. New York: Joint Council on Economic Education, 1978.

Wergin, J. F. "Basic Issues and Principles in Classroom Assessment." In J. H. McMillan (ed.), *Assessing Students' Learning*. New Directions for Teaching and Learning, no. 34. San Francisco: Jossey-Bass, 1988.

31

Short-Answer and Essay Tests

Short-answer items ask students to define a term or concept, list three reasons why..., or state the importance of some idea or event (Lowman, 1984). Essay tests let students display their overall understanding of a topic and demonstrate their ability to think critically, organize their thoughts, and be creative and original. While essay and short-answer questions are easier to design than multiple-choice tests, they are more difficult and time-consuming to score. Moreover, essay tests can suffer from unreliable grading; that is, grades on the same response may vary from reader to reader or from time to time by the same reader. For this reason, some faculty prefer short-answer items to essay tests. On the other hand, essay tests are the best measures of students' skills in higher-order thinking and written expression. In addition to the suggestions below, see "Designing Effective Writing Assignments" and "Evaluating Students' Written Work" for other ideas about creating topics and grading essays.

General Strategies

Do not use essay questions to evaluate understanding that could be tested with multiple-choice questions. Save essay questions for testing higher levels of thought (application, synthesis, and evaluation), not recall of facts (Sanders, 1966). Appropriate tasks for essays include these from Unruh (1988, p. 47):

Comparing: Identify the similarities and differences between...

Relating cause and effect: What are the major causes of...? What would be the most likely effects of...?

Justifying: Explain why you agree or disagree with the following statement.

Generalizing: State a set of principles that can explain the following events.

Inferring: How would character X react to the following?

Creating: What would happen if . . .?

Applying: Describe a situation that illustrates the principle of . . .

Analyzing: Find and correct the reasoning errors in the following passage.

Synthesizing: Describe a plan for proving that . . .

Evaluating: Assess the strengths and weaknesses of . . .

Give students advice on how to approach an essay or short-answer test. To reduce students' anxiety and help them see that you want them to do their best, give them pointers on how to take an essay exam. The following examples are adapted from Brooks (1990, pp. 15–18), McKeachie (1986, p. 96), Sanders (1966, pp. 167–168), and Walvoord (1986, pp. 11–13):

- Survey the entire test quickly, noting the directions and estimating the importance and difficulty of each question. If ideas or answers come to mind, jot them down quickly.
- Divide the time available among the questions. Allow more time for important or difficult questions. Save some time at the end of the period to review what you have written. Stick to your plan—four partially complete answers will probably receive more credit than two extremely complete answers.
- Analyze each question and its parts. Before you begin writing, decide what is called for and what is not called for in your answer. Let the key nouns in the question suggest the topic and subtopics for your essay. Verbs (*compare* and *contrast*, *define*, *describe*) will tell you how to approach the topic. Observe the limitations (for example, "from 1900 to 1945") expressed in the question.
- Outline each answer before you begin to write. Jot down notes on important points, arrange them in a pattern, and add specific details under each point. A good outline shortens writing time, makes the answer clearer, and provides a check against overlooking part of the answer.
- If you are completely stumped by a question, jot down *anything* you can think of that could possibly be relevant. Free association may prompt your memory, and usually you will find that you know something relevant to the question.

- Write a thesis statement that expresses your main point or conclusion. The thesis should not simply announce the topics you will discuss but should state your overall conclusion. If you are given a question that asks you to discuss or analyze, turn it into a how or why question. Your thesis will be the answer to the question. For example, if the test question is "Discuss the concept of love in D. H. Lawrence's novel *Women in Love*," your first thought might be "This essay will discuss bisexual, homosexual, and familial love in Lawrence's *Women in Love*." A how question might be "How are bisexual, homosexual, and familiar love portrayed?" You then transform this into a thesis statement: "An examination of bisexual, homosexual, and familial love in *Women in Love* reveals that hatred and isolation are present even in the closest love relationships." State your thesis at the beginning of your essay (Walvoord, 1986, p. 11).
- Follow your outline as you write. If you skip every other line as you write, you will have room for additions or changes that occur to you as you reread your response.
- Support your point of view with specific examples and relevant evidence.
- Reread your exam before you turn it in. Check for omissions, repetitions, and errors. Cross out words or phrases or add new information as legibly as you can.
- If you run out of time, outline your main points and examples and write, "ran out of time." The instructor may give you partial credit.

Don't give students a choice of questions to answer. There are three drawbacks to giving students a choice. First, some students will waste time trying to decide which questions to answer. Second, you will not know whether all students are equally knowledgeable about all the topics covered on the test. Third, since some questions are likely to be harder than others, the test could be unfair. (Sources: Jacobs and Chase, 1992; Welsh, 1978)

Ask students to write more than one essay. Tests that ask only one question are less valid and reliable than those with a wider sampling of test items. In a fifty-minute class period, you may be able to pose three essay questions or ten short-answer questions.

Writing Effective Test Questions

State the question clearly and precisely. Avoid vague questions that could lead students to different interpretations. If your question is so general that no two students will answer alike (for example, "Compare the Persian Gulf and Vietnam wars"), you will have serious difficulties equitably grading the responses. If you use the word *how* or *why* in an essay question, students will be better able to develop a clear thesis (Tollefson, 1988). Here are some examples of essay and short-answer questions:

Poor: What are three types of market organization? In what ways are they different from one another?

Better: Define *oligopoly*. How does *oligopoly* differ from both *perfect competition* and *monopoly* in terms of number of firms, control over price, conditions of entry, cost structure, and long-term profitability [*Handbook for TAs in Economics*, 1980]?

Poor: Name the principles that determined postwar American foreign policy.

Better: Describe three principles on which American foreign policy was based between 1945 and 1960; illustrate each of the principles with two actions of the executive branch of government ["Guides to Writing Essay Questions," 1990, p. 1].

Poor: You are the president of the United States. What economic policies would you pursue?

Better: You are the president of the United States. State your goals for employment, price levels, and rate of real economic growth. What fiscal and monetary policies would you implement to achieve your goals [Welsh, 1978, p. 174]?

Poor: Why does an internal combustion engine work?

Better: Explain the functions of fuel, carburetor, distributor, and the operation of the cylinder's components in making an internal combustion engine run [Jacobs and Chase, 1992, p. 114].

Poor: Was the above passage written by a classical or patristic Latin writer? Why do you think that?

Better: Decide whether the above passage was written by a classical or patristic Latin writer. Support your position by identifying and explaining specific phrases or other linguistic features that exemplify the characteristic writing style [Cashin, 1987, p. 2].

Consider the layout of the question. If you want students to consider certain aspects or issues in developing their answers, set them out in a separate paragraph. Leave the question on a line by itself. (Source: Tollefson, 1988)

Write out the correct answer yourself. Use your version to help you revise the question, as needed, and to estimate how much time students will need to complete the question. If you can answer the question in ten minutes, students will probably need twenty to thirty minutes. Use these estimates in determining the number of questions to ask on the exam. Give students advice on how much time to spend on each question.

Decide on guidelines for full and partial credit. Decide which specific facts or ideas a student must mention to earn full credit and how you will award partial credit. For example, consider this essay question (Erickson and Strommer, 1991, p. 144):

> In *Habits of the Heart*, Bellah says that the way most Americans think about life has changed. Bellah claims that "the good things of life, those objects that make up the good life are still important, but they now take second place to the subjective states of well-being that make up a sense of self-worth." Is Bellah right about the relative importance of material success and the development of self-worth? Or has he overstated the case? Your essay should state your position on this issue, provide examples or other evidence to support your position, and defend your position against that alternative.

Here is the scoring guide (adapted from Erickson and Strommer, 1991, p. 147):

- *Full credit—six points:* The essay clearly states a position, provides support for the position, and raises a counterargument or objection and refutes it. Evidence is both persuasive and original. Counterargument is significant. The essay contains no extraneous information.
- *Five points:* The essay states a position, supports it, and raises a counterargument or objection and refutes it. The essay contains one or more of the following ragged edges: evidence is not uniformly persuasive, counterargument is not a serious threat to the position, some ideas seem out of place.
- *Four points:* The essay states a position and raises a counterargument, but neither is well developed. The objection or counterargument may lean toward the trivial. The essay also seems disorganized.

- *Three points:* The essay states a position, provides evidence supporting the position, and is well organized. However, the essay does not address possible objections or counterarguments. Thus, even though the essay may be better organized than the essay given four points, it should not receive more than three points.
- *Two points:* The essay states a position and provides some support but does not do it very well. Evidence is scanty, trivial, or general. The essay achieves its length largely through repetition of ideas and inclusion of irrelevant information.
- *One point:* The essay does not state the student's position on the issue. Instead, it restates the position presented in the question and summarizes evidence discussed in class or in the reading.

Here is another example (Ory, 1985, p. 23): "Americans are mixed-up people with no sense of ethical values. Everyone knows that baseball is far less necessary than food and steel, yet they pay ball players a lot more than farmers and steelworkers. Why? In two or three sentences, indicate how an economist would explain the above." The scoring guide might allocate a total of seven points for this question:

Three points: Salaries are based on the demand relative to the supply of a service.

Two points: Excellent ball players are rare (low supply).

Two points: Many ball clubs want excellent players (high demand).

Grading and Evaluating Students' Exams

Read the exams without looking at the students' names. Try not to bias your grading by carrying over your perceptions about individual students. Some faculty ask students to put a number or pseudonym on the exam and to place that number/pseudonym on an index card that is turned in with the test. Other faculty have students write their names on the last page of the blue book or on the back of the test.

Skim all the exams quickly, without assigning any grades. Before you begin grading, you will want an overview of the general level of performance and the range of students' responses. (Source: McKeachie, 1986)

Choose examples of exams to serve as anchors or standards. Identify exams that are excellent, good, adequate, and poor. Use these papers to refresh your memory of the standards by which you are grading and to ensure fairness over the period of time you spend grading. (Source: McKeachie, 1986)

Grade each exam question by question rather than grading all questions for a single student. Shuffle papers before scoring the next question to distribute your fatigue factor randomly. By randomly shuffling papers you also avoid ordering effects (that is, Tanya's B work always follows Lasa's A work and suffers from the comparison). (Sources: Fuhrmann and Grasha, 1983; Ory, 1985)

Avoid judging exams on extraneous factors. Don't let handwriting, use of pen or pencil, format (for example, many lists), or other such factors influence your judgment about the intellectual quality of the response.

Write comments on students' exams. Write brief notes on strengths and weaknesses to indicate what students have done well and where they need to improve. The process of writing comments also keeps your attention focused on the response. And your comments will refresh your memory if a student wants to talk to you about the exam. Some faculty ask students to write on every other page of the blue book, leaving the opposite page blank for instructors' comments (Cashin, 1987). Strive to balance positive and critical comments and to focus on the organization and flow of the response, not on whether you agree or disagree with the students' ideas. Experienced faculty note, however, that students tend not to read their returned final exams, so you probably do not need to comment extensively on those. (Sources: Cashin, 1987; Jedrey, 1984; McKeachie, 1986; Sanders, 1966)

Read only a modest number of exams at a time. Most faculty tire after reading ten or so responses. Take short breaks to keep up your concentration. Also, try to set limits on how long to spend on each paper so that you maintain your energy level and do not get overwhelmed. However, research suggests that you read all responses to a single question in one sitting to avoid extraneous factors influencing your grading (for example, time of day, temperature, and so on) ("Guides to Writing Essay Questions," 1990).

If you can, read some of the papers twice. Wait two days or so and review a random set of exams without looking at the grades you assigned. Rereading helps you increase your reliability as a grader. If your two scores differ, take the average. (Source: "Guides to Writing Essay Questions," 1990)

Place the grade on the last page of the exam. This protects students' privacy when you return or they pick up their tests.

If graduate student instructors assist in grading, set up standardized procedures. McKeachie (1986, p. 103) offers advice to faculty who have readers or teaching assistants to help with grading:

- Meet as a group to discuss the answers to each question. Decide how many points will be given for what types of answers. Review the scoring criteria and model answers prepared by the faculty member.
- Establish two- or three-person teams for each essay question. Give each team eight or ten exams and have each team member independently grade the team's question on each exam. Compare the grades that team members assigned and discuss the discrepancies until consensus is reached.
- If needed, have the teams grade and discuss a second batch of exams so that teams feel confident that they have arrived at common criteria.
- From this point on, each member grades independently. If any team member is unsure about a particular exam, it is passed to another team member for an opinion.

Returning Essay Exams

Return exams promptly. A quick turnaround reinforces learning and capitalizes on students' interest in the results. Try to return tests within a week or so.

Review the exam in class. Give students a copy of the scoring guide or grading criteria you used. Let students know what a good answer included and the most common errors the class made. If you wish, read an example of a good answer and contrast it with a poor answer you created. Give students information on the distribution of scores so they know where they stand. (Source: McKeachie, 1986)

Use groups to discuss test questions. Some faculty break the class into small groups to discuss answers to the test. Unresolved questions are brought up to the class as a whole. (Source: McKeachie, 1986)

Get feedback from the class about the test. Ask students to tell you what was particularly difficult or unexpected. Find out how they prepared for the exam and what they wish they had done differently. Pass along to next year's class tips on the specific skills and strategies this class found effective. (Source: Walvoord, 1986)

Keep a file of essay questions. Include a copy of the test with your annotations on ways to improve it, the mistakes students made in responding to various questions, the distribution of students' performance, and any comments that students made about the exam. If possible, keep copies of good and poor exams. (Source: Cashin, 1987)

References

Brooks, P. *Working in Subject A Courses*. Berkeley: Subject A Program, University of California, 1990.

Cashin, W. E. "Improving Essay Tests." *Idea Paper*, no. 17. Manhattan: Center for Faculty Evaluation and Development in Higher Education, Kansas State University, 1987.

Erickson, B. L., and Strommer, D. W. *Teaching College Freshmen*. San Francisco: Jossey-Bass, 1991.

Fuhrmann, B. S., and Grasha, A. F. *A Practical Handbook for College Teachers*. Boston: Little, Brown, 1983.

"Guides to Writing Essay Questions." *Instructional Exchange*, 1990, 2(3). (Publication of the Office of University Assessment and Intellectual Skills Program, Western Michigan University)

Handbook for TAs in Economics. Berkeley: Economics Department, University of California, Berkeley, 1980.

Jacobs, L. C., and Chase, C. I. *Developing and Using Tests Effectively: A Guide for Faculty*. San Francisco: Jossey-Bass, 1992.

Jedrey, C. M. "Grading and Evaluation." In M. M. Gullette (ed.), *The Art and Craft of Teaching*. Cambridge, Mass.: Harvard University Press, 1984.

Lowman, J. *Mastering the Techniques of Teaching*. San Francisco: Jossey-Bass, 1984.

McKeachie, W. J. *Teaching Tips*. (8th ed.) Lexington, Mass.: Heath, 1986.

Ory, J. C. *Improving Your Test Questions*. Urbana: Office of Instructional Resources, University of Illinois, 1985.

Sanders, N. M. *Classroom Questions: What Kinds?* New York: Harper & Row, 1966.

Tollefson, S. K. *Encouraging Student Writing*. Berkeley: Office of Educational Development, University of California, 1988.

Unruh, D. *Test Scoring Manual: Guide for Developing and Scoring Course Examinations*. Los Angeles: Office of Instructional Development, University of California, 1988.

Walvoord, B. F. *Helping Students Write Well: A Guide for Teachers in All Disciplines*. (2nd ed.) New York: Modern Language Association, 1986.

Welsh, A. L. "Essay Questions and Tests." In P. Saunders, A. L. Welsh, and W. L. Hansen (eds.), *Resource Manual for Teacher Training Programs in Economics*. New York: Joint Council on Economic Education, 1978.

32

Grading Practices

There are no hard-and-fast rules about the best ways to grade. In fact, as Erickson and Strommer (1991) point out, how you grade depends a great deal on your values, assumptions, and educational philosophy: if you view introductory courses as "weeder" classes—to separate out students who lack potential for future success in the field—you are likely to take a different grading approach than someone who views introductory courses as teaching important skills that all students need to master.

All faculty agree, however, that grades provide information on how well students are learning (Erickson and Strommer, 1991). But grades also serve other purposes. Scriven (1974) has identified at least six functions of grading:

- To describe unambiguously the worth, merit, or value of the work accomplished
- To improve the capacity of students to identify good work, that is, to improve their self-evaluation or discrimination skills with respect to work submitted
- To stimulate and encourage good work by students
- To communicate the teacher's judgment of the student's progress
- To inform the teacher about what students have and haven't learned
- To select people for rewards or continued education

For some students, grades are also a sign of approval or disapproval; they take them very personally. Because of the importance of grades, faculty need to communicate to students a clear rationale and policy on grading.

If you devise clear guidelines from which to assess performance, you will find the grading process more efficient, and the essential function of grades—communicating the student's level of knowledge—will be easier. Further, if you grade carefully and consistently, you can reduce the number of students who complain and ask you to defend a grade. The suggestions below are designed to help you develop clear and fair grading policies. For tips on calculating final grades, see "Calculating and Assigning Grades."

General Strategies

Grade on the basis of students' mastery of knowledge and skills. Restrict your evaluations to academic performance. Eliminate other considerations, such as classroom behavior, effort, classroom participation, attendance, punctuality, attitude, personality traits, or student interest in the course material, as the basis of course grades. If you count these nonacademic factors, you obscure the primary meaning of the grade, as an indicator of what students have learned. For a discussion on why not to count class participation, see "Encouraging Student Participation in Discussion." (Source: Jacobs and Chase, 1992)

Avoid grading systems that put students in competition with their classmates and limit the number of high grades. These normative systems, such as grading on the curve, work against collaborative learning strategies that have been shown to be effective in promoting student learning. Normative grading produces undesirable consequences for many students, such as reduced motivation to learn, debilitating evaluation anxiety, decreased ability to use feedback to improve learning, and poor social relationships. (Sources: Crooks, 1988; McKeachie, 1986)

Try not to overemphasize grades. Explain to your class the meaning of and basis for grades and the procedures you use in grading. At the beginning of the term, inform students, in writing (see "The Course Syllabus") how much tests, papers, homework, and the final exam will count toward their final grade. Once you have explained your policies, avoid stressing grades or excessive talk about grades, which only increases students' anxieties and decreases their motivation to do something for its own sake rather than to obtain an external reward such as a grade. (Sources: Allen and Rueter, 1990; Fuhrmann and Grasha, 1983)

Keep students informed of their progress throughout the term. For each paper, assignment, midterm, or project that you grade, give students a sense of what their score means. Try to give a point total rather than a letter grade. Letter grades tend to have emotional associations that point totals lack. Do show the range and distribution of point scores, and indicate what level of performance is satisfactory. Such information can motivate students to improve if they are doing poorly or to maintain their performance if they are doing well. By keeping students informed throughout the term, you also prevent unpleasant surprises at the end. (Sources: Lowman, 1984; Shea, 1990)

Minimizing Students' Complaints About Grading

Clearly state grading procedures in your course syllabus, and go over this information in class. Students want to know how their grades will be determined, the weights of various tests and assignments, and the model of grading you will be using to calculate their grades: will the class be graded on a curve or by absolute standards? If you intend to make allowances for extra credit, late assignments, or revision of papers, clearly state your policies.

Set policies on late work. Will you refuse to accept any late work? Deduct points according to how late the work is submitted? Handle late work on a case-by-case basis? Offer a grace period? See "Preparing or Revising a Course."

Avoid modifying your grading policies during the term. Midcourse changes may erode students' confidence in your fairness, consistency, objectivity, and organizational skills. If you must make a change, give your students a complete explanation. (Source: Frisbie, Diamond, and Ory, 1979)

Provide enough opportunities for students to show you what they know. By giving students many opportunities to show you what they know, you will have a more accurate picture of their abilities and will avoid penalizing a student who has an off day at the time of a test. So in addition to a final exam, give one or two midterms and one or two short papers. For lower-division courses, Erickson and Strommer (1991) recommend giving shorter tests or written assignments and scheduling some form of evaluation every two or three weeks.

Consider allowing students to choose among alternative assignments. One instructor presents a list of activities with assigned points for each that take into account the assignments' educational and motivational value, difficulty, and probable amount of effort required. Students are told how many points are needed for an A, a B, or a C, and they choose a combination of assignments that meets the grade they desire for that portion of the course. Here are some possible activities:

- Writing a case study
- Engaging in and reporting on a fieldwork experience

- Leading a discussion panel
- Serving on a discussion panel
- Keeping a journal or log of course-related ideas
- Writing up thoughtful evaluations of several lectures
- Creating instructional materials for the course (study guides, exam questions, or audiovisual materials) on a particular concept or theme
- Undertaking an original research project or research paper
- Reviewing the current research literature on a course-related topic
- Keeping a reading log that includes brief abstracts of the readings and comments, applications, and critiques
- Completing problem-solving assignments (such as designing an experiment to test a hypothesis or creating a test to measure something)

(Source: Davis, Wood, and Wilson, 1983)

Stress to students that grades reflect work on a specific task and are not judgments about people. Remind students that a teacher grades only a piece of paper. You might also let students know, if appropriate, that research shows that grades bear little or no relationship to measures of adult accomplishment (Eble, 1988, p. 156).

Give encouragement to students who are performing poorly. If students are having difficulty, do what you can to help them improve on the next assignment or exam. If they do perform well, take this into account when averaging the early low score with the later higher one. (Source: Lowman, 1984)

Deal directly with students who are angry or upset about their grade. Ask an upset student to take a day or more to cool off. It is also helpful to ask the student to prepare in writing the complaint or justification for a grade change. When you meet with the student in your office, have all the relevant materials at hand: the test questions, answer key or criteria, and examples of good answers. Listen to the student's concerns or read the memo with an open mind and respond in a calm manner. Don't allow yourself to become antagonized, and don't antagonize the student. Describe the key elements of a good answer, and point out how the student's response was incomplete or incorrect. Help the student understand your reasons for assigning the grade that you did. Take time to think about the student's request or to reread the exam if you need to, but resist pressures to change a grade because of a student's personal needs (to get into graduate school or maintain status on the dean's list). If appropriate, for final course grades, offer to write a letter to the student's adviser or to others, describing the student's work in detail and indicating any extenuating circumstances that may have hurt the grade. (Sources: Allen and Rueter, 1990; McKeachie, 1986)

Keep accurate records of students' grades. Your department may keep copies of final grade reports, but it is important for you to keep a record of all grades assigned throughout the semester, in case a student wishes to contest a grade, finish an incomplete, or ask for a letter of recommendation.

Making Effective Use of Grading Tactics

Return the first graded assignment or test before the add/drop deadline. Early assignments help students decide whether they are prepared to take the class (Shea, 1990). Some faculty members give students the option of throwing out this first test (Johnson, 1988). Students may receive a low score because they did not know what the instructor required or because they underestimated the level of preparation needed to succeed.

Record results numerically rather than as letter grades, whenever possible. Tests, problem sets, homework, and so on are best recorded by their point value to assure greater accuracy when calculating final grades. (Source: Jacobs and Chase, 1992)

Give students a chance to improve their grades by rewriting their papers. Many faculty encourage rewriting but do not count the grades on rewritten papers as equivalent to those of papers that have not been rewritten. See "Helping Students Write Better in All Courses."

If many students do poorly on an exam, schedule another one on the same material a week or so later. Devote one or more classes to reviewing the troublesome material. Provide in-class exercises, homework problems or questions, practice quizzes, study group opportunities, and extra office hours before you administer the new exam. Though reviewing and retesting may seem burdensome and time-consuming, there is usually little point in proceeding to new topics when many of your students are still struggling. (Source: Erickson and Strommer, 1991)

Evaluating Your Grading Policies

Compare your grade distributions with those for similar courses in your department. Differences between your grade distributions and those of your colleagues do not necessarily mean that your methods are faulty. But glaring discrepancies should prompt you to reexamine your practices. (Source: Frisbie, Diamond, and Ory, 1979)

Ask students about your grading policies on end-of-course questionnaires. Here are some sample questions (adapted from Frisbie, Diamond, and Ory, 1979, p. 22):

To what extent:

- Were the grading procedures for the course fair?
- Were the grading procedures for the course clearly explained?
- Did you receive adequate feedback on your performance?
- Were requests for regrading or review handled fairly?
- Did the instructor evaluate your work in a meaningful and conscientious manner?

References

Allen, R. R., and Rueter, T. *Teaching Assistant Strategies*. Dubuque, Iowa: Kendall/Hunt, 1990.

Crooks, T. J. "The Impact of Classroom Evaluation Practices on Students." *Review of Educational Research*, 1988, *58*(4), 438–481.

Davis, B. G., Wood, L., and Wilson, R. *The ABCs of Teaching Excellence*. Berkeley: Office of Educational Development, University of California, 1983.

Eble, K. E. *The Craft of Teaching*. (2nd ed.) San Francisco: Jossey-Bass, 1988.

Erickson, B. L., and Strommer, D. W. *Teaching College Freshmen*. San Francisco: Jossey-Bass, 1991.

Frisbie, D. A., Diamond, N. A., and Ory, J. C. *Assigning Course Grades*. Urbana: Office of Instructional Resources, University of Illinois, 1979.

Fuhrmann, B. S., and Grasha, A. F. *A Practical Handbook for College Teachers*. Boston: Little, Brown, 1983.

Jacobs, L. C., and Chase, C. I. *Developing and Using Tests Effectively: A Guide for Faculty*. San Francisco: Jossey-Bass, 1992.

Johnson, G. R. *Taking Teaching Seriously*. College Station: Center for Teaching Excellence, Texas A & M University, 1988.

Lowman, J. *Mastering the Techniques of Teaching*. San Francisco: Jossey-Bass, 1984.

McKeachie, W. J. *Teaching Tips*. (8th ed.) Lexington, Mass.: Heath, 1986.

Scriven, M. "Evaluation of Students." Unpublished manuscript, 1974.

Shea, M. A. *Compendium of Good Ideas on Teaching and Learning*. Boulder: Faculty Teaching Excellence Program, University of Colorado, 1990.

33

Calculating and Assigning Grades

Grades may be assigned in a variety of ways, each with its own strengths and weaknesses. Which model you choose depends on your department's policies, the size and type of course you teach, and your views of education and the purpose of grades. The suggestions below are designed to increase your understanding of your options and point out the pitfalls of certain types of grading strategies. See "Multiple-Choice and Matching Tests" and "Short-Answer and Essay Tests" for information about grading those types of exams.

General Strategies

Familiarize yourself with department standards. Check to see how grading has been handled for the course in past semesters; if possible, see whether you can obtain past class grade distributions. Ask colleagues who have taught the course before about their grading criteria and general class performance.

Relate department standards to your own conception of the course. Identify the objectives or goals you want your students to meet. What skills and knowledge are absolutely essential for students to pass the course? What would you wish from an A student?

Weight various course components in proportion to their importance. Quizzes should count less than a three-hour exam, but if you make the final exam worth 60 percent of students' final grade in the course, you encourage students to cram at the end rather than work at an even pace throughout the term (Lowman, 1984). As a rule of thumb, the final should count for no more than one-third of the course grade.

Make the institution's definitions of grades known to students. Refer students to the school catalogue for an explanation of your institution's grading scales. Here is the scale used at the University of California at Berkeley:

A, A −	Excellent
B + , B, B −	Good
C + , C, C −	Fair
D + , D, D −	Poor; barely passed
F	Fail
P	Passed (the equivalent of a C − or better)
NP	Not passed (the equivalent of a D + or worse)
S	Satisfactory (for graduate students only: passed at the level of B − or better)
U	Unsatisfactory (for graduate students only: the equivalent of C + or worse)
I	Incomplete (work of passing quality but a small portion is incomplete, such as a lab experiment or term paper; the student must make arrangements to complete the work with the instructor before an incomplete can be issued)
IP	In progress; final grade to be assigned upon completion of two-term course sequence

Use software to compute and keep track of students' grades. Some faculty keep students' grades on spreadsheets, such as Microsoft Excel, that permit sorting, statistical analysis, graphing, and other computations. Faculty who use computerized grading report that it saves considerable time and effort, and many prefer the flexibility of commercially available spreadsheets to customized grading programs. Straka (1986) evaluates the applicability of various computer spreadsheet programs for use as computerized grade books. Magnan (1989) identifies key characteristics of effective software programs (for example, able to handle missing values or temporary zeros for assignments not yet turned in or exams to be made up; able to drop the lowest grade) and offers advice on how to select software.

Approaches to Grading

Criterion-referenced grading versus norm-referenced grading. The principle underlying *criterion-referenced grading* is that a student's grade reflects his or her level of achievement, independent of how other students in the class have performed. If all the students in a seminar give strong oral presentations, they will all receive A's or B's. Conversely, if none of the students in a class scores better than 80 percent on a midterm exam, then no one in the class receives a grade higher than, say, B − on the exam. Under *norm-referenced grading*, in contrast, a student's grade reflects his or her level of achievement relative to other students in the class. Only a certain percentage of the class will receive A's, a good portion will receive C's, and at least some will receive D's and F's. Norm-referenced models are often called grading on the curve.

Researchers conclude that when students' test scores are fairly well distributed across the range of possible points, it does not necessarily matter which model you employ (Svinicki, n.d.). However, when the overall performance of the class is low or high, it matters a great deal which model you use. When many students have done well on an exam, they would want some form of criterion-referenced grading so that everyone who did well will receive an A or B. When many students have done poorly, they would want grades assigned by curve so that at least some would receive A's or B's. Of course, other factors besides the performance of the class will affect the model you choose, including your educational philosophy and the importance of students' mastering the content being tested. In general, however, grading systems based on criterion-referenced standards are more defensible than those that rely strictly on the curve.

Grading on the basis of improvement. Some faculty believe that course grades should take into account the amount of growth and development a student shows over the course of a semester. Otherwise, these faculty argue, a student who enters the course fairly knowledgeable will receive an A even if he or she learns very little or demonstrates little effort or improvement. McKeachie (1986), Pollio and Humphreys (1988), and Terwilliger (1971) point out that grading largely on the basis of progress produces dire inequities: a student who comes into the course with the least background might still be the poorest student in the class at the end of the course but might get an A for progress; a student who shows little growth may still be outstanding and yet get a C for progress. Grading on the basis of improvement also makes it difficult for students to interpret what their grades mean: does a B mean that their work is above average or that their *improvement* is above average? It is also a disservice to students whose knowledge is inadequate for a higher-level course to receive a B in your course. McKeachie (1986) recommends that a student who performs poorly but has tried and has made some progress be given a D rather than an F; assign the F's to students who demonstrate low achievement and have made little progress. Some faculty take improvement into account by giving extra points if a student scores higher on the second midterm than on the first, and by giving a modest number of bonus points at the end of the term if a student's improvement has been steady throughout the semester.

Self-grading and peer grading. Some faculty let students grade themselves. These faculty ask students to justify in detail the reasons for the grade, taking into account their performance on exams and assignments, their perceived grasp of the material, the amount of time spent on the course, and the amount of reading completed. Though this approach does develop students' abilities to evaluate their work, it takes away from faculty one of their chief responsibilities: to make professional judgments about students' learning and tell students how well they are performing. A variation of self-grading is peer grading, where students grade one another's work. This procedure works best in classes that feature a lot of small group work that enables students to judge how well other students are performing. If you wish to try this strategy, see "Collaborative Learning" for suggestions. (Sources: Jacobs and Chase, 1992; Fuhrmann and Grasha, 1983)

Models of Grading Student Performance Relative to Others in the Class

Grading on a curve based on the class's performance. In this norm-referenced model, grades are determined by comparing a student's overall performance with that of other students. Students' scores are arrayed from highest to lowest, and the grades students receive depend on where they land in the array. The key, of course, is where to set the cutoff points. Some instructors determine beforehand which percentages of students will receive A's, B's, C's, D's, and F's. So, for example, if you determine that 20 percent of the class will receive A's, you simply count down from the highest score until you reach the number of students that corresponds to 20 percent. The choice of percentages is left to your judgment. Some faculty use the mean and standard deviation to determine cutoff points. For example, A's and B's are assigned to students who score a specific amount above the mean, C's to students whose scores fall close to the mean, and D's and F's to those whose scores fall a specific amount below the mean. Some researchers (for example, Gronlund, 1974) provide guidelines, such as 10 to 20 percent A's, 20 to 30 percent B's, 40 to 50 percent C's, 10 to 20 percent D's, 0 to 10 percent F's.

This model has the advantage of rewarding students whose academic performance is outstanding in comparison to their peers, but it has several major drawbacks (Frisbie, Diamond, and Ory, 1979). The grade doesn't really indicate how much or how little students have learned—only where they stand in relationship to the class. In addition, no matter how strong the class is, some students will receive low grades; or, no matter how weak the class is, some students will receive high grades. Further, your grading standards will fluctuate with each group of students—a student whose work earns a C+ in the fall term might have received a B− the spring term before. Some faculty try to compensate for inequities by adjusting the cutoff scores or by assigning a higher percentage of A's than usual if the class is really good. But these adjustments still arbitrarily limit the number of A's, so that no matter how much students actually learn, only so many of them will receive A's. (In contrast, other methods of grading permit all students who work hard to earn high grades.) Moreover, researchers Hanna and Cashin (1988) believe that grading on the curve seems to encourage exclusion, isolation, and competitiveness.

Grading according to course or departmental practices or according to faculty consensus. Some faculty try to have their grade distributions reflect the averages reported in their department. Brown (cited in Johnson, 1989) reports that faculty tend to distribute grades as follows: 22 percent A's, 35 percent B's, 29 percent C's, 10 percent D's, and 4 percent F's. Hanna and Cashin (1988) suggest that all faculty who teach the same course might develop a consensus on the distribution of grades suitable for a typical class, say, 20 percent A's, 25 percent B's, 30 percent C's, 20 percent D's, and 5 percent F's, although the instructors would be expected to deviate from the typical distribution to reflect the uniqueness of their class (higher than average performance or less well prepared).

Grading according to breaks in the distribution. In this model, you array the scores from highest to lowest and look for natural gaps or breaks in the distribution. For example, on a midterm six students score 80 or higher and two students score 72; no one scores between 79 and 73. Instructors using this model will assign A's to students who scored 80 and above, and start the B's at 72. The assumption here is that these breaks represent true differences in achievement. However, given the unreliability of teacher-designed tests, the breaks could occur purely by chance, or they could be caused by guessing or poorly written items. Further, the grade distribution depends on judgments made after students have taken the test rather than on preestablished guidelines that can be stated prior to testing. This model is not recommended. (Source: Jacobs and Chase, 1992)

Grading on a bell-shaped curve. A bell curve, or a "normal" distribution curve, is a symmetrical statistical model. A small percentage of the class receives A's and F's, a larger percentage receives B's and D's, and most students receive C's. If you were to use a pure normal curve, the distribution of grades would be 7 percent A's, 24 percent B's, 38 percent C's, 24 percent

D's, 7 percent F's. Though bell curves have their uses, they are wholly inappropriate for grading. Student performance is not necessarily normally distributed within a class, and teacher-made tests are almost never so well designed as to yield such distributions. (Sources: Gronlund, 1974; Terwilliger, 1971)

Models of Grading Student Performance Relative to a Standard

Grading according to absolute standards. In this criterion-referenced model, a student's performance is compared to a specified, fixed standard set by the instructor. For example, according to McKeachie (1986), if a test has 150 possible points and you want to set standards of 90 to 100 percent = A, 80 to 89 percent = B, and so on, the distribution might look like this:

140 and above (93 percent of 150) = A
135 to 139 (90 percent) = A −
131 to 134 (87 percent) = B +
125 to 130 (83 percent) = B
120 to 124 (80 percent) = B −
and so on

An advantage of this approach is that any number of students may earn A's and B's. You might also indicate to students that you may grade more generously than the announced standards but never tougher. A major problem with the model is how to set the standards in a rational, legitimate way. Another problem arises if many students perform very poorly (say, only one student scores above 120). At that point, an instructor could reset the standards to reflect students' performance, but such tinkering confuses the meaning of grades and may frustrate students. (Source: Terwilliger, 1971)

Grading according to highest scores earned and percentages thereof. This model (developed by Carter as reported in Fuhrmann and Grasha, 1983, p. 184, and also described in Svinicki, n.d.) is a hybrid criterion-referenced and norm-referenced approach that combines the advantages of each. You assign grades on the basis of the highest scores earned in the class. It works like this:

- Compute a score for each student.
- Compute the mean score of the best-performing portion of the class. If you have a superior class, you may want to use the scores of the upper

15 or 20 percent; if the class is less capable than previous classes, you might use the top 5 to 8 percent of the distribution. For an average class, use 10 percent. To calculate the mean, add together all the scores in the best-performing portion of the class and then divide by the number of scores in this sample.

- Assign grades according to some predetermined scale; for example: A = 95 percent of the mean of the best-performing portion of the class, B = 85 percent of the mean, C = 75 percent of the mean, D = 65 percent of the mean.

In this model, class performance plays a role in determining the score needed for each grade, but the number of students who can earn each grade is not limited. Some faculty take shortcuts with this model by simply using the highest score (rather than the mean of the highest scores) so that 90 to 100 percent of the highest score is awarded an A, 80 to 89 percent a B, and so on. The drawback of this shortcut is that it is too dependent on a single student's score.

Grading according to mastery of objectives. For this criterion-referenced model, you first prepare a list of detailed objectives, the measurable skills and knowledge students are expected to attain. Students' performance is evaluated on whether or not they have mastered these objectives. The premise here is that a grade indicates how much a student knows rather than how many other students have mastered more or less of that domain. It is possible that all students in a class could receive A's and B's. There are two clear advantages of this model of grading (Frisbie, Diamond, and Ory, 1979): (1) most students who work hard enough and receive good instruction can obtain good grades; (2) the focus is on achieving course goals, not on competing with the other students. The drawbacks of this model, however, are that the instructor must be able to specify clearly the levels of knowledge and skills students must master to earn a given grade and that the instructor must be able to determine the minimum level of performance necessary to attain each grade (Frisbie, Diamond, and Ory, 1979). In many college courses, as Hanna and Cashin (1988) point out, the content is so extensive that an instructor cannot specify the requisite knowledge and skills with precision.

Calculation of Final Grades for the Course

Begin with numerical scores. Calculate final grades by converting letter grades to numerical equivalents if you need to. If you have assigned points throughout the term to students' papers and tests, use those scores. If you need to convert, say, a grade on a research paper, use A = 95, A – = 90, B + = 87, and so on.

When course tests and assignments are all equally weighted, add them all up to obtain a total score. Many faculty calculate final grades by totaling the scores obtained by each student on each of the course requirements (for example, midterms, papers, final exams), putting these total scores in numerical order, and setting a cutoff point for each final letter grade. However, there are some technical drawbacks to this straightforward procedure (Jacobs and Chase, 1992). For example, a test with a wide spread of scores will more heavily influence the final grades than a test with a narrower spread. This problem can be overcome by converting students' raw scores into standardized scores. (See Fuhrmann and Grasha, 1983, pp. 186– 188, for a formula for transforming raw scores into standardized scores. Computerized test grading and analytic programs greatly ease the calculations.) Some researchers argue against transforming raw scores, believing that little is gained by such arithmetic maneuvering, and the probability of error increases. McKeachie (1986), for example, stresses that adding raw scores is adequate for most courses.

When course tests and assignments are *not* equally weighted, calculate weights for each course component and convert individual scores on course tasks. Here's a method for calculating weights (adapted from Frye, 1989, pp. 187–189). First, write down the weights you announced to your class; for example:

Two midterms	50 percent
Two lab projects	30 percent
Final exam	20 percent

Then convert these percentages to points, allowing 100 percent to equal 1,000 points. Thus, the two midterms are worth 500 points, the two lab projects 300 points, and the final exam 200 points. Since each of the midterms is worth 250 points (500 divided by 2), you need to adjust students' actual scores on the midterm to weight them for the final course grades. Suppose the first midterm had 40 items and the second midterm had 50 items:

midterm 1	250 divided by 40 = 6.25 points per item
midterm 2	250 divided by 50 = 5.00 points per item

If a student has 31 correct answers on the first midterm, she would receive $31 \times 6.25 = 193.75$ points; for having 42 correct answers on the second midterm, she would receive $42 \times 5 = 210$ points. Convert the lab projects and final exam in a similar fashion, and use the point totals to compute final grades.

One professor adjusts the weights assigned to various course components to reflect students' performance. For example, if a course has two midterms and a final, the student's highest score on the three tests is weighted 50 percent, the middle score 30 percent, and the lowest 20 percent. The advantage is that students know their best work counts more heavily in their final grade. The disadvantage is that students do not know in advance how much each course component will be weighted.

Set cutoff points. There are four general ways to set cutoff points: straight percentages, standard deviations, percentages of the highest ranges of scores, or absolute standards. With *straight percentages*, you set the grade distribution on the basis of your judgment of department norms or faculty practices. For example, suppose you decide that 15 percent of your students will receive A's, 20 percent B's, 45 percent C's, 15 percent D's, and 5 percent F's. Then you count down the total scores and assign the grades. Because this procedure limits the number of A's and B's, it is not recommended.

For the same reason, using *standard deviations* to calculate cutoff points is also not recommended. This approach, which requires some mathematical skill or computer software, entails calculating the mean score and the statistical standard deviation from the mean. Students whose point total is within, say, one-half a standard deviation from the mean receive C's. The cutoff between A's and B's would lie one standard deviation above the upper cutoff of the C's, and the cutoff between D's and F's would lie one standard deviation below the lower cutoff of the C's.

A better way to set the cutoff points is to use a *percentage of the distribution* (similar to grading according to highest scores earned and percentages thereof, described earlier). This strategy does not restrict the number of A's and B's. Here, you take the upper 10 or 20 percent of the distribution, calculate the mean, and then calculate a percentage of the mean to set the cutoff points (90 percent of the mean is an A, 80 percent a B, and so on). The width of the band and the percentages of the mean for each letter grade are up to you. In calculating grades, you may wish to take into account natural breaks in the distribution that are slightly off from your ideal percentages.

Another way to set cutoff points is to adopt an *absolute standard* rather than relying on the performance of the class. The premise here is that you can specify the point totals necessary for student achievement at various grade levels, representing various levels of mastery of the material.

Consider students' progress over the term. For students on the margin, you could consider such factors as improvement over the course of the semester. One math professor quantifies students' improvement over the semester. Say a class has two midterms worth 100 points each and a final worth 200 points. Ole's score is 50 out of 100 on the first midterm, 80 out of 100 on the second midterm, and 190 out of 200 on the final. His unadjusted total score for the course is 320. To take into account Ole's steady improvement, the professor weights Ole's scores for the second midterm and final more heavily. The weight of the second midterm is calculated by subtracting Ole's score on the first midterm from the total points available for both first and second midterms, or $200 - 50 = 150$. His actual score on the second midterm is then multiplied by this weighting factor. Thus his adjusted score for the second midterm is $(200 - 50)(80/100) = 120$. His first score and his second, adjusted score are then added together, $50 + 120 = 170$. His adjusted score on the final is calculated using the same process. Ole's cumulative total score (170) is subtracted from the total points available for both midterms and the final (400). His actual score on the final is then multiplied by this new weighting factor, or $(400 - 170)(190/200) = 218.5$. To calculate the total adjusted score, add his adjusted score on the midterms (170) to his adjusted score on the final (218.5) for a total of 388.5.

References

Frisbie, D. A., Diamond, N. A., and Ory, J. C. *Assigning Course Grades.* Urbana: Office of Instructional Resources, University of Illinois, 1979.

Frye, B. J. "Planning Student Evaluation, Constructing Tests, and Grading." In D. Grieve (ed.), *Teaching in College: A Resource for College Teachers.* (Rev. ed.) Cleveland: Info-Tech, 1989.

Fuhrmann, B. S., and Grasha, A. F. *A Practical Handbook for College Teachers.* Boston: Little, Brown, 1983.

Gronlund, N. E. *Improving Marking and Reporting in Classroom Instruction.* New York: Macmillan, 1974.

Hanna, G. S., and Cashin, W. E. "Improving College Grading." *Idea Paper*, no. 19. Manhattan: Center for Faculty Evaluation and Development, Kansas State University, 1988.

Jacobs, L. C., and Chase, C. I. *Developing and Using Tests Effectively: A Guide for Faculty*. San Francisco: Jossey-Bass, 1992.

Johnson, G. R. "Throwing Darts at Tests." *Network Newsletter on College Teaching*, 1989, 7(8), 1–4. (Newsletter available from the Center for Teaching Excellence, Texas A & M University)

Lowman, J. *Mastering the Techniques of Teaching*. San Francisco: Jossey-Bass, 1984.

McKeachie, W. J. *Teaching Tips*. (8th ed.) Lexington, Mass.: Heath, 1986.

Magnan, B. "How to Make the Grade." *Academic Leader*, 1989, 5(10), 1–3, 5, 10.

Pollio, H. R., and Humphreys, W. L. "Grading Students." In J. H. McMillan (ed.), *Assessing Students' Learning*. New Directions for Teaching and Learning, no. 34. San Francisco: Jossey-Bass, 1988.

Straka, W. C. "Spreadsheet-Gradebook Connection." *Teaching at the University of Nebraska, Lincoln*, 1986, 7(3), 1–3, 7. (Newsletter available from the Teaching and Learning Center, University of Nebraska, Lincoln)

Svinicki, M. D. *Evaluating and Grading Students*. Austin: Center for Teaching Effectiveness, University of Texas, n.d.

Terwilliger, J. S. *Assigning Grades to Students*. Glenview, Ill.: Scott, Foresman, 1971.

Preventing Academic Dishonesty

34

Between 40 and 70 percent of all college students have reported cheating sometime during their academic career (Aiken, 1991; Davis, Grover, Becker, and McGregor, 1992). Researchers have begun to identify the factors that influence academic dishonesty (Aiken, 1991; Barnett and Dalton, 1981; Davis, Grover, Becker, and McGregor, 1992; Roberts and Rabinowitz, 1992). These include competition and pressures for good grades, instructional situations that are perceived as unfair or excessively demanding, faculty who are perceived as uncaring or indifferent to their own teaching or to their students' learning, lax attitudes on the part of faculty toward academic dishonesty, peer pressure to support a friend, and a diminishing sense of academic integrity and ethical values among students. Not all these factors are under an instructor's control, but there are specific steps you can take to prevent academic dishonesty:

- Inform students of academic standards for scholarship and conduct.
- Explain how cheating harms students and describe campus sanctions.
- Minimize the opportunities for cheating and plagiarism.
- Take visible actions to detect dishonesty so that students know you will not tolerate cheating. (Even if you don't actually carry out all the actions you say you will take, honest students will appreciate knowing that you care enough about academic integrity to take precautions.)
- If cheating occurs, respond swiftly with disciplinary measures and formal action.

The following ideas are designed to help you impart to your students the values of academic honesty and to help you set policies that encourage academic integrity.

General Strategies

Spend time at the beginning of the term discussing standards of academic scholarship and conduct. Cheating may mean different things for faculty and students ("Academic Dishonesty in our Classrooms," 1990). For example, students are often unclear about how much they can work with other students and under what circumstances. Describe for your students acceptable and unacceptable behavior, giving examples of plagiarism, impermissible collaboration, and other practices relevant to your class. Explain that cheating will not be tolerated, and discuss university policies, procedures, and penalties for academic violations. Some departments hand out written materials that define cheating and plagiarism and require students to sign a statement that they have read and understood the material. Here is an example of material that is distributed to students:

> *Cheating* means getting unauthorized help on an assignment, quiz, or examination. (1) You must not receive from any other student or give to any other student any information, answers, or help during an exam. (2) You must not use unauthorized sources for answers during an exam. You must not take notes or books to the exam when such aids are forbidden, and you must not refer to any book or notes while you are taking the exam unless the instructor indicates it is an "open book" exam. (3) You must not obtain exam questions illegally before an exam or tamper with an exam after it has been corrected.

> *Plagiarism* means submitting work as your own that is someone else's. For example, copying material from a book or other source without acknowledging that the words or ideas are someone else's and not your own is plagiarism. If you copy an author's words exactly, treat the passage as a direct quotation and supply the appropriate citation. If you use someone else's ideas, even if you paraphrase the wording, appropriate credit should be given. You have committed plagiarism if you purchase a term paper or submit a paper as your own that you did not write.

Make sure students know the criteria for evaluating their performance. Review students' work throughout the term so that they know you know their abilities and achievement levels. (Source: Malehorn, 1983)

Develop a climate and group norms that support honesty. For example, you may wish to take a vote in class to conduct the exams under the honor system (without proctors). (Source: McKeachie, 1986)

Learn to recognize signs of stress in students. Make students aware of campus resources that they can turn to for help if their grades are low or if they feel under pressure. Familiarize yourself with the services of your campus's student learning center and counseling center, as well as tutoring provided by student honor societies.

Ensure equal access to study materials. Establish a file in the library or department office of old homework assignments, exams, and papers. Or attach a sample of past exam questions to the syllabus. (Source: Singhal and Johnson, 1983)

Make students feel as though they can succeed in your class without having to resort to dishonesty. Give more rather than fewer tests. Encourage students to come talk with you if they are having difficulties. Minimize the threat of exams and grades. See "Allaying Students Anxieties About Tests" and "Grading Practices." (Source: Eble, 1988)

If you suspect students of cheating or plagiarizing material, confront them directly. Deal with the problem immediately. Don't join the 20 percent of faculty members who tend to ignore evidence of cheating (Tabachnick, Keith-Spiegel, and Pope, 1991). Talk with a student about your suspicions and listen carefully to the student's response. Here is some specific advice (adapted from "Handling a Plagiarism Interview," 1987, p. 10):

- If you have qualms or hesitations, talk with an experienced colleague or your department chair before you meet with the student.
- Consult your campus student conduct office for specific guidelines and due process procedures.
- When you meet with the student, objectively explain the problem as you see it.
- Describe why this is a problem in grading or evaluating the student's work.
- Avoid using the words *cheating* or *plagiarism*.
- Project an air of concern for the student as an individual, but communicate the seriousness of the situation.
- Listen to the student's explanation.
- If a student denies any wrongdoing, question him or her about specific aspects of, say, the paper by asking for definitions of terms, interpretations, or restatements.
- Be prepared for pleas, excuses, and tales of hardship and extenuating circumstances.

- Show some sympathy if a student is distraught or upset. Suggest a referral to the counseling center, if appropriate.
- Explain what will happen next to the student.
- Take whatever official action your institution prescribes for handling student academic dishonesty.

Plagiarism

Clarify the distinctions between plagiarism, paraphrasing, and direct citation. Provide students with instances of correct and incorrect ways to use others' ideas and words. You might want to seek permission to distribute the following example from *The Random House Handbook*, 6th ed., by Frederick Crews (New York: McGraw-Hill, 1992, pp. 181–183):

Consider the following source and three ways that a student might be tempted to make use of it:

Source: The joker in the European pack was Italy. For a time hopes were entertained of her as a force against Germany, but these disappeared under Mussolini. In 1935 Italy made a belated attempt to participate in the scramble for Africa by invading Ethiopia. It was clearly a breach of the covenant of the League of Nations for one of its members to attack another. France and Great Britain, as great powers, Mediterranean powers, and African colonial powers, were bound to take the lead against Italy at the league. But they did so feebly and half-heartedly because they did not want to alienate a possible ally against Germany. The result was the worst possible: the league failed to check aggression, Ethiopia lost her independence, and Italy was alienated after all.[1]

[1] J. M. Roberts, *History of the World* (New York: Knopf, 1976), p. 845.

Version A: Italy, one might say, was the joker in the European deck. When she invaded Ethiopia, it was clearly a breach of the covenant of the League of Nations; yet the efforts of England and France to take the lead against her were feeble and half-hearted. It appears that those great powers had no wish to alienate a possible ally against Hitler's rearmed Germany.

Comment: Clearly plagiarism. Though the facts cited are public knowledge, the stolen phrases aren't. Note that the writer's interweaving of his own words with the source's does not render him innocent of plagiarism.

Version B: Italy was the joker in the European deck. Under Mussolini in 1935, she made a belated attempt to participate in the scramble for Africa by invading Ethiopia. As J. M. Roberts points out, this violated the covenant of the League of Nations.[1] But France and Britain, not wanting to alienate a possible ally against Germany, put up only feeble and half-hearted opposition to the Ethiopian adventure. The outcome, as Roberts observes, was "the worst possible: the league failed to check aggression, Ethiopia lost her independence, and Italy was alienated after all."[2]

[1] J. M. Roberts, *History of the World* (New York: Knopf, 1976), p. 845.
[2] Roberts, p. 845.

Comment: Still plagiarism. The two correct citations of Roberts serve as a kind of alibi for the appropriating of other, unacknowledged phrases. But the alibi has no force: some of Roberts' words are again being presented as the writer's.

Version C: Much has been written about German rearmament and militarism in the period 1933–1939. But Germany's dominance in Europe was by no means a foregone conclusion. The fact is that the balance of power might have been tipped against Hitler if one or two things had turned out differently. Take Italy's gravitation toward an alliance with Germany, for example. That alliance seemed so very far from inevitable that Britain and France actually muted their criticism of the Ethiopian invasion in the hope of remaining friends with Italy. They opposed the Italians in the League of Nations, as J. M. Roberts observes, "feebly and half-heartedly because they did not want to alienate a possible ally against Germany."[1] Suppose Italy, France, and Britain had retained a certain common interest. Would Hitler have been able to get away with his remarkable bluffing and bullying in the later thirties?

[1] J. M. Roberts, *History of the World* (New York: Knopf, 1976), p. 845.

Comment: No plagiarism. The writer has been influenced by the public facts mentioned by Roberts, but he hasn't tried to pass off Roberts' conclusions as his own. The one clear borrowing is properly acknowledged.

Watch out for electronic plagiarism. With the growth of electronic bulletin boards, information servers, and electronic mail, students can obtain papers from students at other universities or have on-line access to encyclopedias, Monarch notes, or other source material. While there is little you can do to prevent abuse, letting students know you are aware of the possibility may deter potential cheaters. (Source: Bulkeley, 1992)

Tell students that resubmitting their previous academic work as a new product for your course is inappropriate. Ask students to check with you if they have a paper or project they submitted for another course that may be appropriate for yours. Some faculty work with students who wish to use a recycled research paper by allowing students to use a different statistical method to analyze data already collected or by letting students use the conclusions of their previous papers as springboards for topics for new papers. (Source: "About Plagiarism," 1990)

Paper Topics

Assign specific topics. Design topics that are likely to require new research, that stress thought and analysis more than recall of facts, and that are challenging but not overwhelming. Topics that are too difficult invite cheating, as do boring, trivial, and uninteresting topics. See "Designing Effective Writing Assignments." (Sources: Eble, 1988; "Preventing Plagiarism," 1987; Singhal and Johnson, 1983)

Limit students' choices of broad paper topics. If given complete freedom, students may flounder and turn to commercially produced term papers or "file" papers as an easy out. (Source: "Preventing Plagiarism," 1987)

Change the assignments for each offering of a course. Changing the topics or assignments prevents students from simply appropriating an essay from someone who has already taken your course. (Source: "Preventing Plagiarism," 1987)

Writing Demystified

Give a short lecture on how to research and write a paper. Let students know what you expect of them and how they can proceed. Some campus libraries offer consultation services to students on developing research skills.

Discuss in class the difficulties of writing. Help students understand that the anxieties or blocks they face are a normal part of the writing process. "If, in the classroom, you emphasize the stages of the composing process and the normal tribulations of every writer, your students may be less likely to conclude that cheating is the only feasible way of getting from an assigned topic to a finished paper" (*Handbook for TAs*, n.d., p. 18).

During the term schedule a variety of short in-class papers. In-class assignments help students develop their writing skills and help you determine their abilities. Instructors who assign only one paper a term have a hard time judging whether that assignment is the student's own work. See "Helping Students Write Better in All Courses." (Source: Malehorn, 1983)

Early in the course require students to come in to discuss their paper topics. Again, later in the course, ask them to share outlines and to discuss how they plan to organize and present their ideas and findings. This approach not only helps students write better papers but also allows you to see students' ideas develop. (Source: "Preventing Plagiarism," 1987)

Preparation and Submission of Papers

Require students to submit first drafts. Quick comments on first drafts can help students improve their writing skills. See "Evaluating Students' Written Work."

Request that final versions of papers be handed in with drafts. Ask for note cards and outlines as well. Also ask students to turn in the original version and one duplicate. Keep the copies for your files so that you can consult them to identify pirated or purloined papers the next time you teach the course. (Source: Malehorn, 1983)

If possible, collect papers from students during class. This will only work if your course size is not too large. If papers are turned in at a department or faculty office, consider using locked mailboxes with slots for collection.

Consult the catalogue descriptions of term paper firms. If you suspect a student has purchased a term paper, you may wish to review the catalogues of paper factories. Ask your campus office of student conduct for any catalogues on file.

Exam Questions

Change exam questions as often as is practical. Ask students and (graduate student instructors, if you have them) to submit prospective questions. With judicious editing, some will be appropriate for the exam and others could form the basis of an item pool. See "Quizzes, Tests, and Exams."

For multiple-choice exams, use alternate forms. Scramble the order of questions, and color code the different exams. Some researchers suggest rearranging both test questions and answers (Aiken, 1991). Or collate the pages in different orders, if possible. (Source: Singhal and Johnson, 1983)

Create individualized tests for students, if appropriate. Using a computer, a faculty member in business creates customized assignments for students. In a tax accounting course, he varies the sales price and monthly payment amounts to generate unique problems for each student (using four sales prices and four monthly payment amounts yields 64 different problems; upping each of these variables to six results in 216 different problems). Using software with word-processing, spreadsheet, and mail-merge capabilities makes it possible to create unique problems and the solutions for each so that scoring can be readily handled. (Source: Burns, 1988)

Keep exams, grade books, and rosters safe. Store all exam materials in locked cabinets, desks, or file drawers in your office. Make copies of computer grade files. (Source: "Preventing Cheating on Exams," 1985)

Test Administration

Make certain that you (or proctors) are in the room at all times. During an exam arrange for proctoring or plan to monitor the test yourself, unless your class is run on an honor system. Periodically walk up and down the aisles to actively watch students. Students have developed ingenious ways of cheating during exams: using systems of hand and feet positions, tapping corners of the desk to represent responses to multiple-choice questions, surreptitiously opening books or trading papers, using tiny cassette recorders filled with information. (Source: Davis, Grover, Becker, and McGregor, 1992)

Seat students randomly in alternate chairs. Have students place personal belongings on the floor rather than in empty seats. If needed, schedule an additional room.

In large classes, check students' photo IDs. Check photo IDs displayed on desks against class lists to be certain that each student takes his or her own exam. If you do this, let students know in advance you will be checking IDs. Or seat students in preassigned groups. For example, students could sit by section so that graduate student instructors can determine whether all their students are in attendance and that "ringers" are not taking tests. (Source: "Preventing Cheating on Exams," 1985)

In rooms with seat numbers, keep a seating chart. Hand out blue books or exams with prerecorded seat numbers. In rooms without seat numbers, pick up the exams in the sequence of rows. (Source: Singhal and Johnson, 1983)

Make certain that students have cleared the memories on their calculators. Before you distribute the exam or as students enter the room, check the calculators' memories to be sure they are erased. Also make sure that crib notes are not concealed in a calculator's cover. (Source: Putka, 1992)

Supply scratch paper. Do not permit students to use their own paper or pages of their blue books. One intrepid student reported writing answers on a paper flower and pinning it to her blouse. (Sources: Davis, Grover, Becker and McGregor, 1992; Singhal and Johnson, 1983)

Take action if you observe "wandering eyes." If you notice "wandering eyes," go up to the offending student unobtrusively and ask that he or she move to another seat where it is less crowded. If the student seems reluctant, whisper in his or her ear that you would prefer that the student move. If you observe cheating, position yourself near the offenders to discourage them. Or make a general public announcement: "Please do your own work." If you have suspicions about students, allow them to complete the exam, but take notes on what you observe. (Source: McKeachie, 1986)

Spend some time in the back of the room. Students who are thinking about cheating will have to turn around in their seats to see where you are. (Source: Singhal and Johnson, 1983)

Do not allow students to rush chaotically to turn their bluebooks in at the end of the period. Require students to sign an attendance sheet when they turn in their exams, or collect exams from students. Count those present at the exam to make certain that the number of examinees matches the number of exams. This will prevent students' claims that their exam was lost or misplaced but that they took it. (Source: "Preventing Cheating on Exams," 1985)

Blue Books

Have students turn in blue books prior to the exam. Collect blue books at an earlier class meeting or as students enter the exam room, and then redistribute the blue books at random. (Source: "Preventing Cheating on Exams," 1985)

Require students to write only on the left-hand pages. Or ask students to leave a certain number of pages blank at the beginning of their blue books. (Source: "Preventing Cheating on Exams," 1985)

Examine all the blue books before leaving the classroom. One scam for cheating described by Moore (cited in Flint, 1992) involves a student's pretending to take the test but submitting a blank blue book without his or her name. The student then completes the test at home in a spare blue book using notes and materials. The completed blue book, with the student's name, course, and professor's name on the front, is then dropped outside the classroom, in the hallway, or outside the professor's office. The student depends on someone finding the blue book and returning it to the faculty member, who is supposed to think that it slipped out from the pile.

Scoring and Returning of Exams

Clearly mark incorrect answers. Use an inked X or slash mark to indicate wrong answers or blank spaces.

Let students know that you will be using computer programs to detect cheating on multiple-choice tests. Programs such as "Cheat-1" and "Cheat-2" compare students' responses and determine probabilities that pairs of students by chance will show the same distribution of answers (Aiken, 1991). Even if you do not actually use the software, telling students you may, may be sufficient to deter cheating.

If you permit regrading of exams, take precautions. Throughout the term photocopy the exams or quizzes of students who initially ask for regrading. Or photocopy a sample of all exams before returning them to students. (Source: "Preventing Cheating on Exams," 1985)

Return exams and assignments to students in person. This will work only if your course is small enough. Do not leave exams in the department office or on your desk for students to pick up. For large courses with GSIs, distribute exams in section. For large courses without GSIs, use techniques described in "Preparing to Teach the Large Lecture Course."

Fraudulent Excuses

Distinguish between fraudulent, legitimate, and unacceptable excuses. A legitimate excuse is based on events beyond a student's control; a fraudulent excuse is one fabricated solely to avoid an academic responsibility. In one study, researchers found that over two-thirds of college students admitted to using at least one fraudulent excuse to postpone an exam, turn in a paper late or not at all, or miss class. An unacceptable excuse, such as forgetting when a paper was due, may be truthful but is not a justifiable reason for failure to do the assigned task. (Source: Caron, Whitbourne, and Halgin, 1992)

Clearly state your policies about accepting excuses. Let students know at the beginning of the term what you consider as acceptable and unacceptable excuses. Tell students that no excuse will be accepted without some type of proof of its validity. While it is clearly impossible to obtain evidence that all excuses are legitimate, just saying you will ask for documentation may discourage potential excuse makers. Better yet, try to structure your course so that students are not placed in situations where they might be tempted to lie. For example, allow students to miss a quiz without penalty. See "Allaying Students' Anxieties About Tests." (Source: Caron, Whitbourne, and Halgin, 1992)

Recognize that the excuse "my grandmother died" is more likely to be valid than fraudulent. Research shows few significant distinctions between the content of fraudulent excuses and legitimate excuses. Don't become so cynical that you dismiss every family emergency as an invention. (Source: Caron, Whitbourne, and Halgin, 1992)

References

"About Plagiarism." *Instructional Exchange*, 1990, 2(1), 3. (Newsletter available from the Office of University Assessment and Intellectual Skills Program, Western Michigan University)

"Academic Dishonesty in Our Classrooms." *Instructional Exchange*, 1990, 2(2), 1–4. (Newsletter available from the Office of University Assessment and Intellectual Skills Program, Western Michigan University)

Aiken, L. R. "Detecting, Understanding, and Controlling for Cheating on Tests." *Research in Higher Education*, 1991, 32(6), 725–736.

Barnett, D. C., and Dalton, J. C. "Why College Students Cheat." *Journal of College Student Personnel*, 1981, 22(6), 545–551.

Bulkeley, W. M. "High Tech Aids Make Cheating in School Easier." *Wall Street Journal*, Apr. 28, 1992, pp. B1, B6.

Burns, J. G. "Computers in Class." *Teaching Professor*, 1988, 2(7), 2.

Caron, M. D., Whitbourne, S. K., and Halgin, R. P. "Fraudulent Excuse Making Among College Students." *Teaching of Psychology*, 1992, 19(2), 90–93.

Davis, S. F., Grover, C. A., Becker, A. H., and McGregor, L. N. "Academic Dishonesty: Prevalence, Determinants, Techniques, and Punishments." *Teaching of Psychology*, 1992, 19(1), 16–20.

Eble, K. E. *The Craft of Teaching*. (2nd ed.) San Francisco: Jossey-Bass, 1988.

Flint, A. "'Cheating 101' Becomes a Campus Best-Seller." *San Francisco Examiner*, Feb. 23, 1992, p. B-6.

Handbook for TAs. Berkeley: English Department, University of California, n.d.

"Handling a Plagiarism Interview." *The TA at UCLA Newsletter*, 1987, no. 20, p. 10. (Available from the Office of Instructional Development, University of California at Los Angeles)

McKeachie, W. J. *Teaching Tips*. (8th ed.) Lexington, Mass.: Heath, 1986.

Malehorn, H. "Term Papers for Sale and What to Do About It." *Improving College and University Teaching*, 1983, 31(3), 107–108.

"Preventing Cheating on Exams." *The TA at UCLA Newsletter*, 1985, no. 15, p. 2. (Available from the Office of Instructional Development, University of California at Los Angeles)

"Preventing Plagiarism: Some Tips." *The TA at UCLA Newsletter*, 1987, no. 20, p. 6. (Available from the Office of Instructional Development, University of California at Los Angeles)

Putka, G. "A Cheating Epidemic at a Top High School Teaches Sad Lessons." *Wall Street Journal*, June 29, 1992, pp. A1, A4–A5.

Roberts, D., and Rabinowitz, W. "An Investigation of Student Perceptions of Cheating in Academic Situations." *Review of Higher Education*, 1992, *15*(2), 179–190.

Singhal, A., and Johnson, P. "How to Halt Student Dishonesty." *College Student Journal*, 1983, *17*(1), 13–19.

Tabachnick, B. G., Keith-Spiegel, P., and Pope, K. S. "Ethics of Teaching: Beliefs and Behaviors of Psychologists as Educators." *American Psychologist*, 1991, *46*(5), 506–515.

IX.

Instructional Media and Technology

Chalkboards

35

Most instructors take chalkboards for granted. That's unfortunate, because board work can be an extremely effective teaching tool and visual aid. The following suggestions will help you use the board to reinforce and enrich your classroom presentations.

General Strategies

Use the chalkboard to highlight the organization of your presentation and to emphasize your main points. You can use the board to do any of the following:

- Outline the day's topics
- List major points of a lecture
- Summarize ideas raised during class discussion
- Spell out difficult names, unfamiliar vocabulary, and new terminology
- Present diagrams, graphs, and time lines
- Show formulas, computations, or steps in a proof

Have a plan for your board work. Most students copy into their notebooks exactly what appears on the board. Haphazard or chaotic board work only confuses students. If possible, arrange your board work so that you can erase details and leave the key points as a summary.

Give students time to copy what you have written. Students cannot copy and listen to new information at the same time. Let them catch up with you before you resume lecturing or continue a discussion. (Source: White, Hennessey, and Napell, 1978)

Visual Reinforcement

Outline the topics or activities planned for the day. An outline on the board will help students see where the lecture is headed and help them find their place if their attention drifts from the discussion. You can put the entire outline on the board at once or topic by topic as the subject matter is discussed. (Source: Garcia, 1991)

Draw diagrams or pictures. Practice drawing your diagrams before class: erasing and rewriting is easy for instructors but not for students taking notes in pen. If a diagram will grow larger as the lecture progresses, let students know how much room to leave in their notes (Grayson and Biedenbach, 1975). If you are modifying a drawing, use dotted lines or colored chalk to show the changes, and give students enough time to draw the modified diagram in their notes (White, Hennessey, and Napell, 1978).

In quantitative classes, write complete statements of what you propose to prove. When writing out proofs, define any special notation. Include all important steps. Do not simplify steps by erasing them; instead, use a single strike. (Source: Mathematical Association of America, 1979)

Be selective. Write down only the basic principles and indicate the omission of details ("Computation omitted"). If your board work will involve complex diagrams or detailed derivations, distribute a handout so that students will have an accurate rendering of what is on the board.

Explain any mistakes you have made in your board work before correcting them. If you write something down incorrectly, make sure your students know exactly which part of the board work is incorrect before you erase and correct it.

Record students' comments verbatim. When using the board to summarize a discussion, record verbatim comments. If the comment is dubious, put it in the form of a question with the speaker's okay.

Visually highlight important points. Before you leave a topic, emphasize the major points, assumptions, or conclusions by underlining or circling key words on the board. If you are recording students' comments and ideas and a student makes a particularly insightful remark, write "Great" next to it. (Source: Garcia, 1991)

Hands-On Tips

Avoid squeaking. To avoid spine-tingling screeches, hold the chalk at a 45-degree angle and press it firmly against the board. Breaking the chalk in half will also stop an annoying squeak.

Write legibly. To make sure your writing is legible, check a sample from the back of the room before class. If there is glare on the board, draw the blinds or shades. If you write with your arm fully extended and to the side, students can read the board as you write. When you have finished writing, stand to the side so that the board is visible to the entire class. (Source: White, Hennessey, and Napell, 1978)

Read aloud while you are writing on the board. Reading aloud is especially important for math and science instructors who write formulas on the board. This technique allows students to write while you do, helping them keep up with the presentation. But try not to discuss other points while you are at the board with your back turned to your students.

Erase old chalk work completely. Erase the board as you enter the classroom and throughout class when you change topics. This gives students a chance for reflection or to catch up with you. Make sure, though, not to erase essential information before students have had a chance to copy it.

Structure your board work. Use titles, headings, underlining, circling, boxing, and capital letters to differentiate and emphasize items. You can also organize your work by dividing the board into sections; for example, work out proofs and computations on the right-hand panel, and list major theorems on the left. Or list students' arguments on the right, and summarize the conclusions on the left.

Use the most visible parts of the board for the most important points. The upper left-hand corner of the board is the most prominent spot. Remember, too, that the bottom of the board might not be visible to students in the back of the classroom. Be sure not to block the board by piling materials on your desk or lectern. During class, notice whether students are craning their necks or shifting positions as they write—a sure sign that your board work is hard to see. (Source: White, Hennessey, and Napell, 1978)

With sliding three-layer chalkboards, fill the middle panel first. After the middle panel is full, push it up and pull down the front board—this keeps what you have written in sight. Finally, push up the front board and use the back board. (Source: White, Hennessey, and Napell, 1978)

Evaluation of Your Board Work

Ask students to tell you whether your board work is unclear. Or step back yourself during class and examine the board.

Ask two of your students to lend you their notes. Explain that you want to get a sense of how well you are doing. Note how much the students are copying from the board and what they are copying. Are the essential points clear? (Source: White, Hennessey, and Napell, 1978)

View a videotape of your presentation. Put yourself in the place of a student taking notes. How legible is your board work? How easy is it to follow? Is it well organized and clear? Do you speak too much to the board? Do you erase work too quickly?

At the end of class, erase the board completely. Take a moment to leave a clean board for the next instructor.

References

Garcia, R. "Twelve Ways of Looking at a Blackboard." *Teaching Professor*, 1991, *5*(8), 5–6.

Grayson, L. P., and Biedenbach, J. M. *Teaching Aids in the College Classroom*. Washington, D.C.: American Society for Engineering Education, 1975.

Mathematical Association of America. *College Mathematics: Suggestions on How to Teach It*. Washington, D.C.: Mathematical Association of America, 1979.

White, S., Hennessey, R., and Napell, S. "Blackboardsmanship for Neophytes." *Journal of College Science Teaching*, 1978, *7*(3), 178–179.

Flipcharts

36

A flipchart is a large pad of newsprint paper that sits on an easel or display stand. Flipcharts can be used to display a series of prepared sheets or for impromptu jottings. Flipcharts may be preferable to chalkboards if you are allergic to chalk, if you want to prepare your visual materials before class, if you want to display material continuously, or if you are conducting an outdoor field class. Because of their size, flipcharts are best used with small groups; for larger groups, consider using a slide projector or an overhead projector instead.

General Strategies

Use flipcharts to highlight the organization of your presentation, to emphasize its main points, and to stimulate students' interest. Whether you prepare a flipchart before class or write on it during class, you can use it to reinforce your verbal presentation. For example:

- Outline the day's topics or schedule
- Write difficult names, terminology, or unfamiliar vocabulary
- Show diagrams, charts, graphs, drawings, or illustrations
- List important dates
- Work through formulas, proofs, or theorems
- Summarize major points

Make your flipchart legible and graphically clear. Select a pad that is at least $22'' \times 32''$. In small rooms, two-inch lettering should suffice; in larger rooms, use four-inch lettering. Limit the amount of material on each sheet to a few key words or main points. Highlight important points by underlining, boxing, or using colored pens. Graphs or pie charts are preferable to tables when you want to represent numerical data.

Don't turn your back to the class to look at the flipchart. With practice you can flip the pages without breaking eye contact. If you use a pointer and stand off to the side, you will be able to face the class without obstructing your students' view of the chart.

Using a Flipchart as a Chalkboard

Write on the flipchart systematically. Start at the top left-hand corner and work across and then down to the next line, as you would on a blank piece of paper. Place important material at the top of the page, the most visible portion of the flipchart.

Use the same principles for writing on flipcharts as you would for the chalkboard or overhead transparencies. For example, use titles and headings to structure your work, underline or box off key statements, give students time to copy what you have written, pass out complex diagrams or drawings rather than have students try to copy them. See "Chalkboards" and "Transparencies and Overhead Projectors."

Using Prepared Flipcharts

Place the sheets in order. Some flipcharts are designed to be shown from the top page to the last; others from the last page toward the front. If you will be referring to a particular chart or diagram at several points during your presentation, it may be easier to include a copy of that page at each point rather than having to flip back and forth to find it. If you do plan to flip through the pad, tab key pages with masking tape to help you find important material quickly. (Source: Ellington, 1985)

Don't spend too long on each page. Plan each sheet so that you change pages within a couple of minutes. If you want to spend some time on one point, devote more than one page to it.

Follow the practices for using prepared transparencies. Many of the same principles apply: after revealing a flipchart, hesitate briefly before speaking to give students time to scan the material you are showing; don't read material on the flipchart that students can read for themselves. For other tips, see "Transparencies and Overhead Projectors."

Reference

Ellington, H. *Producing Teaching Materials*. New York: Nichols, 1985.

Transparencies and Overhead Projectors

37

An overhead projector projects onto a screen words or drawings that have been placed on $8\frac{1}{2}'' \times 11''$ plastic transparencies. (The transparency is laid on the projector's glass surface, which has a strong light beneath it, and the image is reflected by mirrors and enlarged by lenses.) A tabletop overhead projector is easy to operate and can be used in a well-lighted or partially darkened room.

In addition to showing transparencies you have prepared or purchased, you can use the projector as a demonstration stage for silhouettes or clear devices such as rulers and protractors (Svinicki and Lewis, n.d.). You can also write on blank transparencies in class, as you would on a chalkboard. Indeed, some faculty prefer overhead projectors to chalkboards because (1) the projected images are clearer and easier to view, (2) one can write on a transparency without turning one's back to the students, and (3) one can turn the projector on and off during the presentation to focus the students' attention on the lecture or on the visual materials (Ellington, 1985). Also, transparencies can be reused, enabling an instructor to build up a systematic collection of material that complements or replaces conventional teaching notes. If you use a projector equipped with a continuous roll of transparency plastic, you can easily rewind the roll to review earlier material.

In contrast to these advantages are two inconveniences: noise from the projector and the need to remain next to the projector while using it.

General Strategies

Use transparencies as you would use a chalkboard. You can highlight the organization of your presentation, emphasize its main points, and stimulate students' interest. For example, use transparencies to present the following information:

- The day's outline or schedule
- Difficult names or terminology or unfamiliar vocabulary

- Diagrams, charts, schematics, maps, graphs, drawings, or other illustrations
- Chronology or time line of important dates
- Formulas, theorems, computations, or steps in mathematical proofs
- Major points of your lecture

Use an overhead projector to present material. For example, display a relevant newspaper headline, cartoon, drawing, or commercially prepared transparency. To avoid overwhelming students, limit yourself to a dozen or so transparencies during a fifty-minute lecture.

Make certain that students can view the screen and the image. Focus the projector before class begins and check to be sure the classroom lighting does not interfere with the image. Placing the projector at the side rather than in the center of the room gives better sight lines. Keep an extra lamp handy (and know how to replace it) in case the bulb burns out during class.

Don't turn your back to the class to look at the screen. Stand to the side of the projector so you don't block the screen. Maintain eye contact with your students, glancing at the screen only to check the focus or visibility.

Be aware of how pointer movements are magnified by projection. Move your pointer slowly and steadily over the transparency. Rapid movements will be startling, and small shakes can look like major tremors through an overhead projector. For a quick reference, point to the screen, not the transparency.

Turn off the projector when you are no longer referring to a transparency. After students have copied the information, turn off the machine or place opaque paper on the projector. A lighted screen can be distracting.

Limit the amount of material on a single transparency. Restrict the content of each transparency to a single concept, and use a series of simple transparencies to cover a complicated topic (Ellington, 1985). As a rule of thumb, Svinicki and Lewis (n.d.) recommend limiting your text to twenty to fifty words or twenty-four to thirty pieces of data unless you have made a copy of the transparency as a handout for your students.

Use color and graphics to add interest and emphasis. Highlight important points by underlining, boxing, or using colored washable inks. You can also affix commercially available transparent color adhesives, in various geometric shapes, to the underside of transparencies. Moreover, you can use off-the-shelf computer software to help you prepare visually engaging transparencies.

Using an Overhead Projector as a Chalkboard

Use pens with water-soluble ink to write. Place clear plastic on the overhead projector and write as you would on the board, but using pens with water-soluble ink or wax-based audiovisual pencils (grease pencils). Avoid using regular felt-tip pens, because their ink does not adhere to the plastic. If you make a mistake or want to reuse the sheet, erase the material with a damp tissue or cloth.

Make your writing legible. Print in upper- and lowercase letters rather than all capitals (Ellington, 1985). Letters one-inch high should be legible at a distance of thirty-two feet (Svinicki and Lewis, n.d.); in a smaller room use smaller lettering. Since the size of projected lettering decreases as the projector is moved closer to the screen, test out various sizes of lettering in your classroom under typical viewing conditions (Lewis, 1982).

Use the same principles for writing on transparencies as you would use for the chalkboard. For example, write systematically, starting at the top left-hand corner and working across and then down to the next line; use titles, headings, and underlining or colors to emphasize key statements; give students time to copy what you have written; pass out complex diagrams or drawings. See "Chalkboards."

Making Your Own Transparencies

For handwritten transparencies, use water-soluble ink or a grease pencil. Use permanent ink if you plan to reuse the transparency. The best colors are black, blue, and green (Ellington, 1985). Place a sheet of lined paper underneath the transparency to serve as a guide as you write on the sheet. To prevent smudging, place a clean sheet of paper under your hand.

Use commercially available "presentation" software to prepare material for overhead transparencies. Software packages produce compelling renditions of even the most tedious material. The software also permits you to make two-per-page or six-per-page reduced format handouts of all transparencies for distribution to students. (Source: Head, 1992)

For professional-looking results, use laser printers or special equipment to prepare the transparency. There are machines especially designed to create transparencies. Some photocopy machines also allow you to reproduce a paper original onto a plastic transparency, and some laser printers can produce transparencies. Check with your institution's media center for information about production processes.

Use large letters, upper- and lowercase, in a plain typeface. Letters approximately one-quarter to one-half inch tall will project well in a small classroom. (If you are using a computer, use sans serif fonts of 24 to 48 points.) (Source: Svinicki and Lewis, n.d.)

Line spacing should be 150 percent of the letter height. For easier viewing, leave a border around the body of the material: for a $10'' \times 10''$ projector, work within a $7\frac{1}{2}'' \times 9\frac{1}{2}''$ space, projecting the $9\frac{1}{2}''$ dimension horizontally. (Sources: Fuhrmann and Grasha, 1983; Svinicki and Lewis, n.d.).

Using Prepared Transparencies

Arrange your transparencies in the order you will be using them. Make sure that your notes match the sequence of the prepared transparencies. Make a notation in the margin of your notes indicating when to put up the next transparency. To avoid exposing the light when you change transparencies, hold the new one above and drop it as you remove the old one.

After displaying a transparency, wait briefly before speaking. Give students time to scan the material; don't read it for them. Leave the transparency up long enough for students to copy the material, but let them know if you are going to distribute a handout that duplicates the image.

Place a clear plastic sheet on top of transparencies you will use repeatedly. On the plastic overlay, you can highlight or emphasize key parts of the permanent transparency or add details to it. (Source: Fuhrmann and Grasha, 1983)

Overlay several transparencies to illustrate changes, processes, or alternatives. By stacking transparencies, you can show how a graph changes, how a plant grows, or how an equation is derived. You can also show several systems simultaneously (for example, the mechanical systems of a building). In preparation you will need to decide which elements belong on the base transparency (projected first) and which belong on each overlay. Overlays can be cumulative or used one at a time on top of the base. Make separate masters for the base and each overlay; special kits can help you create multilayer transparencies. (Source: Drasites, 1975)

When projecting a list, reveal only one item at a time. Cover everything on your transparency except the first point to be discussed. When you are ready to move to the next item, uncover it. This line-by-line display focuses students' attention. (Source: Drasites, 1975)

Insert at least one blank transparency among the prepared set. Use the blank transparency to solicit students' ideas, expand a concept briefly mentioned, or clarify issues raised during class.

Place a copy of your prepared transparencies in the library. Let students know that the overheads are available for them to review.

References

Drasites, J. "Transparencies." In L. P. Grayson and J. M. Biedenbach (eds.), *Teaching Aids in the College Classroom*. Washington, D.C.: American Society for Engineering Education, 1975.

Ellington, H. *Producing Teaching Materials*. New York: Nichols, 1985.

Fuhrmann, B. S., and Grasha, A. F. *A Practical Handbook for College Teachers*. Boston: Little, Brown, 1983.

Head, J. T. "New Directions in Presentation Graphics: Impact on Teaching and Learning." In M. J. Albright and D. L. Graf (eds.), *Teaching in the Information Age: The Role of Educational Technology*. New Directions for Teaching and Learning, no. 51. San Francisco: Jossey-Bass, 1992.

Lewis, K. G. *Taming the Pedagogical Monster*. Austin: Center for Teaching Effectiveness, University of Texas, 1982.

Svinicki, M. D., and Lewis, K. G. *Media Aids for the Classroom*. Austin: Center for Teaching Effectiveness, University of Texas, n.d.

38

Slides

For faculty teaching art history or architecture, slides are a staple, but faculty in other disciplines can also use slides to add interest, detail, and variety to lectures. The chief disadvantage of showing slides is that the room must be darkened, which makes it hard for some students to take notes and easy for others to doze off.

General Strategies

Use slides to reinforce concepts, illustrate ideas or stimulate students' interest. You can use slides to do the following (Fuhrmann and Grasha, 1983):

- Show specific examples of general concepts
- Aid students' memory
- Demonstrate detailed steps of a process
- Show spatial or visual relationships
- Provide illustrations of difficult or complex theories

Vary the slides in your presentation. If most of your slides show graphs and charts, insert some slides of people, places, or things or use title slides to announce a new topic.

Make sure the slides are legible. Too much detail or too much copy is difficult to read. Simplify the material. Preview the slides under conditions similar to those in your classroom. As a quick check, if you can read a 2″ × 2″ slide by holding it up to the light without a magnifier and without squinting, students will be able to see it in the classroom. (Sources: Bryce, 1985; Daniel, 1975)

Mark the cardboard or plastic mount of each slide so that you can load it correctly into the projector. With most projectors, slides must be loaded upside down. So place a dot on the bottom left-hand corner of the *front of the* *slide*, and load the slide so that the dots appear at the top right-hand corner. The front side is sometimes hard to identify, but it is usually the side with a date. You can also identify the front side by holding up the slide against the light to see that it reads correctly left to right.

Design your presentation around your slides. Your slides and lecture should complement each other. If you only have fifteen minutes worth of slides, group them all together rather than dispersing them throughout a fifty-minute lecture.

Photocopy your slides on paper and place these pages in your lecture notes. You can avoid having to look at the screen to know what image is on view or which is coming up next if you have photocopies of all the slides. Place copies of three or four slides along one side of an 8½″ × 11″ page or photocopy and enlarge each slide to 8½″ × 11″. If you later repeat the same presentation, the photocopies will help you reconstruct the correct sequence for the slides. You can also use the photocopies to rehearse your presentation. If the slides are detailed, consider distributing paper copies of them to the class.

Making Your Own Slides

Decide what you want to show as slides. Almost any printed material can be photographed for slides. You can also draw (or have drawn) diagrams, graphs, or other visual aids. Since the images need not be on the screen for a long period of time, the production values can be somewhat rough. Detailed maps reproduce poorly, however, and are seldom legible (Bryce, 1985). Instead, redraw maps to emphasize important details. Newer technologies are making it easier to produce higher-quality slides (Head, 1992). For guidance about procedures and costs, check with your institution's reprographics or multimedia unit.

Leave a blank border around your copy. The standard 35mm slide has a 2:3 horizontal format. Keep these proportions in mind as you lay out your work. Experienced photographers suggest using black paper around the borders to mask out portions that will not fit in the slide format and to eliminate white edges. (Source: Bryce, 1985)

Carefully apportion the lines of text. For slides to be shown horizontally, limit text to five or six printed lines with five to six words per line. Use a plain typeface (upper- and lowercase) and a single font. The lettering should be at least one-fifteenth the height of the slide. (Sources: Ellington, 1985; Svinicki and Lewis, n.d.)

Keep the text simple and concise. Express headings, summaries, or main ideas in five to ten words. Keep in mind that while students are reading a slide, they are not listening to you speak. To prepare quick titles, write with a grease pencil on a blank glass slide. Limit handwritten materials to one or two words or simple images. (Source: Bryce, 1985).

Use graphs and diagrams instead of tables. Graphs are easier to read and comprehend than tables. Be sure to define the variables, label each axis, and as necessary, label the units (for example, each tick mark represents ten thousand people).

Choose colors carefully. Avoid dark blue and dark red lettering. Instead, use bright yellow, orange, or pink — colors that move forward visually. Dark-colored backgrounds (blue, green, or black) are preferable to white. (Source: Svinicki and Lewis, n.d.)

Be aware of copyright regulations. The fair-use provisions of the 1976 copyright law allow copyrighted materials to be copied for educational purposes. You can make one copy of a copyrighted image from a book or periodical without asking permission. However, keep track of the source of the slide in case you want to illustrate an article, essay, or monograph. Permission must be obtained for publication or commercial purposes.

Using Slides in the Classroom

Use slides to emphasize the structure of your presentation. For example, show a title slide at the start of each major section and subsection. Use slides to reinforce your major points, using a new slide for each point you make. Do not, however, read the slide aloud. (Source: Ellington, 1985)

Place the slides in the carousel tray before class. Lay out your slides in order, transfer them to the projector's carousel tray, and make sure the locking ring is in place. An 80-slide tray is less likely to jam than a 140-slide tray. If a single tray will not hold all your slides, change trays at a logical breaking point rather than in the middle of a sequence. (Source: Bryce, 1985)

Consider using two projectors. Project two images simultaneously to compare and contrast objects or to show two perspectives of the same object. Two-projector presentations are easy to do: lay out the slides in two columns, side by side. The left one of each pair goes into the left carousel, the right into the right. In older carousels, you may need to insert blank cardboard whenever there are unmatched pairs.

Use horizontal rather than vertical slides. Most screens are designed to show horizontal slides; vertical slides tend to project past the top and bottom edges of the screen. If you want to show both horizontal and vertical slides in the same presentation, place a vertical slide at the very beginning of your tray so that you can correctly position and focus the projector. (Sources: Bryce, 1985; Ellington, 1985)

In large lecture classes, show slides of review material, cartoons, or questions while students are arriving. This technique directs the attention of students toward the front of the auditorium and makes it easier to call the class to order. Remember the lights will be on, so use simple images. (Source: McKeachie, 1986)

Arrange for a small light for your notes. Check to see whether the podium is equipped with a light. If there is no podium light in the room, bring a flashlight.

Make certain that the slide on view corresponds to what you are saying at the moment. Otherwise students will be distracted by trying to puzzle out the relationship between your words and the image before them. Use title slides to cover portions of your presentation that are imageless.

Keep a slide on the screen for no more than ten or fifteen seconds. Studies show that when a new image appears on a screen, most viewers spend no more than fifteen seconds actively exploring it. If you are using dual projectors, keep the slides up for thirty seconds. In either case, do not leave a slide on the screen after discussing it. (Source: Daniel, 1975)

Avoid backing up to a slide already shown (unless in response to a question). If you want to refer to one image at several points in your presentation, use duplicate slides. Also avoid turning the projector off and on during your talk.

Spur students' active viewing skills by occasionally describing the next slide before it appears. Students will try to imagine what is coming, and the slide will either reinforce or correct their expectations. (Source: Daniel, 1975)

Use an electric pointer. A manual pointer or hand gesture will be lost in the projected image.

Use a projector with a wireless remote control. For maximum mobility, select a newer projector with a wireless remote control. Most remote devices have three buttons (forward, reverse, focus) and are easy to operate.

If you use an old projector, end your presentation with a dark slide. To avoid a screenful of blinding brightness and also to protect your last slide from excessive heat, place a dark slide at the end of the set. Newer projectors automatically remain dark after the last slide. (Source: Bryce, 1985)

If you use a newer projector, be careful with glass-mounted slides. The ventilating system of some brands may not be sufficient to cool the emulsion sandwiched between two pieces of glass. Check the product literature first.

Keep in mind that students may not be able to take notes during your slide presentations. If you want students to have a permanent record, prepare a handout to support the lecture or discussion. (Source: Ellington, 1985)

References

Bryce, G. "Suggestions for Slide Presentations." In Office of Instructional Development, *Notes for TA Consultants: A Sourcebook of Suggestions and Guidelines for Improving Undergraduate Education*. Los Angeles: Office of Instructional Development, University of California, 1985.

Daniel, J. S. "Uses and Abuses of Slides in Teaching." In L. P. Grayson and J. M. Biedenbach (eds.), *Teaching Aids in the College Classroom*. Washington, D.C.: American Society for Engineering Education, 1975.

Ellington, H. *Producing Teaching Materials*. New York: Nichols, 1985.

Fuhrmann, B. S., and Grasha, A. F. *A Practical Handbook for College Teachers*. Boston: Little, Brown, 1983.

Head, J. T. "New Directions in Presentation Graphics: Impact on Teaching and Learning." In M. J. Albright and D. L. Graf (eds), *Teaching in the Information Age: The Role of Educational Technology*. New Directions for Teaching and Learning, no. 51. San Francisco: Jossey-Bass, 1992.

McKeachie, W. J. *Teaching Tips*. (8th ed.) Lexington, Mass.: Heath, 1986.

Svinicki, M. D., and Lewis, K. G. *Media Aids for the Classroom*. Austin: Center for Teaching Effectiveness, University of Texas, n.d.

Films and Videotapes

39

Films and videotapes can bring a variety of experiences into your classroom. You can use films and videos to show movement over time, speed up or slow down motion, view processes that cannot be seen by the unaided human eye, present historical footage or re-creations of events, show an artistic performance, and transport students to new places and surroundings (Fuhrmann and Grasha, 1983).

Films offer better visual quality than some videotapes, but videos are easier to use, more readily available, and can be stopped at any point. Also, when showing a video, you can start at any point, selecting only the most relevant portions of the program. To see what materials are available on your campus, contact the media center or audiovisual librarian. If you are considering recording a television broadcast off the air, ask your campus copyright officer or media staff whether you can show the videotape in class without first receiving written permission from the copyright holder.

General Strategies

Prepare your students to see the film or video. Explain why you are showing the program and what you expect students to learn from it (Lewis, 1982). Relate the program to what your students already know about the subject, and introduce new terms or proper names on the board. Does the program demonstrate examples of key concepts, review material previously covered, or pose a new problem? You could also develop a list of questions students should be able to answer after seeing the program (Svinicki and Lewis, n.d.).

Help your students view the presentation critically and thoughtfully. There are many ways to involve students in active viewing. *In science classes*, stop the film or videotape of an experiment and ask students what will happen next. Or show the end of an experiment and ask students to describe its beginning. Tie the visual presentation to print sources on the same topic by preparing bibliographies or research guides to accompany the presentation. *In social science classes*, show two films or tapes that present different points of view of the same subject and ask students to evaluate the perspectives. Or stop a film or tape before its resolution and ask students to defend their stance on the issue. Use theatrical movies or documentaries to illustrate issues and concepts. *In literature or drama classes*, ask students to compose their own ending to the story being shown. Or show films or videotapes of plays, stories, or novels and ask students to compare the visual treatment to the original in terms of character development, tone, and theme. (Source: Brown, cited in Fuhrmann and Grasha, 1983, p. 237)

Be cautious in developing your own films or videotapes. Short video clips of scientific experiments, interviews, guest speakers, and performances are relatively easy to produce—ask the media staff on your campus for advice. But to develop a quality film or video is an expensive, time-consuming process that should be undertaken only after careful consultation with media specialists.

Using Films and Videos in Class

Practice operating the equipment. Keep a supply of spare bulbs nearby if you are using a film projector; know how to work the VCR. Make sure videotapes are compatible with the machine.

View the film or video before you show it to the class. Become thoroughly familiar with the content. How does the film or video fit your objectives for the class? Is it the best way for students to learn the concepts you want to teach? Take notes on possible discussion questions to raise with the class after the showing. (Source: Svinicki and Lewis, n.d.)

Mention whether or not students should take notes. If you are showing a video, the lights can remain on and students can take notes if they wish. But showing a film in a darkened room makes note taking more difficult.

View the film or video with your students. You can learn a great deal by observing your students as they watch the presentation. Refrain from showing films or videos as a way of occupying students while you miss class or do other things.

Interrupt the video, as necessary, to enhance learning. If it is appropriate to call attention to some point, stop the tape and make your comments.

Keep in mind, however, that too many interruptions can be distracting and disruptive.

Conduct a follow-up activity. After the presentation, engage students in assessing the meaning of what they have seen and its relationship to the course content. You could lead a discussion, ask students to write a brief analysis, or have them form small groups to resolve problems or discuss issues raised in the film or video. For example, ask students to comment on the following:

- What were the major sequences or events?
- What are the key points of each sequence?
- What are the consequences of the actions depicted?

Include content from the film or video on tests or exams. If the film or video is important enough to show in class, it is important enough to be the source of test questions. By letting students know this in advance, you give legitimacy to the film or video. (Source: Fuhrmann and Grasha, 1983)

References

Fuhrmann, B. S., and Grasha, A. F. *A Practical Handbook for College Teachers*. Boston: Little, Brown, 1983.

Lewis, K. G. *Taming the Pedagogical Monster*. Austin: Center for Teaching Effectiveness, University of Texas, 1982.

Svinicki, M., and Lewis, K. G. *Media Aids for the Classroom*. Austin: Center for Teaching Effectiveness, University of Texas, n.d.

40

Computers and Multimedia

Increasingly, faculty members are using computers and interactive multimedia to make their teaching more efficient, effective, powerful, and flexible. Faculty members are also finding that computers and multimedia tools can provide students with individualized activities that accommodate differences in students' levels of preparation. Computers can help you transform course notes into overheads, create high-quality complex illustrations, do real-time calculations and processing, engage students in interactive collaborations, and bring text, graphics, animation, sound, and video into the classroom.

The foregoing examples refer to ways an individual faculty member can improve instruction within a single classroom. But the promise of technology is its potential for liberating teaching from the constraints of place and time. Experts portray a future in which access to academic programs will no longer be restricted by geography or availability of instructors, rooms, or students. Texts will be supplemented or supplanted by electronic information on laptop, palmtop, or even wrist computers. With the advent of networking, faculty and students will be able to collaborate in a worldwide learning community.

Connectivity, networking, miniaturization, and "liquid libraries" may not be fully here yet, but incorporating instructional technologies into your teaching can enhance the way you teach. The suggestions below are designed to help faculty members who have limited experience in using computers as instructional tools. The technologies are changing so rapidly that the technical material described here may become quickly outdated.

General Strategies

Consider the advantages of using technology in your course. O'Brien (cited in Kaplan-Neher, 1991) identifies four reasons for incorporating computers into instruction:

- To increase the amount of material in the course; for example, providing more illustrations or more in-depth descriptions of some topics; or adding material not previously attempted because the material requires complex calculations
- To treat course content in a different way; for example, instead of lecturing on the civil rights movement, showing a multimedia program of speeches, clips of demonstrations, and the text of legislation
- To present demonstrations that cannot be done with traditional instructional tools, such as simulating dangerous or costly lab experiments or modeling very small (atomic) or very large (intergalactic) phenomena
- To enhance course content by presenting hypothetical scenarios (for example, portraying life after global warming), time-lapse animations (a map showing political changes in Europe in the twentieth century), or processes invisible to the naked eye (the movement of a piston)

But avoid using high-end technology to serve low-end instructional practices. For example, refrain from using HyperCard stacks and multimedia as fancy overheads or chalkboards. Overhead projectors may work as well or better at much lower cost. Try to match your instructional needs with the appropriate technology.

Consider how your students might benefit from greater use of technology. Johnston and Gardner (1989) group computer applications into three general categories:

- *Direct instruction:* The software presents new content and information to students or helps them evaluate their mastery of the material. Examples include tutorial programs and interactive simulations.
- *Working tools:* Students are trained to use software programs (such as data-base management, spreadsheets, statistical software, and word processing) as tools for accomplishing a specific task or solving certain types of problems. These programs expedite certain tasks but do not "teach" the student new substantive material.
- *Information exchange:* Students use technology to retrieve or exchange information through electronic mail, computer conferencing, bulletin boards, and on-line data bases such as library catalogues.

Learn about existing software. It is much easier to use existing software than to develop a program from scratch. Computer and software manufacturers publish directories of available software. For example, Apple's *Reference Guide to Macintosh in Higher Education* lists faculty-developed programs by academic discipline as well as commercial products that have broad application in academic and administrative settings. Apple also publishes discipline-specific handbooks that compile software available for the Macintosh relevant to instruction, learning, and research. IBM distributes *Computer Learning*, which describes software and courseware developed by faculty for use in two-year colleges, undergraduate education, and at the graduate level. IBM also supports a free electronic bulletin board on academic computing (ISAAC), which includes abstracts of a variety of software packages (Internet: ISAAC@ISAAC.ENGR.Washington.edu). Kozma and Johnston (1991) and Boettcher (1993) describe faculty-developed award-winning software for use in a variety of disciplines. You can also ask your campus librarian or instructional technology program for help in identifying software.

The *Chronicle of Higher Education*'s regular feature on information technology highlights new software developed by faculty and commercial vendors. In the issue of October 16, 1991, the *Chronicle* listed 101 successful uses of computer technology in classrooms (pp. A26–A38).

Book publishers are also expanding into the field of educational software. For example, one publisher offers student editions of some twenty software packages. These student editions include customized manuals to help students learn to use the software on their own.

Use software in conformance with ethical and legal guidelines. Copyright regulations apply to software: unauthorized copying is illegal. A brochure available from EDUCOM, a consortium of higher education institutions interested in integrating information technology into classrooms, curriculums, and research, describes guidelines for fair, ethical, and legal use of licensed and unlicensed software (bitnet: PUBS@EDUCOM. BITNET; internet: PUBS@EDUCOM.EDU).

Connect with other faculty interested in technology. Contact your campus computer center or office of instructional resources to identify faculty who use computers in instruction. Also use electronic networks to find interested faculty. The Office of Faculty Development and Academic Support of the University of Hawaii reports on four networks for faculty interested in computers, academic software, and instructional technology:

- Educational Technology
  EDTECH@OHSTVMA.BITNET
  Brings together students, faculty, and interested others in the field of
  educational technology to share ideas and information.

- Interpersonal Computing and Technology
  IPCT-L@GUVM.BITNET
  Provides an international forum for pedagogical issues involving teaching with technology. Emphasis is on higher education, connectivity, and networking.

- New Paradigms in Education
  NEWEDU-L@USCVM.BITNET
  Discusses the influences of technology on teaching, learning, and the concept of education.

- Academic Software Development
  ACSOFT-L@WUVMD.BITNET
  Discusses a wide range of topics related to the development of instructional software for computers.

Prepare to spend time integrating technology into your courses. Once you have found the appropriate software, you will need to train students to use the programs, modify your syllabus, and revamp or develop assignments or texts. (Source: Johnston, 1989)

Strengthening Your Lectures Through Technology

Prepare lecture notes, syllabi, tests and exams, and class handouts on computer. Word processing or presentation software enables you to make revisions quickly, to customize notes to suit a particular class, to update and add new material, and to move or combine topics from one set of notes to another. (Source: Kaplan-Neher, 1991)

Produce overhead transparencies for your lectures. You can use overhead transparencies to emphasize or reinforce key points or to add graphics that make your presentation more engaging. Your local copy shop may be equipped to produce the overheads from your disk, or you can do this yourself if you have a letter-quality printer, an application program for producing uniform visuals (such as Microsoft PowerPoint or Aldus Persuasion), and transparencies upon which to print the visuals. For tips on preparing overheads, see "Transparencies and Overhead Projectors." (Source: Head, 1992)

Project computer images onto a large screen. If you can bring a computer, a liquid-crystal display (LCD), and an overhead projector into your classroom, students can see your computer screen as you are working on it. For example, an economics professor uses an LCD and computer to demonstrate financial "what if" projections. During class she manipulates data to show students how changes in one variable affect other variables — for example, how declining interest rates affect housing starts, car sales, and manufacturers' inventories. (Source: Kaplan-Neher, 1991)

Bring interactive multimedia into the classroom. Lamb (1992) and Lynch (1991) describe various examples of bringing video, sound, and animation together with text and still illustrations for demonstrating processes that happen too quickly (the physics of sound) or too slowly (the action of glaciers) to be observed by the normal eye. You can also demonstrate concepts too difficult to explain in words (the mechanics of a bird's wing or the various ways directors have interpreted a scene from *Macbeth*). The most common (and the most primitive) way to incorporate multimedia is to use HyperCard. More sophisticated presentations are possible on new multimedia workstations currently under development. Though intrinsically appealing, multimedia setups are not yet readily available on college campuses; the equipment is expensive, competing devices are incompatible, copyright issues are sticky, and preparation can be time-consuming (Yoder, 1991). As experts have pointed out, however, once the technology is perfected and made cost-effective, faculty will have ready access to a wide collection of digitalized slides, compact discs, and videos for incorporation into their lectures.

Using Technology to Accommodate Individual Differences

Let students learn at their own pace. Software has been developed to help students master a variety of subjects, and many programs have search and browse features that let students freely move through the material in whatever way they want. However, experts caution faculty to select such computer programs carefully. Uninteresting or unmotivating programs will only alienate and disenchant students.

Complex HyperCard programs addressing topics in Western civilization include Project Perseus at Harvard, which covers the Greek classics; Intermedia at Brown University, on works of English literature; and CULTURE, a guide to 3,700 years of Western civilization (Kozma, 1991). Kaplan-Neher (1991) describes a professor of German who has developed software on HyperCard that lets students learn German by reading a story, viewing vocabulary, or taking a short quiz to see what they do and do not know. When students are reading the stories, they can stop at any word and request a screen that offers explanatory materials—for instance, an explanation of a grammar point. Students can also review the material as many times as they want.

Let students work on interactive simulations. Interactive simulations require students to participate in the enactment of procedures impossible or unlikely in the "real world"—because of logistics, expense, or safety concerns. For example, a faculty member in biology has used STELLA to illustrate biological models for estimating the deer population in the wild. A faculty member in archaeology has created a simulation that helps students understand the key life decisions that must be made by people living in a subsistence agricultural society. (Source: Kaplan-Neher, 1991)

Provide accommodations for students with disabilities. Adaptive computer equipment is available for accommodating students with disabilities; guidelines and descriptions may be requested from EDUCOM through their project Equal Access to Software for Instruction. In addition, Apple has compiled a resource listing of books and materials for students with disabilities, including information on adapting computer labs. IBM has established the National Support Center for Persons with Disabilities, which provides information and advice about products and services for specific disabilities.

Using Technology to Strengthen Instruction: Examples

Establish electronic mail (e-mail) accounts for your class. With e-mail, you can send messages at any time of day or night to a computer that is connected to an on-campus or off-campus network. E-mail can be used to make assignments, to comment on work, and to communicate important class information. You can post homework assignments through e-mail, and students can submit homework and papers through the network. E-mail allows users to forward entire memos or papers to others and to file away particularly interesting communications for later review or editing. A professor who uses e-mail to extend classroom discussions outside the classroom finds that electronic discussions avoid the common classroom problem of one or two students always dominating the discussion.

Consider incorporating collaborative writing software into your course. If you assign writing and have the opportunity to work within a networked classroom or on a networked campus, you may want to use one of several software programs that allow a peer or an instructor to attach comments to a student's electronically submitted essay or that allow students to access grammar tutorials. You can also have students send drafts electronically to you for comments before they submit their papers. *Computers and College Writing: Selected College Profiles* (available from the National Project on Computers and Colleges based at the City University of New York) describes forty-nine writing programs across the country that incorporate computers in teaching composition.

Identify multimedia materials for topics not adequately demonstrated by print, lectures, or traditional audiovisual media. Multimedia presentations are particularly appropriate for searching, animating, linking, and visualizing information. Interactive videodiscs give users control over both full-motion video and CD-quality stereo sound tracks. With videodiscs you can search and find any video sequence or still frame almost instantly (unlike videotape). There are videodiscs on physics, chemistry, Middle East conflicts, AIDS, presidential elections, the 1989 Loma Prieta earthquake, and many other topics. Lynch (1991) lists references on the topics of multimedia computing and teaching with multimedia, sources of educational videodiscs (such as the National Geographic Society, Smithsonian, and Voyager Company in Santa Monica, California), and ways to customize the discs to suit your own needs. Lamb (1992) describes multimedia applications in a variety of disciplines.

Create an electronic information server for student use. Consult with your campus computer center to find out ways to make course material readily available to students electronically. For example, you could place on a server the course syllabus, reading lists, past exams, your lecture notes, solutions to problem sets, answers to commonly asked student questions, or other course information. Students could have electronic access to these materials anytime they wished. Unlike e-mail, in which all users simultaneously receive the same messages, with information servers, the users control which information they want to access by "navigating" through the system. Material need not be viewed in sequence; users can explore any topic in the system at their own pace and at a level of detail dictated by their interests. Some campuses are experimenting with these electronic information services and have placed on the network the campus telephone directory, class schedules and campus calendars, campus job listings, the general catalogue, grants and funding opportunities, campus publications, a list of student organizations, and guides to services and facilities.

References

Boettcher, J. V. (ed.). *101 Success Stories of Information Technology in Higher Education.* New York: McGraw-Hill, 1993.

Head, J. T. "New Directions in Presentation Graphics: Impact on Teaching and Learning." In M. J. Albright and D. L. Graf (eds.), *Teaching in the Information Age: The Role of Educational Technology.* New Directions for Teaching and Learning, no. 51. San Francisco: Jossey-Bass, 1992.

Johnston, J. "The Computer Revolution in Teaching." *Accent*, 1989, *5*, 1–3. (Publication of the National Center for Research to Improve Postsecondary Teaching and Learning, University of Michigan)

Johnston, J., and Gardner, S. *The Electronic Classroom in Higher Education: A Case for Change.* Ann Arbor: National Center for Research to Improve Postsecondary Teaching and Learning, University of Michigan, 1989.

Kaplan-Neher, A. *Teaching with Computers.* Sunnyvale, Calif.: PUBLIX Information Products for Apple Computers, 1991.

Kozma, R. B. "Learning with Media." *Review of Educational Research*, 1991, *61*(2), 179–211.

Kozma, R. B., and Johnston, J. "The Technological Revolution Comes to the Classroom." *Change*, 1991, *23*(1), 10–23.

Lamb, A. C. "Multimedia and the Teaching-Learning Process in Higher Education." In M. J. Albright and D. L. Graf (eds.), *Teaching in the Information Age: The Role of Educational Technology.* New Directions for Teaching and Learning, no. 51. San Francisco: Jossey-Bass, 1992.

Lynch, P. *Multimedia: Getting Started.* Sunnyvale, Calif.: PUBLIX Information Products for Apple Computers, 1991.

Yoder, S. K. "Reading, Writing & Multimedia." *Wall Street Journal*, Oct. 21, 1991, pp. R12, R14.

X.

Evaluation to Improve Teaching

Fast Feedback

41

The most widely used method for evaluating teaching is the end-of-course questionnaire. The questionnaires arrive too late, however, to benefit the students doing the evaluation. Nor do the questionnaires usually encourage students to give the specific comments an instructor might need either to identify how well students have been understanding the material or to spot weaknesses in classroom presentation, organization, pacing, and work load.

Much more effective are fast feedback activities that take place *during* the semester. The term *fast feedback* is derived from management practices but can be applied to instruction (Bateman and Roberts, 1992). Informal sampling of students' comprehension of the subject matter will enable you to gauge how and what students are learning. And informal requests for constructive criticism will help you identify which teaching methods best contribute to your students' understanding of the material. Faculty who use such techniques report learning more about ways to improve their courses than they have ever discovered from end-of-term student rating forms (Bateman and Roberts, 1992). The fast feedback techniques described here require modest effort, are easy to carry out, and use little class time.

General Strategies

Decide what you want to assess. You can gather information on how well students are learning the material, on the effectiveness of your teaching strategies, or on other topics of interest to you. When looking at your instructional methods, focus on what can be changed during the semester — for example, the pace of the course, turnaround time on exams and assignments, or the level of difficulty of the material — and ask your students for specific responses about particular issues rather than a general evaluation of the course or your teaching. (Source: "Effectively Using Informal Early Semester Feedback," 1987)

Schedule fast feedback at times appropriate to the course. If you are teaching a course for the first time or have significantly revised a course you have taught previously, you may want to canvass students as early as three or four weeks after the semester begins. If you are teaching a course you have taught many times before, you may want to wait until midsemester before asking for student assessments. (If you solicit feedback immediately after a midterm, however, most of the comments will relate to the exam.) In addition, if you observe that students are having difficulty with the material or course requirements, you may want to probe the issue immediately. (Source: "Effectively Using Informal Early Semester Feedback," 1987)

Use different techniques throughout the semester. Many of the techniques described below are quite simple and take very little time; a few require planning or technical assistance. Of course, you won't want to use all these techniques in any one course; nor would you want to use the same one again and again. Experiment with the ones that appeal to you and see which provide the most helpful information. Or consider developing your own techniques for obtaining feedback; use these ideas to spark your thinking.

Soliciting Students' Opinions About the Course

Distribute blank index cards during the last five or ten minutes of class. Pass out 3″ x 5″ cards to students and ask them to respond anonymously to two questions, one on the front of the card, the other on the back. You can pose general questions about what is going well in the course and what needs to be improved or changed. Other general questions: "What do you want more of? Less of?" "How are you finding the course?" "Any suggestions for improving the course?" "Any problems?" "What do you need before the end of the term?" You may prefer to ask more specific questions about aspects of the course, such as whether the problem sets are too difficult or whether the pace of the class is causing difficulties. Leave the room while students write their comments. Ask a student volunteer to collect the forms and return them to you or the department assistant.

Ask students to complete a brief informal questionnaire. During the last few minutes of class, distribute a short, simple questionnaire to students or to a random sample of students in a large lecture class. Limit the questionnaire to four to six short-answer or multiple-choice questions. The issues posed should be ones you can respond to during the term; otherwise your students may develop false expectations about the remainder of the course. You might ask about the level of difficulty of course content, the quality and quantity of assignments, the use of class time, the nature of student preparation outside of class, or the pace of the class. Consider asking students to list the one or two specific behaviors or incidents that weighed most heavily in their ratings. To assure that students respond candidly, leave the room while they complete the questionnaire anonymously, and ask a student volunteer to collect the forms and return them to you or the department assistant. (Source: Fuhrmann and Grasha, 1983)

Arrange for your students to be interviewed. Invite a colleague or staff member to conduct an oral evaluation with your students during the last ten or fifteen minutes of class. After you leave, the evaluator asks students to cluster into groups of five or six and to take several minutes to do the following:

- Select a spokesperson who will also write down the groups' comments.
- Name something in the course that they find helpful or worthwhile or that has helped their learning.
- Name something that has hindered their learning and that they would like to see changed.
- Suggest how the course could be improved.

The evaluator circulates among the groups as they work to remind them how much time they have left and to make certain that they are staying with the task. The evaluator then asks each spokesperson to report the group's findings, and the evaluator records the results on the board. After all groups have reported, the evaluator summarizes for the class the points of consensus and asks for clarification on points of disagreement. The evaluator collects the written comments from the spokespersons and prepares an oral or written summary for you. (Source: Clark and Redmond, 1982; Coffman, 1991)

Establish a student liaison committee. Ask two to four students to meet with you periodically outside of class to discuss difficulties or dissatisfactions with the course. Membership on the committee may be rotated from a list of volunteers, as long as the entire class knows who the liaison students are at any given time and how and why they should use them to relay information. If you teach a course with a large number of discussion sections, invite each section to select a delegate. Be sure, too, that the liaison students understand their function and encourage them to circulate and seek out information formally or informally from other students. Report back to your class about your meetings with the liaison committee. (Source: Fuhrmann and Grasha, 1983)

Form a student management team to work with you and recommend improvements. After the first three or four weeks of class, ask for student volunteers to serve as the management or resource team for the course. The team meets regularly, and you attend their meetings periodically. The charge of the team is to identify problem areas and make suggestions for improvement. Faculty who use this strategy have found it effective for improving course quality and are enthusiastic about the results (Kogut, 1984). Student teams have suggested improvements in procedural aspects of the course, instructor's management style, course organization, readings, assignments, level and extent of student participation in discussion, board work, and pace of lecturing, among other topics. For a list of manuals on how to implement student management and resource teams and how to help students function effectively as team members, see Nuhfer, Perkins, Simonson, and Colleagues, 1992.

Use electronic mail. If your campus has an electronic mail (e-mail) system, establish a computer account so that you can receive and send electronic mail. Let students know that if they have questions, concerns, or comments about the course, they can mail them directly to you. If you wish, you may also arrange for students to have individual accounts so that you can respond to their questions or comments. If you do institute electronic mail in your class, be prepared to answer queries daily. Faculty at the University of California, Berkeley, who have used electronic mail report that they spend about ten to fifteen minutes a day, for a lecture class of two hundred to three hundred students, responding to students' questions and comments. You can also write open letters to students throughout the course, inviting them to answer specific questions about the class. Of course, e-mail is not a replacement for office hours; it is simply another way for faculty to hear from students.

Install a telephone answering machine or voice mail. By attaching an answering machine or voice mail to your office telephone, you can hear about students' course-related difficulties at the time they are having them—for example, at 10 P.M. when they are trying to solve a problem or understand a difficult section in the text. Voice mail and answering machines also permit students to register anonymous gripes. Be sure to review the messages daily so that problems can be taken up in class. (Source: Lewis, 1988)

Make available a suggestion box. Place a manilla envelope in the back of the classroom, in the department office, or on your office door, and encourage students to drop off questions, comments, or problems.

Responding to Students' Feedback

Respond quickly to students' comments. Ideally, you will want to respond to your students' comments at the next class meeting. So schedule fast feedback activities, such as index cards, informal questionnaires, or interviews, at those times during the semester when you will have the opportunity to immediately review the class's comments. For other fast feedback activities, such as e-mail or student teams, report back to the class as appropriate.

Consider carefully what students say. First, look over the positive things your students have said about the course. This is important because it is too easy to get swayed by negative comments. Then consider their suggestions for improvement and group them into three categories:

- Those you can change this semester (for example, the turnaround time on homework assignments)
- Those that must wait until the next time the course is offered (for example, the textbook)
- Those that you either cannot or, for pedagogical reasons, will not change (for example, the number of quizzes or tests)

You may want to ask a colleague or a teaching consultant to help you identify options for making changes.

Let students know what, If anything, will change as a result of their feedback. Thank your students for their comments and invite their ongoing participation in helping you improve the course. Students appreciate knowing that an instructor has carefully considered what they have said. Clarify any confusions or misunderstandings about your goals and their expectations. Then give a brief account of which of their suggestions you will act upon this term, which must wait until the course is next offered, and which you will not act upon and why. Let students know what they can do as well. For example, if students report that they are often confused, invite them to ask questions more often. Keep your tone and attitude neutral; avoid being defensive, indignant, or unduly apologetic.

Checking Students' Understanding of the Material

Ask students to write a "minute paper." Davis, Wood, and Wilson (1983) describe a Berkeley physics professor who, in the late 1970s, developed this technique, which can be used in any discipline. At the end of a class period, ask your students to write for a minute or two on the following two questions: "What is the most significant thing you learned today?" and "What question is uppermost in your mind at the end of today's class?" The resulting minute papers, submitted anonymously, will enable you to evaluate how well you have conveyed the material and how to structure topics for the next class meeting. Angelo (1991) and Mosteller (1989) describe a Harvard statistics professor who asks students, "What was the 'muddiest point' in my lecture today?" A Florida State business professor asks three questions (Bateman and Roberts, 1992, p. 18):

1. Did you get what you came for today?
   a. If yes, what did you get?
   b. If no, what was missing?
   c. If not sure, please explain.
2. What was the muddiest point remaining at the end of today's class?
3. What percent of mud was due to:
   a. Unclear presentation by instructor?
   b. Lack of opportunity to ask questions?
   c. Your lack of preparation?
   d. Your lack of participation in class discussion?
   e. Other?

Ask students to list key concepts or ideas. At the conclusion of a series of lectures or readings about a particular topic, ask students to write short phrases summarizing the three to five key concepts or main ideas about the topic. You can review these lists to verify whether your students have grasped the important ideas. Students can also use their lists to review for exams. You may want to initiate a class discussion that asks students to compare and contrast their entries or define and apply the concepts. (Source: Angelo and Cross, 1993)

Ask students to give definitions, associations, and applications for difficult concepts or ideas. During the last ten minutes of class, hand out a short questionnaire on the basic concepts covered that day. You might ask students to complete the following or similar statements:

- As I understand it, the main idea (concept or point) of today's session was . . .
- A good example of an application of this idea is . . .

- In my mind, the main point of today's lecture is most closely related to the following concepts, ideas, people, places, processes, events, or things... (Have students list several items.)

(Source: Lancaster, 1974)

Ask students whether they are understanding you or not. But avoid the generic "Any questions?" Instead ask, "How many are following me?" or "How many are with me on this point?" Also refrain from posing general questions that might put students on the spot: "Who is lost?"

Have students briefly paraphrase a lecture or a reading assignment. At the beginning of the class period, you can request oral or written paraphrases and then judge whether students have understood the assigned reading or the last lecture. Or you can request paraphrases at the end of the period to check on whether students understood the material you presented.

Ask students to provide a closing summary. At the end of a class session, ask students, individually or in pairs, to write a very brief summary of the main ideas you covered in class. Have students turn in their summaries—making sure they understand this is not a quiz. Or at the beginning of class, ask students to summarize the main ideas from the previous class or the reading and to write one question they expect to be answered during class.

Circulate a chain note. If your class is small, pass around a notebook or sheets of paper midway through the session, and ask students to jot down the main point or issue of what is being discussed at the moment. At the end of the period you will have a listing of what students thought were the key concepts and important ideas from that session. (Source: Angelo and Cross, 1993)

Encourage students to form study groups. Invite representatives of the study groups to meet with you to discuss any difficulties with the subject matter. Study groups provide students with opportunities to learn from one another, and some students may find it easier to seek assistance as a group rather than as individuals. For pointers about study groups, see "Collaborative Learning."

Hold a debriefing session. Reserve the last ten minutes of a class discussion for an analysis of the effectiveness of the preceding discussion. You can ask for general responses or pose specific questions. It is also helpful to hold a debriefing after the midterm exam, when you can probe students' reactions to the exam questions and the adequacy of their preparation for the midterm.

Borrow students' class notes. Ask student volunteers to let you look over their class notes. The notes will show whether you are getting your main points across—although the volunteers are likely to come from the ranks of your better students. Or give carbon sheets to a few students and ask that they be put underneath the paper on which the students are taking notes; collect the carbon copies at the end of class. (Source: Katz, 1989)

Have students turn in class notes as an assignment. Before a midterm or final exam, require students to turn in their lecture notes, course assignments, homework, and quizzes accompanied by a detailed table of contents. You will be able to get a sense of how well students are understanding the material and to identify who is having trouble in the class and needs help. Students will find that compiling a good set of detailed notes and a table of contents will help them study for the exam. Make sure you let your students know, early in the course, that this will be required.

Undertake your own simple assessments to ascertain how well your students are learning. Rather than waiting to see how students perform on a test, you can frequently sample their progress. For example, an instructor teaching Spanish devised a memory matrix to see how quickly and easily students could categorize the irregular and regular verbs they had learned:

	-AR	-ER	-IR
Irregular			
Regular			

Angelo and Cross (1993) describe a variety of classroom assessment techniques (including the one above) that are easy to implement and will give you feedback on how well students are learning. They also describe how you can develop your own assessments.

Using Videotape, Colleague, and Graduate Student Instructor Evaluation

Videotape one of your class sessions. Watching yourself on videotape is a valuable experience. You can see for yourself whether you dominate the discussion, whether you allow students enough time to think through questions, whether you maintain adequate eye contact, and so on. For pointers on how to plan and use videotaping, see "Watching Yourself on Videotape."

Invite an observer to visit your class. Invite a colleague or a teaching consultant to observe one of your classes and make suggestions on specific aspects of your presentation. You will find observation most helpful if you inform the visitor in advance of your specific goals for the class meeting or the particular technique you are trying to perfect. For example, you may want the observer to focus on the level and method of questioning or on demonstration and chalkboard technique. Meet with the observer immediately after the class visit, while the experience is fresh in both your minds. For more information about colleague observers, see "Watching Yourself on Videotape." Katz and Henry (1988) describe a more formal system in which faculty are paired for a year and conduct observations of each other's classes, interview each other's students, and meet regularly to discuss their teaching.

Have a colleague review your course syllabus, assignments, exams, or other materials. Ask a colleague who teaches a comparable course or who is knowledgeable about the subject matter to take a look at your teaching materials. Ask your colleague to make overall suggestions or to answer specific questions: Is the amount of assigned reading appropriate? Do the exams adequately cover the subject matter? Do the homework assignments give students the opportunity to apply concepts and demonstrate their understanding? (Source: Davis, 1988)

Encourage graduate student instructors to give you comments about the course. If you have GSIs, they can be a valuable source of information on how the course is progressing and whether students are learning the material. Most student complaints eventually find their way to a GSI. Ask GSIs to give you brief written reports on any problems the students may be having in the course (for example, have them list the one or two things that caused students the most difficulty in class last week). (Source: Davis, 1988)

References

Angelo, T. A. "Introduction and Overview: From Classroom Assessment to Classroom Research." In T. A. Angelo (ed.), *Classroom Research: Early Lessons from Success*. New Directions for Teaching and Learning, no. 46. San Francisco: Jossey-Bass, 1991.

Angelo, T. A., and Cross, K. P. *Classroom Assessment Techniques: A Handbook for College Teachers*. (2nd ed.) San Francisco: Jossey-Bass, 1993.

Bateman, G. R., and Roberts, H. V. "Total Quality Management for Professors and Students." Unpublished paper, the Graduate School of Business, University of Chicago, 1992.

Clark, J., and Redmond, M. *Small Group Instructional Diagnosis Final Report*. Seattle: Department of Biology Education, University of Washington, 1982. (ED 217 954)

Coffman, S. J. "Improving Your Teaching Through Small-Group Diagnosis." *College Teaching*, 1991, *39*(2), 80–82.

Davis, B. G. *Sourcebook for Evaluating Teaching*. Berkeley: Office of Educational Development, University of California, 1988.

Davis, B. G., Wood, L., and Wilson, R. *ABC's of Teaching with Excellence: A Berkeley Compendium of Suggestions for Teaching with Excellence*. Berkeley: Office of Educational Development, University of California, Berkeley, 1983.

"Effectively Using Informal Early Semester Feedback." *Illinois Instructor Series*. Urbana: Instructional Management and Services, University of Illinois, 1987.

Fuhrmann, B. S., and Grasha, A. F. *A Practical Handbook for College Teachers*. Boston: Little, Brown, 1983.

Katz, J. "Helping Faculty to Help Their Students Learn." In A. F. Lucas (ed.), *The Department Chairperson's Role in Enhancing College Teaching*. New Directions for Teaching and Learning, no. 37. San Francisco: Jossey-Bass, 1989.

Katz, J., and Henry, M. *Turning Professors into Teachers*. New York: American Council on Education and Macmillan, 1988.

Kogut, L. S. "Quality Circles: A Japanese Management Technique for the Classroom." *Improving College and University Teaching*, 1984, *32*(3), 123–127.

Lancaster, O. E. *Effective Teaching and Learning*. New York: Gordon and Breach, 1974.

Lewis, K. G. "Getting Informative Feedback from Your Students." *CTE Newsletter*, 1988, *9*(3). (Available from the Center for Teaching Effectiveness, University of Texas, at Austin)

Mosteller, F. "The 'Muddiest Point in the Lecture' as a Feedback Device." *On Teaching and Learning*, 1989, *3*, 10–21.

Nuhfer, E., Perkins, M., Simonson, J., and Colleagues. "Improving Courses with Student Management Teams." *Teaching Professor*, 1992, *6*(3), 5–6.

Watching Yourself on Videotape

42

Watching a videotape of yourself is an extremely valuable experience. Videotaping allows you to view and listen to the class as your students do; you can also scrutinize your students' reactions and responses to your teaching. By analyzing a videotape of the dynamics in your classroom, you can check the accuracy of your perceptions of how well you teach and identify those techniques that work and those that need revamping.

Faculty members at all levels and in all disciplines have benefited from seeing videotapes of themselves. The suggestions below are designed to help you use videotape to gain insights that will help you improve your teaching.

General Strategies

Arrange for videotaping through your campus media office. Many colleges and universities offer free classroom videotaping services to faculty members. Contact the media office to find out what services are available. If your campus does not offer such services, ask a colleague to observe you in the classroom. See the section on colleague observation later in this tool.

Select a typical class. Choose a class in which you are teaching as you generally do, using the chalkboard, overheads, handouts, and so on. If possible, try to pick a class that is a mix of lecture and discussion.

Let students know in advance that the class will be videotaped. Explain that the taping is a way for you to review *your* performance—not theirs—and improve your teaching. Assure them that the tape will not be preserved.

Ask the camera operator to tape the students as well as you. The cameraperson will know not to disrupt the class in any way. But feel free to remind the camera operator to break away from focusing on you in order to show your students' reactions to you and to each other. (Source: Krupnick, 1987)

While you are being videotaped try to focus on your teaching, not on the camera. Video equipment is not intrusive; no extra lighting is required.

Though you may feel uncomfortable and awkward at the beginning of taping, these feelings wear off quite quickly. Keep in mind that no one will see the tape except you, unless you choose to invite others to view it with you. Remember, too, you can erase the tape whenever you wish.

Viewing the Videotape

View the videotape as soon as possible. Plan to view the tape on the day it is made or the next day so that your memory is fresh and you can readily recall what you were thinking or feeling during class. Run the tape through once or twice just to get used to seeing yourself on tape. During these first viewings, be prepared for a dose of "video-induced despair" (Krupnick, 1987), a common ailment brought about by the visual distortions of the medium. Most people tend to notice their voice, appearance, gestures, and mannerisms—Do I really sound like that? Is my hair always this disheveled? Why didn't I notice that my shirt was untucked? It is important to realize that these details are exaggerated on tape and are far less noticeable and distracting in real life. In any case, a wrinkled blouse or a crooked tie has nothing to do with effective teaching. (Source: Krupnick, 1987)

Plan to spend twice as long analyzing the tape as it took to tape your class. Once you've adjusted to seeing yourself on tape, set aside sufficient time to analyze it, about two hours to review a one-hour class session. As you start to analyze the tape, remember to focus on your strengths as well as aspects needing improvement. The problem areas are likely to jump out at you, but don't overlook those things that you are doing well: talking to the class, not the board; answering questions clearly; and so on.

View the tape with a supportive consultant. Many campuses have offices of faculty development or instructional improvement whose staff members can assist you in identifying your strengths and areas for improvement. In addition to providing helpful suggestions, the consultant can help you temper your natural tendency to be hypercritical.

Go for the gestalt. Run the tape straight through and answer the following questions:

- What are the specific things I did well?
- What are the specific things I could have done better?
- What do students seem to enjoy most?
- What do students seem to enjoy least?

- If I could do this session over again, what three things would I change?
- How could I go about making those three changes?

(Source: Fuhrmann and Grasha, 1983)

Focus on selected aspects of your performance the next time you view the tape. For example, review the tape looking solely at the kinds of questions you pose or noticing your voice characteristics or presentation style. Identify both your strengths and those areas that need improvement. (Source: Acheson, 1981)

Chart the frequencies and types of classroom interactions. One simple method for analyzing classroom talk in discussion classes is called Contracted BIAS (Brown's Interaction Analysis System). As you watch a segment of the tape, stop every five seconds to make a tic mark in one of three columns: Teacher Talk, Student Talk, Silence. The totals will show you how much time was devoted to your comments and to students' comments. For a more detailed analysis, record a Q, for question, each time you or a student poses a question. (Source: Brown and Atkins, 1988)

Write down verbatim comments of a given type. Useful types of comments to copy down include teacher's questions, students' responses to teacher's questions, students' questions, teacher's responses to students' questions, teacher's responses to students' statements, teacher's reward and praise statements, and teacher's criticism. For example, if you are concerned about your use of questions, view the tape and write down all the questions you asked. Then you can examine such issues as these:

- How many questions actually requested a response from students?
- Did all the questions start with the same phrase?
- Did they all require yes/no or short answers?
- What level of thinking was required in the responses?
- Did you allow sufficient time between questions for students to respond?

In reviewing your videotape, you may find that you are asking too many questions or not pausing to give students time to answer. You can then work on improving your questioning skills. (Source: Acheson, 1981)

Use checklists to focus your analysis. Create your own checklists that reflect your particular areas of interest or select items relevant to your teaching style and subject matter from the following checklists (adapted from Davis, 1988, based on questionnaires from the University of California, Berkeley, University of California, Los Angeles, University of Illinois, Urbana-Champaign, University of Texas at Austin, and Northwestern University).

Organization and Preparation
Do you

- State the purpose of the class session and its relationship to the previous class?
- Present, on the board or in a handout, a brief overview or outline of the content at the beginning of the session or state the problem to be solved or discussed?
- Emphasize or restate the most important ideas?
- Make smooth transitions from one topic to another?
- Restate, at the end of the class, what students are expected to gain from the session?
- Summarize the main points or ask students to do so?
- Relate the day's session to upcoming presentations?
- Include neither too much nor too little material in a class period?
- Seem at ease with the material?
- Begin and end class promptly?

Style of Presentation
Do you

- Speak in a clear, strong voice that can be easily heard?
- Speak neither too quickly nor too slowly?
- Speak at a rate that allows students to take notes?
- Talk to the class, not to the board or windows?
- Listen carefully to students' comments and questions without interruption?

Clarity of Presentation
Do you

- Define new terms, concepts, and principles?
- Give examples, illustrations, or applications to clarify abstract concepts?
- Explicitly relate new ideas to familiar ones?

- Seem to know whether or not the class is understanding you? whether students are puzzled or confused?
- Use alternate explanations when students do not understand?
- Slow down when discussing complex or difficult ideas?
- Refrain from needlessly digressing from the main topic?
- Use handouts and audiovisual aids effectively?
- Write legibly and clearly on the chalkboard?

Questioning Skills
Do you

- Ask questions to determine what students know about the topic?
- Ask different levels and kinds of questions to challenge and engage students?
- Periodically ask questions to gauge whether students need more or less information on a topic?
- Pause sufficiently after all questions to allow students time to respond?
- Encourage students to answer difficult questions by providing cues or rephrasing?
- When necessary, ask students to clarify their questions?
- Ask follow-up questions if a student's answer is incomplete or superficial?
- Request that difficult, time-consuming questions of limited interest be discussed during office hours?

Student Interest and Participation
Do you

- Encourage students' questions?
- Accept other points of view?
- Provide opportunities for students to practice what they are learning?
- Engage students' intellectual curiosity?

Classroom Climate
Do you

- Address some students by name (and with the correct pronunciation)?
- Call on men and women students in equal numbers?
- Call on students of different ethnic groups in equal numbers?
- Evenhandedly listen attentively and respond to students' comments and questions?

- Give feedback, encouragement, criticism, and praise evenhandedly?
- Avoid language patterns or case examples that exclude or derogate any groups?

Discussion
Do you

- Encourage all students to participate in the discussion?
- Draw out quiet students and prevent dominating students from monopolizing the discussion?
- Refrain from monopolizing the discussion yourself?
- Encourage students to challenge one another?
- Mediate conflicts or differences of opinion?
- Bring closure to the discussion?

Having Colleagues Observe Your Class

Invite a faculty development consultant or a colleague to observe you teach. If your campus has an office of faculty development or instructional improvement, one of the staff members can observe you teach. If your campus has no faculty development office, ask a supportive colleague to sit in on your class. If possible, try to select someone who is familiar with the course's content. If no single class is representative of your course, ask the observer to attend two sessions. Let the students know in advance that you have invited an observer to sit in.

Plan for the observation. You and the observer should meet before the visit to discuss class goals, students, and teaching strategies. Offer the observer a copy of your course syllabus and an outline of topics for the class period, and mention which particular features you would like the observer to focus on during class. At this initial meeting you and the observer can also decide on the method of observation (for example, checklist, rating form, open-ended comments). Some researchers recommend limiting the observation form to six or eight open-ended questions that will provide a narrative description of aspects of your teaching, such as organization of presentation, instructor-student rapport, clarity of explanations, and so on (Millis, 1992).

Meet with the observer within a week or so after the visit. A good way to begin the session is for you to identify your own impressions about the class and those aspects that went well and those that did not. Then ask the observer to comment on various aspects. It is sometimes helpful if the observer has prepared a brief written report that includes examples. Ask the observer to be concrete and specific, focusing on behavior and actions. You and the observer can also discuss the degree to which your goals for the class were accomplished. At the conclusion of the session, you may want to ask the observer for any suggestions for improvement in two or three specific areas. (Source: Davis, 1988)

References

Acheson, K. A. "Classroom Observation Techniques." *Idea Paper*, no. 4. Manhattan: Center for Faculty Evaluation and Development, Kansas State University, 1981.

Brown, G., and Atkins, M. *Effective Teaching in Higher Education*. London: Methuen, 1988.

Davis, B. G. *Sourcebook for Evaluating Teaching*. Berkeley: Office of Educational Development, University of California, 1988.

Fuhrmann, B. S., and Grasha, A. F. *A Practical Handbook for College Teachers*. Boston: Little, Brown, 1983.

Krupnick, C. G. "The Uses of Videotape Replay." In C. R. Christensen with A. J. Hansen (eds.), *Teaching and the Case Method*. Boston: Harvard Business School, 1987.

Millis, B. J. "Conducting Effective Peer Classroom Observations." In D. H. Wulff and J. D. Nyquist (eds.), *To Improve the Academy*. Vol. 11. Stillwater, Okla: New Forums Press, 1992.

43

Self-Evaluation and the Teaching Dossier

Creating a teaching dossier, or portfolio, by compiling your teaching materials and related documents, gives you a chance to reflect on your accomplishments and teaching achievements. Dossiers can be submitted as documentation of the quality of your teaching for merit and promotion decisions, in which case the materials will be selective, or they can be used solely for your own edification, in which case the materials can be more comprehensive. Seldin (1991) and Edgerton, Hutchings, and Quinlan (1991) believe that the act of compiling a dossier can help instructors improve their teaching because it gives them a chance to review their instructional priorities and strategies.

The guidelines below, adapted from Davis (1988), address the components of a teaching dossier you might compile for yourself. A dossier forwarded for merit and promotion review would need to be more formal and contain additional sources of information as required by your department (for example, letters from students or letters from colleagues). Brinko (1991) and Edgerton, Hutchings, and Quinlan (1991), drawing from the work of the Canadian Association of University Teachers (1986), provide detailed lists of items that can be used to demonstrate instructional excellence within several broad categories: the products of good teaching (such as students' lab books, essays, or creative work), steps taken to evaluate and improve one's teaching (such as exchanging course materials with colleagues), and information from students (such as student rating forms). Urbach (1992) poses questions to address in compiling a portfolio for external review, and Seldin (1991) and Edgerton, Hutchings, and Quinlan (1991) provide case examples of teaching portfolios.

In preparing a dossier for your own use, consider it as an opportunity to describe and candidly judge your teaching and as a chance to compile in one source course-related information that may be useful in subsequent revisions. Such a dossier could also demonstrate merit (for promotion). It is best if you assemble the dossier shortly after the end of the term, while your experiences are still fresh and your memory vivid.

Preparation of a Teaching Dossier

Describe the course. List the course title and course number. How many times have you taught this course? Is the course required or an elective? How does it fit within the department's curriculum? Were there any course activities that placed special demands on your time (for example, field trips, student projects, and so on)?

Describe the students in the class. What were the general characteristics of students enrolled in the course? How do students compare in this class to others you have taught? Was there a significant difference between the number of students who preregistered for the course and the number who ultimately enrolled? How would you characterize attendance throughout the term? Did you undertake extra efforts to work with students who were not well prepared for the course? Did you undertake extra efforts to work with your best students?

Write a brief reflective self-assessment of your teaching in this course. Divide your assessment into four parts: the goals of the course, your teaching methods and philosophy, the effects of your course on students, and your plans for improvement. For each section provide specific concrete examples. In the *goals* section, address the following kinds of questions: What were you trying to accomplish? Why were these goals selected? How well did the course meet these goals and how do you know? What problems, if any, did you encounter in attempting to meet these goals? Under *methods*, discuss your choice of teaching strategies: How did you conduct the course and challenge students? How did your methods take into account the level and abilities of your students? What were your grading policies? What changes did you make in topics, readings, or assignments for a course you have taught repeatedly? How well did those changes work?

In terms of *effects*, speculate or provide evidence on how your teaching encouraged independent thinking, intellectual development, and enthusiasm for the subject matter. How did you know whether students were gaining competence and learning the material? What evidence do you have of student learning? Finally, under *improvement*, address these kinds of questions: How satisfied were you with this course? What do you think were the strong points of the course and your teaching? The weak points? What would you change or do differently if you taught this course again? What did you find most interesting about this course? Most frustrating? Comment about any efforts you might make to improve the course or your teaching abilities. If you are short of time, simply address the questions under *improvement*. This will give you a written record of your overall impressions.

Comment on student ratings from the course. Include a copy of the form (if the raw data are not available), noting the response rate—the percentage of your students who turned in questionnaires. Look at the overall ratings of the course and your teaching. Review students' open-ended comments. Respond briefly and candidly to the students' evaluations and critiques, commenting on those aspects with which you agree and will change in the next offering and those with which you disagree. See "Student Rating Forms."

Compile course material. You can include copies of the course syllabus, course descriptions, required and recommended reading lists, examinations and assignments, handouts, and your teaching notes. Annotate the materials to give details about how you used them and your candid assessment of their effectiveness. Look critically at the materials to identify the kinds of intellectual tasks you set for students. Do the materials reflect adequate breadth and depth? You may also want to include photocopies of students' work with your comments and grades. Your self-reflective commentary on your materials might respond to the following kinds of questions:

- Is the treatment of the subject matter, as represented in the course material, consistent with the latest research and thinking in the field? Is this material valuable and worth knowing?
- Are the topics logically sequenced? Does each topic receive adequate attention relative to other topics?
- Do the readings represent the best work in the field? Do they offer a diversity of up-to-date views? Are the reading assignments appropriate in level and length for the course?
- Are the assignments effectively coordinated with the syllabus and well integrated into the course? Are they appropriate in frequency and length?
- Do the tests and exams give students a fair opportunity to demonstrate their abilities? Do they focus on important aspects of the course and adequately cover the subject matter? Are there questions that assess students' abilities to apply concepts as well as questions that test students' memory?
- Are the standards for grading clearly communicated to students? Is the grading fair and consistent? Are written comments on papers constructive and helpful?

Describe any instructional innovation or experiments you undertook. Whether the activities were successful or not, discuss what you tried to do, how it turned out, and the effect on students and on your own teaching.

Assess your role with your graduate student instructors. If your course had graduate student instructors (GSIs), review your role in their guidance, supervision, and evaluation. What did you do that was especially effective in helping them learn how to teach? What did they do that was especially helpful to students or to you? How satisfied were you with the GSIs' teaching performance? What would you change or do differently if you taught this course again? See "Guiding, Training, and Supervising Graduate Student Instructors."

Add any evaluations by reviewers or observers. If colleagues or instructional consultants observed your course, interviewed your students, or reviewed your teaching materials, include their written notes in your dossier.

Self-Evaluation Strategies

Conduct a before-and-after assessment. Before you begin the term, write brief comments about the types of students for whom your course is intended, the most important course goals or objectives, and the teaching strategies or course components (laboratory, lecture, and discussion sections) designed to achieve each goal. After the course, write a brief description of the types of students who actually enrolled, the instructional methods and assignments you employed, and the methods you used to assess students' achievement of major goals. Then focus the body of your evaluation on the goals and objectives you feel were achieved and the evidence of students' achievements; the goals or objectives you feel were not realized; and the nature of any discrepancies between your intentions for the course and the actual outcome. (Source: Task Force on Teaching Evaluation, 1980)

Complete an end-of-course questionnaire similar to the one used by your students. Before looking at the ratings your students submitted, complete the form yourself on the basis of your perceptions of your behavior or on what you expect, on average, that your students will say. In most cases, your self-evaluation will be more positive than students' ratings. In comparing students' ratings and your self-evaluation, focus on any discrepancies and on deficiencies you marked on the form. Discussions with faculty colleagues or a teaching consultant can be helpful in exploring strategies for improvement.

Keep a teaching journal or log. Take five or ten minutes immediately after each class to jot down some quick comments on how the session went. Identify places where students seemed puzzled or asked questions, note how well the activities you planned worked out, and comment on your use of time. Add a test question that came to mind and any other impressions of the session. Then list two or three simple things you could do to improve this session. Review these notes when you are preparing to teach this course again. (Source: "Teaching Journals: A Self-Evaluation Strategy," 1988)

References

Brinko, K. "Documenting Excellence in Teaching." *Teaching Professor*, 1991, *5*(8), 3–4.

Canadian Association of University Teachers. *The Teaching Dossier: A Guide to Its Preparation and Use*. Ottawa, Ontario: Canadian Association of University Teachers, 1986.

Davis, B. G. *Sourcebook for Evaluating Teaching*. Berkeley: Office of Educational Development, University of California, 1988.

Edgerton, R., Hutchings, P., and Quinlan, K. *The Teaching Portfolio: Capturing the Scholarship in Teaching*. Washington, D.C.: American Association of Higher Education, 1991.

Seldin, P. *The Teaching Portfolio*. Boston: Anker, 1991.

Task Force on Teaching Evaluation. *Report of the Task Force on Teaching Evaluation*. Oakland: Office of the President, University of California, 1980.

"Teaching Journals: A Self-Evaluation Strategy." *Teaching Professor*, 1988, *2*(6), 2.

Urbach, F. "Developing a Teaching Portfolio." *College Teaching*, 1992, *41*(2), 71–74.

XI.

Teaching Outside the Classroom

Holding Office Hours

44

Office hours are an important adjunct to college-level courses, allowing you and your students the chance to go over material that could not be addressed during class, to review exams or papers in more detail, to discuss questions at greater length, or to explore future courses or careers (see "Academic Advising and Mentoring Undergraduates"). Office hours also give you and your students a chance to get to know one another, and students are often motivated to work harder for teachers they have come to know (Marincovich and Rusk, 1987). Finally, office hours provide you with an opportunity to gauge how the course is going and how well students are understanding the material. If several students ask you the same question during office hours, you know it is a point you need to cover in class.

General Strategies

Ask about department policies. If your department has no set policy, begin by holding two to four office hours a week. Vary the times and days of your office hours; for example, instead of M 10–12 or MWF 11–12, try M 9–10, Tu 3–4, and Th 9–10, or schedule an office hour from 9:30–10:30 so you will be available to students who have either a 9 A.M. or 10 A.M. class. Let students know that you are also available by appointment. In addition, remember to stagger your office hours with your graduate student instructor, if you have one, to provide maximum coverage. (Source: "Office Hours," 1989)

List your office hours on the course syllabus and post them outside your office door. The course syllabus should include your office room number, office telephone number, electronic mailing address, fax number, and office hours. If your office is hard to find, draw a map on the board or in the syllabus (Marincovich and Rusk, 1987). Mention your office hours on the first day of class and at particularly important times during the semester (that is, before major exams or deadlines for papers). Post your office hours outside your office and report them to your department's administrative assistant.

In class, explain to your students the purpose of office hours. New students may have only vague notions of what office hours are for. Let students know that they can come to talk to you informally, to ask questions about the material or assignments, to review graded work, to get suggestions for further reading, or to discuss other topics related to the course or to your field. Encourage students who are having trouble with their course work to come in to review their status and receive, as needed, referrals to campus tutoring resources.

Be disciplined about keeping your office hours. If you will be unavailable during a scheduled office hour, ask the department's administrative assistant to post a note on your office door. Students get upset with instructors who are not present for the full period of their posted office hours, and these feelings can impair their motivation to do the course work. (Source: "Office Hours," 1989)

Refer students for additional help. Students sometimes ask for advice about personal problems. In most cases it is best to express your concern, convey a sense of caring, but remind students that you are not a counselor and refer them to campus counseling services.

Encouraging Students to Attend Office Hours

Be friendly and accessible and stay after class. Students may be intimidated by the thought of speaking directly and privately to their instructors or may feel they do not need attention. The more approachable you are, the more likely students are to come around. Invite students to visit you during office hours and repeat the invitation several times during the term. (Source: Marincovich and Rusk, 1987)

Make at least one office visit a course requirement. If your class is not too large, schedule each student in the class for a ten- to twenty-minute appointment during the early weeks of the course. Use these appointments to find out more about your students (their reasons for taking the course, problems they anticipate or are having), to consult with students before they begin projects or essays, or to discuss recent quizzes or exams. Once students have come to your office, they will be more comfortable seeking you out in the future.

Use an office hour as an orientation for students who missed the first day of class. For students who add your course after the first week, schedule a group office hour to go over requirements, expectations, and course operations.

Return student work with a "Please see me during office hours." Comments on returned exams and papers often motivate students who are performing poorly in class to come to office hours. You might also ask particularly shy students to see you: seeing you in your office may put them at ease and make them more willing to speak during class. The comment "See me about this" will bring about a 75 percent response rate. (Source: Unruh, 1990)

Have students satisfy a course requirement during office hours. For example, ask students to make a brief oral presentation or bring an outline of their paper for review.

Post answers to quizzes or homework by your office door. Some instructors find that posting answers inside the door is an effective means of attracting students during office hours. (Source: Unruh, 1990)

Consider scheduling appointments for your office hours. Place a sign-up sheet on your office door, dividing your office hours into fifteen- or twenty-minute blocks. If you do this, keep to the schedule. Appointments minimize the amount of time students spend waiting to see you. Keep some blocks open for drop-in or emergency requests.

Contact students who fail to show up for scheduled appointments. If a student misses an appointment, call to find out what happened or ask the student in class. Let students know that if they schedule appointments, you expect them to appear or to advise you of any change. (Source: "Office Hours," 1989)

Making Office Hours Productive

Advise students to prepare their questions. Students who come in asking you to explain Chapter 9 need to do more preparation on their own. Ask them to come back as soon as they have figured out what points are stumping them. Or before papers are due, explain that you are available to help students *develop* their ideas but that they must come prepared with a preliminary thesis statement or outline. One instructor gives students a handout on guidelines for office hours. Students are advised to do the following ("Office Hours," 1989):

- Come to the office with specific written questions
- Bring any reading or materials for discussion, with the appropriate sections marked
- Be prepared to argue ideas, not scores, when discussing exams

Group students with similar concerns or questions. If a large number of students arrive just before or after an assignment or exam, poll them to see whether you can group students who have similar problems. That way you will not have to repeat information, and they can share ideas and learn from one another.

Remind students that office hours are not the time for a recap of a class lecture they missed. Encourage students to know the telephone number of at least one other member of the class, and instruct them to call each other for missed assignments or lecture notes.

In quantitative courses, focus on problem-solving strategies rather than on the answer to a given problem. Ask students to make an effort to solve the problem on their own. It is helpful to jot down your answers to questions on a sheet of paper so that the student has something to study later. It is also helpful to solve problems aloud so that students see the steps you took in arriving at the solution. (Source: Honjo, 1989)

Identify special topics for your office hours. Announce that you will devote particular office hours to reviewing certain difficult topics. If enough students want to attend these help sessions, schedule a classroom for the office hour.

Conducting Office Hours

Create a relaxed mood in which communication is natural and easy. Make your students feel welcome. Some faculty members use a bit of small talk to help students relax. Students may feel less intimidated if you sit in front of or to the side of your desk rather than behind it. It is also a good idea to keep the door open at all times. (Source: Lowman, 1990)

Let the student tell you the purpose of the visit. If the student needs prompting, ask, "What can I do for you?"

Try to give your students your undivided attention. Some students may fear that they are wasting your time; by listening carefully you can help dispel their concerns. Put aside your papers or your work. Try not to let phone callers or visitors interrupt student conferences. (Source: "Office Hours," 1989)

If more than one student is in your office at a time, introduce them to each other. If you have just explained something to one student and another comes in with the same question, ask the first student to explain to the second, while you listen in or help a third. If too many students arrive at once, try to group those with similar questions and ask students to limit themselves to the most pressing questions. Invite students to return when you are less busy. (Source: Heine and others, 1981)

If no other students are waiting, ask students how they feel about the course in general. After you have answered your students' questions, ask them their opinions of the lectures, assignments, readings, and other aspects of the course.

Be tactful with latecomers. If students arrive five minutes before the end of your office hour, thank them for coming but add that you have only a few minutes right now. Encourage them to return near the beginning of your next office hour.

References

Heine, H., and others. *The Torch or the Firehose? A Guide to Section Teaching*. Cambridge: Undergraduate Academic Support Office of the Dean for Student Affairs, Massachusetts Institute of Technology, 1981.

Honjo, R. T. *Speak of the GSI: A Handbook on Teaching*. Berkeley: Department of Mechanical Engineering, University of California, 1989.

Lowman, J. *Mastering the Techniques of Teaching*. San Francisco: Jossey-Bass, 1990.

Marincovich, M., and Rusk, L. *Excellence in Teaching Electrical Engineering*. Stanford, Calif.: Center for Teaching and Learning, Stanford University, 1987.

"Office Hours." *Teaching Professor*, 1989, *3*(7), 7–8.

Unruh, D. (ed.). *The TA Handbook at UCLA*. Los Angeles: Office of Instructional Development, University of California, 1990.

45 Academic Advising and Mentoring Undergraduates

Most faculty members regularly engage in several kinds of advising activities. As academic advisers, faculty offer students guidance on selecting courses and majors. As career advisers, faculty help students explore career choices and opportunities for further education and training. Some faculty also serve as extracurricular advisers to student groups or organizations. As Nathans (1988) points out, every instructor, whether formally assigned advising responsibilities or not, is also an adviser.

Faculty tend to view advising casually, and the fact that faculty receive little training in advising and little recognition for their advising efforts reinforces this ad hoc approach (Erickson and Strommer, 1991). But research has found that advising plays an influential role in students' academic success: faculty who interact with students outside of the classroom have a more accurate sense of students' intellectual capabilities and higher expectations for their performance (Voorhees, 1990). The frequency of informal interaction, outside of class, between students and genuinely interested faculty is a potent predictor of student retention, student satisfaction, and student achievement (Chickering and Gamson, 1991; Pascarella and Terenzini, 1991).

Research has shown (Metzner, 1989) that an effective strategy for improving student retention is to offer good advising to students. Even providing poor advising is better than no advising in helping to improve retention rates. In addition, advisers can help students clarify their educational goals and relate these goals to the curriculum; can encourage academic success by assisting students with a selection of course work that is compatible with their interests, abilities, and outside commitments; and can facilitate referrals to support services.

Effective advising relies on some of the same skills as effective teaching. Erickson and Strommer (1991) and Voorhees (1990) have identified the following attributes of successful advisers: demonstrated concern for and interest in students, availability and accessibility, ability to listen nonjudgmentally, willingness to take an active role in helping students make deci-sions, ability to create an open and accepting climate, and respectfulness for students from diverse backgrounds and with diverse goals. Effective advisers should also be able to answer questions about degree requirements, recom-mend courses, provide letters of recommendation, be aware of institutional resources, and keep regular office hours. The following suggestions will help you advise students with confidence and purpose. See also "Holding Office Hours" for ideas about day-to-day informal advising.

General Strategies

Check with your chairperson to determine how advising is handled in your department. In some departments, each faculty member is assigned a certain number of students (from ten to thirty, depending upon the size of the department) for whom they are responsible. Some departments require students to see their faculty advisers once each term to sign off on study lists and other forms. Others leave the timing of meetings to the discretion of students and faculty members. If your department does not have a set policy, experienced observers recommend that you require your students to see you at the very least at three key "checkup" points (Halgin and Halgin, 1984): (a) prior to freshman or transfer entry (summer)—when students need help making the transition to college life, (b) second semester of sophomore year (spring)—as students begin to establish a sense of direction and a major, and (c) first semester of senior year (fall)—when students need guidance on postbaccalaureate plans.

Keep the relationship professional. Be friendly, open, welcoming, and informal, but try not to compromise your ability to make judgments that students may find difficult to accept (for example, rejecting a student's course choices). Your role is to help students help themselves—so view your students as partners in advising, not merely the recipients of advice. Avoid making decisions for students. (Sources: Kramer and Spencer, 1989; Nathans, 1988)

What to Know and What to Do

Know your campus policies about the confidentiality of student rec-ords. Release of student records to third parties is limited by federal law and in most cases requires a written release signed by the student. This means that you cannot inform a student's parents, for example, of their child's academic progress without the student's written consent. With narrowly defined exceptions, students are entitled to see their records. Check with your department chairperson to determine your campus's policies on the release of student information.

Know your stuff. Most campuses have handbooks that are packed with specific information: departmental and institutional degree requirements; prerequisites for admission to majors; preprofessional courses of study; procedures for changing majors; policies on academic warning, probation, and suspension; procedures for adding and dropping courses; information about leaves of absence, withdrawals, and transfer units; graduate and professional school requirements and procedures; special programs (education abroad, undergraduate research opportunities, honors programs, and so on); and sources of academic assistance for students. You do not need to memorize all the rules and regulations as long as you know where to look or which office to call for answers to students' questions. To keep up-to-date, read your departmental and college bulletins, and develop the habit of filing brochures, bulletins, and memos that update the handbook. (Sources: Kramer and Spencer, 1989; Nathans, 1988)

Take the first step. Students profess to want good advising, yet in practice few students visit their advisers other than to seek signatures on required forms. To encourage your advisees to meet with you, consider inviting a small group to lunch or for coffee or send each one a note mentioning something you have noticed in their transcripts or records that might initiate a discussion (for example, outstanding grades, interesting pattern of courses). You can use electronic mail or the telephone to keep in touch with students: a one-on-one office visit is not always necessary. (Source: Nathans, 1988)

Be accessible and available. Never miss an appointment, if you can help it, and try to be prompt for scheduled meetings. When students arrive, do whatever you can to help them feel you are genuinely interested in their welfare.

Keep notes on student conferences. For each student, jot down his or her class level, major, dates and topics of conferences, and any decisions or special issues. By taking a moment to glance at your notes before a student arrives, you can refresh your memory and follow up on questions or issues from the last time you met. (Sources: Erickson and Strommer, 1991)

Use computer technology to free you from routine checks. Computerized tracking systems can monitor students' academic requirements and progress toward a degree or alert you to send students letters at regular or specified intervals (for example, when grade-point averages drop below a certain level). Some faculty members have developed data bases with a file for each student (Appleby, 1989). The file contains background information, campus and departmental requirements completed and to be completed, and relevant material for a letter of recommendation and résumé (for example, awards or honors, research activities, employment, and volunteer activities). Some campuses are developing networked systems that allow faculty easy access to student records and mechanisms for keeping notes on students' progress. (Sources: Appleby, 1989; Kramer and Spencer, 1989)

Take advantage of what you learn from advising to rethink your teaching. Listen to what your advisees say about instruction in your department. You can learn a good deal about the relative difficulty and appropriate sequencing of courses, the skills taught in prerequisite classes, and the like — information useful for your own teaching. (Source: Erickson and Strommer, 1991)

Solicit feedback about your effectiveness as an adviser. Send students a questionnaire that they can complete anonymously. Davis (1988) presents an example of an evaluation form. Here are four main criteria of effectiveness:

- *Knowledge:* How well informed are you as an adviser?
- *Availability:* Do you post and maintain office hours and encourage follow-up visits as needed? Are you accessible during the term?
- *Rapport:* Do you put students at ease and treat each student as an individual? Are you interested in their academic progress?
- *Methods:* Do you communicate clearly and use conference time efficiently?

Advising of Freshmen and Undeclared Students

Find out what campus resources are available for advising freshmen and undeclared students. Some large universities have professional advisers who are familiar with the campus rules, regulations, and procedures and provide students with technical and academic advice. In these circumstances, your role may be more that of a mentor, a new student's first personal contact with a professor. Your institution may also have peer advising programs in which upper-division students advise lower-division students. According to research, these programs are very successful (Crockett, 1985; Halgin and Halgin, 1984).

Be prepared to discuss a range of topics. Freshmen are more likely than upper-division students to view the advising process as a forum to discuss problems of a personal nature. Freshmen are also more likely to need direction, structured interviews, and frequent advising contacts. (Sources: Erickson and Strommer, 1991; Voorhees, 1990)

Help students make the transition to college life. Freshmen often need help in assessing their academic needs, in locating academic support services, and in finding out about academic departments, campus student groups, and activities. (Source: Kramer and Spencer, 1989)

Involve freshmen and new transfer students in the institution. Tell your students about your department's student associations, undergraduate research projects, study groups, and career-exploration activities. Personal involvement is a prime motivator for learning, so try to help your students find their place on your campus. (Sources: Frost, 1991; Grites, 1980; Kramer and Spencer, 1989)

Encourage students to take at least one course that is vitally interesting to them. Studies show that students who feel their academic program has at least one gripping course tend to do better and are more likely to persist in college than students who feel their program is composed solely of required courses that they would not have chosen for themselves. (Source: Guskey, 1988)

Encourage freshmen to form study groups and take small classes. Students who are most satisfied with their academic life are those who are involved in study teams or study groups or who take freshman and sophomore seminars (Marchese, 1992).

Advise students on how to manage their time. Help students develop accurate expectations of the time and effort their courses require. New students also need advice on how to acquire effective study strategies and habits. (Source: Kramer and Spencer, 1989)

Be sensitive to the needs of students who are of a different gender, ethnicity, or culture than you are. Experts are divided about the importance of matching students with advisers of the same gender or ethnicity (Jacobi, 1991). But in practice, many programs try to ensure that the advisers are representative of the students they serve.

Consider distributing an "advising syllabus" to freshmen. Like any syllabus, an advising syllabus lists goals and a specific schedule of activities.

It can outline the benefits to students of meeting with their advisers, the expectations of each partner in the advising relationship, the format of individual and group meetings, and even a short reading list. Erickson and Strommer (1991, pp. 192–194) present a model syllabus.

Be especially patient with freshmen. Undeclared students are indecisive, vacillating between a career in architecture or zoology — and all the letters of the alphabet in between. Their moods can range from cocky self-confidence to tormented self-doubt about their chances of succeeding in college. Overlook their shortcomings and show them you truly are interested in helping them succeed. (Source: Nathans, 1988)

Advising of Departmental Majors

Be sure your advisees understand the department's requirements for the major. If your department's requirements are complicated, help your advisees diagram alternative ways of fulfilling each requirement.

Limit the amount of time you spend discussing course selection. According to some observers, course scheduling should occupy no more than 25 percent of your advising time (Grites, 1980). Experienced advisers recommend that faculty help students avoid the pitfalls of courses being taken out of sequence, of postponing required courses until the last possible moment, and of ignoring prerequisites (Halgin and Halgin, 1984).

Let students know about career opportunities in your field. Some campuses have career specialists in offices of career planning and placement, but you can expect juniors and seniors to ask about jobs and opportunities for graduate study. Try to connect students with alumni who are working in the field. (Source: Erickson and Strommer, 1991)

Consider group advising as a supplement to individual meetings. Group advising fosters friendships among students who share similar academic interests and may encourage deeper exploration of career and academic issues. Possible discussion topics for group discussions include what course to take next term (and why), the two or three best tips for studying for a midterm, and a thorny bureaucratic problem and ways to resolve it. (Sources: Erickson and Strommer, 1991; Grites, 1980)

"Intrusive" Advising and Mentoring

Provide "intrusive" advising for students who need it. Intrusive advising consists of structured intervention strategies for new students and students who are having academic problems. Students are required to meet their advisers frequently to discuss their progress and difficulties. Some colleges and universities have established intrusive advising programs for reentry students and students who are academically underprepared, low-income, non-native speakers of English, or physically or learning disabled (Harnish, 1991). Researchers report the success of intrusive advising programs in retaining underrepresented minority students and students on probation (Voorhees, 1990).

Consider serving as a mentor. Mentors are more than advisers and teachers; mentoring is an ongoing one-to-one relationship in which a more experienced individual offers advice, counsel, or guidance to someone less experienced (Johnson, 1989). As Eble (1988) puts it, a mentor does not so much tell students what to do as give them the courage to do it. Jacobi (1991) identifies three general components of a mentoring relationship: emotional and psychological support, direct assistance with career and professional development, and role modeling. Though the research literature has not demonstrated unequivocally that mentoring facilitates academic success, mentoring programs have become popular on college and university campuses, particularly for underrepresented minority students (Jacobi, 1991).

Meet students outside the classroom. Griffin and Ervin (1990) outline possible activities for mentors:

- Meet with the student periodically, occasionally for lunch or coffee.
- As part of a group, invite the student to your home.
- Dine with students in their residence halls or living groups.
- Encourage the student to take advantage of campus resources, including workshops on test taking and study strategies or tutoring, if needed.
- Attend activities in which the student is an active participant.
- Arrange an informal meeting with the student's parents if they visit the campus.
- Send the student notes of encouragement before, during, or after final exam periods; send congratulations for noteworthy achievements.

To this list can be added: encourage students to attend local professional meetings and other events in the field, and involve students in your research or scholarly work.

Matters of Conduct

Be sensitive to matters of conduct when meeting with students outside the classroom. No matter how informal the setting, avoid any suggestive behavior: comments or teasing remarks about a student's clothing, body, gender, or sexual activities; off-color stories or jokes; and unnecessary touching or physical contact.

Obtain a copy of campus policies on sexual harassment and complaint resolution procedures. Ask your campus ombudsman or Title IX office about campus policies on sexual harassment and on romantic relationships with students. In general, unwelcome sexual advances, requests for sexual favors, and other verbal or physical conduct of a sexual nature constitute sexual harassment when (1) submission to such conduct is made either explicitly or implicitly a term or condition of instruction, employment, or participation in other campus activity; or (2) submission to or rejection of such conduct by an individual is used as a basis for evaluating an individual; or (3) such conduct has the purpose or effect of unreasonably interfering with an individual's performance or creating an intimidating or hostile campus environment. As Beidler and Tong (1991) point out, although sexual harassment and intimidation are always wrong, any romantic relationship between a student and an instructor may be suspect, even when it is consensual and there is no overt exploitation. In fact, several colleges and universities across the country have undertaken reviews of this issue and have proposed or approved policies that ban consensual sexual liaisons between teachers and students as unprofessional.

Take steps to prevent misunderstandings and misinterpretations. Enthusiastic behavior on your part might be misperceived by some students as sexual harassment. For example, suggesting that a student take an independent study under your direction could be misread as an expression of personal rather than professional interest. Minimize the chances for misinterpretation by, for example, leaving your office door open during student conferences, meeting with students outside of class and during office hours in small groups rather than one-to-one, and avoiding physical contact with students. Treat students of both sexes evenhandedly so that all have the opportunity for informal contact with you. Do not, however, feel so constrained and anxious about sexual harassment that you sacrifice the basic tenets of good teaching. (Source: "Sexual Harassment," n.d.)

If you feel a student is making advances, speak up immediately. Shrugging off the behavior or remaining silent may be misconstrued as tacit approval. Instead respond, "It is inappropriate for me to discuss these personal issues with you." If a student leans on you or gets too close, move or stand up. If the student persists, keep a record of the incident, including the date, time, place, people involved, and what was said and done. Speak with your department chairperson or ombudsman. (Source: *Avoiding Sexual Discrimination in the Classroom*, n.d.)

References

Appleby, D. C. "The Microcomputer as an Advising Tool." *Teaching of Psychology*, 1989, *16*(3), 156–159.

Avoiding Sexual Discrimination in the Classroom. Los Angeles: Office of the Ombudsman, University of California, n.d.

Beidler, P. G., and Tong, R. "Love in the Classroom." *Journal on Excellence in College Teaching*, 1991, 2, 53–70.

Chickering, A. W., and Gamson, Z. F. (eds.). *Applying the Seven Principles for Good Practice in Undergraduate Education*. New Directions for Teaching and Learning, no. 47. San Francisco: Jossey-Bass, 1991.

Crockett, D. S. "Academic Advising." In L. Noel, R. Levitz, D. Saluri, and Associates (eds.), *Increasing Student Retention*. San Francisco: Jossey-Bass, 1985.

Davis, B. G. *Sourcebook for Evaluating Teaching*. Berkeley: Office of Educational Development, University of California, 1988.

Eble, K. E. *The Craft of Teaching*. (2nd ed.) San Francisco: Jossey-Bass, 1988.

Erickson, B. L., and Strommer, D. W. *Teaching College Freshmen*. San Francisco: Jossey-Bass, 1991.

Frost, S. H. *Academic Advising for Student Success: A System of Shared Responsibility*. ASHE-ERIC Higher Education Report No. 3. Washington D.C.: School of Education and Human Development, George Washington University, 1991.

Griffin, E. V., and Ervin, N. R. *Innovative Practices and Developments in Student Mentoring*. Institute: Division of Student Affairs, West Virginia State College, 1990. (ED 323 893)

Grites, T. J. "Improving Academic Advising." *Idea Paper*, no. 3. Manhattan: Center for Faculty Evaluation and Development, Kansas State University, 1980.

Guskey, T. R. *Improving Student Learning in College Classrooms*. Springfield, Ill.: Thomas, 1988.

Halgin, R. P., and Halgin, L. F. "An Advising System for a Large Psychology Department." *Teaching of Psychology*, 1984, *11*(2), 67–70.

Harnish, D. "Designing Training Programs for Faculty Advisers." *Journal of Staff, Program and Organizational Development*, 1991, *9*(3), 155–162.

Jacobi, M. "Mentoring and Undergraduate Academic Success: A Literature Review." *Review of Educational Research*, 1991, *61*(4), 505–532.

Johnson, C. S. "Mentoring Programs." In M. L. Upcraft, J. N. Gardner, and Associates (eds.), *The Freshman Year Experience*. San Francisco: Jossey-Bass, 1989.

Kramer, G. L., and Spencer, R. W. "Academic Advising." In M. L. Upcraft, J. N. Gardner, and Associates (eds.), *The Freshman Year Experience*. San Francisco: Jossey-Bass, 1989.

Marchese, T. "Assessing Learning at Harvard." *American Association of Higher Education Bulletin*, 1992, *44*(6), 3–7.

Metzner, B. S. "Perceived Quality of Academic Advising: The Effect on Freshman Attrition." *American Educational Research Journal*, 1989, *26*(3), 422–442.

Nathans, E. S. "New Faculty Members and Advising." In A. L. Deneff, C. D. Goodwin, and E. S. McCrate (eds.), *The Academic's Handbook*. Durham, N.C.: Duke University Press, 1988.

Pascarella, E. T., and Terenzini, P. T. *How College Affects Students: Findings and Insights From Twenty Years of Research*. San Francisco: Jossey-Bass, 1991.

"Sexual Harassment: A Hidden Issue." Washington, D.C.: Project on the Status and Education of Women, Association of American Colleges, n.d.

Voorhees, R. A. "A Survey of Academic Advising as an Area of Inquiry." In J. C. Smart (ed.), *Higher Education: Handbook of Theory and Research*. Vol. 6. New York: Agathon Press, 1990.

46 Guiding, Training, and Supervising Graduate Student Instructors

In an important sense, the teaching of undergraduate courses with graduate student instructors (GSIs) is a special form of team teaching. As in any team-teaching effort, the success of the course depends on the quality of team communication in both the planning and the conduct of the course. GSIs often complain that they do not receive the kind of guidance and support from faculty members that would allow them to do their best and to develop as teachers. By serving as a mentor, meeting with GSIs before and during the term, and setting up procedures for evaluation, you can enhance the instruction your students receive and also contribute to the development of future college and university teachers.

General Strategies

Select your graduate student instructors as early as possible. The more notice your GSIs receive, the better they will be able to prepare for their teaching assignments. Appoint and reappoint GSIs on the basis of command of both spoken and written English, command of the subject matter, and potential or demonstrated teaching ability rather than on financial need.

For a large course with many sections, appoint a senior GSI. The senior GSI can coordinate other GSIs' activities, offer orientations or serve as mentors for new GSIs, conduct demonstration classes, observe and monitor GSI performance, and in general, provide a liaison between GSIs and the faculty. (Source: Sprague and Nyquist, 1989)

Hold at least one meeting with your GSIs before the term begins. As soon as they are selected, meet with your GSIs to discuss course content, policies, procedures, and activities. Let your GSIs know that you will provide supervision and guidance to help them as novice teachers. Also make sure your GSIs know what their GSIship involves. The three most common roles for GSIs are these:

- *Leading discussion sections:* In large lecture courses, GSIs may lead weekly discussion sections devoted to working on problem sets or case studies, discussing new material, or reviewing topics covered in lecture.
- *Teaching one section of a course:* In foreign language and composition programs, a GSI may be solely responsible for teaching an introductory class.
- *Teaching a laboratory section of a lecture course:* In lab courses, GSIs are usually responsible for setting up the lab, teaching proper techniques and use of equipment, explaining experiments, and grading lab reports and quizzes.

Working with GSIs

Ensure ongoing open communication between you and your GSIs. To develop and maintain good relations, discuss your expectations with your GSIs. Meet with them regularly, listen carefully to what they have to say about the course and student problems, and give them responsibilities commensurate with their experience. (Source: Lewis, 1982)

Share anecdotes about your own teaching experiences. Tell GSIs about the kinds of problems you experienced when you began to teach, and pass along whatever tips you might have.

Be sensitive to the special needs of international graduate student instructors. Give international GSIs an overview of the American educational system and teaching methods. For example, in some cultures instructors only lecture, and your international GSIs might need detailed advice about how to lead a class discussion. Encourage international GSIs who speak with an accent to repeat important words and phrases slowly and to use handouts and board work. Assign "buddies" and promote collaboration among GSIs in your department to build friendships and provide sources of support, acculturation, and the exchange of information about teaching practices. In some cases you may need to sensitize your students to the roles and value of international GSIs. (Source: Svinicki, 1989)

Treat GSIs as budding colleagues. Be sensitive to GSIs as individuals and as members of an instructional team. Ask GSIs to give you constructive suggestions on ways to improve your lecture presentation, chalkboard work, or speed and tone of voice. By encouraging GSIs to take an active role in articulating their ideas about the course, you increase their involvement and investment in teaching.

Meeting with Your GSIs Before the Term

Introduce yourself to new GSIs. If you don't know the GSIs, you will want to tell them something about yourself, your academic interests, and the place of the course in the curriculum.

Discuss the amount of time GSIs are expected to devote to their teaching responsibilities. Give your GSIs some idea of the hours involved, and remind them that their teaching—although very important—is only part-time and should not overshadow their own academic work. Give GSIs an indication of your priorities on how they should allocate their time among preparation, classroom and laboratory teaching, office hours, and reading student papers and assignments.

Distribute written guidelines on the roles and responsibilities of GSIs and supervising faculty. The list of GSI responsibilities might include these:

- Assisting the faculty member in preparation of course materials
- Teaching in a laboratory or discussion section
- Attending all lectures
- Attending weekly meetings with other GSIs and the course professor
- Reading student work (problem sets, lab reports, papers, examinations)
- Assisting in preparing quizzes and exams
- Assisting in evaluating and grading student performance
- Holding a specified number of office hours
- Participating in the department's GSI training seminar course

The faculty member's responsibilities might include the following:

- Providing GSIs with feedback on their teaching effectiveness
- Meeting weekly with the GSIs to discuss content and preparation for lab or discussion section
- Coaching GSIs on the content and presentation of course material (for example, appropriate emphasis on different topics, questions to ask or points to cover, potential problem areas)
- Making available answer keys for quizzes and exams as well as detailed guidelines for grading papers, problem sets, and other student work
- Overseeing and monitoring how GSIs grade student work

- Helping GSIs set priorities, with the highest priority given to the central duties of preparation for teaching, office hours, and some grading of student work

These written materials should also include a job description, procedures for grievances, your department's policy on GSI evaluations, and procedures for GSI reappointment and promotion. (Source: Unruh, 1989)

Discuss the course in detail. Cover the following important topics:

- *Your role and the role of the GSIs in the course:* What is the relationship between the instructors? What is to be covered in sections: review lecture, present new material, go over homework, discuss the readings, answer student questions? How much autonomy does the GSI have in choosing subject matter, setting policies on attendance, or bringing in new material?
- *Goals of the course:* Explain what you intend to accomplish in the course and what you hope students will achieve.
- *GSIs' course responsibilities:* How many office hours must be held? Are GSIs responsible for preparing and grading exams and assignments?
- *GSIs' nonteaching responsibilities:* Let GSIs know what nonteaching activities, if any, they will be responsible for, such as picking up media equipment or placing books on reserve.
- *Course syllabus:* Give GSIs a copy of your syllabus and readings at least three weeks before the class begins. Go over any unfamiliar topics so that the GSIs feel comfortable with the material.
- *Past exams:* If you have taught the class before, distribute copies of old exams to give GSIs an overview of the important material.
- *Logistics:* What is the maximum number of students that can be admitted in a section? What if the room is too small? What if the books have not yet arrived? Who will handle problems regarding enrollment, assignment to sections, and so on?

Mention what office support services will be provided. Will the GSIs have access to clerical and administrative assistance, computers, copying and fax machines, and electronic mail?

Review campus policies with GSIs. Distribute copies of campus policies on academic dishonesty, sexual harassment, and grade complaints, and review standards for GSI conduct and professional behavior. Advise GSIs to be fair and balanced in dealing with all students, and remind them that neither favoritism nor prejudice has a place in the classroom.

Inform GSIs about campus resources for learning about teaching. Make sure your GSIs are informed about campus GSI training programs, orientation conferences, handbooks, files of materials on teaching in the discipline, and other resources. Let them know, too, of exemplary teachers or experienced GSIs in or outside the department who can be of assistance.

Discuss effective teaching practices. Help novice GSIs prepare for the first day of class. See "The First Day of Class." If possible, arrange for new GSIs to talk to experienced GSIs about typical problems.

Inform GSIs about campus resources for students. GSIs need to know where to refer students with emotional, personal, health, or academic problems.

Review time sheets. Ask GSIs to keep track during the semester of how many hours they are devoting to lecture, discussion section, lab session, office hours, staff meetings, and miscellaneous activities. Use their time sheets to make sure GSIs are not overworking themselves and are allocating their time effectively.

Meeting with Your GSIs During the Term

Set up regular meetings throughout the term. Depending on the experience of your GSIs, the nature of the course, and the GSIs' work load, set weekly or biweekly meetings. Distribute a brief agenda for each meeting. For example:

- Discussion of students' problems with the last homework assignment
- Overview of next assignment and potential pitfalls
- GSIs' reports on discussion sections and lab sessions
- Suggestions for questions to be used on the midterm

Discuss how the course is going. Ask GSIs whether their students are understanding the lectures and keeping up with the reading. GSIs are a good source of information about problems your students are having with the course.

Review past content and new material. Review topics presented in previous classes and topics to be introduced in the coming ones, and discuss teaching strategies. (Source: Instructional and Management Services, 1986)

Develop common criteria for grading students' assignments and exams. Review GSIs' comments and grades on the first set of essays, problem sets, quizzes, or lab reports and discuss the need for common criteria. Advise GSIs on ways to give students constructive comments. See "Evaluating Students' Written Work" and "Grading Practices."

Ask GSIs to help identify students having difficulties. You might ask your GSIs to jot down the one or two things that caused students the most difficulty in class last week. Find out how many and which students are having trouble, and give GSIs advice on how to help these students, including referrals to the student learning center, writing center, or tutoring center. GSIs will also appreciate suggestions on how to handle students who are causing difficulties, such as ways to prevent students from dominating the discussion or ways to encourage shy students.

Evaluating and Improving Your GSIs' Performance

Arrange for GSIs to be evaluated by their students at the middle and end of the semester. All instructors can benefit from student evaluations, especially first-time GSIs. Encourage GSIs to solicit informal written comments from their students during the fourth or fifth week of the semester. On the basis of these evaluations, give your GSIs specific suggestions for improving their teaching. It is also helpful at the beginning of the term for GSIs to see the end-of-semester questionnaire students use to rate their instructors. See "Fast Feedback."

Arrange for GSIs to be observed teaching. If you have a modest number of GSIs, plan to attend at least one of their sections during the term. Schedule the visits in advance with the GSIs, and set aside a time to discuss your observations. If you have a large number of GSIs, ask that GSIs visit one another's sections. Both the observer and the instructor can benefit from such visits. See "Watching Yourself on Videotape" for suggestions on how to conduct observations.

Arrange for GSIs to be videotaped. Many campuses have offices that provide classroom videotaping. Suggest that GSIs be taped at the beginning of the semester and again near the end, and offer to review the tapes with your GSIs, if they wish. See "Watching Yourself on Videotape."

If appropriate, invite GSIs to deliver a short lecture to the entire class. Give GSIs comments on key aspects of their presentation: organization, explanations or examples, speed and tone of voice, use of chalkboard, handling of questions, and so on.

At the end of the term, prepare a written evaluation of each GSI's performance. Evaluation is an essential component of your responsibilities as a supervisor. A brief written review that highlights the GSI's strengths and shortcomings will help assure accountability and give your GSIs ideas for improving their teaching skills.

References

Instructional and Management Services. "Working with Teaching Assistants." *Illini Instructor Series*, no. 2. Urbana: Instructional and Management Services, University of Illinois, 1986.

Lewis, K. G. *Taming the Pedagogical Monster*. Austin: Center for Teaching Effectiveness, University of Texas, 1982.

Sprague, J., and Nyquist, J. D. "TA Supervision." In J. D. Nyquist, R. D. Abbott, and D. H. Wulff (eds.), *Teaching Assistant Training in the 1990s*. New Directions for Teaching and Learning, no. 39. San Francisco: Jossey-Bass, 1989.

Svinicki, M. D. "The Development of TAs: Preparing for the Future While Enhancing the Present." In A. F. Lucas (ed.), *The Department Chairperson's Role in Enhancing College Teaching*. New Directions for Teaching and Learning, no. 37. San Francisco: Jossey-Bass, 1989.

Unruh, D. *Teaching Assistant Training: A Guide for Developing Department Programs*. Los Angeles: Office of Instructional Development, University of California, 1989.

XII.

Finishing Up

The Last
Days of Class

47

The end of the term is hectic for everyone: faculty are rushing to make sure they get through the last topics in the course; students begin thinking about finals and are less receptive to new information (Goldsmid and Wilson, 1980). In addition to finishing the syllabus, there are three other tasks you may want to undertake during the last days of class: (1) hold a review session before the final exam, (2) give your students a sense of closure, and (3) administer an end-of-course student rating form. This tool covers the first two topics. For information on designing and administering student rating forms, see "Student Rating Forms."

Review sessions can serve two important functions for students: focus their attention on course content and reduce exam anxiety ("Exam Review Sessions," 1988). Such a session can also offer students the opportunity to practice skills needed on the exam, to verify what is expected of them on the final, or to gauge the knowledge and skills they have acquired over the term. Though empirical evidence is sketchy, faculty who offer review sessions believe that students who attend them tend to do better on the final ("Exam Review Sessions," 1988). Providing a sense of closure is also important during the last days of class. Most students appreciate having time to acknowledge the end of the term, either informally or by completing an end-of-course questionnaire.

Planning a Review Session

Explain how the review session will be conducted. Will the session be voluntary or required? What will students accomplish? When and where will it be held, and how long will it last? A handout, distributed with the syllabus or near the end of the term, will help students understand your expectations for the review session.

Conduct the review yourself. Asking graduate student instructors to lead the reviews can cause problems. If their interpretation of the material does not match yours, the session will confuse students right at the very end of the course. And you wouldn't want to hear students complain about their grades on the final by challenging, "But the GSI said that in the review session." (Source: Sahadeo and Davis, 1988)

Ask your students about scheduling the review. Sahadeo and Davis (1988) recommend holding your review sessions in the evening one or two days before the final exam. They report that students perform better on the final if the review is held after classes end, when students have had a chance to study and are ready to review. If you hold the review during the last class session or two, students may put off studying until they have been told what the test will cover. Scheduling a review outside of regular class hours, however, makes it hard for some students to attend because of work obligations, family commitments, or other conflicts. (Source: Sahadeo and Davis, 1988)

Create a relaxed, informal atmosphere for the review. Put nervous students at ease by reassuring them that they can succeed on the final. Help students develop confidence. (Source: Sahadeo and Davis, 1988)

Conducting a Review Session

Begin the session by going over exam logistics. Give students a handout listing the time and place of the exam, what to bring, assignments due prior to the exam, the specific readings or topics the exam will cover, and the number and format of questions. (Source: Sahadeo and Davis, 1988)

Consider giving a simulated exam. You can give students thirty to sixty minutes to work on typical or previous exam problems or questions and then discuss the answers as a group or in subgroups. (Source: "Exam Review Sessions," 1988)

Use a game show format. A professor of psychology reports success in structuring his review sessions like "Jeopardy." (In this game, contestants are given an "answer" and must come up with the correct question.) Before the session, students are divided into teams and given six broad categories to study (for example, reliability, the scientific method). The instructor generates "answers" of increasing difficulty within each category. During the review session, he serves as the emcee and student teams amass points by answering correctly. Just as in "Jeopardy," he includes daily doubles and a final jeopardy. (Source: Gibson, 1991)

Have students brainstorm about key concepts or ideas. Ask students to identify the most important topics, themes, or points from the course. Record all the students' responses on the board and then sift through the list with students for connections, convergences, or points of confusion. (Source: *Teaching Assistance*, n.d.)

Pull together the main themes or issues in a brief lecture. Focus your overview / review on the connections among the topics covered in the course. For example, you might list the major topics in the sequence in which you taught them (or have the students generate such a list). Then briefly discuss the important concepts within each major topic and show how they relate to each other. Or ask questions that will help students identify these relationships. The challenge of preparing this kind of review is to distill the essence of the course into one relatively short presentation. (Sources: "Exam Review Sessions," 1988; Goldsmid and Wilson, 1980; Sahadeo and Davis, 1988)

Leave at least some time for students' questions. You can structure the entire session as an open question-and-answer period: Students can ask specific questions, describe the types of problems they would like to solve, or name the topics they want to review. If their questions take only fifteen or twenty minutes, you can end the review at that point or move on to another activity that helps them establish priorities or a focus for their studying. Don't let the session deteriorate to "Do we have to know x for the exam?" (Source: "Exam Review Sessions," 1988)

End by offering advice on how to prepare for the final. For example, discuss the value of studying in groups, give students strategies for pacing themselves, and alert them to common pitfalls (for example, read the instructions carefully; remember to leave time to reread your essays). See "Multiple-Choice and Matching Tests," "Short-Answer and Essay Tests," and "Allaying Students' Anxieties About Tests" for suggestions on how to advise students to prepare for tests. (Source: Dubrow and Wilkinson, 1984)

Providing Closure

Ask students to write notes to each other and to you. During the last days of a seminar or discussion course, give students index cards on which to write messages to you and their classmates, commenting on each other's presentations or participation in the course, noting what they liked best about the class, and so on. (Source: Pfeiffer and Jones, 1973)

Ask students to write their regrets. Sometime during the last week of class, ask your students to write down what they regret not having said during the course. Then go around the room talking about these items. (Source: Pfeiffer and Jones, 1973)

Hold a debriefing session. If your class is small enough, devote some time to discussing such issues as, What would have made the material easier to learn? What one or two concepts or ideas do students remember most from the semester? What do students wish had happened during the term that did not?

References

Dubrow, H., and Wilkinson, J. "The Theory and Practice of Lectures." In M. M. Gullette (ed.), *The Art and Craft of Teaching.* Cambridge, Mass.: Harvard University Press, 1984.

"Exam Review Sessions." *Teaching Professor*, 1988, 2(9), 1–2.

Gibson, B. "Research Methods Jeopardy: A Tool for Involving Students and Organizing the Study Session." *Teaching of Psychology*, 1991, *18*(3), 176–177.

Goldsmid, C. A., and Wilson, E. K. *Passing on Sociology: The Teaching of a Discipline.* Belmont, Calif.: Wadsworth, 1980.

Pfeiffer, J. W., and Jones, J. E. *Handbook of Structured Experiences for Human Relations Training.* Vol. 4. Iowa City, Iowa: University Associates, 1973.

Sahadeo, D., and Davis, W. E. "Review—Don't Repeat." *College Teaching*, 1988, *36*(3), 111–113.

Teaching Assistance: A Handbook of Teaching Ideas. San Diego: The Teaching Assistant Development Program, University of California, n.d.

Student
Rating Forms

48

Student rating forms, also called student end-of-course questionnaires or student evaluation forms, are traditionally administered at the end of the term to solicit student evaluations of a course. (For suggestions on using student rating forms midsemester, see "Fast Feedback.") Typically such end-of-course information is used by faculty committees and administrators to make personnel decisions regarding an instructor: merit increases, promotion, tenure.

At one time, it was considered controversial to administer student rating forms. Now such forms have become commonplace because it makes sense to survey students to find out what they think about their experiences in the class over the term and also because a substantial body of research has concluded that administering questionnaires to students is both valid and reliable. Here is some of what we know about student rating forms from the research (adapted from Davis, 1988):

- Ratings of overall teaching effectiveness are moderately correlated with independent measures of student learning and achievement. Students of highly rated teachers achieve higher final exam scores, can better apply course material, and are more inclined to pursue the subject subsequently. (Sources: Abrami, Apollonia, and Cohen, 1990; Braskamp, Brandenburg, and Ory, 1984; Cohen, 1981; Kulik and McKeachie, 1975; McMillan, Wergin, Forsyth, and Brown, 1986; Marsh and Dunkin, 1992)
- An instructor's ratings for a given course tend to be relatively consistent over successive years; there is not much variation in student ratings for an individual instructor regardless of whether the form is administered to current students or to alumni. (Sources: Braskamp, Brandenburg, and Ory, 1984; Centra, 1979; McMillan, Wergin, Forsyth, and Brown, 1986; Marsh and Dunkin, 1992)
- There is little or no relationship between the following characteristics of students and their ratings of instruction: age, grade point average,

year in college, and academic ability. No consistent relationships have been found between student ratings and such variables as the amount of homework assigned or grading standards. (Sources: Braskamp, Brandenburg, and Ory, 1984; Centra, 1979; Kulik and McKeachie, 1975; McKeachie, 1979; McMillan, Wergin, Forsyth, and Brown, 1986; Marsh and Dunkin, 1992)

- Researchers do report the following relationships:

  Students tend to rate courses in their major fields and elective courses higher than required courses outside their majors. (Sources: Kulik and McKeachie, 1975; McKeachie, 1979; Marsh and Dunkin, 1992)

  Faculty tend to receive more positive ratings than graduate student instructors. (Source: Marsh and Dunkin, 1992)

  The gender of a student has little effect on ratings. The gender of an instructor, however, may have an impact. Though some studies report no relationship between a professor's gender and student ratings, others show that adhering to a gender-appropriate teaching style may be rewarded by higher evaluations. (Sources: Basow and Silberg, 1987; Bennett, 1982; Kierstead, D'Agostin, and Dill, 1988; Marsh and Dunkin, 1992; Statham, Richardson, and Cook, 1991)

  Ratings can be influenced by class size (very small classes tend to receive higher ratings), by discipline (humanities instructors tend to receive higher ratings than instructors in the physical sciences), and by type (discussion courses tend to receive higher ratings than lecture courses). (Sources: Cashin, 1992; Feldman, 1984; Marsh and Dunkin, 1992)

  Students' expectations affect their ratings: students who expect a course or teacher to be good generally find their expectations confirmed. (Sources: Marsh and Dunkin, 1992; Perry, Abrami, Leventhal, and Check, 1979)

Many campuses have standard rating forms that all faculty administer and centralized procedures for analyzing the data. Check with your department to find out what policies exist on your campus. If you are free to design and administer your own questionnaire, the suggestions below (adapted from Davis, 1988) will help you make the most of student rating forms. If you use the standard campus questionnaire, these suggestions can improve the way you administer the forms and interpret the results.

Use forms that give students the opportunity to provide quantitative ratings and to comment narratively on an instructor's performance. Forms that include both quantitative and narrative data are the most useful for getting the broadest picture of students' reactions. Davis (1988) presents sample student rating forms and items that can be used in end-of-course questionnaires, grouped by such categories as accessibility, organization and preparation, and interaction. Kulik (1991) describes the catalogue of items for instructor-designed questionnaires (IDQs), grouped by categories such as student development, course elements, and student responsibility. Theall and Franklin (1990) offer cautions in developing your own questionnaire: it is a time-consuming process to produce a valid and reliable form. They recommend using specific, unambiguous items. For example: "instructor defines new or unfamiliar terms," "repeats difficult concepts," "provides frequent examples." Especially if you are using these forms for your own improvement, the items you select or develop should capture specific behaviors that are amenable to change.

Select items that reflect your department's and institution's criteria of effective teaching and that are within students' range of judgment. For example, current students can judge how well prepared instructors are, how effectively they make use of class time, how well they explain things and with what level of enthusiasm, and how responsive they are to difficulties the students may be having in the course. Students can also comment on whether the instructor promotes original thinking and critical evaluation of ideas. In contrast, current students are not qualified to judge whether instructors are up-to-date in their field or to rate how adequately a course prepares them for advanced course work in the field.

State each item clearly. For example, "The instructor routinely summarizes major points" is unambiguous, while "The instructor is well prepared and gives fair exams" confounds two different issues.

For at least some of the key items, provide a numerical rating scale. The use of quantifiable items enables you to calculate a class's average response and to note the distribution of responses, both of which are useful in interpreting the results of the evaluation. Use either a 5-point or 7-point scale, with 1 representing "not at all descriptive" and 5 (or 7) "very descriptive." Also provide a "Don't know or doesn't apply" option that students can check.

Include at least one item that asks students about the effects of the course. For example, ask students to describe or rate the knowledge, appreciation, or skills they acquired in the course or their intellectual, personal, or professional growth as a result of the instructor's teaching.

Include at least one quantitative measure on the overall effectiveness of the instructor. For example:

Considering both the limitations and possibilities of the subject matter and course, how would you rate the overall effectiveness of this instructor?

Not at all effective			*Moderately effective*			*Extremely effective*
1	2	3	4	5	6	7

Include at least one open-ended item that asks about the overall effectiveness of the instructor. For example, "Please identify what you perceive to be the greatest strengths and weaknesses of this instructor's teaching."

Limit the number of questions about student characteristics. Student characteristics have relatively little influence on ratings of overall effectiveness (Cashin, 1990a). You might want to know, however, whether students are taking the course as an elective or to fulfill a requirement.

Keep the form short. Since students may fill out evaluation forms for all their instructors, questionnaires should be brief.

Administering the Questionnaire

Announce in advance the date on which rating forms will be handed out. Schedule the time sometime during the last two weeks of the term; allow ten to fifteen minutes for this activity. Encourage students to attend that day and complete the form. Do not distribute forms at the final exam, when students are preoccupied with other matters.

Inform the students about the purpose of the questionnaire. It is helpful to stress to students that their ratings and comments are important and will be used by both you and your department. Students may want to know how the completed forms will be handled. Here are some sample instructions that can be placed on the rating forms and read aloud:

We hope you will take the time to answer each question carefully. The information you provide will be part of our ongoing efforts to improve the curriculum and the teaching in this department. In addition, your comments will be summarized and used in faculty promotions and reviews [if this is true on your campus]. To maintain confidentiality, these forms will be collected by someone other than the instructor and will not be available to the instructor until after the course grades have been submitted.

Ask students to complete the forms anonymously. Research shows that requiring students to sign the forms inflates the ratings (Cashin, 1990b). In addition, anonymity can eliminate students' concerns about possible retribution (Ory, 1990).

Designate a student from the class (or a department staff member) to supervise questionnaire administration. You may hand out the forms (always bring several more than the official number of students enrolled), but you should not be present while students complete the questionnaires, and you should not collect the forms. Ask the designated collector to place the forms in a large manilla envelope, noting on the outside your name, the course number, the total number of students present, the total number of forms collected, and the date. The sealed envelope should be delivered to the department office.

Do not look at the forms until after you have submitted final grades for the course. Some campuses provide the faculty with summaries of their rating forms, including computer printouts that show trends and comparative data. If your campus does not provide such a service, you will want to analyze and summarize the data yourself.

Summarizing Responses

Look at the number of students who completed forms and the total class enrollment. Ideally, you would like a response rate (number of completed forms divided by number of enrolled students) of 80 percent or higher. When less than two-thirds of the enrolled students in classes of one hundred or fewer students or less than one-half of the enrolled students in classes of more than a hundred students have submitted forms, the data should be interpreted cautiously if the questionnaires are being used for personnel decisions, such as merit, tenure, or promotion. (Sources: Cashin, 1990b; Theall and Franklin, 1990).

Keep the data separate for each course offering. Aggregating data for several different courses may obscure differences in teaching effectiveness for various kinds of instruction and may raise questions of proper weighting of the responses in each course. Aggregating data for several offerings of the same course may obscure long-term trends toward increased or decreased student satisfaction.

Do not summarize data if there are fewer than ten questionnaires. Student questionnaires from independent reading courses or seminars with very small enrollments may be accumulated over several terms and summarized when their numbers are sufficiently large. (Source: Cashin, 1990b)

If your department does not already do so, prepare summary statistics for the quantifiable questions. The summary should include the following:

- The frequency distribution of student ratings for each item (the number and percentage of students selecting each response)
- The average response, either the mean (calculated to one decimal point), mode, or median
- The standard deviation (an index of agreement or disagreement among respondents)
- Departmental norms (averages) or comparison norms, if available, on key items for courses of a similar size, level, and type of instruction (for example, laboratory, seminar, studio, lecture)

Summarize the narrative comments. The summary should reflect the entire range of comments as well as their preponderance. To prepare such a summary, read all the students' comments about a single question, develop categories or headings that meaningfully group most of the comments, and record the number of comments made in each category. In deciding what to ignore and what to consider, take into account your goals for the course, your values and emphases, and your teaching style (Lunde, 1988). Also remember that it is human nature to focus on that piercing negative comment to the exclusion of the positive remarks from most of the class. An outside teaching consultant or supportive colleague can help you put students' comments in perspective.

Interpreting Responses

For quantifiable questions, determine the percentage of omitted responses. Some items may be left blank because they do not apply. Items with low response rates should be interpreted cautiously. (Source: Theall and Franklin, 1990)

Look at the average ratings for the quantifiable questions. Average ratings can be interpreted on an absolute scale and in relation to the ratings of other similar courses and instructors. For example, a mean rating of 4 on a 7-point scale for overall course evaluation may be labeled "moderately effective." However, if half of all *similar* courses receive mean ratings above 4, then this 4 rating falls in the lower half. There is some debate within the field on whether such comparisons are meaningful (Theall and Franklin, 1990), even among courses similar in level (lower division, upper division, graduate), size, format (lecture, laboratory, and so on), and student demographics. Cashin (1992) argues for using comparative data, pointing out that because students tend to rate most items high, a score of 3.5 on a 7-point scale is not really an indicator of "average" effectiveness. In using student ratings to improve your teaching, try to incorporate some comparative information to better understand your own strengths, weaknesses, and accomplishments (Kulik, 1991). Perhaps the best comparative information, as Kulik suggests, comes from noticing changes in the ratings of a course you have taught several times.

Look at the range of student responses for the quantifiable questions. The range provides important information. For example, the average of all ratings for your course may be 5 on a 7-point scale. But notice whether all students rated the course as 4, 5, or 6 or whether some 2 and 3 ratings were balanced out by some 7s. If ratings cluster at the two ends of the scale, then some aspects of your teaching work for one group of students but not for another — an area to explore. The standard deviation also provides useful information. A standard deviation of less than 1.0 (on a 5-point scale) indicates relatively good agreement among the respondents. Deviations above 1.2 indicate a divided class on that item. (Sources: Cashin, 1990b; Theall and Franklin, 1990).

Note your highest and lowest rated items. One way to analyze student ratings is to calculate the averages for individual questions and note your highest and lowest rated items. See whether your strengths and weaknesses cluster in patterns on any of the following topics: organization and clarity, enthusiasm and stimulation of student interest, teacher-student rapport, teaching and communication skills, course work load and difficulty, fairness of exams and grading, classroom climate. As a rule of thumb, it is usually cause for concern when a third of the students give low ratings to some aspect of a course (Kulik, 1991). In looking at your highest and lowest rated items, try to identify specific behaviors of yours that might have caused students to give you those ratings. If you do this exercise with a colleague who has administered the same form to his or her students, you can exchange examples of behaviors that lead to high ratings.

From the open-ended comments, identify specific problems. Lunde (1988) recommends reading the comments to pinpoint specific complaints—for example, student anxiety about the degree of structure in the course or your expectations for students. Then determine whether the complaint is justified (in this case by looking at the syllabus and handouts). If the worry is legitimate, identify specific steps you can take to address the weakness. Keep in mind that students give few detailed suggestions on how to improve a course; they are better at spotting problems (Braskamp, Brandenburg, and Ory, 1984). If you have the time or can prevail upon an experienced teaching consultant, you could analyze open-ended comments using a grid technique, a method for determining whether students who rate a course highly are saying the same things as those who rate the course lower (Lewis, 1991).

Consider how characteristics of courses can influence ratings. Small classes, electives, and courses in the humanities tend to receive more favorable ratings. For each characteristic the differences are minimal, but together they may be meaningful (Sorcinelli, 1986). It may also be helpful, in interpreting the results, to take into account whether this course is your favorite, one you frequently teach, or a course that you are teaching at the request of the department chair.

Ask a knowledgeable consultant or a colleague for assistance. Some teachers can read their students' ratings and map out strategies to improve teaching. Others find it helpful to review the ratings with a knowledgeable colleague or teaching consultant, available on some campuses. Consultants can help you interpret the results and explore strategies for improvement.

Consider making your ratings available to students. Several departments on campuses around the country—and some entire institutions—have a tradition of making their course ratings public. Many faculty members in these departments or on these campuses believe that because faculty members work harder at their teaching when they know the results are on view to their peers and to students, teaching is of higher quality when the rating forms are publicly available.

References

Abrami, P. C., Apollonia, S., and Cohen, P. A. "Validity of Student Ratings of Instruction: What We Know and What We Do Not." *Journal of Educational Psychology*, 1990, *82*(2), 219–231.

Basow, S. A., and Silberg, N. T. "Student Evaluations of College Professors: Are Male and Female Professors Rated Differently?" *Journal of Educational Psychology*, 1987, *79*(3), 308–314.

Bennett, S. K. "Student Perceptions of and Expectations for Male and Female Instructors: Evidence Relating to the Question of Gender Bias in Teaching Evaluation." *Journal of Educational Psychology*, 1982, *74*(2), 170–179.

Braskamp, L. A., Brandenburg, D. C., and Ory, J. C. *Evaluating Teaching Effectiveness: A Practical Guide.* Newbury Park, CA: Sage, 1984.

Cashin, W. E. "Students Do Rate Different Academic Fields Differently." In M. Theall and J. Franklin (eds.), *Student Ratings of Instruction: Issues for Improving Practice.* New Directions for Teaching and Learning, no. 43. San Francisco: Jossey-Bass, 1990a.

Cashin, W. E. "Student Ratings of Teaching: Recommendations for Use." *Idea Paper*, no. 22. Manhattan: Center for Faculty Evaluation and Development in Higher Education, Kansas State University, 1990b.

Cashin, W. E. "Student Ratings: The Need for Comparative Data." *Instructional Evaluation and Faculty Development*, 1992, *12*(2), 1–6. (Available from Office of Instructional Research and Evaluation, Northeastern University)

Centra, J. A. *Determining Faculty Effectiveness.* San Francisco: Jossey-Bass, 1979.

Cohen, P. A. "Student Ratings of Instruction and Student Achievement." *Review of Educational Research*, 1981, *51*(3), 281–301.

Davis, B. G. *Sourcebook for Evaluating Teaching.* Berkeley: Office of Educational Development, University of California, 1988.

Feldman, K. A. "Class Size and College Students' Evaluations of Teachers and Courses: A Closer Look." *Research in Higher Education*, 1984, *21*(1), 45–116.

Kierstead, D., D'Agostin, P., and Dill, W. "Sex Role Stereotyping of College Professors: Bias in Students' Ratings of Instructors." *Journal of Educational Psychology*, 1988, *80*(3), 342–344.

Kulik, J. A. "Student Ratings of Instruction." *CRLT Occasional Paper*, no. 4. Ann Arbor: Center for Research on Learning and Teaching, University of Michigan, 1991.

Kulik, J. A., and McKeachie, W. J. "The Evaluation of Teachers in Higher Education." In F. N. Kerlinger (ed.), *Review of Research in Education.* Itasca, Ill.: Peacock, 1975.

Lewis, K. G. "Gathering Data for the Improvement of Teaching: What Do I Need and How Do I Get It?" In M. D. Sorcinelli and A. E. Austin (eds.), *Developing New and Junior Faculty.* New Directions for Teaching and Learning, no. 48. San Francisco: Jossey-Bass, 1991.

Lunde, J. P. "Listening to Students Learn: What Are Their Comments Saying?" *Teaching at the University of Nebraska, Lincoln,* 1988, *10*(1), 1–4. (Newsletter available from the Teaching and Learning Center, University of Nebraska, Lincoln)

McKeachie, W. J. "Student Ratings of Faculty: A Reprise." *Academe,* 1979, *65*(6), 384–397.

McMillan, J. H., Wergin, J. F., Forsyth, D. R., and Brown, J. C. "Student Ratings of Instruction: A Summary of Literature." *Instructional Evaluation,* 1986, *9*(1), 2–9.

Marsh, H. W., and Dunkin, M. J. "Students' Evaluations of University Teaching: A Multidimensional Perspective." In J. C. Smart (ed.), *Higher Education: A Handbook of Theory and Research.* Vol. 8. New York: Agathon Press, 1992.

Ory, J. C. "Student Ratings of Instruction: Ethics and Practice." In M. Threall and J. Franklin (eds.), *Student Ratings of Instruction: Issues for Improving Practice.* New Directions for Teaching and Learning, no. 43. San Francisco: Jossey-Bass, 1990.

Perry, R. P., Abrami, P. C., Leventhal, L., and Check, J. "Instructor Reputation: An Expectancy Relationship Involving Student Ratings and Achievement." *Journal of Educational Psychology,* 1979, *71*(6), 776–787.

Sorcinelli, M. D. *Evaluation of Teaching Handbook.* Bloomington: Dean of the Faculties Office, Indiana University, 1986.

Statham, A., Richardson, L., and Cook, J. A. *Gender and University Teaching: A Negotiated Difference.* Albany: State University of New York Press, 1991.

Theall, M., and Franklin, J. (eds.). *Student Ratings of Instruction: Issues for Improving Practice.* New Directions for Teaching and Learning, no. 43. San Francisco: Jossey-Bass, 1990.

Writing Letters of Recommendation

49

As a faculty member, you will be asked to write letters or serve as a reference for students who are applying for fellowships, graduate school, or employment. If you do not know a student well or have a lukewarm opinion of his or her work, explain to the student that you will be unable to write a persuasive letter of recommendation and ask the student to turn to another instructor. If you agree to write the letter, here are some suggestions for producing the most effective recommendation.

General Strategies

Let students know the general tone of what you are likely to write. Especially if your letter will include reservations, let the student know in private what you plan to say so he or she can decide whether to use you as a reference.

Make the letter personal. The more the recommendation conveys a full rounded picture of the student's performance, the more effective the letter will be. Avoid simply reporting the student's grade, class rank, or term paper topic. Use anecdotes and specific examples to give substance and shape to your appraisal.

Check with your colleagues for advice on how to phrase negative comments. To avoid any possibility of complaints about libel or discrimination, some observers suggest faculty preface negative remarks with such phrases as "to the best of my knowledge." (Source: Humphreys and Wickersham, 1988)

Keep in mind that students have a right to see a copy of your recommendation. Under the Family Educational Rights and Privacy Act of 1974, a student has the right to see a copy of your recommendation unless he or she signs a waiver. Some admissions officers feel that letters are helpful only if the student has signed the waiver; others don't care one way or the other. If you want your letter to remain confidential, ask the student to sign the waiver.

Obtain the student's consent before you write a letter of recommendation. If a third party requests a letter because you have been listed as a reference, check with the student to see if this is true. Of course, courteous students let you know in advance that they are listing you as a reference. (Source: Swensen and Keith-Spiegel, 1991)

Getting Ready to Write

Ask whether there is a specific form or format. Some graduate schools or fellowship programs request letters of recommendation on a special form. Make sure you have all the information you need, including where to send the letter and the deadline. Try to write the letter promptly because your delay can negatively affect a student's application.

Ask the student for information about the job or school. Ask for the job description or a brief overview of the graduate program if it is a school or field with which you are unfamiliar.

Ask the student to provide you with copies of papers submitted for your course. Have the student include a self-addressed stamped envelope so you can return the written work after you have examined it. In your letter of recommendation, describe the student's paper (topic, method, conclusions, and implications) and its merits as evidence of intellectual ability, academic skills, the like.

Review your old grade books or records. Students may call upon you long after a course is over, so keep your class records. Some faculty make a habit of noting both good and not-so-good points about students in the margins of their grade books immediately after the conclusion of the term to jog their memories later on. (Source: Humphreys and Wickersham, 1988)

Talk with the student about his or her goals and aspirations. Ask the student to bring a brief résumé, or statement of purpose, or a paragraph or two on career goals or ambitions. Discuss specific abilities or topics that the student feels should be highlighted in the letter. Probe the student about specific purposes: "Why are you applying to this graduate school in this field?" "How does this job you are applying for relate to your long-term career goals?" "Which of your qualifications do you think especially stand out?" (Source: Fisher, 1981)

Preparing the Letter

Limit the letter to one or two pages. The letter should be typed on the form supplied or on your department's letterhead. Some experienced letter readers look at the signature, read the last paragraph, and then decide whether to read the rest of the letter. (Source: Palmer, 1983)

Explain how you know the applicant and your relationship. Is the applicant a former student, advisee, research assistant? State how long you have known the student and how well. Have you worked closely with the student or only observed his or her classroom performance? If the student served as a research assistant, describe the specific responsibilities that relate to the job or graduate school criteria.

Tailor the letter to the specific job opening or academic program. Give the reader a sense of whether the student has the potential to succeed at this particular job or school. If a student is applying for a job, try to translate the student's academic skills into business skills—for example, a student's research project demonstrates the capacity to work independently (Fisher, 1981). Point out what is most important for the reader to know about the student:

- *Intellectual ability* compared to that of other students you have taught
- *Capacity for independent and original thought*
- *Academic and analytic skills.* How well the applicant learns and applies information, grasps new ideas, deals with complex or abstract matters?
- *Knowledge of the field of study*
- *Attitude toward academic work.* Intellectual curiosity, attitude toward learning, class participation, promptness and carefulness in completing assignments and tasks
- *Performance in applied settings*, such as laboratories or clinical situations
- *Communication skills.* Strengths and weaknesses in writing and speaking
- *Initiative, motivation, and persistence*
- *Personal characteristics* as they relate to the position or graduate program: maturity and personal adjustment, dependability, integrity, relations with others, sensitivity, sincerity, leadership ability, supervisory skills, responsiveness to constructive criticism
- *Personal achievements* or activities
- *Special circumstances*, such as work or background experiences that may have affected the student's academic record or that might contribute to or hinder future performance

(Sources: Fisher, 1981; Harvard–Danforth Center for Teaching and Learning, 1986; Office of Instructional Development, 1988; Wolke, 1988)

Be specific. For example, instead of saying "an excellent student," offer a comparative assessment: "the best student in a class of twenty-five" or "among the top ten students I have taught at this institution." "Good communication skills" could be sharpened to "articulate in class discussions" or "writes well-organized and forceful analyses." Then illustrate your appraisal with a supporting example or anecdote. For instance, if you are writing a letter of recommendation for a graduate student seeking a teaching position, describe how the candidate draws students into the discussion, responds to students' questions, or handles tough teaching situations (Lacey, 1989). Here is another example (adapted from Swensen and Keith-Spiegel, 1991, p. 1): Rather than say, "Rita performed well in my social psychology course and was one of the best students in the class; she will likely be a good teacher," consider supporting your observations with specific facts and details: "In the research project assignment, Rita developed a well-defined hypothesis and created a design that was more feasible within the time and budgetary constraints than the other students in the course. Her oral presentation of her project was clear and thoughtful. It was illustrated by several interesting and appropriate examples that held students' attention throughout the 15-minute period. Based on these observations, I predict she will be an outstanding instructor."

Present a balanced picture. Include information on the students' strengths and weaknesses. Readers may be suspicious of gushing letters that make the applicant sound perfect; an honest appraisal may carry more weight. Exaggeration will mar your credibility as a recommender. (Sources: Office of Instructional Development, 1988; Palmer, 1983)

Provide evidence for negative comments and offer interpretations if possible. Try to put weaknesses in context: "This person was insecure during the first year, which may account for some low grades, but has since gained confidence and skills and has done quite well" (Palmer, 1983). Another example (adapted from Swensen and Keith-Spiegel, 1991, p. 1): Instead of saying, "Max was a mediocre student, not really interested in class," say "Max scored below 70 percent on the two midterms and the final exam. The class average was more than 80 percent. (Enrollment was 120.) His research paper was not organized and omitted important components, such as a review of the literature and directions for future research."

Avoid personal remarks. Do not mention age, marital status, children, physical characteristics, or other personal attributes. If a student has successfully balanced academic work and family responsibilities, ask the student if he or she wants that information included in the letter.

Guard against ambiguous statements that could be misinterpreted. Here are some examples from Yager, Strauss, and Tardiff (1984) cited in Swensen and Keith-Spiegel (1991, p. 2):

- "He worked hard to improve himself and he did." *(What was he like when he started?)*
- "She demonstrated a commitment to excellence in those areas that draw her interest." *(What about those that don't?)*
- "She showed considerable progress." *(From what to what?)*
- "He was particularly effective in . . ." *(And mediocre or poor in other aspects?)*

Conclude with an overall recommendation. Indicate how well qualified the student is for the job or graduate program. Stress his or her potential or probable performance if you can. Comment on whether you would choose the applicant for graduate study or for a career position.

Add that you welcome requests for more information. Include your telephone number, electronic mail address, and fax number. Veteran letter readers will see this as a sign that you feel strongly about the candidate. (Source: Palmer, 1983)

Carefully proofread your letter. Be sure names are spelled correctly and dates and facts are accurate.

Following Up

Ask about the results. Ask the student to inform you about whether the application was successful.

Save copies of your letters of recommendation. Copies are useful if the recipient contacts you for further information or if the same student requests another letter. You can also use past letters as guides for writing future ones.

References

Fisher, M. (ed.). *Teaching at Stanford*. Stanford, Calif.: Center for Teaching and Learning, Stanford University, 1981.

Harvard–Danforth Center for Teaching and Learning. *Teaching Fellows Handbook.* Cambridge, Mass.: Harvard–Danforth Center for Teaching and Learning, Harvard University, 1986.

Humphreys, L., and Wickersham, B. "Letters of Recommendation." In J. Janes and D. Hauer (eds.), *Now What?* Littleton, Mass.: Copley, 1988. (Reprinted from *A Handbook of Resources for New Instructors.* Knoxville: Learning Research Center, University of Tennessee, 1986)

Lacey, P. A. "Professors Ought to Do Their Homework When They Recommend Graduate Students." *Chronicle of Higher Education*, March 15, 1989, p. B2.

Office of Instructional Development. "Letters of Recommendation." In J. Janes and D. Hauer (eds.), *Now What?* Littleton, Mass.: Copley, 1988. (Reprinted from *Handbook for Graduate Teaching Assistants.* Athens: Office of Instructional Development, University of Georgia, 1987)

Palmer, S. E. "What to Say in a Letter of Recommendation? Sometimes What You Don't Say Matters Most." *Chronicle of Higher Education*, Sept. 7, 1983, pp. 21–22.

Swensen, E. V., and Keith-Spiegel, P. *Writing Letters of Recommendation for Students: How to Protect Yourself from Liability.* Washington, D. C.: American Psychological Association, 1991.

Wolke, R. "Writing Letters of Recommendation." In J. Janes and D. Hauer (eds.), *Now What?* Littleton, Mass.: Copley, 1988. (Reprinted from *A Handbook for Teaching Assistants.* Pittsburgh, Pa.: Office of Faculty Development, University of Pittsburgh, 1984)

Yager, J., Strauss, G. D., and Tardiff, K. "The Quality of Deans' Letters from Medical Schools." *Journal of Medical Education*, 1984, 59(6), 471–478. Cited in Swensen and Keith-Spiegel, 1991.

Name Index

Subject Index